# LEABHARLANNA CHONTAE FHINE GALL
## FINGAL COUNTY LIBRARIES

Items should be returned on or before the last date shown below. Items may be renewed by personal application, writing, telephone or by accessing the online Catalogue Service on Fingal Libraries' website. To renew give date due, borrower ticket number and PIN number if using online catalogue. Fines are charged on overdue items and will include postage incurred in recovery. Damage to, or loss of items will be charged to the borrower

| Date Due | Date Due | Date Due |
|----------|----------|----------|
|          |          |          |

# VIOLATION

By the same author

*Beneath the Mountains*
(with Richard Gregson)

*A Climate of Fear*

*In the Name of the Law*

*Regions of the Heart*
(with Ed Douglas)

*Guantanamo: The War on Human Rights*

DAVID ROSE

# VIOLATION

Justice, Race and Serial Murder
in the Deep South

Harper*Press*
*An Imprint of* HarperCollins*Publishers*

Harper*Press*
An imprint of HarperCollins*Publishers*

HarperCollins*Publishers*
77–85 Fulham Palace Road,
Hammersmith, London W6 8JB
www.harpercollins.co.uk

Published by HarperCollins*Publishers* 2007

1

A catalogue record for this book is
available from the British Library

ISBN 13  978-0-00-711810-6
ISBN 10  0-00-711810-4

Set in Minion

Printed and bound in Great Britain by Clays Ltd, St Ives plc

This book is proudly printed on paper which contains wood
from well managed forests, certified in accordance with
the rules of the Forest Stewardship Council.
For more information about FSC,
please visit www.fsc-uk.org

Mixed Sources
Product group from well-managed
forests and other controlled sources
www.fsc.org  Cert no. SW-COC-1806
© 1996 Forest Stewardship Council
FSC

*For my mother, Susan, who gave me a sense of history*
*And my father, Michael, who taught me the meaning of justice*

# CONTENTS

# ILLUSTRATIONS

for fire-bombing a grocery store in Gainesville, Florida, 17 March 1968.

Carlton Gary after his arrest in Albany, New York, in 1970.

Carlton Gary arriving in Columbus on the night of his arrest, 3 May 1984. *(Michael Mercier)*

Gary on the night of his arrest with Detective Michael Sellers, who was the only cop to testify about his alleged confession. *(Ed Ellis)*

Police Chief Jim Wetherington gives a press conference on the night of Gary's arrest. *(Lawrence Smith)*

Bill Kirby, Carlton Gary's defence attorney May–September 1984.

Gary Parker, a member of Gary's defence team 1984–86, and later a state Senator.

August 'Bud' Siemon, Gary's trial attorney.

Judge John Land, who handled Gary's case pre-trial.

Bud Siemon and Assistant District Attorney Doug Pullen approach Judge Kenneth Followill's bench during Gary's trial. *(Joe Schwartz)*

District Attorney William Smith addresses the jury. *(Allen Horne)*

Sheila Dean on the witness stand. *(Allen Horne)*

Earnestine Flowers testifies at Gary's trial.

Gary in court with his lawyer, Bud Siemon.

Henry Sanderson testifies about his gun, stolen from his car in Wynnton in October 1977. *(Allen Horne)*

John Lee Mitchell, whom Gary falsely accused of murdering Nellie Farmer. *(Allen Horne)*

Malvin Alamichael Crittenden testifies in the stranglings trial. *(Allen Horne)*

A police 'composite' sketch that Gertrude Miller identified as the man who raped and tried to kill her in September 1977.

Carlton Gary's mother, Carolyn, after he was given the death penalty. *(Allen Horne)*

Gary on the way to court for an appeal hearing, 14 December 1989. *(Lawrence Smith)*

# MAPS

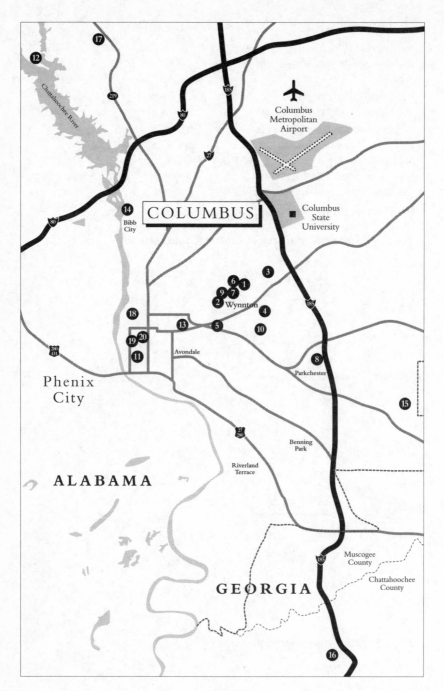

Chattahoochee River

⑰

⑫

219

80

185

✈

Columbus
Metropolitan
Airport

80

⑭
Bibb
City

COLUMBUS

27

■ Columbus
State
University

185

③
⑥ ①
⑨ ⑦
② Wynnton
④

⑱

⑬
⑤
⑩

⑲ ⑳
⑪
Avondale

280
431

⑧
Parkchester

⑮

Phenix
City

27
280

Benning
Park

Riverland
Terrace

ALABAMA

GEORGIA

185

Muscogee
County

Chattahoochee
County

⑯

xii

## Strangling Crime Scenes

1 Ferne Jackson (17th Street)
2 Florence Scheible (Dimon Street/Eberhart Avenue)
3 Jean Dimenstein (21st Street)
4 Martha Thurmond (Marion Street)
5 Kathleen Woodruff (Buena Vista Road)
6 Ruth Schwob (Carter Avenue)
7 Mildred Boron (Forest Avenue)
8 Janet Cofer (Steam Mill Road)
9 Callye East's house – Henry Sanderson's gun stolen (Eberhart Avenue)
10 Gertrude Miller – survived first attack by strangler (Hood Street)

## Other Locations

11 Historic District
12 Big Eddy Club
13 Lynching of Teasy McElhaney 1912
14 Lynching of Simon Adams 1900
15 Carlton Gary's apartment 1977–79
16 Fort Benning
17 Area of Land family holdings 1900–20
18 G.W. Ashburn murdered 1868
19 Dr Thomas H. Brewer murdered 1956

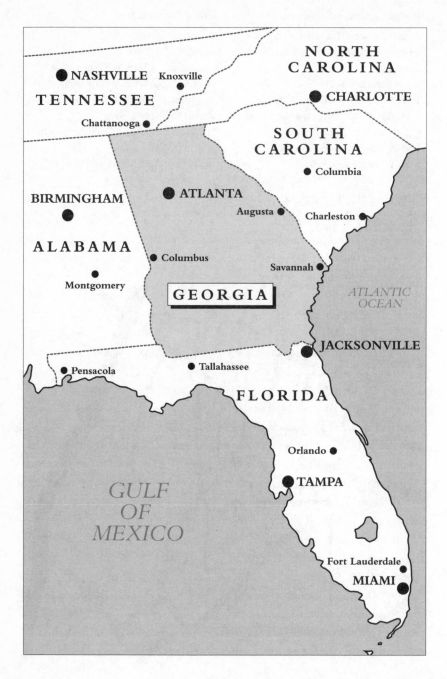

NORTH
CAROLINA

● NASHVILLE  Knoxville
TENNESSEE          ● CHARLOTTE

Chattanooga ●                SOUTH
                            CAROLINA

                                   ● Columbia
BIRMINGHAM      ● ATLANTA
    ●                  Augusta ●    Charleston ●
ALABAMA      ● Columbus
     ●                          Savannah ●      ATLANTIC
Montgomery        GEORGIA                         OCEAN

                                    ● JACKSONVILLE
           ● Pensacola   ● Tallahassee
                    FLORIDA

                         Orlando ●
  GULF
   OF                    ● TAMPA
MEXICO

                              Fort Lauderdale
                              ● MIAMI

# ACKNOWLEDGEMENTS

Early in our association, in the spring of 1998, I was talking on the phone with Wendy Murphy, who more than anyone is responsible for my committing myself to this book. I was thinking aloud about whether to do it: 'I'm just not sure,' I remember saying. 'It's a big decision – after all, it's likely to dominate the next two years of my life.' Although I was out by more than 400 per cent, I thank her first for her constant help and involvement in what has been the most intellectually rewarding project of my working life to date.

Its long gestation has seen both my original editors – Michael Fishwick at HarperCollins in London and Colin Robinson of New York's New Press – move on to new challenges, but I remain indebted to them for their support. Their successors Richard Johnson and Diane Wachtell swiftly reassured me that all would be well, and they and their colleagues went on to prove it by their brilliance and enthusiasm as the book neared press. Special thanks are due to Robert Lacey, whose copy edit of the text was beyond emulation. As ever, I must also thank my British and American agents, Peter Robinson and Jill Grinberg, for whom this is the third Rose literary parturition. If they ever doubted whether I would finish, they did not say so to me. Neil Belton, who has published my work elsewhere, helped me find a way to structure the book with his warm and generous advice.

This book describes great evils, but along the path of its research I have made sustaining friendships with some of the finest people I know. In and around Columbus, Gene Hewell, Earnestine Flowers, Doris Layfield, Bill and Jean Kirby, George and Vicky Williams, Floyd Washington, Tracy Dean,

Anne Blalock, Eddie Florence, Robert Leonard, Marcel Carles, Daniel and Elizabeth Senne, Murphy Davies, Marquette McKnight, Jo-Jo Benson, Randy Loney, Ruby Miles, George Ford, Ronzell Buckner, the late A.J. McClung, Clarence White, Albert Thompson, Ruby James, J.T. Frazier, Freddie White Junior, Malvin Crittenden, Beleta Turner, Carlos Galbreath, Arthur Hardaway, John Allen and John Land opened up their doors, their hearts and their memories, not knowing what might be the result.

Two local writers, Richard Hyatt and Billy Winn, welcomed me with courtesy and comradeship, although both thought the main thrust of my work wrong-headed. Without Winn's seminal work on lynching and the murder of Thomas H. Brewer, this book would not have been written. It began to gestate when I sat in the old W.C. Bradley Library and read the yellowing clippings of Winn's monumental 1987 newspaper series about the killing of Teasy McElhaney. It was this that first made me think that there might be a way to connect Columbus's past with more recent times. Mike Haskey, chief photographer at the *Ledger-Enquirer*, helped me sift through the paper's old photo files and facilitated the use of many of the pictures published here. Special thanks are due to Reagan Grimsley, the archivist at Columbus State University, who found many invaluable materials and sent them across the Atlantic, and to Cathy Fussell, Professor of English at the same institution, who introduced me both to the work of the great Carson McCullers and to her Wynnton former home. John Lupold, recently retired as Professor of History, supplied knowledge, insight and the warmest hospitality and, as both tutor and reader, saved me from countless errors. He also found more photos, and the time to scan and send them all to Britain on compact disk. He and his wife Lynn are friends for life.

The members of the Atlanta death penalty defence bar labour daily against great odds in what can be a distinctly hostile environment. I want to pay tribute to Steve Bright, Jeff Ertel, Bud Siemon, Gary Parker, Beth Wells, Robert McGlasson and Michael McIntyre for years of guidance, friendship and sheer inspiration. All could have become rich many years ago had they not devoted themselves to a less tangible kind of wealth – that derived from the pursuit of justice. Above all, I must thank Jack Martin, his wife Sandra Michaels and their assistant-cum-piano-star Chad Mason for the best fun it is possible to have while researching a book about serial murder and the unjust application of the death penalty.

The forensic tests described in Chapter 11 were financed by *Vanity Fair* magazine, and I must thank its editor Graydon Carter, London editor Henry Porter, and its softball team coach Michael Hogan for their encouragement and support. Michael also happens to edit my articles. I also thank Roger Alton and Allan Jenkins at the *Observer*, whose magazine published an article about this story in 2004. Valerie Kalfrin dug out important facts in upstate New York.

Jesselyn Radack, Emily Whitfield, Tom Williamson, Desmond King and Cathy Caruth read all or parts of the text and made numerous wise comments, without which it would have been greatly inferior. Professors David Garland and W. Fitzhugh Brundage gave me some vital intellectual hints, while Roger Hood, nominally retired as Oxford's Professor of Criminology, one of the doyens of world death penalty studies, has provided friendship and encouragement for many years. By inviting me to give a seminar at All Souls College in early 2000 when my research was at an early stage, he forced me to think hard for the first time about some of what have become this book's underlying themes.

It is not entirely coincidental that the next edition of Hood's essential reference work, *The Death Penalty: A Worldwide Perspective*, will be co-written by my wife Carolyn, Oxford's Criminology Reader. The long years that I have been expecting this have seen her produce our sons Jacob and Daniel, and without her love, understanding and occasional injections of much-needed discipline, we might all still be waiting.

David Rose
Oxford, December 2006

# ONE

## *The Best Place on Earth*

Way down in Columbus, Georgia
Want to be back in Tennessee
Way down in Columbus Stockade
Friends have turned their backs on me.
Last night as I lay sleeping
I was dreaming you were in my arms
Then I found I was mistaken
I was peeping through the bars.

'Columbus Stockade Blues' (traditional)

'We don't take just anybody as a member,' said Daniel Senne, the Big Eddy Club's general manager. 'They have to be known to the community. It's not a question of money, but of standing, morality, personality. And they must be people who conduct themselves well in business. Integrity is important.'

We were talking in the hush of the club's sumptuous lounge, perched on deep sofas, our feet on a Turkoman rug, surrounded by antiques. With the seasons on the turn from winter to spring, the huge stone fireplace was not in use, but there was no need yet for air-conditioning. From the oak-vaulted dining room next door came the muffled clink of staff laying tables for lunch: silver cutlery, three goblets at every setting, and crisply starched napery. The club's broad windows provided a backdrop of uninterrupted calm. Framed by pines that filtered the sunlight, a pair of geese glided across the state line, making barely a ripple. Behind them, across a mile of open water, lay the smoky outline of the Alabama hills.

1

The minutes of the club's founding meeting were framed on the wall, a single typed folio dated 17 May 1920. On that day, ten of the most prominent citizens of Columbus, Georgia, led by the textile baron Gunby Jordan II, had formed a committee 'to perfect an organization for building a suitable club at a place to be determined ... for having fish fries, 'cues and picnics'. A postscript added: 'Arrangements will be made at the club for entertaining ladies and children.'

The Big Eddy's buildings had expanded since that time, but were still on the spot the founders chose, a promontory at the confluence of the Chattahoochee River and its tributary, Standing Boy Creek. In 1920, before the river was dammed, the turbulence formed where the currents came together was an excellent place to catch catfish. Anyone who ate Chattahoochee catfish now would likely suffer unpleasant consequences, thanks to the effluent swept downstream from Atlanta, but the club's location remains idyllic. Escaping the traffic that mars so much of modern Columbus, I'd driven down a vertiginous hill to the riverside, where I followed a winding lane along the shoreline, past grand homes and jetties. Before passing through the club's wrought-iron gates, I pulled off the road to feel the warmth of the sun. The only sounds were birds and a distant chainsaw.

Senne and his wife Elizabeth, dapper and petite, spoke with heavy French accents. They had served their apprenticeship in some of the world's more glamorous restaurants: London's Mirabelle and the Pavilion in New York, at a time when its regular patrons included Frank Sinatra, Bette Davis, Salvador Dalì, Cary Grant and the Kennedys.

'If you had told me twenty years ago that this is the place to be, I would not have believed you,' Elizabeth said. 'But it is. They are nice people, really down-to-earth.'

Membership was strictly limited to 475 families, Elizabeth went on, and applicants must accept that their backgrounds would be carefully investigated by the board. Even in summer, the dress code was strictly observed: a jacket and tie for men, and for women, 'no unkempt hair or wrinkled pants'.

The rules served their purpose, Daniel said. 'It's a good community. People take care of you.' Just as in the 1920s, the club could count many of

Columbus's most distinguished inhabitants as members: the leaders of business, and local, state and national politicians. Former President Jimmy Carter was an honorary member for life.

In the week of my visit in March 2000, another of the city's more venerable institutions, the Columbus Country Club, had announced the admission of its first two African-American members – both of them women who worked for the public relations departments of local corporations. I turned to Daniel and mentioned this news, then asked: 'Do you have any black people yet in the Big Eddy Club?'

He shifted his posture awkwardly. 'No. Not yet.' He looked appealingly at his wife. 'We don't have black members, because none have applied.'

Later that day, as the light was starting to fade, I sat on the veranda of a Victorian house on Broadway, in the heart of Columbus's downtown 'Historic District', with George and Vicky Williams, admiring their profligate springtime flowers. The area had once been in steep decline, but years of careful restoration had made it again a highly desirable neighbourhood. The Williamses were the first middle-class black family on their block, but Vicky said they'd encountered little overt prejudice. 'Most of them just leave us alone.'

George, some twenty years older than his wife, was a highly decorated Vietnam veteran, and since leaving the military had built up several thriving businesses. Vicky had a university degree and worked at Columbus's huge commercial bank, CB&T. She had lived in Columbus all her life: attended its schools; socialised widely; watched its local TV news and read its newspaper, the Columbus *Ledger-Enquirer*. How important did she think the Big Eddy Club was in the way the city was run?

Vicky looked at me blankly. 'What's the Big Eddy Club?'

Columbus, population a little less than 200,000, is Georgia's second city, 110 miles south of the state's capital, Atlanta. Running across it is a racial fissure, a rift with an exact geographical position, its line marked by the east–west thoroughfare known for most of its length as Macon Road. With exceptions unusual enough to be noticeable, white people – about 65 per cent of the total – live to the north, and black to the south. No longer legally segregated, they will mingle at work and use the same stores and restaurants, but in general they do not mix in their social lives, or at home. This *de facto* segregation still divides other American cities, on both sides of the Mason-Dixon line. But in places like Columbus it tends to be more noticeable. One of its lesser implications is the fact that a well-educated, middle-class black family has never even heard of the fine dining club where their white counterparts take their families for Sunday brunch, marry off their daughters and hold their charity balls; a place where rich and powerful people relax in each other's company. Unbeknown to George and Vicky Williams, their near neighbours included at least one Big Eddy member, a prominent lawyer.

Columbus stands amid the rolling granite landscape of what, before the boll weevil infestation of the early twentieth century, used to be Georgia's cotton belt. In summer, the sun irradiates the city with a lacquered intensity for months on end, bringing with it a plague of bugs. Winters are pleasantly mild, although a shift in the wind can bring plummeting temperatures and even, occasionally, tornadoes. The city takes up far more room than its inhabitants need. Its low density has allowed them to cultivate generous, handsome gardens, and there are so many trees that viewed from above, from atop one of the hills on the eastern perimeter, it barely looks like a city at all, but an expanse of forest. At ground level, the foliage turns out to hide a sprawling hinterland of strip malls and snarling expressways, built to connect mazes of suburban subdivisions which on superficial inspection could be almost anywhere in America. Beyond the Victorian downtown enclave, anyone crossing a road on foot takes their life in their hands.

To the west, across the Chattahoochee, is Alabama, here represented by Phenix City, long a centre for gambling and illicit alcohol. In the 1950s the gangs of Phenix City took to murdering elected officials who were trying to clean it up, and it remains the only town in the United States where martial law has had to be imposed in peacetime. Some of those gangsters' descendants now occupy positions of the greatest respectability in both Georgia and Alabama.

For many Americans, Columbus has a fame and importance out of proportion to its size. It was in his Columbus drugstore during the 1870s that the chemist John Stith Pemberton first mixed the ingredients for his patent soda drink, Coca-Cola. (That original formula is said to have included a stimulating ingredient which is missing from its later versions – cocaine.) To the immediate south of the city lies Fort Benning, the world's largest infantry base, a place familiar to millions who have served in the military. Its short-haired inhabitants can often be seen in Columbus on weekends, in the dive bars and strip lounges on Victory Drive, a venue for occasional drunken shootings, and with their girlfriends at the motels clustered round the exit ramps on the road to Atlanta, Interstate 185. On my very first night in Columbus, I found myself in the Macon Road Days Inn, where some recent recruits had decided to hold a party in the room above mine. At 3 a.m. it sounded as if they were rounding off their celebrations by repeatedly throwing a heavy refrigerator against the walls and onto the floor. A few hours later, as I blearily went in search of breakfast, there were two used condoms, pale translucent jellyfish, on the concrete stairs.

In Oxford, my English home city, which has a population about two-thirds of Columbus's, the Yellow Pages phone book entries under the heading 'Places of Worship' take up less than a page. In Columbus, they require fourteen, listed under a rich array of denominations: from 'Churches, African Methodist Episcopalian' to 'Churches, Word of Faith'. There are five separate headings to cover the different varieties of Baptist, and seven for Methodists. In Columbus can be found many kinds of Reverend. At the fancy places, such as the imposing neo-classical First Baptist Church of Columbus on Twelfth Street, they are solemn men in silken robes. At the other end of the market is Eddie Florence, a former cop who turned to religion after a short spell in the penitentiary. Dominating his church, deep in South Columbus, on the day of my visit was a drum-kit and electric organ; the premises doubled from Monday to Friday as the office for Florence's real estate and loans business. A plump, intense, beaming figure, he told me: 'I don't suppose you've had much opportunity to take out a mortgage from a man of God before?'

For many of Columbus's citizens, whose behaviour, I learnt, was not always conventionally devout, Church and community are one and the same. If one only knew a person's choice of place of worship, one would be able to assume much about his or her race, class and social standing. But Columbusites' faith is no veneer. They give generously to charity, and their routine enquiries after one another's health appear to express a genuine concern. As I rapidly discovered, their habit is to welcome strangers, even those armed with a notebook and difficult questions.

Its citizens may be oriented towards the world to come, but Columbus, according to Mayor Bob Poydasheff, with 'its wonderful people and great climate, is simply one of the best places on earth – cosmopolitan but always neighbourly'. The city, states his website, is 'in a period of unprecedented building and development, which is bringing our quality of life to new highs'. He enumerates its blessings: '[The] Chattahoochee Riverwalk, River-Center for the Performing Arts, Springer Opera House, Coca-Cola Space Science Center, Columbus Civic Center, our South Commons Softball Complex including a world-class softball stadium and much, much more.'

The economy, Mayor Poydasheff adds, is buoyant. For more than a century, Columbus has been quietly dominated by a small number of wealthy families. Gunby Jordan, who founded the Big Eddy Club, came from one of them. In 1919, two of these dynasts, Ernest Woodruff and William C. Bradley, bought the Coca-Cola corporation for $25 million. (In Bradley's case, some of this money was originally derived from his father's former slave plantation across the river in Alabama.) Their investment was to multiply several thousand times, and spread among their descendants, it has fructified Columbus. Bradley also founded the CB&T banking conglomerate. Its offshoot, the financial computing firm TYSYS, has been quartered since 2002 in a line of large, reflective buildings just north of the former textile district, and is the world's largest processor of credit cards.

It is only in the south of the city, on the other side of its racial frontier, that the signs of twenty-first-century prosperity are less visible. There, the surfaces of the roads are potholed and pitted. There are junkyards piled with ancient cars, and meagre stores with signs done in paint, not neon. In the poorer districts, lines of low-rise public housing projects stand amid meadows of ragged grass, competing for space with wooden three-room 'shotgun' houses, whose squalor would not look out of place in Gaza or Soweto.

The clubs of south Columbus are different, too. The biggest, a huge, low-ceilinged cavern just off Victory Drive, belongs to the R&B singer Jo-Jo Benson, responsible for a string of hits in the sixties and early seventies, including a national pop chart number one, 'Lover's Holiday'. A big, bearded bear of a man, the day we met he was dressed in a vivid striped caftan. He showed me round the club and took me into his office, taking pains to check that the large-calibre revolver he kept in the drawer of his desk was still there. 'This town is a trip,' he said. 'A lot of people don't want to see you make no money or succeed. Coming here from Atlanta is like leaving earth and going to the twilight zone, or travelling back in time.

'But this is the biggest, the nicest club in town, and I'm a public figure. A lot of people ask me why I stay. Well, I was raised in Phenix City, and more than that, I don't want to go in for that big-city stuff – gangs and shit. At the end of the day, Columbus is a place to sleep, lay down and rest. Most of the time I don't get no trouble.'

Benson led me out of the club into the parking lot, and asked me to sit in the passenger seat of his impressive grey sports utility vehicle. 'I've got sound equipment worth thousands of dollars in here,' he said. He opened the glovebox and removed an unmarked CD. 'We recorded this last week. Ain't finished with it yet.' It turned out to be a romantic duet of heart-breaking sweetness and purity with another local singer, Ruby Miles. Jo-Jo's music filled the car and brought to mind decades of Georgia gospel, blues and soul: Otis Redding, Randy Crawford, Sam Cook. For a moment he looked bashful. 'You like it? Tell your friends.'

I made my first visit to Columbus to investigate what looked like a paradox. It was 1996, and the British newspaper that employed me, the *Observer*, had asked me to go to Georgia to write about the death penalty. My editors were intrigued by the fact that the state's death row held two prisoners who had exhausted every possible appeal, but whose execution had been indefinitely delayed. The reason, it seemed, was that Georgia wanted to wait until after the Olympic Games, which were shortly to be held in Atlanta. In Britain, as in the rest of Europe, capital punishment had been abolished many years earlier, and the paper wanted me to try to find out why parts of America still found it so attractive.

I began by talking to defence attorneys in Atlanta. They all said the same thing: I should go to Columbus. While its overall crime rate was relatively low, since 1976, when a case from Georgia persuaded the US Supreme

Court to reinstate the death penalty, Columbus had sentenced more men to die than anywhere else in the state. By the middle of 1996, four had been executed, all of them African-American, and eight were still on death row. At least another twelve had been condemned by Columbus judges and juries, but had won reprieves in appeals. If one worked out the number of death sentences per head of population, Columbus was one of the most dangerous places to commit a murder in the whole of the United States.

A few days later I found myself in Columbus's second tallest building, a harsh monstrosity in white concrete which would not have looked out of place in Stalinist East Berlin, the eleven-floor Consolidated Government Center. In front of a view across the river sat Judge Doug Pullen of the Chattahoochee Circuit Superior Court, which covers the city and five neighbouring counties. It had been a hot and languorous weekend, and I knew Pullen's reputation: criticised for his record a few years earlier by *Time* magazine, he had told the local media that *Time*'s problem was that it had yet to discover *glasnost*, the new policy of openness pioneered by the Soviet leader Mikhail Gorbachev, and was still a 'lovely pink colour'. Nevertheless, his lusty enthusiasm for capital punishment took me by surprise.

'I would guess that your experience of seeing bodies splattered and mutilated is limited,' he said by way of introduction. 'Unfortunately, mine is not.' A spreading, heavy-set man with round eyes too small for his face, he moved a little stiffly. 'In all honesty, abolishing the death penalty would have a negligible effect on crime. But the effect on the American people would be horrific. It would be symbolic, like flag-burning.

'We like to talk tough on crime, but we're soft. And every time you get an execution, you get people picketing, saying it's so cruel. Phooey. The first man I prosecuted for capital murder, even if he'd been executed on his due date, it would have been nine years to the day after he committed the crime. And then he got a stay, and all the anti-death penalty people went out dancing. In my view, there should be one appeal, and one only, then that's that: homeboy goes.'

'What about life without parole?' I asked.

Pullen shook his head. 'It's a weak sister, my friend. A horribly weak sister.'

As we talked, a big, stooped man with unusually bright blue eyes entered the room without knocking. The two of them stood, whooped, and made high fives. 'Meet Gray Conger, my successor as District Attorney,' Pullen said.

'We still on for that barbecue this weekend?' Conger asked him. Pullen replied in the affirmative. Before Pullen became a judge, the two men had worked together as prosecutors for more than twenty years: Pullen had been DA, and Conger his assistant. That was the way things had been done for decades in Columbus, they explained: an orderly progression from District Attorney to Superior Court judge meant that four of the five judges then sitting had spent most of their careers in the prosecution office.

'They're friends of mine, and they employed me,' Conger said. 'But don't get the idea that that means I get any advantages in court. All it does is give us a smooth transition when a new DA comes in.'

'Why do you think the city has sent so many men to death row?' I asked.

'I just don't know,' Conger shrugged. 'Maybe it's just that we've had some awful horrible murders around here.'

One thing he was sure of. 'In deciding which cases to seek the death penalty, and in the way we work in general, race is not a factor. In the South in my time, over the last thirty years, there's been the most amazing transformation. Southerners are very conscious of race. They go out of their way not to be accused of racial bias.'

Later that afternoon, Pullen took me in his battered Volvo down to Fort Benning, where he taught a class in criminal law and capital punishment to soldiers and police patrolmen. I still had no real idea why he was wedded so strongly to capital punishment, but there was obviously nothing confected about the strength of his feeling. 'I love people,' he remarked happily as we sped through the gates of the vast military base. 'You can probably tell that. So if you hurt one of my people, I'm going to come after you.'

In the past, he said, he had received dozens of letters asking him to reconsider death sentences. 'The strange thing was, they all seemed to come from Holland and Wales. Don't think I can't recognise an organised letter-writing campaign when I see it. I got news for you. My education puts me in the top 3 per cent in this country, but I couldn't name a single city in Wales. Folks round here don't necessarily care what folks in Wales think of them. I guess those letters came from Amnesty International or something. They should be concentrating on real human rights abuses, like in the Third World.'

Pullen's class, in an echoing room easily big enough to contain his hundred students, was a bravura performance. 'Let me give you a little insider tip,' he began. 'Our fine Attorney General, Michael Bowers, is planning to run for Governor.'

'How do you know?' someone asked.

'Bowers made his intentions plain to me personally. When we met up recently.' Pullen paused, then winked: 'At an execution.'

An Alabama state trooper, so fat he seemed almost triangular, asked how lawyers got to be judges. Pullen chuckled. 'You may rest assured that anyone successful in defence litigation need not apply. At least not on the Chattahoochee circuit.'

After the seminar, Pullen took me to dinner in a barbecue restaurant downtown. As we consumed a small pork mountain, I asked him about one of the cases that had attracted those letters from Holland and Wales, a capital murder he'd prosecuted in 1976. The defendant had been a mentally retarded man named Jerome Bowden, an African-American aged twenty-four. The body of his victim, Kay Stryker, a white woman of fifty-five, was found in her house, knifed and beaten, several days after her death. Afterwards, the police searched the home of her sixteen-year-old neighbour, Jamie Graves, and found an old pellet gun, its butt stained with her blood, together with her jewellery. Graves admitted burgling her home, but claimed she was killed by his friend Bowden. In return for his help, he was sentenced to life rather than being given the death penalty.

Bowden soon heard the police were looking for him. He walked up to a squad car he saw in the street, and asked if he could be of help. He was arrested on the spot, and less than two months after the murder, he stood trial. Pullen's case rested on Bowden's confession. He tried to retract it on the witness stand, saying he hadn't been in Stryker's house at all, and that a police detective had promised 'to speak to the judge' to save him from the electric chair in return for his signature. At the start of the hearing, Pullen had exercised his right to strike prospective jurors, so removing all eight African-Americans from the panel and ensuring that Bowden was tried only by whites. They did not believe him, and found him guilty on the second day of the trial.

In Georgia, as in many American states, capital trials consist of two phases. The first is the 'guilt phase', when the jurors have to decide guilt or innocence; in the event of a guilty verdict, they will go on to the 'sentencing phase', when it becomes their responsibility to decide whether a murderer should live or die. Here Bowden's attorney, Samuel Oates, begged the jury not to impose the death penalty, arguing that his client was of low intelligence and had a 'weak mind'.

Pullen dismissed this suggestion, arguing that it had been cooked up 'so someone can jump up and say, "Poor old Jerome, once about ten years ago his momma told somebody he ought to see a psychiatrist." He is not a dumb man, not an unlearned man … He certainly knows right from wrong.' In his view, Bowden was 'a defendant beyond rehabilitation', for whom death was the only possible sentence, because he had been sent to prison – for burglary – before. He held up a photograph of Stryker's body. 'How do you take a three-time loser who would take a blunt instrument and beat a harmless fifty-five-year-old woman's head into that? You can look through the holes and see the brains.'

In the nineteenth century, slavery's apologists had justified human bondage by equating black people with animals. Appealing to the jury to decree the death of a mentally retarded teenager, Pullen invoked this tradition: 'This defendant has shown himself by his actions to be no better than a wild beast – life imprisonment is not enough. Why? Because he has killed. Because he has tasted blood.' It would take courage for the jury to vote to have Bowden put to death, Pullen averred; much more courage than giving him a life sentence. But 'it took more courage to build this great nation, and it will take more courage to preserve it, from this man and his like'.

Almost ten years later, in June 1986, Bowden had lost his every appeal, and his last chance lay with Georgia's Board of Pardons and Parole. However, evidence had now emerged that Pullen had overstated Bowden's mental capabilities. In fact he had an IQ of fifty-nine, and was well within the clinical parameters of mental retardation.

Bowden's pending execution became a *cause célèbre*. The international music stars Joan Baez, Peter Gabriel, Lou Reed and Bryan Adams signed a petition to stop the killing, and sang at a protest concert in Atlanta. A flurry of last-minute legal petitions bought a few days' stay of execution, but on 23 June the Pardons and Parole board decided that he had indeed, in Pullen's phrase, 'known the difference from right and wrong' at the time of Kay Stryker's murder. The following morning, Bowden was led into the death chamber, his head and right leg shaved. The prison warden held out a microphone to carry his last words to an audience of lawyers, reporters and officials.

'I am Jerome Bowden and I would like to say my execution is about to be carried out,' he said. 'I would like to thank the people of this institution. I hope that by my execution being carried out it will bring some light to this thing that is wrong.' His meaning was ambiguous, but most observers thought he was referring to his own electrocution. Then he sat down in the electric chair. There was a short delay when the strap attaching a leather blind to hide his face from the audience snapped, and had to be replaced. But when the executioner threw the switch, the chair functioned smoothly. Eighteen months after Bowden's death, the Georgia legislature passed a new statute barring state juries from sentencing the mentally retarded to death.

Pullen told me he still slept easy over Bowden's execution. 'I never heard Jerome Bowden was retarded until Joan Baez had a concert in Atlanta and said he was retarded. Jerome Bowden was no rocket scientist, but he knew words like "investigation" and "detective" and was kind of articulate. On death row, they said he was a deep thinker in Bible class. He was fit to execute.'

When we left the restaurant, it was already late. The cicadas were out in force, their strange chorus loud enough to overcome the noise of the distant traffic. We strolled back towards Pullen's car, the shadows of the historic district's houses shifting under a blurry moon. Not far from the Government Center, Pullen stopped.

'This is the site of the old courthouse. This is where they seized a little black boy and took him up to Wynnton, right by where the library is now. He wasn't more than twelve or thirteen and they shot him thirty times. The son of the man who led that mob grew up to become a judge. Kind of interesting, isn't it?'

\* \* \*

I left town next day intrigued but also bewildered, and with no real answers as to why Doug Pullen and his colleagues had such a passion for putting men to death. But notwithstanding Gray Conger's protestations, I was beginning to suspect that if there was a place where the 'amazing transformation' in race relations that he claimed to have witnessed had been least effective, it was within the criminal justice system.

In police stations, prosecutors' offices and the criminal courts, societies attempt to deal objectively with their most traumatic events. But the horrifying nature of those events sometimes makes objectivity impossible to achieve, and creates opportunities for ancient hatreds and primeval fears to reassert themselves. Stories about crimes and criminal trials, writes the British historian Victor Gatrell, permit 'a quest for hidden truths, when obscure people have to articulate motives, interests, and buried values and assumptions ... They expose fractured moments when people were in exceptional crisis, or observers were moved to exceptional passion.' They may say more about the way societies function than any number of broader surveys.

Before I left Georgia on that first visit I drove out to DeKalb County, at the foot of Stone Mountain, the great, bald dome of granite where giant sculptures of Confederate leaders have been carved into the rock face. I was there to see Gary Parker, an African-American attorney and former state Senator who'd spent most of his career doing criminal defence work in Columbus. Parker, a tall, slim man of forty-six whose hazel eyes seemed to brim with energy, had fought some famous legal battles, both civil and criminal, against tough odds. 'In Columbus,' he said, 'usually there's only two blacks in the courtroom. Me and the defendant.'

We talked about the city and his work there long into the evening. I was about to leave when he took a pull on his menthol cigarette and paused, as if debating whether to say what was on his mind. Outside the windows of his spacious, homely den, thickets of trees cast dusky shadows. Recently, he told me, he had left Columbus for good, unable to bear an atmosphere that he had begun to find intolerably oppressive.

'Sometimes I think something really bad happened in Columbus,' he said quietly. 'That there's some terrible secret from the past. Like a massacre or something. I keep on expecting someone to go digging foundations at a construction site and find a mass grave. Raised as I was in the South, images of lynching come to mind all the time, and there have been times when I've sat in court there and felt as if I was witnessing a lynching in my lifetime. I don't know what it was, but something happened there. It's like a curse.'

I got up to go. I knew I had come nowhere near to understanding Columbus's paradoxes and mysteries. I suspected that their solutions must lie deep in the city's history, and in the way it had been remembered and set down, and had thus helped form contemporary outlooks and mentalities. I also knew I'd be back.

Most of the remains of antebellum Columbus are to be found in Wynnton, the neighbourhood Doug Pullen had mentioned at the end of our evening. It was once known as the 'millionaires' colony', and its placid exclusivity dates back to the time when Columbus was first laid out in 1828, and its richer citizens began to construct their homes there, on the slopes of Wynn's Hill, a safe distance from the downtown stews and factories springing up by the side of the Chattahoochee. They were joined by cotton planters from the surrounding countryside, who saw in Wynnton the ideal location for an urban retreat. Their Palladian temples and mansions decked with Louisiana-style wrought-iron tracery were once at the heart of a social whirl that is said to have rivalled more famous centres of Old South, slave-holding glamour, such as Charleston, Richmond and New Orleans. There were lavish picnics, barbecues, marching bands and orchestras, full-dress hunts and glittering balls.

As late as the 1970s, Wynnton remained a kind of Arcadia, writes the Columbus journalist and author William Winn. His nostalgic description carries more than a whiff of *Gone with the Wind*: 'Nearly every house, however modest, has a lawn, and every spring Wynnton is ablaze with pink and white azaleas, the neighbourhood's particular glory.' Later, the district was to become synonymous not with colourful flowers, but with rape and murder. But until then 'it had always been a calm, peaceful neighbourhood, almost entirely free of crime except for an occasional cat burglar. Generations of black nurses rolled perambulators containing generations of white children down the shady sidewalks, and every June the air became so redolent with the fragrance of magnolias and fading gardenias it almost made one dizzy.'

The economic strength of Columbus has long enabled it to wield disproportionate political influence in Georgia, and the torrid months that preceded the South's secession from the United States were no exception. By 1859, just thirty-one years after the time when it lay on the ragged American frontier, the city is said to have contained eleven churches, four cotton factories, fourteen bars, forty-five grocery stores, four hotels, thirty-two lawyers, three daily newspapers and a magnetic telegraph office. Cotton spun in Columbus could be taken by paddle steamer down the Chattahoochee all the way to Apalachicola on the Florida Gulf Coast, a distance by river of almost five hundred miles. In May 1853, the closing of a last ten-mile gap saw the completion of the Muscogee-Southwestern railroad. 'It was then that a great railroad jubilee was held in Columbus,' writes the local historian Etta Blanchard Worsley. 'Mayor J.L. Morton mingled water from the Atlantic Ocean with the waters of the Chattahoochee, typifying the union of Savannah and Columbus.' In the whole of what was about to become the Confederate States of America, the industrial production of Columbus was second only to that of Richmond, Virginia.

In the 1860 census, the population of Muscogee County (including Columbus, its suburbs such as Wynnton and the surrounding rural districts) was made up of 9,143 whites, 165 free blacks and 7,921 slaves. It was on this human property that the city's wealth depended, as its civic leaders recognised. As the abolitionist movement gathered strength in the North and Midwest, the lawyer Raphael J. Moses argued as early as 1849 in favour of leaving the Union in order to protect the right to own slaves. Five years later, America's first secessionist journal, the *Corner Stone*, began publication in Columbus. Another early supporter of secession was the local attorney Henry Lewis Benning, later to become the Confederate General whose name is still borne by the military fort. In 1859 he warned that if Lincoln were elected President, all who resisted the end of slavery would be summarily hanged by the 'Black Republican Party'. Immediate secession was the only way to escape the 'horrors' of abolition. 'Why hesitate?' Benning asked. 'The question is between life and death.'

As the political temperature rose, individuals suspected of abolitionist sympathies faced violent retribution. In December 1859, William Scott, the representative of a New York textile company, was run out of Columbus by a vigilante committee, which claimed he displayed 'more interest in the nigger question than in the real object of his visit'. Like the French aristocracy before the Revolution, Georgia's whites had been seized by a *grande peur*. Their terror of a slave insurrection was fuelled by the distant memory of Nat Turner's bloody revolt in Virginia in 1831, and the recent raid by the Christian radical John Brown on the federal armoury at Harpers Ferry in the same state, planned as a means of arming a putative slave rebellion. In the wake of the raid, which had been crushed by the future Confederate general Robert E. Lee, the 1859–60 session of the Georgia Assembly enacted harsh new measures against free blacks, who were seen as potential focuses for discord. Blacks from outside the state were forbidden to enter it on pain of being sold into slavery, and any current free black resident found 'wandering or strolling about, or leading an immoral, profligate course of life' could be charged with vagrancy and also sold. It was thenceforth forbidden for a master to free his slaves posthumously in his will, making slavery in Georgia somewhat less escapable than in ancient Rome.

From this febrile milieu sprang the Columbusite US Senator Alfred Iverson. 'Slavery, it must and shall be preserved,' he proclaimed in a speech in 1859, going on to argue that the only way to achieve this end was to form an independent confederacy. By the end of 1860, after Lincoln's victory in the presidential election, the second Georgia Senator, Robert Toombs, who owned a plantation south of Columbus and later became the Confederacy's Secretary of State, had also backed secession. On 23 December, the night South Carolina became the first state to leave the Union, Columbus celebrated with a torchlight procession, bonfires and fireworks. The city had already spawned several companies of a paramilitary 'Southern Guard', which joined the march in their freshly designed uniforms, rifles at their shoulders. J. Harris Chappell, aged eleven, a future President of Georgia College, wrote to his mother: 'I think nearly all the people of Columbus is for secession as they are wearing the cockade. There are several small military companies one of which I belong to … the uniform is red coats and black pants. Lenard [sic] Jones is captain. I'm a private. Tommy's first lieutenant. Sammy Fogle has got the measles.'

Georgia's Ordinance of Secession passed the State Constitutional Convention on 21 January 1861, to be greeted in Columbus with a mass meeting of citizens, another torchlight procession, and the firing of cannon salutes. The common people shared the zeal of the small, slave-owning elite. The State Governor, Joe Brown, was warning them that if Lincoln were to free the slaves, blacks would compete for jobs with poor whites, 'associate with them and their children as equals, be allowed to testify in court against them, sit on juries with them, march to the ballot box by their sides ... and ask the hands of their children in marriage'. (Georgia's laws against miscegenation were not struck down by the US Supreme Court until 1967.) In the first months of the war that began that April, Columbus sent eighteen companies to the front – 1,200 men, more than a fifth of its pre-war white population.

The war both blasted and, at least for a time, enriched Columbus. One family, that of the pioneering entrepreneur Colonel John Banks, whose seventh- and eighth-generation descendants were still occupying the magnificent Wynnton mansion known as The Cedars in 2006, lost three sons. As they fought what increasing numbers came to perceive as a 'rich man's war', ordinary Confederate soldiers not only died in combat, but fell prey in vast numbers to malnourishment, cold and disease. N.L. Atkinson, who lived on the Alabama side of the Chattahoochee, wrote in a letter to his wife, 'this inhuman war is putting our whole country in mourning'. But while its youth fought and fell at Gettysburg, Antietam and Manassas, Columbus's industry boomed. By 1862, the Eagle textile mill was running non-stop, and producing two thousand yards of worsted for uniforms each day, as well as cotton cloth for tents, thread, rope and rubberised fabric. The city's ironworks rapidly expanded, to become the Confederacy's second-largest source of swords, pistols, bayonets, artillery pieces, steam engines, boilers and ammunition. The newly established Confederate Navy Yard made a gunboat 250 feet in length.

Of the industrial quarter that was the scene of this feverish activity, not a trace remains. As the war reached its closing stages, the Union's Major General James Harrison Wilson was ordered to sap the Confederacy's resistance by striking at its last centres of manufacturing. Having dealt with the cities of Selma and Montgomery in Alabama, his force of thirteen thousand reached the west bank of the Chattahoochee on 16 April 1865 – a week after Lee's surrender at Appomattox. Neither Wilson nor the ragtag of militia units defending Columbus had received this news; they were likewise unaware that Lincoln had been murdered on 14 April. After a short battle on the Alabama shore, the Yankees swarmed across the Fourteenth Street bridge and took the city that Wilson had called 'the door to Georgia' in just over an hour. Next day, Wilson ordered that 'everything within reach that could be made useful for the continuance of the rebellion' must be destroyed. Mills, foundries, warehouses and military stockpiles were put to the torch, together with three gunboats, which drifted for miles down the river in flames. While the Union army went about its work, civilian mobs looted stores and small businesses. Even respectable, well-dressed women were said by one witness to have participated: 'They frantically join and jostle in the chaos, and seem crazy for plunder.' As Wilson moved on towards Macon on 18 April, leaving only a small garrison, Columbus was 'a mass of flame and coals'.

For many years, Columbus's business and political elites have gently looked down on their counterparts in the parvenu state capital to the north, Atlanta, which was still a featureless rural tract when Columbus was building its grid of downtown streets. Perhaps their superior attitude stems in part from their ancestors' differing response to Yankee-inflicted devastation. While Atlanta complained about its treatment at the hands of General William Tecumseh Sherman during his notorious march to the sea, Columbus got on with building new factories. Most of the imposing red-brick buildings downtown date from the late 1860s and seventies. One of them is built on the site of its predecessor, the Eagle mill. Above its mullioned arches, a banner in brickwork picks out the legend 'Eagle and Phenix'. Within a month of Wilson's fire, the iron foundries were open again for business. Louis Halman, formerly the proprietor of a sword works, retooled his charred and shattered premises and began, symbolically enough, to manufacture ploughs.

Impressive as this physical rebuilding was, in the period after the South's defeat, Columbus also engaged in a process of psychic reconstruction. In common with other communities whose long-term material suffering was much more severe, an important part of the city's attempt to come to terms with its role in America's bloodiest war was its adoption of a narrative myth – the legend of the Lost Cause. On the one hand, this was a way of making the past seem acceptable. At the same time, it contained the ideological seeds for the region's defining social characteristic far into the twentieth century – white supremacy.

There is a line in William Faulkner's play *Requiem for a Nun* which has become a cliché in writing about the South: 'The past is never dead. It's not even past.' Faulkner meant it to apply to the enduring consequences of an individual's actions, not the influence of history – and in any case, the past affects the present in regions other than the states of the former Confederacy. But ultimately the past doesn't die because it is remembered, and memory, as historians have recently begun to understand, is a potent influence on contemporary events, an analysis that seems especially true of the American Civil War. 'Americans have needed deflections from the deeper meanings of the Civil War. It haunts us still; we feel it, but often do not face it,' writes the Amherst professor David Blight. Instead of a titanic struggle over principle, America preferred to remember the war through 'pathos and the endearing mutuality of sacrifice among soldiers', so that 'romance triumphed over reality'. The consequence, Blight concludes, has been 'the denigration of black dignity and the attempted erasure of emancipation from the national narrative'.

In the Lost Cause account of the Civil War, partially created and vividly expressed in Columbus, slavery, racial oppression and the struggle against them have all but disappeared. The Confederate soldiers' courage and independence were to be celebrated, but not the realities of the 'peculiar institution' – slavery – they had happened to be defending. If slavery were to be mentioned at all, it was to be as something decent and necessary, grounded in mutual respect.

Histories of Columbus by authors from the city are steeped in the different aspects of this myth. For Nancy Telfair, a local journalist whose *History of Columbus, Georgia* was published in 1928 and recently reissued, the only principles involved in secession and the war were 'states' rights' to determine whether or not to permit slavery, and the prerogative of owners 'to assert their rights to equality and the protection of their property'.

19

It simply did not occur to her that the fact that this property happened to consist of human beings made it different from bales of cotton or farmland. According to Telfair (her real name was Louise Jones DuBose), slavery was merely 'a characteristically Southern industry' destroyed by the war.

Etta Blanchard Worsley's *Columbus on the Chattahoochee* was published in 1951, at an early stage of the modern civil rights era, when Georgia's African-Americans were fighting in court for the right to vote and other basic liberties. Like Telfair's, her book was published by the Columbus Supply Company, and taught in the city's schools. Both works can still be found on the shelves of Columbus's libraries. The Reverend Joseph Wilson, father of the US President Woodrow Wilson, had argued that bondage was an 'ameliorative' institution, which could improve the spiritual welfare of slaveholders and slaves alike. Echoing his logic, Worsley characterises slavery as 'part of the evolutionary process of the civilisation of the African tribes'. There might, she adds, have been isolated examples of abuse by 'low-class overseers'. In general, however, 'there had been the kindliest feelings between the whites and the Negroes ... the tie that bound the slave to the master with whom he was closely associated was one less of law than of mutual need, confidence and respect'. As for abolition, it was but a 'fanatical demand' orchestrated mainly by Northern Quakers, peddled by means of 'inflaming editorials', and 'little did it help for the South to plead for conciliation. The agitation went on for forty years.'

If Worsley is indignant about the end of slavery, Sterling Price Gilbert, long a member of Georgia's Supreme Court and arguably the most distinguished jurist Columbus has produced, is both egocentric and mawkishly sentimental. In his 1946 memoir *A Georgia Lawyer*, he writes of the liberation of his own family's property:

> The earliest recollection that I have of my home takes me back to the age of about three ... Our cook and her son, Anderson, who was the yard boy and who had 'looked after' me were leaving. I had a strong attachment, almost love, for Anderson. He had been my bodyguard and my playmate. My heart was filled with sorrow, and I cried because he was leaving me. I went to the road with him and his mother. I can remember standing

with feet apart, in the middle of the road, with tears streaming down my face, waving goodbye to my two friends. Every hundred yards or so, they would turn round and wave.

Justice Gilbert does not ask why his father's chattels, given a choice for the first time in their lives, had elected to leave.

Telfair, Worsley and Gilbert were all writing in the twentieth century, but the Lost Cause legend had emerged much earlier, and Columbus played a direct and significant role in its formation. On 12 March 1866, less than a year after Wilson's raiders torched the city's factories, Miss Lizzie Rutherford, her cousin Mrs Chas. J. Williams and their friends in the Soldier's Aid Society of Columbus began what was to become a totemic institution, Confederate Memorial Day. Mrs Williams, the daughter of a factory and railroad magnate, was married to a soldier who had, as Worsley writes, 'served bravely in the war'. She composed 'a beautiful letter', which she had distributed to women, newspapers and charitable organisations throughout the South. Williams proposed

> to set apart a certain day to be observed from the Potomac to the Rio Grande, and be handed down through time as a religious custom throughout the South, to wreath the graves of our martyred dead with flowers … Let every city, town and village join in the pleasant duty. Let all alike be remembered, from the heroes of Manassas to those who expired amid the death throes of our hallowed cause … They died for their country. Whether or not their country had or had not the right to demand that sacrifice is no longer a question for discussion. We leave that for nations to decide in the future. That it was demanded – that they fought nobly, and fell holy sacrifices upon their country's altar, and are entitled to their country's gratitude, none will deny.

Here was the core of Lost Cause mythology, what Blight describes as 'deflections and evasions, careful remembering and necessary forgetting', defined in a few sentences, as candid as they were succinct. If the true reason for the war was too painful to contemplate, then let it be dropped from discourse. Instead of asking whether all the devastation, loss and sacrifice had been justified, let them be venerated by the South's revisionist history.

The seed sown in Columbus flourished and multiplied. By the end of the 1860s, there was barely a town which did not observe Mrs Williams's ritual, with newly constructed memorial monuments, sometimes built in the greatly expanded cemeteries, as its focus. Similar observances began to be held in the North. Underlying them was a rhetoric of national reconciliation, of brotherhood renewed, in which Mrs Williams's plea that the causes of the bloodshed be 'no longer a question for discussion' was accepted wholeheartedly. As the *New York Herald* put it in an editorial on Memorial Day 1877, 'all the issues on which the war of the rebellion was fought seem dead'.

The only people written out of the script, in Columbus as elsewhere, were the former slaves. To them, in a Georgia stained by murder, exclusion, organised intimidation and a legal system of segregation that became more oppressive by the year, the issues for which the war had been fought did not seem dead at all. For black freedmen, reconciliation was possible only through submitting to white supremacy almost as completely as they had done before the torchlight parades and salutes that had heralded the war.

The Lost Cause legend did not die with the gradual entrenchment of civil rights, nor with the rise of a South where African-Americans have begun to serve as judges and elected politicians, and to gain access to business and social circles that were once impenetrably closed. In Columbus, hidden signs of a vision of the Confederacy as something heroic, a bulwark against the North's alien values, lie as if woven into the streets. The local TV station, its logo reproduced on signs and billboards, is called WRBL – W-Rebel. It took a strike by black students in the 1980s to get the authorities at the local college (now Columbus State University) to see that to use 'Johnny Rebel' as the mascot for sports teams, black and white alike, and to ask them to parade before games to the strains of the Confederate anthem 'Dixie', was, at least for African-Americans, unacceptable.

On the shelves of the city's bookstores I found the Lost Cause legend reproduced in an entire literary sub-genre of works such as *The South Was Right*, by James and Walter Kennedy, published in 2001. Railing against Northern historians' 'campaign of cultural genocide', it maintains that the true story of the War Between the States is that 'the free Southern nation was invaded, many of our people raped and murdered, private property plundered at will and their right of self-determination violently denied'.

Always lurking beneath Georgia's surface, the strange and anachronistic wounded anger expressed by such discourse burst into the open in a protracted political struggle in the first years of the twenty-first century. In early 2001 I spent several weeks in Columbus, and daily studied the *Ledger-Enquirer*'s letters page. The State Assembly was debating a proposal to replace the Confederate battle flag as the official flag of the state, on the grounds that African-Americans saw it as a symbol of servitude and oppression; just as pertinently, transnational corporations which would otherwise have been investing in the state were expressing their reluctance unless the flag were changed. Not the least bizarre aspect of the debate was the fact that far from representing historical continuity, the Stars and Bars had only been readopted in 1956, as part of the state's militant response to the US Supreme Court's attempt to desegregate education. But to change the flag again, the *Ledger-Enquirer*'s incensed correspondents claimed, would be an intolerable act of vandalism.

'The issue over the state flag is not altogether about heritage or hate or slavery. It is all about the blacks trying to force the white southerners to remove all symbols of the Confederacy from their sites, and they do not have the right to do that. If they choose to live in the South, they WILL have to look at it. Keep the flag flying!' wrote Mr Danny Green. 'The Confederate emblem should remain. There is [sic] no racial problems I know of. We gave blacks the right to ride in the front of the bus. Let's not give them everything they want,' added J.R. Stinson. A Mr Raymond King was more extreme: 'Where does it end? It's OK for a terrorist [sic], Jesse Jackson, to be revered as some kind of saint ... but it's not OK for us to honour our great Southern heritage. Bull! As far as I'm concerned, it's the African-Americans that are full of hate because people like me will not bow down and give them a free ride in life.'

In 2001, the flag-reform measure passed. Almost two years later, a Republican candidate for State Governor named Sonny Perdue ended many decades of Democrat stewardship after making a pledge to restore the Confederate flag the central plank of his campaign.

I bought a copy of *The South Was Right* and took it home to England. It was only there, as I browsed one afternoon, that I noticed that someone had left a business card inside it, hidden between two pages. 'National Alliance', read a heading on the front, above a logo made up of a cross and oak leaves. 'Towards a New Consciousness, a New Order; a New People'. Further details, complete with numbers for 'Georgia hotlines' and an address for a website, were printed on the reverse:

We believe that we have a responsibility for the racial quality of the coming generations of our people. That no multi-racial society is a healthy society. That if the White race is to survive we must unite our people on the basis of common blood, organize them within a pro-gressive social order, and inspire them with a common set of ideals. That the time to begin is now.

*   *   *

I returned to Columbus in the autumn of 1998, two years after my first trip. This time, and for many subsequent visits, some of which lasted several weeks and others just a few days, my enquiries had a focus: the city's most notorious series of crimes – the serial killings known as the 'stocking stranglings'.

In the late 1970s, a time when Jimmy Carter's arrival in the White House was being said to mark the emergence of a new, racially harmonious, post-civil rights 'sunbelt' South, the fabric of the city was rent by seven exceptionally horrible rapes and murders. The victims – the youngest fifty-nine, the oldest eighty-nine – were all white women who lived alone, and all were strangled, most with items of their own lingerie. All but one had lived in the neighbourhood of Wynnton, and some were members of the city's highest social echelons. From an early stage, while he still rampaged without apparent hindrance, the Columbus authorities had been con-vinced that the perpetrator was black.

In the course of my research, I found myself keen to know more about the Big Eddy Club, the exclusive private social club on the banks of the Chattahoochee. The membership lists were confidential. But former staff told me that five of the women murdered by the strangler had been members or frequent visitors, together with many of the public officials whose job it became to capture and punish the man responsible for their deaths.

It took time, and the assiduous cultivation of local contacts, before I was able to acquire an invitation to venture beyond the big iron gates bearing the legend 'B.E.' that guard the entrance to the club's driveway. My lunch, as the guest of a delightful, politically liberal couple who made me promise not to jeopardise their social standing by thanking them in print, was adequate, if not exceptional – a salmon filet with wilted greens, slightly overdone, and a chocolate torte with mixed berries for dessert. It would not have won a Michelin star, but on the other hand, I had been living amid the fast-food and chain restaurants of Columbus, and it was the tastiest meal I had eaten for weeks. The service – from a pair of young black waiters – was efficient and polite, without being over-attentive. As for the surroundings, as one gazed through the dining room's panoramic windows at the scene of utter tranquillity, it was difficult to imagine that Columbus had a long history of violence.

After coffee in the lounge, I picked up my coat and made ready to leave. Elizabeth Senne, the *maîtresse d'hôtel*, saw me from the passageway and hurried over, detaining me at the door. She seemed awkward, agitated. 'Please don't make anything of the fact we haven't got black members,' she said, 'and they do come as visitors. Really, they are very welcome.' She touched my arm confidentially. 'I think perhaps it's the joining fee: it's a lot to pay if you're not sure you're going to fit in.'

'How much is it?' I asked.

'I can't tell you that. But you know, most of the members are old families, and although newcomers are very welcome, there is a distinction. There is one guy who worked his way up from selling insurance. And although he's seventy now, he's still a newcomer. So maybe they sense that. You know what I mean?'

The joining fee, I discovered later that day, was $7,500. On her veranda that same evening, I described the club to my African-American friend Vicky Williams, and mentioned Elizabeth's closing remarks. Vicky laughed, surprised at the way some people chose to spend their money, then came up with an alternative hypothesis. Mrs Senne, of course, was an employee:

she could not be held responsible for following the club's policies. But Vicky said, with a bitter little shrug, 'It's like, you're a reporter, and you're good at getting people to tell you their stories, and maybe you can tell when they're lying. That's how it is as a black person, when you encounter racism. People can seem ever so nice, but sometimes, you can smell it.'

# TWO

# We've Got a Maniac

The black fiend who lays unholy and lustful hands on a white woman in the state of Georgia shall surely die!

REBECCA FELTON (1897)

Hours after nightfall, when the last lights are going out and the only sound is the rustle of the pines and sweetgums on the balmy Georgia wind, the terror that enveloped Wynnton seems closer, more palpable. I'd planned to take a slow drive, to pause and stare at these moon-shadowed dwellings as once the killer saw them, in the moments before he pounced. My guide, a local architectural historian, kept hurrying me on. 'People here might not like it if we dawdle,' she said. 'You don't want to have to explain yourself to the police. Besides, a lot of people here have guns.'

If one knew nothing of its history, Wynnton after dark might feel no different from any American neighbourhood. But knowledge cannot be undone, and despite myself I shared her unease. I had seen the crime scene photographs, and the passage of more than two decades had done nothing to diminish their horror. It wasn't just the bodies, their swollen faces seeming to betray a heart-rending mix of fear and resignation. What conveyed the sense of violation most was the ordinariness of their surroundings.

Inside the houses we were driving past, policemen's cameras had captured life's final debris. In one home, the story of a death struggle was told by large-print books, some still stacked neatly on their shelves, others strewn across a patterned carpet; in another, the floor was covered with an old lady's intimate garments, ripped from closets, then used by the killer to

27

fashion his weapon. Most poignant of all were the family photographs, still on their tables and dressers. Amid this everyday banality lay the victims: twisted, bruised, exposed.

The horror began to surface at 10 a.m. on Friday, 16 September 1977. Dixon Olive worked in the city's public health department and had been fretting indecisively for more than an hour. Mary 'Ferne' Jackson, his boss and colleague, had failed to show up for work. She was a woman of meticulous and unchanging routine, and Olive had already spoken to Ferne's best friend, Lucy Mangham. Early the previous evening, Lucy said, she had picked up Ferne from her red-brick bungalow on Seventeenth Street in Wynnton, and they had gone together to what Lucy called 'an enrichment school' at St Luke's United Methodist Church on Second Avenue, a spacious neo-Georgian edifice. Afterwards, Lucy took Ferne directly home, and waited by the kerb while she unlocked her door. She had noticed, she told Olive, that Ferne's bronze-coloured Mercury Montego was parked in its usual space outside. Lucy was away to her own house, only a street away, by 9.45 p.m. Having spoken to her, Olive decided to phone the police.

Mrs Jackson, who was fifty-nine, had been Columbus's Director of Public Health Education for twenty-six years. A widow, she had no children, and in her head-and-shoulders portrait she looks a little austere, as if the years of giving lectures on the dangers of smoking or the need for a healthy diet had begun to weary her. But she was much admired. She was about to be named Public Health Educator of the Year by the American Public Health Association. Her nephew, Harry Jackson, a successful businessman, was planning to run for Mayor.

When Jesse Thornton, the first police officer to respond to Dixon Olive's call, arrived at Ferne Jackson's house, he could see no sign that anyone had forced an entry. The doors were locked, the windows unbroken, and had he not been alerted by Mr Olive and some of Ferne's neighbours, he would have been tempted to leave. But her car, they pointed out, was missing. Thornton spoke by radio to his patrol commander, who advised him to get inside the house and look around. He used the knife he always carried to remove the mesh insect screen from the living-room window, and to jiggle the lock until he could get it open.

Many years later, Thornton would tell a murder trial jury what he did next. The first space he came to was the hallway, and straight away, 'I could see something that wasn't right.' Ferne's approach to tidiness was as meticulous as her time-keeping. But in the hall, said Thornton, 'There was stuff laying on the floor, papers, articles, just scattered all over the floor. There was a pillow on the floor, there was a suitcase that was opened, the drawers had been opened on the dresser, and stuff was pulled out and hanging out of it.' He continued, very slowly, down the passage towards Ferne Jackson's bedroom, his hand poised over his weapon. 'Once I got to the bedroom, I looked inside,' Thornton said. 'That's when I saw the body on the bed.'

Ferne's sheets had been pulled up round her head, and her nightgown tugged upwards, in order to expose her hips, pubic area and waist. Thornton could see there was blood on the sheets.

It fell to the Columbus medical examiner, Dr Joe Webber, to conduct a post mortem. The killer, he wrote in his subsequent report, had tied a nylon stocking and a dressing-gown cord together to make a single ligature, which was wrapped around Mrs Jackson's neck three times, leaving three 'very deep crevasses'. There was a large area of haemorrhage and bruising on the left side of her face and head, so that the white of her left eye was 'almost obliterated' by bleeding; the result, he believed, of a massive blow to her head. The white of her right eye was a mass of tiny, pinpoint petechial haemorrhages where her blood, deprived of oxygen, had burst from its vessels close to the surface, a common sign of strangulation. The small hyoid bone at the front of the throat was fractured, and there was more bleeding inside her neck. Her brain was swollen, another symptom associated with an interruption to the blood supply. Her sternum, or breastbone, had been fractured, an act which would have required the application of enormous force: 'It apparently had been flexed and pressure applied to the point that the bone snapped about midway between the upper and lower ends.' Finally, her vagina was bloodied, torn and bruised. Although Dr Webber could not find spermatozoa, he felt it would be reasonable to conclude that Ferne Jackson had been raped. Later, traces of seminal fluid would be found on her sheet.

There was no obvious motive for Ferne's murder. Despite ransacking her house, the killer had left her jewellery and other valuables untouched. She was still wearing two diamond rings. Nor did she have any enemies, and her popularity as a selfless public servant made her death all the harder to bear. 'She was one of the unsung heroes who quietly, gently and persistently worked for the betterment of her community,' Dr Mary Schley, a local pae-diatrician, told the Columbus *Ledger*. 'Ferne Jackson fought for the under-privileged, the minority groups, and against poverty and for better mental health,' added A.J. Kravtin, one of many readers who wrote to the paper after she died. While no one knew who was responsible, 'if it turns out to be one of the above, they killed the wrong person. They killed a friend.'

Three days after the discovery of her body, the *Ledger* published an edi-torial in her memory. 'It's always tragic when an innocent person becomes the victim of a violent crime,' it began, somewhat prosaically. 'It's even more tragic when the victim is someone who has devoted his or her life to helping others.' What could be done about the kind of crime that had taken Mrs Jackson's life, the paper asked, and how could further such acts be pre-vented? Increased police patrols would help. 'Vigorous efforts to apprehend the assailant and assure him a swift trial and appropriate punishment, if found guilty, might deter others from committing similar crimes ... Greater emphasis on respect for law and expanded educational and job opportunities might get at some of the underlying factors.' It was not to be that simple.

Ferne Jackson was murdered barely a month after the capture of David Berkowitz, the sexually driven 'Son of Sam' who killed or seriously injured a dozen women in New York. Partly in response to Berkowitz's bloody but compulsive career, Robert Ressler, the founder of the FBI's Behavioral Science Unit at Quantico, Virginia, had coined a new term to describe the perpetrators of such actions – they were, he suggested, 'serial killers'. The phrase had swiftly gained widespread currency. It took just eight days after the murder of Mrs Jackson for it to become apparent that one was at large in Columbus.

Jean Dimenstein was seventy-one, a wealthy spinster from Philadelphia who owned and ran a small department store, Fred and Jean's, with her brother. She spent the evening of 24 September with two friends at a steakhouse on Macon Road. They drove her home a little before 10 p.m., and watched from the car as she let herself into her house on Twenty-First Street, about half a mile from the residence of Mrs Jackson. As usual, she used the door at the side of the house, which led into her kitchen from her carport. Some time later that night, working in absolute silence, the killer removed the pins from the door's hinges, laid them to one side and entered Miss Dimenstein's house. Her sister-in-law, Francine, arrived there for coffee at ten the following morning. She noticed at once that Jean's car was missing, saw the open doorway, and called the police.

Like Ferne Jackson, Jean Dimenstein had been beaten about the head, strangled with a ligature made from a stocking wrapped around her neck three times, and raped. She was wearing the two diamond rings and, beneath the ligature, the diamond necklace she had worn the previous night. Although her house was also ransacked, it appeared that again, nothing had been stolen. To the chagrin of the police, who were cautiously claiming that they couldn't be sure that Jackson and Dimenstein had been killed by the same assailant, J. Donald Kilgore, Columbus's coroner, told the *Ledger* of the similarities between the two murders. He was, he said, quite certain that there was only one Columbus strangler. As if the bubbling panic that began to seize the city needed further encouragement, Kilgore informed journalists of supposed details that were not borne out by later investigations: that 'some sort of inflexible object was used to violate the women', and that 'a pillow was used to muffle their horrified screams while [they were] being tortured sexually before their death'. The motive for the crimes, he proclaimed, was torture.

In the autumn of 1977, Kilgore had been in his post for a year. He was not, however, a qualified forensic scientist, nor a pathologist, but the former director of a funeral home who had been embalming bodies with unusual enthusiasm since his teens. 'By the time I was twenty-one, I had participated with embalming 1,500 bodies,' he once told a Columbus reporter. 'You've got to disassociate yourself from the body at such times, even if the body has been mutilated. You try to associate with something positive. For instance, I don't see blood. I see ketchup.' Kilgore said that 'I treat every person's body with respect. I always have.' But as time went on, growing numbers of police officers came to disagree, accusing him of 'aggressive investigation and handling of the remains' at murder scenes. Some filed official complaints. In 1989, the tension between Kilgore and the Columbus Police Department (CPD) reached a new peak when he was accused of and investigated for allegedly decapitating a suicide victim. Under Georgia law, only a qualified medical examiner could cut into a body during a post mortem, and Kilgore was forced to admit that he often did so before such a person arrived. However, he insisted that he had not removed the victim's head. He had merely 'performed a procedure that involved the opening of the top portion of the skull'.

Told of Jean Dimenstein's murder while he was attending Sunday worship, Columbus's Mayor, Jack Mickle, addressed reporters on her lawn, ringed by ten police cars. 'We've got a maniac,' he said. 'I hope we get this guy. We gotta get this guy.'

The police had not been slow to notice that the cars belonging to both of the victims were found abandoned in Carver Heights, a black district on the southern side of Macon Road. Having examined the crime scenes and bodies, Donald Kilgore supported the CPD's growing suspicion that the strangler was black. Later, he told reporters he had looked under the microscope at pubic hairs left at the crime scenes, and in his view, being black and curly, they displayed 'Negroid characteristics'. In the Deep South of the United States, this was not an incidental matter.

In 1941 the Southern writer Wilbur J. Cash diagnosed what he termed the 'Southern rape complex', a social neurosis that originated long before the Civil War, and that continued to dominate whites' approach to race relations for many decades afterwards. In the collective mind of the South, Cash argued, white women's status was exalted to a bizarre and extraordinary degree, while their virtue was seen as at constant risk from the marauding, violating power of black sexuality. In part, he suggested, this was the product of guilt on the part of white male slave-owners at their own numerous illicit relationships with slave women, who often gave birth to mixed-race, light-skinned children. Soiled and shamed by their own desires and their inability to restrain them, white men projected an image of pristine chastity onto their wives and daughters, while assuming that black males must inevitably share their own lust for erotic miscegenation. By the time the Civil War broke out in 1861, writes Cash, 'she was the South's Palladium, the Southern woman – the shield-bearing Athena gleaming whitely in the clouds, the standard for its rallying, the mystic symbol of the nationality in the face of the foe ...

Merely to mention her was to send strong men into tears – or shouts.'

Columbus shared this dangerous fantasy. It could be found in purest form at the climax of Mrs Chas. Williams's 1866 appeal on behalf of the city's Soldiers' Aid Society to newspapers and other kindred spirits that heralded the start of Confederate Memorial Day. In rousing, heartfelt language, Mrs Williams had claimed that the need to safeguard white female honour provided the noblest justification of all for the deaths of so many Southern men in pursuit of the doomed Lost Cause:

> The proud banner under which they rallied in defence of the holiest and noblest cause for which heroes fought, or trusting woman prayed, has been furled forever. The country for which they suffered and died has now no name or place among the nations of the earth. Legislative enactments may not be made to do honour to their memories, but the veriest radical that ever traced his genealogy back to the Mayflower could not refuse thus the simple privilege of paying honour to those who died defending the life, honour and happiness of the Southern women.

After the South's defeat, the slaves' emancipation posed a new and terrible threat. Before the war, men such as Georgia's Governor Brown had warned that if the slaves were freed, they would soon be asking for white women's hands in marriage. Now that day had come to pass. In the summer of 1865, writes Nancy Telfair in her history of Columbus, 'white women could not go alone on the streets'. The reason was that they were filled by black former slaves. As W.J. Cash put it, by 'destroying the rigid fixity of the black at the bottom of the scale, in throwing open to him at least the legal opportunity to advance', the abolition of slavery opened up a fearful vista in the mind of every Southerner. A war had been fought and lost to preserve white female honour. Though defeated, the white Southern male must fight still harder to protect it in time of peace. 'Such,' writes Cash, 'is the explanation of the fact that from the beginning, they justified – and sincerely justified – violence towards the Negro as demanded in defence of women.'

Cash, of course, was white. African-Americans had noticed the effects of this rape complex long before his book was published in 1941. Towards the end of the nineteenth century, the black activist writers Ida B. Wells and

W.E.B. du Bois revealed how spurious rape allegations were used time and again by Southern whites to justify the wave of lynching, then at its terrible peak. Du Bois began his campaign when he investigated the torture and killing of Sam Hose in 1897 near Newnan, Georgia, a small farming town between Atlanta and Columbus. Hose, a farm labourer, had killed his employer, Alfred Crawford, in the course of a fight that started when he complained that he had not been paid his wages. When Hose disappeared, the local newspapers claimed he had also raped Crawford's wife, Mattie, described before her marriage as 'one of the belles of Newnan'. As vigilantes mounted a state-wide manhunt, the Newnan *Herald and Advertiser* warned the authorities not to interfere with the summary justice that must surely follow. Hose, it said, must be 'made to suffer the torments of the damned in expiation of his hellish crime', to demonstrate to all 'that there is protection in Georgia for women and children'.

After his arrest near Marshallville, seventy-five miles to the south-east, Hose was transported to Newnan, where his death was deliberately delayed in order to magnify its spectacle. In front of a crowd of four thousand, many of whom had arrived aboard special trains from Atlanta, the mob slowly tortured him by slicing off his ears, nose, fingers and genitals, then burnt him at the stake. Already covered in blood, he was heard to cry 'Sweet Jesus' as the smoke entered his nose, eyes and mouth, and the flames roasted his legs; in a final, desperate struggle to break the chain which bound his chest, he burst a blood vessel in his neck.

Although an attempt had been made to get Mattie Crawford to identify Hose as her supposed rapist, she did not do so, and it seems improbable that she was raped at all. Du Bois commented: 'Everyone that read the facts of the case knew perfectly well what had happened. The man wouldn't pay him, so they got into a fight, and the man got killed – then, in order to rouse the neighbourhood to find this man, they brought in the charge of rape.'

The orator and writer Frederick Douglass, a former slave and arguably the greatest chronicler of the black experience of Emancipation and its aftermath, saw how the effects of bogus rape claims spread far beyond the places and people they directly involved. In the last speech of his life, delivered in Washington in January 1894, he argued that white propaganda about rape by blacks had become a device to justify their continued subjugation. 'A white man has but to blacken his face and commit a crime, to have some negro lynched in his stead. An abandoned woman has only to start the cry that she has been insulted by a black man, to have him arrested and summarily murdered by the mob.' Douglass quoted the recent words of Frances Willard, leader of the Women's Christian Temperance Union: 'The coloured race multiplies like locusts in Egypt. The safety of women, of childhood, of the home, is menaced in a thousand localities at this moment, so that men dare not go beyond the sight of their own roof tree.'

The truth, Douglass pointed out, was that when most of the South's white men had been away at the war, their women went unmolested. There was simply no substance to this 'horrible and hell-black charge of rape as the peculiar crime of the coloured people of the South'. But its unchallenged prevalence in white society had terrible consequences, not only for the victims of lynch mobs but for black people as a whole: 'This charge ... is not merely against the individual culprit, as would be the case with an individual culprit of any other race, but it is in large measure a charge against the coloured race as such. It throws over every coloured man a mantle of odium.' It underpinned the exclusion of blacks from politics and the right to vote, and the racial segregation of the so-called 'Jim Crow' laws then being enforced throughout the South. The fear of rape had become the 'justification for Southern barbarism'. Douglass ended by quoting the former Senator, John T. Ingalls. There need be no 'Negro problem', he said. 'Let the nation try justice, and the problem will be solved.'

Another perspective emerges from *Portrait in Georgia*, a short and terrifying stanza by the black writer of the 1920s, Jean Toomer, in which he casts his erotic attraction for a white woman in the light of its likely consequence should his desire be fulfilled:

> Hair – braided chestnut
> Coiled like a lyncher's rope
> Eyes – faggots
> Lips – old scars, or the first red blisters,
> Breath – the last sweet scent of cane,
> And her slim body, white as the ash
> Of black flesh after flame.

The Southern rape complex could manifest itself with startling power when grounded in baseless fantasy. But even before Ferne Jackson's murder, in the Columbus of the late 1970s, it was beginning to seem as if its racist account of African-American sexuality was a simple description of fact. On 30 November 1976 Katharina Wright, the nineteen-year-old bride of a military officer, who had lived in Columbus for only a fortnight, was raped, robbed and murdered by a man who entered her house on Broadway by posing as a gas company employee. The killer stole $480 in cash, and was said to have shot her as he left. The following September, just before the first stocking strangling, a mentally retarded black man named Johnny Lee Gates was convicted and sentenced to death for these crimes. (After many legal vicissitudes, his sentence was commuted to life without parole in 2003.)

Katharina Wright was German, and although the case attracted its share of news coverage, its impact was limited. Much more shocking to white Columbus was the killing of Jeannine Galloway on 15 July 1977, two months before the death of Ferne Jackson. In Galloway's brutal slaying, it seemed that whites' primordial fears had achieved realisation.

Galloway, aged twenty-three, was a blonde and beautiful virgin who still lived with her parents, and who devoted much of her leisure time to directing the choir at the St Mary's Road United Methodist Church. A talented musician, she played the piano, organ, clarinet, saxophone and guitar, and was as happy playing jazz as Christian hymns. Her fiancé, Bobby Murray, met her when they were both students at the Columbus College music school. Before enrolling, he'd been on the road with a rock band; after taking advice from one of her friends, he cut his hair and shaved his beard in order to impress Jeannine. On trips with the college jazz big band, other musicians 'would sneak a beer or smoke marijuana', Bobby told the *Ledger*. 'Partaking of neither, Jeannine would still be in the middle of the action. Somebody would say, "Have a drink. Have fun." She'd get real quiet and tell them right quick, "I am having fun." She got high on life.'

For years after her murder, the Columbus newspapers continued to run long feature articles about her, on significant anniversaries of her passing, or when some development occurred in the case of her killer, a young African-American criminal named William Anthony Brooks. In these memorials, her qualities came to be described as belonging more to heaven than earth. 'She was just an angel, a bright and shining light who was just every father's dream,' her church's Reverend Eric Sizemore told reporters after one legal milestone in 1983.

There is no way to mitigate the horror of her murder. Early in the morning of her death, Jeannine was putting out the garbage, chatting to her mother, who stayed inside the house. She bent down to leave the bin, then straightened and came face to face with William Anthony Brooks, a young African-American. He was holding a loaded pistol, which he used to force her into her own car and drive to an area of marshy wasteland behind a school two miles away.

'She was continually asking me to let her go – to take her money and the car and let her go,' Brooks told the police after his arrest, a month later, in Atlanta. Instead, he marched her into a wood: 'I told her to take her clothes off and she said no, and I yelled at her to take her clothes off.' After raping her, Brooks's statement continued, he asked if this had been the first time that she had had sex. 'She said yes, and I said I didn't believe it. She started screaming and wouldn't stop and I pulled out my gun so she'd know I was serious … she kept screaming and the pistol went off. She kept trying to scream but she couldn't get her voice.' Jeannine died slowly, bleeding to death from a small-calibre bullet wound in her neck.

Brooks was tried in November 1977, two months after the first stocking strangling. At the start of the case, District Attorney Mullins Whisnant objected to every African-American in the jury pool, in order to ensure that the twelve men and women who would decide Brooks's fate were white. At the end of the penalty phase he made his closing appeal, imploring the jury to send Brooks to the electric chair: 'You have looked at William Anthony Brooks all week, he's been here surrounded by his lawyers, and you've seen him.' Having seen him, of course, the jury knew he was black.

Brooks, Whisnant said, had treated Jeannine 'worse than you would a stray animal'. Not content with 'raping her, with satisfying his lust', he had let her die 'very slowly, drip by drip, drop by drop … if you sat down and tried to think up a horrible crime, could you think anything more horrible than what you've heard here this week, that this defendant committed on this young lady? Could you think of anything more horrible?'

The defendant, Whisnant said, might be only twenty-two, but rehabilitation was quite impossible: he had been in trouble since he was a child. (As a teenager, Brooks had been arrested for car theft.) Fellow prisoners and guards would be at constant risk of a murderous attack if he lived. The defence was asking for mercy because Brooks had been brutally abused as a child, but for Whisnant this was just an excuse: 'His sisters talked to you about him being beaten by his stepfather, but they never did say what his stepfather was beating him for. Maybe he needed it. There's nothing wrong in whipping a child. Some of them you have to whip harder than others. And there's been children who have been abused and beaten, but they don't turn to a life of crime on account of it.'

He concluded by appealing to the jurors' social conscience. Columbus was fighting a war, and men like Brooks were the enemy:

> And you can do something about it. You can bring back the death penalty and you can tell William Brooks, and you can tell every criminal like him, that if you come to Columbus and Muscogee County, and you commit a crime … you are going to get the electric chair. You can think of it this way. You know from time to time, if you were a surgeon, and you have people coming to you and maybe they have a cancer on their arm, and you look at it, and you say, 'Well, the only way to save your life is to take your arm off.' Or maybe he's got cancer of the eye, and you have to take his eye out. Sure, that's terrible, but it's done because you save the rest of the body. And I submit to you that William Brooks is a cancer on the body of society, and if we're going to save society and save civilisation, then we've got to remove them from society.

Amid the sea of white faces inside the courtroom, that last 'them' might easily have been interpreted as a reference not to tumours but to African-Americans. In less than hour, the jury voted to put Brooks to death.

Six years later, in 1983, the Federal Court of Appeals for the US Eleventh Circuit stayed Brooks's execution eighteen hours before his scheduled death, because of its concern about Whisnant's rhetoric and the exclusion of blacks from the jury. After another six years of bitterly contested hearings, Brooks was sentenced to life without parole. Removed from death row, the man whom Whisnant had deemed beyond rehabilitation took his high school diploma, and then began to study for a university degree.

The racial connotations of the murders of 1977 were not lost on those who had to investigate them. In a cavernous, oak-panelled suite at his thirty-seventh-floor office in Manhattan, blessed with a dazzling view of Central Park, I interviewed Richard Smith, once a Columbus detective, now the chief executive of the Cendant Corporation's property division, Coldwell Bankers – the largest real-estate business in the world. The former cop was now responsible for twenty thousand employees, and an annual turnover of $6.5 billion.

The son of a soldier based at Fort Benning, Smith said he'd been faced with a choice of flipping hamburgers or joining the police to pay his way through college. He chose law enforcement, serving from 1973 until 1979 and acquiring two degrees. By 1976 he was a detective, and soon rose to working the robbery-homicide section. Smith spoke in a soothing, under-stated manner which matched his well-tailored light grey suit and navy shirt. Though he had a very different life now, he stayed in touch with his friends and colleagues from Columbus, which he visited several times a year. He had worked on both the Galloway and the stocking strangler cases, and his obvious intelligence had made him the effective operational leader of the 'task force' established to investigate them.

'Did the fact that it appeared to be an African-American raping and killing white women add to the impact of the crimes?' I asked.

The easy flow of Smith's conversation became more broken. 'Probably. A bit. Yes: that added to the trauma.' He cleared his throat, and his face began to colour. 'The old South has great respect and admiration for elderly people, and to see someone treated that way was incredibly offensive. Retired women are supposed to be untouchable people. Nothing is sup-posed to happen to them. Most of us took it very personally.'

White women shared his sense of revulsion. At the time of the murders, Kathy Spano, who went on to work in Columbus's courts, was living with her parents in Wynnton. 'I knew some of the women who died,' she told me. 'They were typical Southern gentlewomen, used to being put on a pedestal. I remember them as very gracious women, and also my mother saying, "Oh, it's awful what they've gone through. I cannot imagine laying there as a black man did those things to me." Because it was a black man, in the eyes of the neighbourhood, it made his crimes much, much worse.'

The body that had to deal with this mayhem, the Columbus Police Department, had not been a happy organisation for many decades. In the 1960s and early seventies, a series of corruption scandals saw officers fired for accepting bribes and taking part in large-scale burglary rings. Earlier, during the 1940s, no one got a job with the CPD without a nod from Fate Leebern, a bootlegging gangster who ran Columbus's rackets. Among African-Americans, the CPD had had a reputation for racism since the days of Jim Crow, directed both at black Columbus citizens and at the minority of black officers within its ranks, who were forbidden to arrest white suspects, and worked only 'black beats'. In the late 1960s, just one of the city's fifty-two black officers had been promoted to sergeant, and none above that rank. Whites received higher pay.

One freezing January night I drove to south Atlanta to meet Robert Leonard, an African-American former Columbus patrolman. A stooped, haunted figure, he told me that together with some of his black colleagues, he had joined the force after returning from service in Vietnam. There they had grown used to something like equality. It was warm inside Leonard's house, but as he recalled his experience, he shivered.

'We'd been out there fighting for our country. When we got to the Department, they wouldn't let us drink from the water fountains. They were reserved for whites. We had to go down to the basement, and drink the water they used for washing patrol cars.'

In 1971, Leonard was going to night school, studying for a degree in police science.

'There were only two blacks in the class, and it seemed to me that the captain who was taking the class was deliberately marking us down. So a white cop and me, we had a discussion, and agreed to swap papers. I knew my paper was good, and when he turned it in under his name, he got an A. His paper was pretty good too. When I turned it in under my name, I made a C.'

Leonard and the other African-American officers tried to tackle the rampant discrimination by founding a new organisation – the Afro-

American Police League. They attempted to make formal representations to the CPD, but its chiefs retaliated swiftly. One black cop was arrested for contempt by his white colleagues when he failed to make a court date, despite having called in sick, said Leonard; another was fired for damaging patrol-car tyres – after risking his life chasing a suspect.

'They started chopping us off, one by one. It got to the stage where relations between black and white cops had gotten so bad that we were pulling guns on each other. White cops I knew were calling me at home and making threats to me and my mother.'

Finally, in the spring of 1971, Leonard decided 'it was time to get something done'. He arranged to fly to Washington DC and meet officials from the Justice Department. As he boarded his plane, he realised he was being tailed – by two CPD detectives.

'I explained to the Justice Department that we wore the flag of the United States on our uniforms, that it stood for liberty and justice, and we weren't getting any.' The officials promised to look into it. But soon after Leonard's return, he was called one night to the Columbus Medical Center, the city's main hospital, where a doctor had got drunk and was threatening patients and nurses.

'I told him he was under arrest. He turned to me and said, "Nigger, you can't say that." So I cuffed him. Then a captain came and called another white colleague. They suspended me from duty for eight days.'

On the afternoons of 29 and 30 May 1971, Leonard and some of the Afro-American League members held a small demonstration outside the police headquarters. Their protest reached its climax the following day, when ten of them, including Leonard, carefully removed the US flag from their epaulettes, stitch by stitch.

'We had the media there, and we tried to explain that the flag represented what we'd fought for in Vietnam and couldn't find in Columbus. There was no liberty or justice inside the CPD, and it was treating black people in the city with brutality. The chief came out of the building and faced us. He looked at us with hate in his eyes and said, "You're fired." He went along the line and took our shields and our weapons.'

Later that day, the CPD held a press conference, confirming that Leonard and six others had been dismissed for 'conduct unbecoming an officer'. Columbus's Safety Director, Joseph W. Sargis, told reporters: 'These officers have repetitiously made baseless allegations of unlawful conduct, racism and discrimination against their fellow officers.' The chief and his men had 'exercised patience and forbearance concerning the conduct individually and as a group by these officers who call themselves the Afro-American Police League'. Beside him on the platform, two senior cops nodded vigorously – the CPD chief, B.F. McGuffey, and his future successor, Curtis McClung.

The black officers' dismissal triggered a wave of protest, which was further fuelled in early June when the police shot dead a twenty-year-old African-American whom they claimed had been a robbery suspect. On Saturday, 19 June, the civil rights leader Hosea Williams of the Southern Leadership Christian Council led a demonstration by about a thousand people in support of the fired seven, demanding the reorganisation of the CPD on racially equal lines. Mayor J.R. Allen denounced his proposals as 'an attack upon this city and its citizens' by 'a group of outsiders with no legitimate concern here'. The demands being made by Williams and the former patrolmen 'could only be described as an extortion note'.

Mayhem followed. For three nights, Columbus was afflicted by rioting and arson, with grocery stores, a lumberyard and a confectionery company fire-bombed and set ablaze. Firemen and their trucks were shot at, and their hoses cut. At 1.10 a.m. on 22 June, Mayor Allen declared a state of emergency. In Columbus, Allen – who died a few months later in a plane crash – is remembered today as a reformer who believed in racial integration. On this occasion he acted like a medieval monarch, and issued an 'ordinance' by proclamation. Bars, liquor stores and shops selling guns and ammunition would be closed until further notice. Notwithstanding the Constitution of the United States, and its First Amendment protecting free speech, any gathering on the streets of Columbus of more than twelve people would be illegal, and its members subject to arrest. Protest marches would only be allowed if their organisers had obtained a permit from the Mayor's office in advance. Allen was buoyed by a message of support from Georgia's Governor, the Democratic future President Jimmy Carter. He too denounced Hosea Williams: 'There is no evidence he wants to solve problems. He wants to create one.'

As sporadic rioting and arson continued, Columbus's long hot summer reached its violent zenith on 24 July, with a march – banned under the Mayor's emergency ordinance – to the CPD headquarters. Later, the police – inevitably – claimed that they were trying to disperse it peacefully, and only used force when they came under attack. Equally inevitably, accounts by surviving black participants are very different.

'Before we started, pickaxe handles had been handed out to the cops, and they just beat us,' Leonard said. 'Men, women and children. Some of the kids and women got real scared, started running. I was walking with a woman who was pregnant and this cop said, "Hey Leonard, you hiding behind a pregnant woman?" He beat me on the head, knocked me to the ground, fractured my skull. Somehow I got away and ran to an old lady's house. I was taken to hospital in Fort Benning, because I was a veteran. They arrested me in hospital, for assaulting a cop.'

By the end of the day, five police officers and five marchers had been hospitalised with serious injuries. The following week, another demonstration was broken up and eighty-one people arrested and jailed. Trouble simmered for the rest of the summer: by the time of the last conflagration, on 6 September, Columbus had seen 161 fires set by arsonists – some of them, it was widely believed, by whites, motivated not by anger at police brutality but by the prospect of making insurance claims.

As for the seven fired patrolmen, they launched a federal lawsuit that took twenty-two years to resolve. Three times Columbus's Federal District Judge, Robert Elliott, an old-time segregationist, refused to entertain it; three times the US Supreme Court and other appeal judges insisted that he should. Finally, the case was settled out of court, and the former patrolmen were each awarded $133,000. But the emotional cost had been overwhelming.

'I was warned by my own lawyer: leave town or face getting killed,' said Leonard. 'So I came here to Atlanta. All of us lost our jobs, our wives, our homes. My first wife was a schoolteacher in Columbus, and she was threatened, told she'd lose her job. One time I was unemployed and couldn't make my child support payments. Columbus had me jailed.'

\* \* \*

The Columbus Police Department badly needed a new broom, and with the appointment of Curtis McClung as its chief in 1976, one seemed to have arrived. Possessed of a degree in police sciences, he was skilled at handling the media, and wanted to be seen as a new model police chief, not a backwoods lawman. On first taking office, he told reporters that he was determined to expunge the stains left by the events five summers before. Nevertheless, experienced black investigators, who might have had much to contribute to the hunt for the stocking strangler, were swiftly excluded from it. Early in his service in 1967, Arthur Hardaway had been the first black patrolman assigned to the downtown Broadway beat, responsible for a business district that was then entirely white: 'The chief called me in and told me no black officer had ever walked Broadway,' Hardaway said. 'He wanted to determine the reaction of the whites and he thought I had the personality to be able to do it.' That experiment passed off successfully: 'The business people accepted me pretty good; treated me with respect, invited me in and offered me Cokes, like I guess they did the white officers.'

The stranglings were a very different matter. Hardaway had been a detective since 1968, working mostly in robbery-homicide, and had solved several murders. 'When the stranglings began, I did a few door-to-door interviews. But when they formed a special task force to investigate them, I wasn't picked for it, though I was one of the top investigators, and I'd worked on that squad a long time. I didn't know then if it was a white man or a black man who had committed those crimes. But the victims were influential people and they still had that racial concern in their heart in Columbus. The people who were making decisions still had that racist mentality.'

Hardaway spent years acquiring an impressive list of academic qualifications, only to see a long line of less experienced and less well-educated white officers promoted over his head. A methodical, unassuming man, he answered my questions in his south Columbus living room with the same precision he had once applied to murder cases, despite having become partially deaf. He left the force a disillusioned man in 1992, to scratch out a living as a small-time building contractor.

He was not the only skilled black investigator to be left out. There was no more experienced fingerprint expert on the Columbus force at the time of the stocking stranglings than Eddie Florence, the cop who later turned to real estate and religion after leaving the force. He told me that he'd always kept abreast of the latest developments in identification techniques, and ensured that the city had the most modern technology. Yet he wasn't called to any of the strangling crime scenes. He had left the police in 1984, but his bitterness was still near the surface.

'You had to be part of that madness to know what it was really like. The pressure, not just in the Police Department, but across the whole city was incredible, and it was being applied right in the middle of the racial divide. But the shit they put on me: not trusting me to take part in the investigation because they thought the killer was black!' He shook his head. 'I suppose they thought I'd try to fudge the evidence.'

After the second strangling, the murder of Miss Dimenstein, Chief McClung announced that all police leave was cancelled indefinitely. Staff who normally worked on administrative duties were moved to the streets to join new, intensive patrols, especially in Wynnton. Both the city and the state pledged money for a reward fund. Within a week it stood at $11,000, a substantial sum in 1977. And then, nine days after Dimenstein's death, came the break Columbus had been praying for.

Jerome Livas, an African-American odd-job man aged twenty-eight, lived in south Columbus with a much older woman – Beatrice Brier, who was fifty-five. Early on Sunday, 2 October, she was found by the porch of her home, beaten and unconscious. As her partner, Livas immediately became a prime suspect. He was arrested and questioned by two detectives, Gene Hillhouse and Warren Myles. Livas, a short, muscular man who looked older than his years, was illiterate and easily confused. The detectives, he said years later, told him that if he confessed to beating Beatrice Brier, he could go home. He quickly fell for this transparent ploy, and told them that he had. Six days later she died from her injuries, and although he retracted it, his confession was enough to secure him a life sentence for murder.

Hillhouse and Myles were intrigued by the wide age gap between Livas and Brier, and wondered whether his interest in older women might mean he had strangled Ferne Jackson and Jean Dimenstein. They began to question him about their murders, and as they talked, they made notes of everything they told Livas about what had happened. They were well aware of the danger of generating a completely bogus 'confession' to the crimes, containing nothing but recycled information their suspect had learned from them. Unbeknown to Myles and Hillhouse, after they went home at the end of the day, three more detectives – Ronald Lynn, Robert Matthews and Robert Coddington – continued the interrogation. They were much less careful, and made no note of their questions. Their interrogation lasted for much of the night.

Around midnight, the cops bundled Livas into a police car and drove him to the scenes of the murders. Along the way, they also drove by the Wynnton home of another possible victim of the strangler, Gertrude Miller, aged sixty-four, who had been beaten and raped, but not murdered, five days before Mrs Jackson was attacked. At each house, the detectives made Livas get out, lighting the shadows with powerful torches in the hope that this would enhance his recollections, and make them more vivid.

By 2.45 a.m. on 3 October, they had a full, typed confession. In the bare police interrogation room they read it back to Livas, and he marked it with the one thing he knew how to write, his name. It was an impressive document, filled with details about the murders which had not been made public, and which, journalists were later told, 'only the killer could have known'.

Livas's statement began with an account of the rape of Gertrude Miller – a crime that had been given no publicity. He said he managed to enter her home by pulling the screen off her back-room window, hit her on the side of the head with a mop handle, and tied her hands and feet with stockings. Then, Livas supposedly said, 'I took her clothes off. I fucked her for a little while and pulled my dick out and ate her pussy a little bit and then fucked her some more. When I got through fucking her, I hit her some more with the stick.'

According to Livas's confession, he decided to attack Ferne Jackson after seeing her get out of a car being driven by someone else and go inside her house. The police, of course, knew she had been dropped at her home by her friend Lucy Mangham. The rest of Livas's account was a close match with other known facts:

The strangler's first victim, Mary 'Ferne' Jackson.

Mayor Harry Jackson at the home of his aunt, Ferne Jackson, 15 September 1977.

Jean Dimenstein, the owner of a small department store, the second victim.

Columbus coroner Don Kilgore (right) confers with a rabbi and a policeman after the murder of Jean Dimenstein, 25 September 1977.

Jerome Livas, who confessed to the first two stranglings and to a string of other murders – including those of two US Presidents.

Florence Scheible, murdered in October 1977 when she was eighty-nine, blind and able to walk only with the aid of a zimmer frame.

Martha Thurmond, the fourth victim of the stocking strangler. A neat sample of the killer's semen was recovered from her body.

Kathleen Woodruff, a close friend of the writer Carson McCullers who married into one of Columbus's business dynasties. She was murdered in December 1977, shortly after special police patrols mounted to prevent another attack had been stood down.

I waited down the street on the corner until I didn't see no lights on at the house. I went to the house and went up on the porch where some glass doors were. I had a screwdriver with me. I stuck the screwdriver in the right side of the door and forced the lock. I went in the door and looked around the house and found an old woman asleep in the bed in the bedroom. She had on some type of gown. I put my hand over her mouth and she tried to move. I hit her pretty hard in the eye with my fist. I raised her gown up. I started fucking her in the pussy and then I ate her pussy. She was crying while I was fucking her. I was buck fucking her with her legs pulled up toward her head. I looked around in some drawers and found a stocking. I wrapped the stocking around her neck and pulled it tight and tied it in a knot.

Livas said he stole his victim's car and left it on a dirt road off Lawyers Lane in south Columbus, exactly where Mrs Jackson's vehicle had been found. His confession to murdering and raping Jean Dimenstein was equally vivid and, seemingly, accurate. Having tried to open a window, he said, he went round to the port where her car, a blue Chevrolet, was parked:

I took the hinges off the door. I threw them out in the backyard. I took the door off and set it to the side ... I found an old woman in the bedroom asleep. I put my hand over her mouth and she was trying to wake up. I hit her with my fist. I don't remember where I hit her. She had on some kind of housecoat. She had on a pair of panties. I took her panties off and threw them down. Then I pushed her legs back and buck fucked her. Then I ate her pussy a little bit. I got a stocking from a chair and wrapped it round her neck and choked her ... I went out the same door I came in and got in [her] car and left. I put the radio station on WOKS because I always listen to it. I took the car pretty close to where I left the last car but left it on a paved street this time.

Dimenstein's car radio – as the police, but not the press, knew – had indeed been tuned to WOKS when it was found on a paved road in Carver Heights.

Three days later, on 6 October, the police showed Gertrude Miller, the woman who had apparently survived the strangler's attack, an array of photographs. She picked out Livas. His picture, she said, was the one that looked most like the man who raped her, and had 'all the right features'. It looked as if the case was nailed. On 14 October, the Deputy Police Chief C.B. Falson, the robbery-homicide squad director Ronnie Jones, and his deputy, Herman Boone, called a press conference. Jerome Livas, they announced, was officially a suspect for the stranglings. If convicted, he could expect to be sentenced to death.

Even then, there were some members of the CPD who had their doubts. Carl Cannon, a young reporter with the Columbus *Ledger-Enquirer*, spoke to an anonymous police source who told him Livas was a 'twenty-four-carat idiot with the intelligence level of a five-year-old'. Another said Livas had not understood the contents of his own confession, let alone the implications of signing it without having seen a lawyer: 'Explaining that to him is like explaining Einstein's quantum theory of physics [sic] to a three-year-old.' Livas's employer, William Renfro, told Cannon he was 'slow, illiterate and stupid', and would 'say anything'. But Chief McClung was confident the police had got their man. The special patrols in Wynnton were stood down.

Florence Scheible was a widow of eighty-nine, almost blind, and walked only with the aid of a Zimmer frame. Originally from Iowa, she moved to Columbus because she liked its warm weather. On the morning of 21 October, while Livas remained in custody, her neighbours saw her outside at about 11 a.m., shuffling in the garden in front of her two-storey house on Dimon Street, a few blocks from the murders. Three-and-a-half hours later, her son Paul, a colonel in the military, called the police, saying he had come to visit and found her dead.

Ed Gibson, a CPD patrolman, went inside, into the tidy living room. Antique furniture and a rug stood on a polished hardwood floor; there was a television in the corner. Mrs Scheible was lying on her bed in the bed-room next door, next to her walker. Her dress had been pulled above her waist, exposing her pubic area, which was covered in blood. She was wearing one nylon stocking. The other had been wrapped around her neck.

In the wake of Florence Scheible's murder, Columbus was seized by dread. The special patrols reappeared, joined by soldiers from Fort Benning and volunteers from other jurisdictions. Like many women who lived alone, Martha Thurmond, a retired teacher aged sixty-nine, decided not to risk relying on these measures. The day after the discovery of Mrs Scheible's body, she had deadbolt locks fitted to the doors, and burglar bars fixed to the windows of her house on Marion Street, a small, wood-framed dwelling just off Wynnton Road. Her son Bill, who lived in Tucker, a suburb of Atlanta, came down with his wife and son to stay for the weekend, wanting to be certain that she would be safe. They left for home at about 3.30 p.m. on Monday, 24 October.

At 12.30 p.m. next day, a neighbour noticed that Mrs Thurmond's front door was open. The new lock had not been properly fitted, and working in silence, the killer had forced it during the night. She was inside, on her bed, wearing a pink pyjama top; taped to the wall above her was a large sheet of paper with a phone number written in large characters: 322-7711 – the number for the Columbus Police Department. Like Florence Scheible, she had been hit with enormous force, by a blow that fractured the base of her skull. The stocking ligature had been tightened so fiercely against her skin that it had caused a friction burn, a brownish red, blistered trough against her windpipe. In and around her vagina were copious quantities of seminal fluid.

Driven to desperation, Mayor Mickle tried to reduce the chances of another murder by cancelling Halloween. Parents, he told reporters, should ensure their children were home by 6 p.m. on 31 October. Trick or treating was forbidden.

With the police investigation and the reputation of his department in disarray, Chief McClung continued to claim that Jerome Livas might still have killed the first two victims. 'The evidence against him still exists,' he told reporters. I met the *Ledger*'s former crime correspondent Carl Cannon in a cellar bar in Washington DC, where his career has prospered as the White House correspondent for the *National Journal*. Warm and approachable, he vividly recalled the events of his reporting youth twenty-five years earlier. His father had been a big-time Washington reporter before him, and unlike most Columbus journalists, he always knew he was only passing through, and could afford to make enemies.

'They were still using that hoary old line – Livas had said things that only the killer could have known – and when Mrs Scheible was killed, they added another: that there had to be a copy-cat killer. I'd already had some experience with the Columbus cops and their tendency to rush to judgement. But I had a source in the department who used to call me at home. He told me it was bullshit: the murders were the work of the same guy. He said Livas had this urge to please. He'd confess to anything.'

Cannon managed to enlist the help of a judge to get him access to Livas in jail. Left alone with Cannon, Livas signed another statement within a couple of hours. This time, he not only confessed again to the first two Columbus stranglings, but admitted that it had been he who had assassinated two Presidents, John F. Kennedy and William McKinley; that he had been with Charles Manson the night his followers murdered the actress Sharon Tate; that he had known when Charles Lindbergh's baby was going to be kidnapped in the 1930s; and that he knew Elizabeth Short, the victim of the notorious 'black dahlia' murder in Cannon's home state of California the following decade. Cannon asked him if knew what the word 'suspect' meant. Livas replied: 'That means you're trespassing on private property or something.' The one crime he vehemently denied was the only one for which he was to be convicted – the murder of his girlfriend, Beatrice Brier.

Twenty-three years old, Cannon had the scoop of his career thus far. After staying up all night transcribing his notes and tapes, he had his story ready to run for the evening edition of 17 November 1977. Shortly before his deadline, he called on Chief McClung. Cannon recalled: 'He got up, walked to the window, looked out. He said, "You know, Carl, I've got a lot of people here but no one doing public affairs to get our stories out to the public, not like the Army has." He asked me what I earned, and suggested he might be able to double it. I told him: "I tell you what, Chief. This story's going to come out in two hours, and everyone's going to know that this guy didn't do it. But I'm not, on this occasion, going to tell the readers about our conversation." '

Meanwhile, Columbus's maniac remained on the loose.

# THREE

# *Ghost-Hunting*

And the Negro. Do not forget the Negro. So far as I and my people are concerned the South is Fascist now and always has been … The history of my people will be commensurate with the interminable history of the Jew – only bloodier and more violent.

Benedict Mady Copeland in CARSON McCULLERS,
*The Heart is a Lonely Hunter* (1940)*

At his hilltop home at the upscale end of south Columbus, Gene Hewell was tending his garden. Now sixty-five, he moved smoothly, wielding his hoe without apparent effort, his only concession to the heat and humidity a straw boater. I was sweating the moment I got out of my car, but his breathing was rhythmic, his skin dry. In the distance, the towers used for parachute training at Fort Benning seemed to shimmer above the trees. Gene gestured towards the west. 'That's where my great-grandmother worked as a slave,' he said. 'On a plantation at a place called Oswichee, in Russell County, Alabama. It was owned by the first W.C. Bradley's father.'

---

* Carson McCullers (1917–67) was born and raised in Wynnton. After her extraordinary first novel, *The Heart is a Lonely Hunter*, became a best-seller in 1940 when she was twenty-three, she lived mainly in New York, but often returned to Columbus to write. A visceral egalitarian, her last and most overtly political novel was *Clock Without Hands* (1961). As the black writer and critic Richard Wright has noted, among the most impressive aspects of her work is the 'astonishing humanity that enables a white writer, for the first time in Southern fiction, to handle Negro characters with as much ease and justice as those of her own race'. Benedict Mady Copeland, a radical black physician, is among the most memorable of all.

Gene, the brother of the singer Jo-Jo Benson, owned a men's fashion store on Broadway, the Movin' Man – the first, and for many years the only, black-owned business on the street. Inside his house, in the welcome cool of his living room, Gene eased himself into a sofa beside an impressive collection of guitars. Like his brother, he had lived in Columbus or Phenix City for most of his life, and his family had been in the district for much longer than that.

'My great-grandmother told my grandma about the day they freed the slaves, and she told me and Jo-Jo,' Gene said. 'She said that she was out in the fields, chopping cotton – chopping at the stalks to let the plants get more nutrients. Then she heard this noise. A crackling, was how she explained it. She looked up at the ridge above the field where she was working and all she could see was a blue line of white people, running by the master's house. Some of the people there were trying to shoot at them, and they were trying to get in. She said she'd never seen so many whites killing so many whites.'

Afterwards, with the plantation secure, the Union soldiers called the slaves from the fields in order to tell them that Lincoln had set them free. Addressing a hushed semi-circle of African-Americans in the shade of a tree, an officer read the Emancipation proclamation. As he did so, Gene said, one of his men idly bounced his rifle on the toe of his boot. 'The gun went off and clean shot off his toe. My great-grandmother pulled his boot off and dressed the wound. Then he pulled it right back on.'

When the federal army left later that afternoon, some of the former slaves followed it, because they were scared of reprisals from whites. According to the oral history handed down among the Chattahoochee Valley's African-Americans, their fears were justified.

'My grandma told us that the day after the Yankees left, all down through the woods near the plantations, there were black people nailed to trees,' Gene said. 'They were dead, like butchered animals. Instead of being set free, they were killed.'

In the National Archives in Washington DC, in the Georgia section's records of the federal agency set up to assist the former slaves, the Bureau of Refugees, Freedmen and Abandoned Lands, I found a ledger, compiled regularly from information sent from every county to the state headquarters. Entitled *Reports Relating to Murders and Outrages*, its pages document what can only be described as the beginning of Georgia's white terror.

Written in the elegant copperplate of the Victorian bureaucrat, the ledger sets out its accounts of ethnic assault and homicide under logical headings. There are columns for the 'name of person assaulted or killed'; whether they were white or coloured; the 'name or person killing or assaulting', together with their race; whether anything was done to bring the perpetrators to justice; and any further 'remarks'. In Columbus's Muscogee County, and the five surrounding counties that today comprise the Chattahoochee judicial circuit, I counted the names of thirty-two victims attacked, most of them fatally, between March 1866 and November 1868. All but one were black. All the named perpetrators were white.

Even before the Civil War, writes W. J. Cash, the law and its institutions were weaker in the South, where slave-owners had displayed 'an intense distrust of, and, indeed, downright aversion to, any actual authority beyond the barest minimum essential to the existence of the social organism'. In the turmoil of the Reconstruction era after the war's end, these traditions found expression in a new wave of extralegal violence. 'At the root of the post-war bloodshed was the refusal of most whites to accept the emancipated slaves' quest for economic and political power,' writes W. Fitzhugh Brundage, the historian of lynching in Georgia and Virginia. 'Freed from the restraints of planter domination, the black man seemed to pose a new and greater threat to whites. During a period when blacks seemed to mock the social order and commonly understood rules of conduct, whites turned to violence to restore their supremacy.'

The details of these forgotten killings were not always recorded, although some bring to mind the later, more famous wave of lynching that swept the South from the 1880s on. One example took place in Harris County, just to the north of Columbus, now the site of rich dormitory suburbs, where the body of Jordan Nelson was found in June 1866, 'in the woods, hanging by the neck'. But from the beginning, many such murders seem to have displayed a degree of organisation, a coordinated premeditation that revealed their underlying purpose. The Ku Klux Klan did not spread to Georgia from its home state of Tennessee until 1868. But the racist vigilantism that the Klan embodied was already in evidence when the

Freedmen's Bureau ledger opened its record in March 1866. On the fifteenth day of the month, an African-American named only as Samuel was 'shot in bed by party of white men, organized' in Talbotton, east of Columbus. His unknown killers, says the Freedmen's Bureau ledger, called themselves 'regulators'.

The bare accounts contained in the ledger also convey what must have been a terrifying sense of randomness, an absence of motive other than race which must, all too rationally, have led any black person to feel they were at risk. In Harris County in August 1866, an unnamed black woman 'was beaten by a white man by the name of Spicy. She died next day, and he escaped.' 'There was no cause for the assault,' the ledger states of the shooting of K. Hocut by Nathaniel Fuller in Muscogee County on 20 January 1868. Of the slaying of Samuel Clemins in Harris County by 'unknown whites' on 7 September 1868, it records: 'Clemins was murdered by four white men because he had sent his son away to avoid a whipping.' Hiram McFir died in the same county at the hands of Bud Vines five days later. 'Vines shot McFir while holding his horse,' says the ledger, 'without the least cause.' As for Tom Joiner, he was stabbed by Jesse Bennett in Troup County on 17 September 'for refusing to let his dog fight'.

The national politics of the late 1860s were dominated by the struggle over 'radical Reconstruction', the attempt by the Republicans, the party of Abraham Lincoln, to persuade the former slave states to ratify new amendments to the Constitution – the Fifteenth, enshrining black citizens' right to vote, and the Fourteenth, which promises 'equal protection under the laws'. In and around Columbus, the absence of such protection was manifest. According to the ledger, only one of the perpetrators in the region's thirty-two listed attacks was convicted and sentenced in court, a man named John Simpson, who killed Sammy Sapp in Muscogee County on 27 November 1867. Simpson, however, who was 'tried, found guilty and sentenced to hang', was 'coloured'. Where white perpetrators were concerned, the outcomes of the cases described in the preceding paragraph typify the rest. K. Hocut's killer, Nathaniel Fuller, was at least tried, but was acquitted. Although an inquest was held into the murder of Samuel Clemins, 'no further action was taken by the civil authority'. Likewise, 'the authorities have taken no action' against Bud Vines, the man who shot

Hiram McFir, and Vines 'is supposed to be in Alabama'. The Freedmen's Bureau officer who recorded the stabbing of Tom Joiner by Jesse Bennett knew that Bennett 'lives near LaGrange', but in his case too, 'no action [was] taken by the civil authorities'.

One of the most odious aspects to the ethnic terror of the 1860s was the maiming and murder of African-Americans by the same individuals who had once owned them as property, and who seemed unable to adjust to the fact that if they still wished to put their former slaves to work, they would have to pay them. The first such case recorded in the ledger dates from July 1866, when an unnamed coloured man from Talbotton was 'shot by his employer'. When Andrew Rawick stabbed John Brown in Troup County on 3 July 1868, 'the difficulty originated about some work', and when Austin and Dennis Hawley were 'severely cut with [a] knife' in Harris County two months later, it was because 'the Hawleys demanded a settlement for work [they had] done'. In the same county on 20 October, Isaac Smith was killed by three unknown white men because he had 'left a [work]place in the spring'.

Two brothers from Harris County, William and Lewis Grady, appear to have taken special pains to exact vengeance from their former human property. On 4 August 1868 they 'whipped very severely' a man named David Grady; the fact that he shared their last name suggests that he had been their slave. The reason, states the ledger, was that 'David had left [their] place because he did not get enough to eat.' In this case, warrants were issued for William and Lewis Grady to attend court, but they did not answer them. A month later they again revealed their contempt for the law when they 'shot and very severely whipped' another African-American who bore their name, George Grady. As usual, 'no action [was] taken by the civil authority'. When the ledger closed at the end of 1868, the Grady brothers were still living with impunity a few miles north of Columbus in Harris County, Georgia.

A pattern that would last many decades was beginning: racial violence and inequalities were simply matters beyond the rule of law. Long after the end of the 1860s, the fact that the law did not treat the races equally was among the first lessons black parents taught their children.

'Sassing,' said Gene Hewell, 'you know what that means? To be rude, disrespectful. Our parents warned us about sassing from the cradle up. That didn't just mean being careful what you said. It meant, you don't mess with white people; you don't talk to them, and you don't talk back. If they do something you don't like, you get out of their way. You could be walking down Broadway and if three white people came towards you, you got off the kerb. And if you didn't, they could make it real ugly for you – arrest you, beat your brains out in jail.'

In 1950, Gene said, a favourite uncle, 'a big, muscular guy', was murdered after getting into some kind of trouble with a white grocer – 'They said he'd sassed him.' After his death, his body was laid across the railroad tracks, and 'cut up and pushed in pieces along the bridge towards Phenix City'.

This climate of fear and vulnerability allowed other kinds of oppression and exploitation to flourish.

'We'd come out of slavery, but we had to find a place to stay, and they owned the houses. You had to buy clothes, and they owned the stores. You had just about enough chump change to feed your children and go back to work each Monday. If you didn't like your job, you couldn't quit at one place and find work at another. That was blue-collar slavery.'

The story of Gene's own liberation, of how he came to buy his own downtown store and made it succeed, was a long saga of struggle against prejudice and hostility, against banks which refused to lend him money, and a Police Department that twice tried to ruin him by laying bogus charges – once for theft, and on another occasion for possessing planted drugs.

For a few months before and after the end of 1977, at the time of the stocking stranglings, he'd employed a man named Carlton Gary, first as a sales assistant, and then as a TV advertisement model. 'It was the Superfly era when clothes were flamboyant. Big boots, tassels, silk shirts and hats,' Hewell said. 'I used Carlton for the simple reason that he looked good. Real good. He was a very well built, extraordinarily attractive man, and he knew how to move, you know what I'm saying? He was a charmer, and when it came to women, he had the pick of the litter.'

'How often did you show your adverts?' I asked.

'At busy times, like the weeks before Christmas, Carlton would have been appearing in five TV spots a night. I guess that made him kind of easy to recognise.' Nine years after working for Hewell, Gary would find himself standing trial for the Columbus stocking stranglings.

The rapes and murders of Florence Scheible and Martha Thurmond in October 1977, followed by Carl Cannon's exposure of the CPD's incompetence, plunged Columbus into a new abyss of fear. More than two decades later, in his chambers in the Government Center tower, I met Andrew Prather, a State Court judge who had lived alone in Wynnton at the time of the murders. Despite the belief that the killer was black, he said, any single man was regarded as a possible suspect: 'There was a police car parked outside and I knew they were watching me. I thought of moving to Atlanta but then I thought, "What if I leave town and the killings stop?"'

One night he found an old lady's dog in the street. 'I was scared to give it back. I thought I was going to get shot. I yelled through the door, "It's Andy Prather! I live down the street and I've got your puppy!" ' His fears were well founded. In one reported incident, a woman fired a pistol through her glass front door when she saw the shadow of a friend and neighbour who was calling to check her well-being.

As the police stumbled to make progress, they asked for help from the famous FBI criminal psychology profile expert, Robert K. Ressler. In his memoirs, Ressler writes of attending a social gathering during his visit: 'A group of middle-aged and elderly women were at a party together, and the main topic of conversation was the mysterious series of killings. At one point in the evening, in a demonstration of how completely the fear of the killer had gripped the city, seven of the women guests emptied their purses, revealing seven handguns that fell out on to the carpet.' Meanwhile, the local media advised single and widowed women to move in with male relatives, and if that were not possible, to form 'communes' for their own protection.

Aware that he and his colleagues had no suspect, Detective Richard Smith and his partner, Frank Simon, decided to try prevention. Before the murders began, Smith had been responsible for a programme designed to protect store-owners from robbery – the Columbus Anti-Robbery Enforcement System, or CARES. Possible targets were identified, and then equipped with panic button hotlines to the police, who were supposed to respond immediately.

'Now,' said Smith in his New York office, gazing into the middle distance through a mist over Central Park, 'I had to profile the elderly women and widows who lived alone in Wynnton, then go to them and tell them, as if they didn't already know, that they were likely victims of the strangler. The harder task was to convince them that they were going to be safe, that we were going to protect them. They didn't have family, so we were it.'

Smith fitted dozens of these possible victims' homes with alarms activated by panic buttons and pressure pads placed under the carpets outside their bedrooms. 'They were very expensive units, hooked directly up to police radio bands. Unfortunately, the only result was very, very many false alarms.' Time and again, a woman would hear something, then press her button almost reflexively. Some did it so often that the police had to take their alarms away.

'I got to know some of those women quite intimately,' Smith said. 'What I do remember is that when one of them raised the alarm, what seemed like the whole world of policing would show up within seconds. One night I was on patrol with a guy from the GBI [the Georgia Bureau of Investigation]. A call went out that a guy had heard screaming from the home of his neighbour, a widow. We weren't more than half a mile away, but by the time we got there, we had to park three blocks from the house, there were so many law-enforcement vehicles there already.'

Working with the help of official records, it took Smith hours of work to produce his list of possible victims.

'How do you think the strangler managed to carry out his own profiling?' I asked. 'How did he work out where elderly women were living alone?'

Smith paused for a long time. 'We don't know. Until the day I left the force, I had no idea how he selected his victims.'

Anyone – especially anyone African-American – walking through Wynnton was likely to be stopped and asked to submit to a pro-forma 'field interview', with their personal details and movements for the past few days taken down and filed. Some were asked to give saliva and hair samples. Many of those stopped were students, on their way to the black high school in Carver Heights, and when they were questioned again and again, it aroused fierce resentment. However, flooding Wynnton with law-enforcement officers seemed to work.

'We were not *allowed* in that neighbourhood – there's no way that I could have gone through Wynnton after six or seven at night without being jumped on by every police car in the city,' Gene Hewell said. 'As a black man, you would have been *asking* for it – you could have driven through, but even now, twenty-seven years later, you couldn't walk through without attracting attention.'

Kathy Spano, a courthouse clerk, used to lie in her Wynnton bedroom, her radio tuned to the police communications channel. 'There were so many people on the alert, constantly moving, responding to alarms, following leads with their dogs. I do not know how they could not have seen any black man in the neighbourhood. It would have been very difficult for him to move around. One night I heard they were chasing someone. Next day I asked how he'd got away. An officer told me they'd found some ground hollowed out beneath a bush.'

Through the end of October, the whole of November and past Christmas, the strangler did not strike. As 1978 approached, Columbus began to hope that the murders had drawn to a close. In fact, the city's serial killer was about to choose his most prominent target.

If the intermarried Bradleys and Turners are the mightiest of all Columbus's great families, close behind has been the dynasty of Woodruffs. Founded when George Waldo Woodruff moved south from Connecticut in 1847, the clan of his numerous descendants rose to become financiers, mill-owners, bankers and philanthropists. It was a Woodruff who put together the Columbus syndicate that bought Coca-Cola in 1919, while another later became its chief executive. By the middle of the twentieth century, George C. 'Kid' Woodruff, a fanatical sportsman who once coached his beloved University of Georgia football team for just $1 a year, was serving as President of the Columbus Chamber of Commerce, and was one of the city's most powerful men. After his death his widow, Kathleen, divided her time between a house at the Wynnton end of Buena Vista Road and a mansion in Harris County. As a young woman she had been among the writer Carson McCullers's closest friends, and lived for a time in Paris. Now her two remaining passions in life were her garden and her grandchildren. In the winter of 1977, she was seventy-four.

Kathleen's home has since been torn down, but it used to lie in the open, close to the well-lit junction with Wynnton Road, the busiest in the neighbourhood. Through the autumn and early winter, it remained on the list of houses that the CPD had earmarked for regular checks by its special patrols. Shortly before Christmas, these patrols were scaled back, just as they had been after the arrest of Jerome Livas.

The last person to see her alive apart from the strangler was her servant of thirty-three years, Tommie Stevens. At 5 p.m. on 27 December, Mrs Woodruff called her over to where she was sitting at the kitchen table, chequebook at the ready. The next day was Tommie's birthday, and Kathleen gave her a gift of $20 before Tommie left for her own home in Carver Heights. 'Next morning, when I came back – I always kept my own key – I unlocked the door and I noticed the light was on in her room, which it always be,' she told the trial of Carlton Gary almost nine years later. It was between 10 and 11 a.m., and Tommie noticed nothing out of the ordinary. She was surprised that Mrs Woodruff wasn't yet up, but went into the kitchen to make her some eggs for her breakfast. Only then did it occur to her that her employer 'was sleeping mighty late'.

'I decided to go see whether she was asleep,' Tommie went on, 'because I felt like she was sleeping late. And so, when I went in the bedroom and seen she was lying on the bed with the, you know, scarf around her neck and about half dressed and blood running down her cheek, and after I saw that, then I ran my hand across to see if she would bat her eyes, and she didn't. And after that, I ran to the phone and called Mr Woodruff' – George Junior, Kathleen's son.

Like the other victims, Kathleen Woodruff had bedroom closets and drawers containing numerous pieces of lingerie, yet she had been strangled with an item that had special meaning for her family – a University of Georgia football scarf. Only two years earlier, she and George Junior (another Georgia alumnus) had been photographed for the cover of the programme for a football game against Clemson University. Inside was an article about George Senior's playing and coaching career. His uncle, Harry Ernest Woodruff, a brilliant young man who founded the real estate firm which both George Woodruffs (and the still-surviving George Woodruff

III) went on to run, had also been on the University of Georgia team. (Harry died aged forty-one in a car crash in 1924, en route to the annual homecoming game between Georgia and the University of Tennessee.)

Kathleen's body displayed the same signs of strangulation as the other victims', including the petechial haemorrhages and the fractured hyoid bone. Unlike the earlier victims, she had not been subjected to a massive blow to her head. She had, however, been raped.

Two days after her murder, the enterprising reporter Carl Cannon heaped new humiliation on the CPD in another front-page story for the Columbus *Ledger*, published under the headline 'Police Ended Special Patrol 2 Weeks Ago':

> Special Columbus police patrols which had cruised past Kathleen K. Woodruff's 1811 Buena Vista Road house every night since 25 October were called off two weeks ago because the 'stocking strangler' had been silent, police confirmed.
>
> The patrols were resumed Wednesday.
>
> The special details were ordered in late October following the stranglings of two elderly women within four days – the third and fourth stranglings of elderly Columbus women since September.
>
> Columbus waited in horror to see who the next victim would be, and when week after week passed without the dreaded news, many residents turned their thoughts to family, Christmas and other things …
>
> Commander Jim Wetherington, who was in charge of the special details, confirmed they were stopped a little before Christmas. Wetherington said the patrols would resume now.
>
> A police source said that the fruitlessness of the special patrols and the boredom felt by officers was a factor in calling off the special details.

For the first time, the city's continuing terror was mingled with anger. At a disastrous press conference, Mayor Mickle insisted the police were doing all they could to solve the killings – just as he had already done time and again, the *Ledger* pointed out, since Ferne Jackson's death the previous September. 'We are going to solve this problem,' Mickle said. 'We are going to make arrests.' Next day, the paper published a lengthy attack on Mickle, the CPD and its chief Curtis McClung, in the form of a letter from one E. Jensen:

> We the people of Columbus, Georgia are sick! We have a terminal disease called fear, and soon, it will be the death of us all. But the trouble is, it's justified. My fear stems not so much from the criminal element, but … the ineptness of local law. We are now on centre stage. The world is watching us through the networks. And what do we do? We let the world see our sloppy police work and our praying Mayor! Mickle, get up off your knees and do something!

Stung by the criticism, the CPD tried to mount its own public relations campaign, briefing reporters about the long hours its staff were working and their total commitment to finding the killer. At the behest of Georgia's Governor, the police were forced to cede their autonomy and set up a joint 'task force' with the state-wide detective agency, the Georgia Bureau of Investigation. Twenty GBI agents and support staff moved into a special office that took up the entire basement of the Government Center, bringing with them Columbus's first crime computer system. Ronnie Jones, the CPD's chief homicide detective, told reporters that task force members were making huge personal sacrifices; for his own part, he said he was working up to twenty hours each day, while the strangler had invaded his dreams. For the first time in eight years, Jones revealed, he had gone so far as to disappoint his wife by cancelling their annual wedding anniversary holiday in Gatlinburg, Tennessee.

If shared mentalities are partly formed by shared historical memories, among the white citizens, cops and politicians who strove to deal with the stranglings, there was none more potent than the Reconstruction period. Accounts of this era, after the end of the Civil War in 1865, in the local histories of Columbus describe it in extravagant language, suggesting that until the stranglings, Reconstruction had been the city's deepest wound. They are, of course, written from a white perspective. On the violence and death meted out to African-Americans, the Columbus histories are silent. In their pages, post-war lawlessness and injustice in the South involved whites only as victims.

Like the Lost Cause legend, this narrative, with its wayward, marauding Negroes, 'carpet bagger' Northern radicals and 'scalawag' Southern collaborators, is not unique to Columbus. For decades, the myth of punitive vengeance by the Civil War's victors dominated American historiography, even in the North. Its acceptance helped to legitimise the white supremacist oppression of the Jim Crow era, and was further fuelled by works such as Thomas Dixon's bestselling 1905 novel, *The Clansman*. Dixon characterised Reconstruction's aim of achieving legal equality as 'an atrocity too monstrous for belief', using the language of visceral racial hatred. Underlying it was the familiar Southern rape complex. In Dixon's view, the decision to award the vote to the 'thick-lipped, flat-nosed, spindle-shanked negro, exuding his nauseating animal odour', had rendered every Southern woman at risk of barbaric violation.

In 1914, D.W. Griffith made cinematic history with his film based on Dixon's book, *The Birth of a Nation*. Screened at the White House for Woodrow Wilson and the Supreme Court's Chief Justice, Edward D White, it depicted a version of Reconstruction that bore only the most distant relationship to the truth. A contemporary scene-by-scene review in *Variety* provides a representative taste: 'Soon the newfound freedom of the former slaves leads to rude insolence. Black militiamen take over the streets in a reign of terror. Flashes are shown of helpless white virgins being whisked indoors by lusty black bucks. At a carpetbaggers' rally, wildly animated blacks carry placards proclaiming EQUAL RIGHTS, EQUAL MARRIAGE.'

Much of the film concerns the efforts of Gus, one such 'buck', to defile the innocence of the virginal 'Little Sister'. Terrified, she tries to flee the pursuing Gus, while the orchestra (in the words of a later critic) 'plays hootchy-kootchy music with driving tom-tom beats, suggesting ... the image of a black penis driving into the vagina of a white virgin'. Just as he is about to catch her, she opts for the preferable fate of tumbling over the edge of a cliff. Needless to say, her death is avenged by the heroic redeemers of the Ku Klux Klan, who lynch Gus against a superimposed image of Little Sister in her coffin. At the film's climax, a massed Klan cavalry 'pour over the screen like an Anglo-Saxon Niagara', to Wagner's 'Ride of the Valkyries'.

Across the South, writes the Klan's historian Wyn Craig Wade, *The Birth of a Nation* was greeted as a 'sacred epic', while the film 'united white Americans in a vast national drama, convincing them of a past that had never been'. No moving picture had ever achieved a fraction of its audience and impact before. Against this backdrop, Columbus's parochial, local version of the Reconstruction story is not particularly original, and is somewhat less vivid. But for future race relations in the city, it lacks neither relevance nor power. In paragraphs representative of prevailing white sentiment, Nancy Telfair begins the pertinent chapter of her 1928 *History of Columbus, Georgia* with a ringing condemnation of the South's treatment in the immediate wake of defeat in 1865:

> Half a million negroes had been given their 'freedom', and were drunk with the sound of the word. Thousands of Yankee soldiers had been stationed throughout the state for the purpose of seeing that the negroes received the rights so tumultuously thrust upon them.
>
> Besides these, were the 'carpet baggers', who were said to carry their worldly goods in their carpet bags, and the 'scalawags', low-class Southerners, who were hand in glove with their Yankee confreres in stirring up racial hatred to result in their own affluence and aggrandizement ... there were yet crowds of worthless, lazy darkies in the towns, who lived only by stealing from whites and acted as henchmen for the 'carpet baggers' and 'scalawags' whose power was constantly increasing.

Reconstruction, adds Etta Blanchard Worsley in her later, but equally unapologetic *Columbus on the Chattahoochee*, published at the dawn of the civil rights era in 1951, was a time when Northern radicals sought to impose 'punitive measures' on the broken South. What were these measures? According to Worsley, the worst was the idea that 'the Negroes, though uneducated and not long out of darkest Africa, must have the vote'. The Constitution's Fifteenth Amendment 'took from the states control of their suffrage by bestowing the ballot on the Negro'.

The burning sense of grievance implanted during Reconstruction and magnified in its later retellings had distinct implications for both the rule of law and the idea that the races should be equal under it. The Southern view that parts of the Constitution had been imposed by force, and were therefore illegitimate, had a consequence: decent people could reasonably see the law as something that need not always be obeyed, or as an instrument to be manipulated. Occasionally, even acts of terrible violence that were patently illegal might be justified.

No less a figure than Columbus's one-time Georgia Supreme Court Justice, Sterling Price Gilbert, expresses these thoughts in his memoir *A Georgia Lawyer*. Echoing Telfair, he describes Reconstruction as 'cruel and oppressive', and continues with a eulogy to the Klan, which he compares to the French Resistance:

> These [Reconstruction] measures were often administered in a vindictive manner by incompetent and dishonest adventurers. This situation brought into existence the Ku Klux Klan which operated much like the 'underground' in World War Two ... it is credited with doing much to restore order and protection to persons and property. The Ku Klux Klan of that day resembled the Vigilantes who operated in the formative days of our Western states and territories. The methods of both were often primitive, but many of the results were good.

Those Klan methods had been described over twelve volumes of testimony to a joint select committee of the two houses of Congress in 1871–72. Established in response to a mass of reports that the Klan had brought large tracts of the South close to anarchy, the committee's mission was to gather evidence and investigate *The Condition of Affairs in the Late Insurrectionary States*. In Georgia, a subcommittee of the parent body sat in Atlanta for several months, unearthing a pattern of rape, intimidation and murder, perpetrated not by freed slaves and Yankees but against them. By 1871, the subcommittee heard, the Klan's secret and hierarchical terrorist brigades were committing an average of two murders in Georgia each month.

In the city of Columbus, the defining moment of Reconstruction came in March 1868, a period of intense political ferment. Since December 1867, the Georgia Constitutional Convention, the state's first elected body to include African-Americans, had been sitting in Atlanta. While it deliberated, Georgia remained under federal military rule, a state of affairs expected to last indefinitely, unless and until the state ratified the 'equal rights' Fourteenth Amendment. According to the Columbus *Daily Sun*, the delegates to this 'black and tan' Convention consisted of 'New England outlaws; Sing-Sing convicts; penitentiary felons; and cornfield negroes'.

On 21 March 1868 the *Sun* reported the founding of the Columbus chapter of the Ku Klux Klan. According to some of the witnesses who testified before the Congressional select committee, the Klan was fostered by the presence in the city of no less a figure than the former Confederate cavalry's General Nathan Bedford Forrest, who had become the Klan's 'Grand Wizard' the previous year. As a military leader, Forrest was renowned for his tactical flair and aggression. He was also an alleged war criminal, accused of the massacre of black Union soldiers at Fort Pillow, Tennessee, in April 1864, an event that prompted one survivor to describe him in a letter to a US Senator as a 'foul fiend in human shape', a perpetrator of 'butchery and barbarity'.

As in other towns across the South, the Klan's arrival in Columbus was heralded by strange placards couched in bizarre, Kabbalistic language, printed on yellow paper in clear black type, and posted on doors and walls throughout the city. Their text read:

K.K.K
Horrible Sepulchre – Bloody Moon –
Cloudy Moon – Last Hour.
Division No. 71
The Great High Giant commands you. The dark and dismal hour will be soon. Some live today, tomorrow die. Be ye ready. The whetted sword, the bullet red, and the rights are ours. Dare not wear the holy garb of our mystic brotherhood, save in quest of blood. Let the guilty beware!! In the dark caves, in the mountain recesses, everywhere our brotherhood appears. Traitors beware!

By order of
Great Grand Cyclops, G.C.T.
Samivel, G.S.

Over the next few days the *Sun* named several prominent Republicans and warned: 'The Ku Klux Klan has arrived, and woe to the degenerate ... Something terrible floats on the breeze, and in the dim silences are heard solemn whispers, dire imprecations against the false ones who have proved recreant to their faith and country. Strange mocking anomalies [sic] now fill the air. Look out!' In its editorial on 27 March, the paper warned 'scalawags' and 'radicals' to expect 'terrible doom'.

To General Forrest, the *Sun* and their local followers, there was no 'traitor' hated more than Columbus's most famous scalawag, George W. Ashburn. Among post-war Southern Republicans, he was as close as any to becoming a national figure. Born in Bertie County, North Carolina, in 1814, he spent part of the 1830s working as an overseer of slaves. When Georgia seceded from the Union in January 1861, Ashburn raised a company of Southerners loyal to the Union and fought with the Northern army, attaining the rank of colonel. After the war he settled in Columbus, and in 1867 ran for election to the Georgia Convention, where he played a large part in drafting the proposed new state constitution, including its bill of rights. Ashburn was also planning to stand for the US Senate, and his speeches were reported on several occasions by the *New York Times*. According to Worsley, he was 'a notorious influence among the innocent and ignorant Negroes', and even before the Convention, had been 'most offensive to the whites of Columbus'.

Having travelled back to Columbus after the Convention broke up on 17 March, Ashburn took lodgings at the Perry House, a boarding establishment where he had stayed before, but when the owner forced him to leave he moved to a humble shotgun house on the corner of Thirteenth Street and First Avenue. Its other occupants included the Columbus head of the pro-Republican Loyal League, and the house's owner, a black woman named Hannah Flournoy.

The most detailed contemporary account of what happened next was written up in a dispatch for the *New York Tribune* on 1 April by the Reverend John H. Caldwell, the presiding Elder of the Methodist Episcopal Church in LaGrange, forty miles to the north. Caldwell was a leading 'Christian scalawag', an early white prophet of racial tolerance who worked hard after the war to create a bi-racial church in Georgia. He had even organised special religious camps for freedmen in LaGrange, attended by up to six thousand former slaves. A frequent visitor to Columbus, he was present in the city during the events he described.

A political as well as a religious scalawag, Caldwell addressed a mass meeting of Republicans in the courthouse square on the afternoon of Saturday, 29 March. He pieced together his account of what happened after the meeting by talking with members of the Columbus coroner's jury:

> Between twelve and one o'clock last night a crowd of persons, estimated at from thirty to forty in number, went to the house where Mr Ashburn lodged, surrounded the building, broke open the rear and front doors, and murdered him in his room. He received three fatal shots, one in the head between the eyes, one just below and to the rear of the hip, and another one in the mouth, which ranged upward. His clothing had from ten to fourteen bullet holes in them [sic]. Five persons entered his room and did the murderous deed; the rest were in other parts of the house and yard. The crowd remained from ten to fifteen minutes, during which time no policeman made his appearance. As the murderous crew were dispersing, however, some policemen made their appearance on the opposite side of the street. They could give no account of the affair when examined. This deed was perpetrated on one of the principal streets, in the most public part of the city ... all the assassins wore masks, and were well-dressed.

Ashburn's body was barely cold before those who thought his murder justified began to assail his memory. The *Sun*'s report the following day was the beginning of a series of claims that would be made in many subsequent accounts, none of which, according to Caldwell, was true. Far from being a cold-blooded political assassination by the Klan or its supporters, the paper said, Ashburn's murder owed its origins to his own tempestuous nature, and to his habit of waging disputes with members of his own party.

Caldwell protested in his dispatch for the *Tribune* that the claim that Ashburn's friends were to blame for his murder was merely an attempt 'to cover up and confuse the whole affair ... everyone in Columbus knows for what purpose these vile insinuations are put out. See how *The Sun* abuses and traduces the character of poor Ashburn, even while his mangled corpse lies before the very eyes of the editor. Ye people of America, do ye not understand all this?' In Caldwell's view, the *Sun's* pro-Klan coverage before the killing suggested that its editor 'knew beforehand what was going to happen'. Now, he went on, Columbus's advocates of racial equality were overcome with understandable terror. 'The sudden, horrible, cowardly and brutal murder of Colonel Ashburn, by this infamous band, shows that their purpose is murder. They are bent on midnight assassinations of the darkest, bloodiest and most diabolical character. Union men all over the city now feel that their lives are at every moment in danger. They do not know at what hour of the night they may be massacred in their bed.'

Few other white people saw things quite that way. The Ashburn murder is a perfect example of what the contemporary historian of Southern violence W. Fitzhugh Brundage terms 'flashpoints of contested memory', events whose competing accounts have as much to do with 'power, authority, cultural norms and social interaction as with the act of conserving and recalling information'. In Ashburn's case, old Dixie, the Klan and the Democrats were soon trouncing their opponents in the propaganda battle. By the time the Congressional Committee heard testimony in the summer and autumn of 1871, Ashburn's characterisation as an evil-doer largely responsible for his own, richly merited, demise was much more advanced. Some of the witnesses took their cue from *Radical Rule*, a virulently hostile pamphlet that is thought to have been written by William Chipley, one of the men accused of murdering Ashburn. Its claims and phraseology surfaced repeatedly in their evidence. According to *Radical Rule*, Ashburn had been remarkable as an overseer 'only for his cruelty to the slaves'. None other than Henry Lewis Benning, the Columbus attorney and former Confederate General, told the committee that Ashburn 'was reputed to be a very severe overseer – brutal'. Benning admitted he had never met Ashburn, but happily added further slanders. Again, the influence of *Radical Rule*, which claimed that Ashburn died 'in a negro brothel of the lowest order', is clear. Benning told the committee: 'After the war was over he joined in with the freedmen, and made himself their especial friend – he was ahead of almost every other white man in showing devotion to their interests. He quit his wife and took up with a negro woman in Columbus, lived with her as his wife (so said reputation) and at a public house at that; I mean a house of prostitution.'

Hannah Flournoy, the black woman who owned Ashburn's last residence, and who witnessed his murder, also testified. After the shooting, she said, 'They run me out of Columbus.' Too frightened to return, she 'lost everything I had there'. Shortly before Ashburn's death, she added, she had been given a letter addressed to Ashburn. He opened it in her presence, so that she could see it was 'a letter by the Ku Klux, with his coffin all drawed on it'.

Trying to rescue Ashburn's reputation for posterity, Caldwell told the committee that he had known Ashburn for years before the war, 'and I never heard anything against him'. Far from having been a cruel slave overseer, 'He was a very clever, kind man, and I never heard anything against him personally.' In Caldwell's view, Ashburn fell 'a martyr to liberty', having been 'among the very few men in Georgia who openly resisted the secession mania all through the war'. The experience of serving in the Georgia Convention had tempered his radical views, and he had done his utmost to negotiate political compromise 'in a subdued and conciliatory spirit to the moment of his death'. Other independent witnesses supported his account.

Caldwell's efforts were to no avail. In the Columbus histories by Telfair and Worsley, it is the Ashburn depicted in *Radical Rule*, the divisive, adulterous, former 'brutal overseer', whose death is memorialised, not the principled would-be statesman. As late as 1975, in an article on the case for the *Georgia Historical Quarterly*, Elizabeth Otto Daniell cites the pamphlet produced by Ashburn's enemies as her source for the statement that he had once been a 'cruel overseer of slaves'.

Historical events do not become flashpoints of contested memory without good reasons. One of the explanations for the posthumous vilification of G.W. Ashburn is the political struggle of which his murder formed a significant part: the largely successful terrorist campaign to limit or remove the rights of Georgia's African-Americans. This 'required' their most important white Columbus advocate to be demonised, and at the same time to be seen as having acted over many years against their real interests. In Telfair's phrase, the purpose of Ashburn's assassination was 'merely to remove a public menace'. Generations after his death, the guardians of white Southern memory found that the bleakest assessments of his life and character still fitted with their overall view of Reconstruction as a time of Northern cruelty and injustice.

Behind Ashburn's death was also another agenda, which concerned the matter of his killers. His murder was a scandal of national significance, and the ensuing investigation and eventual trial were widely reported. General William Meade, the former federal commander at Gettysburg who was now in charge of Georgia's military occupation, appointed two famous detectives to bring the assassins to justice – H.C. Whitley, who had investigated the plot to kill Abraham Lincoln, and William Reed, a veteran of the failed impeachment of Lincoln's far from radical successor, President Andrew Johnson. During the spring of 1868 they arrested at least twenty-two persons, most of them whites from Columbus, who were said to be men of the utmost respectability. Twelve were eventually charged with the murder, and their trial began at the McPherson barracks in Atlanta on 29 June – not by an ordinary civilian court, but by a military commission, a panel of federal military officers, because Georgia had not yet been readmitted to the Union.

According to contemporary reports in Northern newspapers, the prosecution presented a formidable case. The Cincinnati paper the *Commercial* claimed, 'The testimony of the prosecution was crushing – overwhelming, and the cross examination, in the hands of eight illustrations of the Georgia bar ... did not in the least damage it.' The only evidence presented by the defence had been alibis which did not stand scrutiny.

However, by the time this assessment was published at the beginning of August, it was too late. The defendants' guilt or innocence was no longer at issue. That spring, elections had been held for a new Georgia Assembly, which until now had resisted the Fourteenth 'equal rights' Amendment, so prolonging the military occupation. On 21 July, its Democrat diehards abruptly changed their minds and ratified the amendment. The fate of Ashburn's alleged killers had been settled by an extraordinary deal between Southern white leaders and the federal government, in which the prisoners' freedom, as Worsley puts it, was 'Georgia's reward'. On 24 July, General

Meade issued orders to dissolve the military commission. Next morning, the prisoners returned to Columbus, to be met at the railroad station by a large, exultant crowd. In theory they had been released on bail, pending future prosecution by the restored civilian authorities. In practice, there would be no further effort to put them or anyone else on trial.

For the former defendants' many Southern supporters, it was not enough that they were free: they had to be seen as utterly innocent, as almost-martyred victims of their enemies' radical zeal. Hence, at one level, the need for the claim that Ashburn might have been killed by African-Americans or white members of his own party: if the Columbus prisoners were innocent, there had to be alternative suspects. Meanwhile, there was another battle for future historical memory to be fought. Upon their release, nine of the prisoners issued a statement, printed next day by the Columbus *Sun*. It said that the prosecution witnesses had been suborned by 'torture, bribery and threats', including the use of the 'sweatbox'. Meanwhile, the defendants had been held at Fort Pulaski in conditions of inhuman cruelty:

> The cells were dark, dangerous, without ventilation, and but four feet by seven. No bed or blankets were furnished. The rations consisted of a *slice of pork fat* [original italics] three times each week. A piece of bread for each meal, soup for dinner and coffee for breakfast, finished the bill of fare. An old oyster can was given each prisoner, and in this vessel both coffee and soup were served … Refused all communication with their friends, relatives or counsel, they were forced to live in these horrid cells night and day, prostrated by heat, and maddened by myriads of mosquitoes. The calls of nature were attended to in a bucket which was removed but once in twenty-four hours.

In some quarters the prisoners' allegations were vehemently denied. According to the Cincinnati *Commercial*, their supporters in Georgia were guilty of 'moral terrorism', which 'made it a crime to entertain any opinion but the one most decided as to the[ir] innocence'. Appalled by the claims of torture and ill-treatment, General Meade issued his own public rebuttal, accusing the Georgia newspapers of making false and exaggerated statements for political purposes, and insisting that they had 'no foundation'. He ended his remarks with some trenchant comments about the city where Ashburn died: 'Had the civil authorities acted in good faith and with energy, and made any attempt to ferret out the guilty – or had the people of Columbus evinced or felt any horror of the crime or cooperated in any way in detecting its perpetrators, much that was seemingly harsh and arbitrary might have, and would have been, avoided.'

There were two further layers of significance to the murder of George Ashburn. In a case of the highest importance and profile, positions had been taken not in response to evidence, but on the basis of partisan beliefs and allegiance. And at its end, resolution had not come about through a court's dispassionate verdict, but through a political deal, itself the result of the vexed and edgy relationship between the Union and the states of the South. Not for the last time in Columbus, the rule of law had been shown to be a contingent, relative concept. *Realpolitik* had taken precedence over justice.

Even in Georgia, cloudless nights in January bring frosts, and bands of mist that collect in hollows, clinging to the trees. The cold muffles sound. As I walked amid the lanes and shrubbery of Wynnton one evening at the start of 2001, I found it easy to imagine how an intruder might have crept undetected between the pools of shadow, moving in on human prey without so much as the crackle of a twig. Twenty-four years earlier, in the weeks after Kathleen Woodruff's death, the Columbus police stepped up their patrols again, joined by their many allies. By January 1978, some of the task force officers were giving in to despair, and hinted to reporters that they were beginning to think that the stocking strangler possessed supernatural powers. Trying to catch him, they suggested, was like trying to hunt 'a will o'the wisp, a ghost'.

If science couldn't stop the killer, the authorities hoped to rely on sheer numbers. Earnestine Flowers, a childhood friend of Carlton Gary, was working as a Sheriff's Deputy. 'There were guys from the hills of Tennessee who knew how to track people; Military Police from Fort Benning; the Ku Klux Klan; people from other Police Departments who wanted to volunteer. We had night lights, people hiding up in trees; that new night

73

vision thing which had just come out; dogs. And yet we were getting so many calls. People were so afraid. I don't mean only the people who lived there. I was terrified, too. I was out on patrol, shaking with fear. I remember thinking, "I can't do this, night after night; I gotta get myself assigned as a radio operator. I gotta get myself inside the building!" '

If there was a point when Columbus became immobilised by fear, it came with what law enforcement staff still call the 'night of the terrors' – the early hours of 11 February 1978. It began with an attempted burglary at the Wynnton residence of a retired industrial magnate, Abraham Illges. An imposing building, a pastiche of a medieval castle, the Illges house had a drive that opened on to Forest Avenue, in the heart of the territory haunted by the strangler. On 1 January the house had been burgled, and while Mr and Mrs Illges slept, a purse containing her car keys removed from the bed next to hers. Next morning, her Cadillac was missing. The couple then installed a sophisticated alarm system, with a pressure pad under the carpet near the front door, and at 5.15 a.m. on 11 February, someone stepped on it, automatically summoning the police. They arrived within a few minutes, and, in the belief that the burglar might be the strangler, summoned help. As officers, some with sniffer dogs, fanned out through the moonlit trees and gardens, the airwaves were alive with officers' communications.

Half an hour after the alarm had been raised at the Illges residence, a second, home-made panic buzzer sounded two blocks away on Carter Avenue, inside the bedroom where Fred Burdette, a physician, lay sleeping. His neighbour, Ruth Schwob, a widow of seventy-four who lived alone, had asked him to install an alarm in her own bedroom, wired through to his, so that he might summon help if she were attacked. When the alarm went, Burdette tried to call Mrs Schwob, and listened as her telephone rang without answer. Then, while his wife phoned the police, Burdettte ran to his neighbour's home. By the time he reached her door, the occupants of several squad cars were already approaching the premises. The first officer to reach Mrs Schwob, Sergeant Richard Gaines, later described what he saw:

> I climbed in through the kitchen window, over the kitchen counter, had my flashlight. I started going through the house room by room, without

turning on any lights, using only my flashlight. And after about two minutes, I got to the back of the house and looked in through the bedroom door and saw Mrs Schwob, sitting on the edge of the bed. She had a stocking wrapped around her neck; it was hanging down between her legs, also laying on the floor was a screwdriver. Then I went over to where she was and when she saw me she said, 'I thought you were him coming back.' And then she said, 'He's still here, he's still in the house.' And I went over and I checked the necklace – I mean the strangling – the stocking that was wrapped around her neck to make sure it was not too tight, and it was loose.

Gaines and his colleagues checked the rest of the house. But Mrs Schwob was mistaken. The stocking strangler had gone.

The Columbus newspapers published next day, 12 February, warmly celebrated Mrs Schwob's survival. Like Kathleen Woodruff, she was a very prominent citizen and patron of the arts. For twenty years after the death of her husband, Simon, in 1954, she had continued to run his textile firm, Schwob Manufacturing, and continued as board chairman emeritus until it was sold in 1976. In 1966 she was Columbus's Woman of the Year, and her other accolades included the local Sertoma Service to Mankind Award. She was, reported the *Ledger*, 'credited with almost single-handedly raising more than $500,000 for the $1.5 million fine arts building at Columbus College', which was named after her husband.

Ruth Schwob, the *Ledger* said, had survived the attack because she was a regular jogger and unusually fit for her age.

I just awakened and he was there. He was on the bed and had his hand on my throat and wrapped pantyhose all the way around. Then he pulled the thing tightly round my neck. He had a mask on his face, I think he had gloves on, and it was dark in my room. There was no flesh showing, and he never uttered a sound. It was quite a struggle. I fought like a tiger. He choked me so bad, I passed out. I think the police just missed him. I don't know how long he was in the house or whether he was gone before the police arrived.

After her rescue, the police sealed off the surrounding streets as officers combed the earth for a scent with bloodhounds and a helicopter equipped with floodlights hovered overhead. There were shoe tracks leading from Schwob's kitchen window, where the strangler had forced his entry with the screwdriver found by her bed. But once again, he escaped. 'If he doesn't have knowledge of the area,' the task force leader Ronnie Jones told the *Ledger*, 'then he's mighty damn lucky.'

Having found Mrs schwob, and having failed to find the strangler, Jones and his staff assumed that he had left the area. In fact, he merely fled two blocks to 1612 Forest Avenue, a house diagonally opposite the Illges castle. It was not until 11.30 in the morning of the following day, 12 February, that Judith Borom called on her way to church to check on the woman who lived there, her mother-in-law Mildred, a lone widow, aged seventy-eight. Earlier that day Judith's husband, Perry Borom, had been discussing Mildred's safety with his business partner, George C. Woodruff Junior, Kathleen Woodruff's son. 'I was telling him, "I'm really worried about your mama,"' Woodruff told reporters later. 'He said he'd sent a man out to put screws in the window to keep it closed.'

Judith was with her three children. She parked her car in the back yard, and rang the back doorbell. There was no answer, but she could hear the television playing. She told her son to go round to the front while she tried to peer into Mildred's bedroom, at the building's side. Then she heard the boy screaming: 'Mama, come here, Mama, come here.' At the front of the house a plate-glass window had been broken, and the front door was ajar, wedged open with a piece of carpet. Judith called the police. Mildred's body, raped and strangled with cord from a Venetian blind, was lying on the hall floor. The autopsy reports suggested that she was being murdered at the very time that dozens of police were keeping busy at Ruth Schwob's house two blocks away, and the bloodhounds and helicopter were conducting their futile search of the neighbourhood.

As usual, the task-force leader Ronnie Jones was among the first on the scene. At the sight of the killer's sixth victim, he collapsed, sobbing uncontrollably. 'Ronald had begun to take it personally,' Detective Luther Miller, who now took over his responsibilities, later recalled. 'He felt like it was his responsibility to stop the strangler. He had – we had all been

76

working day and night to protect these women. He started thinking it was his fault each time one was found dead. It was just an emotional breakdown. Chief McClung decided he needed a break.'

The CPD's relationship with Columbus's eccentric coroner, Donald Kilgore, remained somewhat strained. On the day after Mildred Borom's killing, it took another turn for the worse. Fibres found on her body, Kilgore told reporters, were 'black, Negroid, pubic hairs'. Kilgore, it will be recalled, was a mortician, without scientific training. At the time he made this controversial pronouncement, proper forensic examination of the corpse and the crime scene had barely begun. Presumably, Kilgore had noticed that the hairs were dark and curly.

Four days after the discovery of Mildred Borom's body, the Columbus police turned for help to the realm of the spirits. At the behest of Detective Commander Herman Boone, two officers took John G. Argeris, a well-known psychic who was said to have helped police solve crimes in New England, on a drive through Wynnton. Argeris, the officers' report stated, 'determined that the suspect lives in the area … The suspect was also determined, without a doubt, to be a white male, with large eyes, having a full beard. Suspect either has money or his family is considered well-to-do. Argeris determined that the suspect has the initial "J" … Argeris further stated that "J" should stand for John.'

The pressure on the cops was already almost intolerable, but on 1 March it grew still more severe. Police Chief McClung received a letter, signed 'Chairman, Forces of Evil', purportedly a white vigilante group, saying that if the strangler were not caught before the beginning of June, a black woman named Gail Jackson, whom the group had already kidnapped, would be murdered. If the strangler were still at large in September, the letter went on, 'the victims will double … Don't think we are bluffing.' Gail Jackson, it rapidly became apparent, was indeed missing.

With commendable *sang froid*, McClung separated the 'Forces of Evil' investigation from the stranglings case. Eventually, after the receipt of further letters that demanded a $10,000 ransom, the FBI's psychological profilers suggested that the author of the letters was black, and that Gail Jackson was probably already dead. They were right on both counts. The 'chairman' of 'Forces of Evil' was an African-American soldier from Fort

Benning named William Henry Hance, and he had killed Jackson and two other women. Towards the end of 1978 he was convicted and sentenced to death. Twelve years later he died in Georgia's electric chair.

Perhaps the night of the terrors scared even the strangler. For his last murder, he moved out of Wynnton, to Steam Mill Road, a mile and a half away. There, on 20 April 1978, eight months after his first attack, he killed Janet Cofer, aged sixty-one, a teacher at an elementary school. Her son, who normally lodged with her, had been away for the evening. And then, without apparent explanation, the stocking stranglings stopped.

# FOUR

## *Dragnet*

The first time I met the blues mama,
They came walking through the woods
The first time I met the blues baby,
They came walking through the woods
They stopped by at my house first mama,
And done me all the harm they could.

The blues got at me
Lord they ran me from tree to tree
The blues got at me
Lord they ran me from tree to tree
You shoulda heard me beggin',
'Mister blues, don't murder me.'

'The First Time I Met the Blues',
'LITTLE BROTHER' MONTGOMERY (1906–85)

Even the greatest detectives rarely solve their cases on their own. They need tip-offs, informants, steers from those in the know, especially when the trail they have to follow is cold. One chilly evening in April 2001, across a table in a chain hotel in Gwinnett County, on the northern edge of the metro Atlanta sprawl, the man who cracked the stocking stranglings leant towards me and lowered his voice. The former Columbus homicide investigator Michael Sellers had already told me that his work on the murders had begun with a mysterious phone call in March 1984, almost six years after the last killing. Now, after five hours' intense conversation, he felt ready to reveal his own prize source, the starting point of the hunt for Carlton Gary. 'I think,' he said, 'it was a phone call from God.'

A tall, slim, greying figure, his face dominated by a toothbrush moustache, Sellers was dressed in jeans and a plaid shirt. Born and raised in Columbus, the son of the city's former Treasurer, he described himself as part of a new breed of better-educated officer who began to join the CPD in the 1970s: he even had a degree in policing from Troy State University. The pride Sellers took in the work he had done seventeen years earlier was palpable. He carried an ordered folder of photographs and documents, and I had the impression that he had made presentations of his contribution to this case many times before. But Sellers, fifty at the time we met, also seemed suffused by bitterness, much of it directed at his former boss and CPD chief, Jim Wetherington.

'After the trial in 1986, when Carlton Gary had been convicted, Richard Smith put in an application for me to be nominated as Police Officer of the Year with the Police Chiefs' Association,' Sellers said. 'But for it to go forward, Chief Wetherington had to second it. He refused. He said the case had been a team effort.'

I found it strange that this still rankled after so many years. 'But surely,' I asked, 'bringing Gary to justice was reward enough?'

Sellers shook his head, colouring. 'For two years, I'd been assigned to the District Attorney's office in the Government Center, working up the case. I almost set up home there. I think there was a lot of jealousy from some of the lieutenants and captains. They resented the fact that because I was working on the stranglings, I wasn't doing any of the John shot Mary cases.

'You know what I found hardest? That no one ever said thank you. After the trial, the DA opened up the grand jury room and allowed me to talk to the media. But when I got back to the office, I got my butt chewed off. And after it was all over, all that I was ever assigned was the crap.'

In the spring of 1987, less than a year after Gary's trial, Sellers left Columbus and detective work altogether. When we met, he was earning a higher salary. But instead of solving notorious murders, he was working nights as a Gwinnett Country Patrol Sergeant. I couldn't help thinking it was really a job for a younger man, physically demanding and dangerous.

In 2002 he suffered terrible injuries in a car crash, sustained while chasing a suspect.

After Janet Cofer's murder in April 1978, as the strangler's silence grew from weeks to months, the special police patrols continued, and the strang-lings inquiry remained the overwhelming preoccupation of the CPD. There was more to this than the simple horror of leaving such a murderer at liberty. Always in the background was the social position of many of the victims. The venerable business elites of Columbus did not normally concern themselves with criminal justice, and if they thought about it at all, it was merely as a job that had to be done. But a serial killer who had violated and murdered women such as Kathleen Woodruff, and had done so amid the citadels of Wynnton, represented a different level of threat.

Columbus is a town for joiners, where a person's position in society is advertised by their memberships of clubs and other organisations. In Wynnton, one of the oldest and swankiest is the Columbus Country Club; further north, on the banks of the Chattahoochee, is the Green Island Club – just as expensive, but burdened with a hint that some of its members are what might be considered a little *nouveau riche*. Above them all stands that riverside fine-dining establishment on its little promontory, the Big Eddy Club. Its members are generous contributors to charity, and not a month goes by without some gala dinner or reception there in aid of this or that good cause, together with Columbus's best weddings and debutante balls. For years, such events were chronicled every Sunday in Marquette McKnight's 'Around Town' column in the *Ledger-Enquirer*: 'That's where you find the bluebloods,' she told me, 'the families who settled Columbus, together with what they call newcomers – people who are major players, but who have been in the city for less than twenty-five years.'

For almost thirty years, beginning in 1962, the club was managed by Marcel Carles, a skilled French chef. I went to see him at his home in Wynnton, filled with memorabilia of his years of service to the city's upper class.

'The only other food you could get if you dined out in Columbus in those days was burgers and hot dogs,' Carles said. 'I had *moules* flown in from New York, *langoustines*, châteaubriand, *sole bonne femme* boned at the table. We were easily good enough to merit a Michelin star. We had

Georgia's first air-conditioned wine cellar, and the wines to go with it: *premiers crus*, a complete run of vintages of Château Mouton-Rothschild going back to 1929. There are people in Columbus who have never seen the ocean, never been outside the state. Here the people were more sophisticated. And we had a special *à la carte* service. If you wanted anything that wasn't on the menu, you had only to ask, and we would cook it.' Carles's special talent was for ice sculptures. He showed me photographs taken at weddings and other club functions with huge models on the tables of Rodin's *The Kiss* and Michelangelo's *David*, which he had carved.

'In the Big Eddy, you don't ask regular visitors, "What's your name?",' Carles said, 'even if they are not members themselves. Many of the women who were strangled had been there often enough that all the staff recognised them immediately and knew their names.' Some of the victims had family memberships: Ferne Jackson through her nephew Harry, later Columbus's Mayor; Mildred Borom and her son Perry; and the Woodruffs, the family of murdered Kathleen. According to Carles, Ruth Schwob, who survived the strangler's attack, was a frequent guest, as were Jean Dimenstein and Janet Cofer. Of the seven murdered women, only two had not been seen at the Big Eddy, Martha Thurmond and Florence Scheible. 'You can only imagine what the atmosphere was like when they began to get killed,' Carles said. 'Everyone was on edge, uneasy. They were frightened for their women, and they were angry.'

Leading figures in Columbus's legal establishment were also club members. There was Judge Mullins Whisnant, District Attorney when the murders took place, and William Smith, his successor, the man in post during the hunt for Carlton Gary, and later the lead prosecution counsel at his trial. The family of Judge Kenneth Followill, who would try the case, were members, as was Robert Elliott, judge of the city's Federal District Court, who many years later would start to hear one of Gary's appeals. Successive police chiefs, from Curtis McClung onwards, also dined at the Big Eddy. The pressure these officials felt to find the strangler would have been intense in any case, but the connections they had through their social lives can only have increased it.

Nevertheless, in the absence of further murders, the CPD and the GBI did not have the resources to maintain its huge investigative effort indefinitely. At the end of 1978, eight months after Janet Cofer's death, the task force was closed. By then, its case file contained more than thirty-five thousand separate documents. The contents of some eleven thousand 'field interview' cards, together with details of five thousand vehicles reportedly seen near the murder scenes, had been fed into an IBM computer, the first time such a device had been used by the police in Columbus. The police told reporters they could punch a geographical grid number into the machine, 'and it will show everyone we stopped in that area'. But no amount of technology could hide the fact that they had no suspect. 'This has been one of the biggest career disappointments to me,' the CPD Chief, Curtis McClung, said prosaically. 'I have this fear that somewhere in all that information we've overlooked something.'

The murders had stopped, but there could be no normality until the killer was captured. 'It's not over yet,' wrote the Columbus *Enquirer* columnist Richard Hyatt on the first anniversary of the strangling of Janet Cofer. He built his article around an interview with an eighty-six-year-old widow from Wynnton, who still kept a loaded gun among her family photographs, next to her rocking-chair. 'How can it really end until a final chapter is written, until there's an answer to our questions?' Hyatt asked. Those responsible for the absence of such answers were already paying with their jobs.

Ronnie Jones, the head of the task force at the time of the murders, resigned from the force in the summer of 1978, claiming that he had been hampered by 'political interference'. Next to go was Mayor Jack Mickle, who lost a bid for re-election the following autumn to the murdered Ferne Jackson's nephew, Harry Jackson, after a campaign in which the investigation's lack of success figured heavily. In 1980, Curtis McClung resigned as chief of the CPD to run for election as Muscogee County Sheriff – only to lose by ten thousand votes to a man who had never held public office. By the end of that year, most of the senior detectives who had worked on the investigation under him had either resigned or been demoted. According to William Winn, in an article for *Atlanta* magazine, 'A popular courthouse pastime in Columbus is to attempt to list all the individuals whose careers – lives – were adversely affected by the strangler.'

Occasionally there were hints that the police did have a plausible suspect. In the summer of 1978 a businessman told the police that a young African-American had visited his office, and in the opinion of his female clerical staff, had 'acted strange'. There was no reason to believe this individual had anything to do with the stranglings, but in its desperation the CPD asked the women to help its artist produce a 'composite' sketch of the man they had seen. The sketch depicted a black man with a pointed chin, a curved, somewhat uneven nose, a medium Afro hairstyle and pronounced, bushy eyebrows.

In June 1983, Horice Adams, an African-American aged twenty-four, was arrested and charged in the north Georgia town of Elberton with burgling and attempting to assault an elderly white woman. Having removed her bedroom window screen, he climbed in and began to choke her, but fled when she screamed and rolled off her bed. Three years earlier, Adams had been sentenced to five years in prison for robbing a couple of $15 at a motel and raping the woman, and he had recently been freed on parole. He lived with his mother in Columbus, as he had been doing throughout the months of the murders. With his thick eyebrows and pointed chin, he bore more than a passing resemblance to the composite sketch.

For a few days the city's media explored the details of Adams's life, while the Georgia Bureau of Investigation laboratory tested his hair and bodily fluids against the samples left by the strangler. The most telling physical evidence came from the strangler's semen. Since the late 1980s, police involved in rape investigations have been able to use a powerful new technology, DNA profiling. If semen taken from a victim's body is uncontaminated, forensic scientists will usually be able to state to a high mathematical probability whether its complex DNA molecules match those in a suspect's fluids. But even though these techniques had not been invented at the time of the stranglings, investigators did possess an older method that could be very effective – secretor typing. Most people, about four-fifths of the population, are 'secretors', meaning that in their saliva, semen and other fluids, they secrete the chemical markers which give away their blood group. A 'group O secretor' would be someone from the common O blood group whose semen revealed this fact, because it contained a relatively large amount of the relevant marker.

However, the tests carried out on the stocking strangler's semen indicated that he was a 'non-secretor' – that his body fluids contained only tiny traces of the group O marker. Unfortunately for those who had hoped that the police finally had their killer, Horice Adams turned out to be a regular O secretor. He might have resembled the composite sketch, but he could not be the stocking strangler.

Over the years there had been other ultimately frustrating leads. One of the earliest came even before the last murder, after the night of the terrors. Three days before Ruth Schwob survived the strangler's attack, she had been burgled by a man she claimed to have recognised – a young white neighbour named Chris Gingell, the son of a local television news anchor. Schwob told the police that she thought it was the same man who had attacked her on the later occasion, and when the cops questioned him about the burglary he failed a polygraph test, although he was never charged. Tests on his hair and serology type – he was a blood group B secretor – appeared to exclude him definitively, but there are some in Columbus who remain convinced that Gingell was the real killer. The unjustified damage to his reputation is not hard to understand. If he, a white man who lived in Wynnton, had been guilty, it would have made two of the case's abiding mysteries much easier to explain. Even someone like Gingell might have found it hard to evade the police patrols, but for an African-American it would have been close to impossible. Moreover, a local white man would have been more likely to have known the addresses where elderly women lived alone.

Two more possible suspects came to light during the summer of 1978. The first, Wade Hinson, had been arrested for a minor public order violation in Barbour County, Alabama, just across the Georgia state line. Once in jail, he not only confessed to committing the stranglings, he showed the Sheriff and his Deputies how he had killed his victims by 'throttling' a door handle with a stocking he carried in his duffle bag. He also threatened to kill the Sheriff's wife upon his release, saying he had been 'told by God to take care of old women'.

A few weeks later, Barbara Andrews, the estranged wife of Jesse Rawling, a black man from Columbus, informed the police of her belief that her husband was the killer. One thing she mentioned made the task force take her seriously: Rawling, she said, told her that one of the victims had had breast cancer. This was true: Jean Dimenstein had had a mastectomy, although this fact had not been made public.

Like the strangler, Hinson and Rawling had O-type blood. Initial tests indicated that Hinson's pubic hairs were very like the strangler's. But both men had to be ruled out, because they were O secretors.

After that, new leads in the case became rather sparse. The police tried opening what they called a 'rumour center', a telephone hotline for people who wanted to pass on confidential tips. Hardly anyone called. Taking office in 1982, the new CPD chief, Jim Wetherington, pledged that solving the case remained a high priority. But until the day two years later that Michael Sellers took his mysterious phone call, there was no real progress. For the moment we must leave the question of whether the Almighty really had something to do with it to one side. But if He did, He chose a human being called Henry Sanderson to be His messenger.

In 1977, the autumn of the stranglings, Sanderson was living near Dadeville, Alabama, where he owned and ran a store. On 7 October he and his wife came to Columbus for a family party, and spent the night at the house shared by Sanderson's octogenarian mother, Nellie Sanderson, and her elder sister, Callye J. East. It lay on Eberhart Avenue, in the heart of Wynnton, a short walk from the homes where Ferne Jackson and Jean Dimenstein had recently been murdered. Late that night, the house was burgled.

The intruder first tried and failed to get in through Nellie Sanderson's bedroom window, and then succeeded via the kitchen. But the room he entered next contained not a vulnerable old woman, but the sleeping figures of Mr Sanderson and his wife. Before departing, the burglar removed Sanderson's trousers from the chair by his bed. Next morning, Sanderson said later, 'I got up and started to put my pants on and couldn't find them.' His wallet, which contained his banking cards and $60 in cash, had been in a pocket, together with the keys to his Toyota car, which was missing from the place he'd parked it outside. A few days later the police found the car, abandoned. The thief had gone through the glove compartment, removing some gasoline credit cards and Henry Sanderson's weapon – a blue-steel .22 Ruger automatic.

Nine months later, in July 1978, the then-CPD chief Curtis McClung addressed a press conference about the Ruger. There was, he admitted, 'absolutely no evidence that the strangler committed this particular burglary'. He had never used a gun against any of his victims, and the Eberhart Avenue intruder left no fingerprints or other physical clues. But the burglary had been in Wynnton, and just possibly, McClung said, it had been the strangler's work: 'We are asking for the public's help in this matter because the gun could not be recovered through the normal investigative process.'

Back then, Detective Sellers had been assigned to the pawnshop detail – a long way down the police hierarchy from investigating serial murder. By 1984 he had been promoted to sergeant, and had made the robbery-homicide division, the CPD's elite.

'I'd made a promise,' Sellers told me portentously. 'I was in the mall one day, at J.C. Penney, and I ran into Cindy Scheible. I knew her from school, and [the strangler's third victim] Florence Scheible was her grandma. It must have been four or five years after her death. I said to her, "Cindy, someone killed your grandmother, and I am going to find him." After I'd cleared it [solved the case] I saw her again and she reminded me: "You said you'd find him, and you did." '

Meanwhile, Henry Sanderson had moved to Allen, a suburb of Dallas, Texas. But on the morning of 15 March 1984, Sellers told me, Sanderson dialled the CPD number and spoke to him. 'He calls and he says, "I've been looking for a .22 Ruger," ' Sellers said. 'He said the reason he was calling us was someone had phoned him from the Police Department and left a message that said we had the gun.'

Sellers took down the serial number and told Sanderson he'd look into it. Under normal circumstances, he might not have been interested, but Ruger automatics were big news in Columbus that week in 1984. Four days earlier, a police officer, Charles Bowen, had been shot twice in the face and killed by a robber armed with a Ruger after a car chase. Sellers discussed the phone call with Charlie Rowe, a detective colleague who'd been on the stranglings task force. When he mentioned the weapon, Rowe said later, 'something clicked'. He told Sellers: 'That's the gun stolen at Callye East's house.' Sellers quickly discovered two things. The first was that no one at the CPD seemed to know anything about the gun's current whereabouts. The second was that none of his colleagues had called and left a message for Henry Sanderson.

'I called him back,' Sellers said. 'He was quite specific. He said the message was, "Call Sergeant Sellers at the CPD." ' Perhaps Sellers thought he had somehow been chosen. In any event, he decided to do whatever it took to find Sanderson's gun. His first step was to send out a 'teletype', a telex message containing the Ruger's serial number, in which he asked every police force in America if they had come across it. He was certain, he said, that the key to the unsolved murders now lay with him.

By the closing years of the nineteenth century, whatever hopes Georgia's African-Americans might have had during Reconstruction had been brutally dashed. Outright slavery remained defunct. But in its place had come new forms of political, social, educational, economic and legal discrimination, whose cumulative effects were becoming ever more severe. The brief Atlanta spring of multi-racial legislative assemblies had virtually ended in the 1870s: Georgia's politicians and public officials were once again almost all white. (W.H. Rogers, the last black Assembly man before the civil rights era, clung onto his seat in McIntosh County until 1908.) Formal segregation, codified in the series of statutes known as the 'Jim Crow' laws, maintained blacks' oppressed and inferior status, anticipating the apartheid system introduced in South Africa by many decades.

After 1877, and the so-called 'compromise' by which Union troops were finally withdrawn from the South, the federal courts and government ceased any attempt to enforce the Fourteenth Amendment, and its promises of due process and equal protection under the laws. By 1908, 86 per cent of Georgia's convicted criminals were black. Thousands were victims of trumped-up prosecutions for trivial misdemeanours, brought not to exact justice, but for economic reasons. Under the state's 'convict lease' system, prisoners were leased to private convict-brokers, who hired them out to sawmills, mines, farms and factories, and set them to work in chain gangs on public roads. By 1900 this was bringing the State Treasury revenue of $250,000 a year, and providing employers with a workforce at a fraction of the normal cost. Its black victims faced a bondage effectively indistinguishable from their pre-Emancipation ancestors. Around Columbus, writes William Winn, others were 'held in a form of debt slavery by white farmers, who, in exchange for paying a misdemeanour fine against a black, required him to work off the debt as farm labour'.

Some of this found black cultural expression long ago. Ma Rainey (1886–1939), the 'mother of the blues', was born in Columbus and lived there for much of her life, and was the author of some of her genre's first recordings in the early 1920s. Rainey, who inspired and trained the more famous Bessie Smith, wrote her own songs; as her biographer Sandra Lieb comments, they 'communicate ... some essential truth about the black experience in [the United States]: poverty, suffering, heartbreak and pain, as well as humour, fortitude, strength and endurance'. Most of her lyrics deal with the personal, but in 'Chain Gang Blues' (1926) she sang of the shackled lines of male and female convicts, some just children, who had been leased to toil on public works, and made to wear anklets with needle-sharp points which lacerated their legs:

> Ain't robbed no train, ain't done no hanging crime
> But the judge said I'd be on the county road a long, long time.

Underpinning white supremacy was the constant threat and occasional exercise of mob violence. Often Georgia led the lynching league tables compiled each year by the Tuskegee Institute in Alabama. The historian W. Fitzhugh Brundage provides details of the lynchings of 441 black males and ten black women in Georgia between 1880 and 1930. In only the rarest cases was any attempt made to bring the perpetrators to justice.

Columbus and the surrounding counties were no strangers to this phenomenon. In 1896, Jesse Slayton and Will Miles were taken by a mob from the Muscogee County Jail in Columbus and murdered outside it. Like so many lynching victims, they had been accused of raping a white woman. Few details of their lives and deaths survive. Another case four years later is more copiously documented.

On the Columbus bank of the Chattahoochee, halfway between the Big Eddy Club and the Victorian factory district downtown, there's a rocky bluff about thirty feet high. Known as Lover's Leap, it carries a legend: here, it is said, two native American lovers, forbidden from marrying because they came from different tribes, once jumped to their deaths. Nowadays, just downstream lies a humming hydro-electric dam, but in 1900 it was still under construction and the torrent surged unmolested, tumbling between granite boulders. The shore would have looked much the same as it does now, an obstacle course of rocks and dense scrub. The land above the leap became the site of a mill and its workers' village, Bibb City. At the turn of the century it was known as North Highland Woods, and was a favourite spot for picnics and romantic trysts. It even had a pavilion. The probably mythical native Americans would not be the only ones to die there.

In the small hours of 9 June 1900, Simon Adams, a black farm labourer aged nineteen, was caught trying to burgle the home of his employer, Judge E.H. Almond, who lived a little to the north of Columbus in Muscogee County. (Despite his title, Almond was not a full-time jurist, but a local Justice of the Peace.) Adams made the mistake of trying to enter Almond's home by the window of the bedroom used by his daughters, aged ten and seventeen. When one of them raised the alarm, he tried to hide in their wardrobe. The men of the house swiftly found him, tied him up at gunpoint, and placed a heavy chain around his neck. The likelihood is that the only crime he intended to commit was theft, but his presence in a white girls' bedroom seems to have created the suspicion that he had some sexual motive.

A few hours later, still bound and chained, Adams was entrusted to the care of a bailiff, who was to take him to the county jail in Columbus. The bailiff, from a powerful land-owning family, was a big, jug-eared man named Aaron Brewster Land. Photographs taken later in his life depict him proudly displaying prize-winning vegetables, with a broad and faintly menacing grin.

There was a direct road from Almond's house to downtown Columbus, but Land did not use it. Instead, he took a detour towards the North Highlands pavilion. Later he told a reporter from the Columbus *Enquirer-Sun* that he was aware of the danger Adams ran, and had been hoping to slip into the city unnoticed. However, as Land must have known, the road he took was a dead end. In the woods, a vigilante posse was waiting. They seized Adams, dragged him to the brink of Lovers' Leap and pushed him into the river.

Unlike the lovers, Adams did not die immediately. He landed in a spot where the water was deep enough to swim, and willed the muscles built up though years of hoeing and picking cotton to keep him afloat against the weight of the chain around his neck. There were a few islands back in 1900, boulders in the stream which might have offered refuge; the reports of his death suggest that he thought that if he could only keep fighting long enough, he could snatch lungfuls of air when needed but otherwise stay underwater, being carried by the current until he was out of sight. Perhaps he wondered whether he could somehow reach Alabama, on the other side of the river, where he would have been relatively safe.

For just a few moments, he seemed to be winning. The surging current began to bear him away, and he wasn't sinking as fast as the mob seems to have expected. According to one account, one of the men had told him: 'In you go, nigger, swim for your life.' In the circumstances, perhaps that remark gave him a little hope. As he was swept downstream, the men on the shore found it hard to keep up with him, stumbling and leaping over the flood-polished rocks. One of them stopped and raised his rifle. A puff of smoke; a bullet winged the water. Then another bullet, and another. Adams was wounded, and must have known that the river was carrying him to oblivion, but he started to dive more deeply, looking for cover among the weeds, staying down until the pressure in his chest was overwhelming. The last time he came up for air a round from a Winchester entered his skull behind his ear.

'It is possible that the chain will not be of sufficient weight to keep the body down,' the *Enquirer-Sun* reported, 'and that it will rise in the next day or two.' There is no record that it did. Bailiff Land was asked if he knew any of the men he met in the woods that hot June morning. 'I didn't recognise anybody,' he said. 'I was more concerned with the guns than the men behind them.' Like most lynchings, Simon Adams's murder was officially put down by the coroner as the work of 'persons unknown'.

If, as seems likely, Brewster Land had been in league with the lynch mob, he escaped with impunity. His large and ramified family were not as rich as the industrial magnates who made their wealth downtown and lived in the mansions of Wynnton. But strung out in their prosperous farms along Double Churches Road, an easy ride from the city, the Lands were also a kind of dynasty. Settled in the area long before the Civil War, they have remained a centre of power in and around Columbus for almost two centuries. They will figure largely in this narrative again.

While the lynchings of Jesse Slayton, Will Miles and Simon Adams appear to have been typical products of that dangerous Dixie fantasy, the Southern rape complex, the local tradition of political murder that had been inaugurated by the assassination of G.W. Ashburn still flourished around Columbus, despite the fact that the Ku Klux Klan had been officially banned since the 1870s. In 1909 the newspapers began to carry references to a blind, itinerant African-American preacher, Joseph Hardy, accusing him, in the words of the *Enquirer-Sun*, of making 'dangerous and incendiary sermons' to black plantation workers. On the evening of Sunday, 19 June, the *Enquirer-Sun* reported, a gang of white vigilantes learnt that Hardy was at the home of a man called William Careker, twelve miles from Talbotton, to the east of Columbus. They went there, the paper said,

> to stop a disturbance raised by [the] negro preacher. It seems that the negro preacher was a disorganiser and did very mischievous work among the negro farm hands, stirring up strife between the farmers and their employees. A posse of citizens went to Careker's house with the supposed purpose of dealing with him in such a vigorous manner that he would not meddle in such matters in the future, although it is not supposed that unnecessarily harsh measures were contemplated – just a line of argument that would impress the negro with the necessity of ceasing such harmful and foolish tactics.

The posse had convened after church service that morning, and decided that Hardy's preaching might easily provoke an 'insurrection'. They were led by William Leonard, a prominent young planter who claimed to be descended from the early Virginia settlers, and the 'line of argument' they planned to administer was, in reality, a whipping.

Hardy's friend and host William Careker tried to dissuade them. At first he appealed to their sense of compassion, pointing out that Hardy was an old man who meant no harm: 'He jest ain't got all his wits about him.' Leonard was unimpressed. 'We have come after that voodoo preacher and we don't want no trouble,' he said. Reason having failed, Careker levelled his double-barrelled shotgun and blasted Leonard in the head, killing him outright. His death, the *Enquirer-Sun* reported, was nothing less than an 'assassination'. As for Careker and Hardy, 'the cause of all the trouble', they disappeared.

News of Leonard's death spread rapidly, and over the following day hundreds of whites formed new posses to hunt for the fugitives. One of them found the elderly, blind preacher hiding in a barn. 'Ignoring his pleas for mercy, the men smashed his head with rifle butts, carried him a short distance to a bridge, shot him several times, and threw his weighted body into the creek below,' writes W. Fitzhugh Brundage. According to the *Atlanta Journal-Constitution*, Hardy's death was 'accidental due to his falling from the bridge'. As for Careker, he turned himself in at the Sheriff's office in Talbotton, the county town, hoping against hope for something resembling due process. On the night of 22 June the jailer handed his keys to the leaders of a mob a hundred strong, who opened Careker's cell and hanged him from a telegraph pole in the town square.

Almost a hundred years later, the last place that Careker saw looks much the same as it must have done in 1909. As in many rural Georgia county towns, the middle of the square is almost filled by an imposing neo-classical building – the courthouse, the seat of the law to which Careker turned and from which he failed to find protection. In the environs of Columbus, blacks who dared to protest at their oppression or defy its authors could expect no mercy. According to the *Enquirer-Sun*: 'It was the work of but a few minutes to get the negro. It was all done quietly, and in perfect order.'

The African-American writers and politicians who began the first campaigns against lynching in the 1890s understandably saw the practice as the absolute negation of the rule of law. By definition, a suspect seized from jail or a bailiff's custody and murdered had not been accorded due process rights, and in the view of an Ida B. Wells or W.E.B. du Bois, the solution was new statutes to prevent lynching and provide punishment for its perpetrators. Many of Georgia's whites saw things very differently. If mobs were resorting to extra-legal violence, then the fault must lie with the law, which was too slow in its delivery of justice, too hidebound by suspects' protections and the rules of evidence, and too restricted in the penalties it could impose.

In order to curb the supposed wave of Negro rape, John Temple Graves, editor of the Atlanta *Georgian*, advocated the return of branding and castration. In February 1904, the North Carolina journalist Clarence Poe urged laws to permit the 'surgeon's remedy' in an article for the *Atlantic Monthly*, then as now a national magazine published in New York. Commenting on the recent lynching of a black alleged rapist in Delaware, Poe claimed that the man had been released from prison after an earlier attempted assault: 'Set free with the same lustful mania, a wolf in human form, he brought death to himself and a pure-hearted victim, and shame to a great state.' Castration might be barbaric, but it was better than lynching, while 'we must recognise the fact that we have a peculiar crime, to be dealt with in a peculiar manner'.

Georgia's lawyers were not so crude, but as they wrestled with the problem of lynching at successive annual meetings of their State Bar Association, they appeared no more ready to condemn the practice on principle. Setting the tone for many subsequent lawyers' speeches and writing, the Hon. Seymour D. Thompson, a judge and legal author, addressed the association's gathering in 1888. At the core of the matter, he said, was the pressing need for 'more justice and less technicality'.

Juries, said Thompson, were bewildered by the thickets of rules and restrictions that the law imposed on the evidence they were allowed to hear, and hence unable to exercise their common sense. Even in capital murder cases, convictions were apt to be reversed on appeal – not because there was any doubt that the defendant was guilty, but because some obscure regulation had unwittingly been transgressed. Appeals brought retrials and almost endless delays, which were often 'so great that all benefit of public example has been lost'. Defendants had so many chances to evade their fate through legal technicalities that even when executions were finally carried out, this was 'a matter of sheer luck'. No wonder, Thompson concluded, that 'the number of miserable persons lynched by mobs on accusations of crime, outnumber those who are executed at the hands of the law'. But it was the law, he insisted, not the mobs, that was at fault, and lynchings would continue unless and until the law was reformed.

At the Bar Association meeting of 1899, convened at Warm Springs when lynching was close to its peak, several speakers addressed the subject. The looming question was put most starkly in the title of a paper by the Athens attorney John J. Strickland: 'Are the Courts Responsible for Lynching, and if so, Why?' His answer was an unequivocal yes. 'Good people are leading the van of the lynchers,' Strickland insisted, and in places and times where the courts were doing their job, 'history furnishes no example of outlawry among good people'. Another speaker, J.F. De Lacy from Eastman, said, 'The chief cause of the discontent and disorder that occasionally breaks out is the uncertainty of punishment for the commission of crime.' To restore that certainty would require a wholesale revision of the rules of evidence and procedure. If lawyers could really 'discard scholastic forms and technicalities', De Lacy said, then justice would once again 'diffuse its light through all legal procedure, and permeate all courts'.

Eighty-five years later, as the net began to close around the alleged stocking strangler, much had changed. But as his hunters began to build a case around a suspect, the 'certainty of punishment' would not have looked like a controversial aim.

Sitting in his office at the CPD in March 1984, it took Michael Sellers many hours to send out his teletypes asking for information about Henry Sanderson's stolen gun to every law enforcement agency in America. Such messages, his colleagues told him, were usually futile. On this occasion, however, he got an answer in less than a week – from Lansing, Michigan, a town near Kalamazoo. Two clerks there had gone through their records, and found that a black man named Aaron Sanders had tried to register the weapon there in 1981. American law enforcement agencies were supposed to keep data on missing firearms from all over the country, and the files said this gun was hot. According to Sellers, the Michigan police had inexplicably failed to confiscate the gun, although they sent a teletype to the CPD stating that it had reappeared. In any event, no one in Georgia seems to have noticed this message.

Sellers told me that he called a detective in Lansing, Tom Barder. 'I said to him, "Tommy, I'm going to make you a famous man." I asked him if he would go to Kalamazoo and see if the guy still had the gun. Sanders did still have it. Sanders gave it to Tommy, and then I asked him to ship it to me in Columbus.'

Aaron Sanders told Detective Barder that the gun had been a present from his mother, Lucille, who lived in Indiana. Her maiden name was Gary. She in turn had been given it by her brother, Jim Gary, a building contractor who lived in a ramshackle yard in Russell County, Alabama, a few miles from the Chattahoochee river and Columbus. At the beginning of April 1984, accompanied by two colleagues, Sellers drove up Gary's muddy switchback drive.

As he recalled those days of glory, Sellers's eyes gleamed. 'We went there first on a Friday. He was kind of evasive. He said he'd bought the gun from a stranger at Kinfolks Corner, a place in south Columbus where black folks used to hang out. I told him: "Listen, I have traced this gun all the way from Kalamazoo, and you're telling me you got it from an unknown black male? I know your business, Mr Gary, and your memory had better get a whole lot better when I come back on Monday." ' Sellers said that in an effort to jog Jim Gary's memory, he told him that the weapon had been used to commit a murder. Of course, this assertion was false.

After the weekend, said Sellers, he returned to work on the Monday to find no fewer than three telephone messages from Jim Gary, asking to see him again. This time he was more forthcoming. When Sellers returned to his yard, Gary said he'd bought the gun for $20 from his nephew, Carlton, the son of Jim's late brother William. Carlton Gary was a convicted criminal. As far as Jim Gary knew, he was in prison.

Sellers used the records he found at the CPD to establish that Carlton Gary had been born in Columbus and spent his childhood there, and had lived there again for nearly two years in the late 1970s – including the time of the stranglings. In February 1979 he had been arrested trying to rob a Po' Folks restaurant in the South Carolina town of Gaffney. The cashier there had faced him down and Gary fled, only to blunder into a swamp where he surrendered to the police. Almost immediately he confessed to several similar crimes, pleaded guilty at his trial and was sentenced to twenty-one years. On 10 March 1979, the stocking stranglings task force detective Richard Smith and a colleague had gone to a police station in Greenville and asked Gary whether he had committed some similar restaurant stick-ups in Columbus. In return for a promise of immunity from further prosecution, Gary readily confessed that he had robbed five places there – the first a Burger King on Macon Road in April 1978, just two days after the final strangling, the murder of Janet Cofer. But he went on to become a model inmate, and was eventually transferred to a minimum security prison, the Goodman Correctional Institution near Greenville.

On the same day that Henry Sanderson phoned Sellers about his stolen gun in May 1984, Gary absconded from prison. Later, he would claim that another inmate had been threatening his life: he would have been due for parole two months later had he not walked out. But according to Sellers, Gary's ill-advised escape gave him his next clue. The South Carolina corrections staff had sent a teletype to the CPD, warning that Gary might be headed their way. Sellers contacted the prison in Greenville, and asked for a set of Gary's fingerprints.

It took ten frustrating days before the prints arrived, and when they did, a clerk initially took them to the wrong office. At last the confusion was sorted out, and Sellers and his colleague Lem Miller brought the precious envelope to a print ID officer. Miller stayed while Sellers went back to his office, and the expert compared the prints to a mark found on Kathleen Woodruff's window screen, which her murderer had opened in order to enter her house. A few minutes later, Sellers told me, his phone rang. It was Miller. Two words were enough: 'They match.'

Over the next two days, Gary's prints were allegedly matched with 'latent' marks lifted from two of the other strangling murder scenes, the homes of Jean Dimenstein and Florence Scheible. Sellers, Miller, Charlie Rowe and Ricky Boren, a detective captain who has since risen to become the head of the CPD, went to see Chief Wetherington. 'Our hearts were thumping,' Sellers said. 'Wetherington listened. Then he said, "Put this in overdrive."' District Attorney William Smith later told the Columbus journalist Richard Hyatt: 'The gun made Gary a suspect. The prints made him a defendant.' What followed was a manhunt.

When I met Sellers in 2001, he had been telling his complex story about how the call from Sanderson triggered his investigation for fifteen years. But it has one puzzling gap, right at the start. If none of the cops had left a message with Henry Sanderson about his stolen gun, who did?

The Columbus journalist Richard Hyatt posed that question in an article published at the end of Gary's trial in 1986. 'What about the phone call Henry Sanderson received?' Hyatt wrote, 'Columbus police didn't call. Michigan didn't call. Who called him?' He recorded no answer from Sellers, but he asked District Attorney William Smith, who told him what Sellers would later tell me: 'Our explanation is that God called.'

What on earth did they mean? Talking to me in the Gwinnett County hotel lounge, Sellers tried to explain. Some months after their original conversation, he said, he called Sanderson's home to talk to him again. Sanderson was out, so he spoke to his wife. Sellers asked her the same question that troubled Hyatt and me – who had left the message?

'This is what she told me,' Sellers said. '"Oh, my, Mr Sellers, I don't know if you realise, but my husband has Alzheimer's. He just got it in his mind. He got it in his mind and he called you. No one had really called him about the gun.' That, said Sellers, was why he called it a phone call from God. At this point the trial was still two years away. Sadly, Sellers told me, by the time it got underway Sanderson's mental state had deteriorated further. 'He was too gone to testify.'

By now it was after midnight, and we had the hotel lounge to ourselves. Sellers's voice sank to little more than a whisper. 'Sanderson first called me the day Carlton Gary got out of prison in South Carolina. Isn't that scary? I think it was God saying, "Here's one more chance before the killing starts again." Stuff like that doesn't just happen. And the rest, as they say, is history.'

Sellers fixed me with his bright blue eyes, hardly blinking. He radiated sincerity. But when I got home, I checked my copy of the transcript of Gary's trial. Sanderson *had* testified. His evidence began on page 3,244 and ended on page 3,252, and he had displayed an impressive recall of events that had taken place nine years before the hearing. He described not only the loss of his gun, but its purchase in Orlando, Florida; his reasons for buying it; and how he knew that the weapon eventually recovered by the CPD was his. He spoke about his store in Alabama, and how he'd borrowed a car from a relative to get back to Dadeville, returning it to Columbus when his own vehicle had been recovered. At one point, when District Attorney Smith stumbled over a question, making a mistake about when the police first showed serious interest in his gun, Sanderson politely corrected him. If he had been suffering from Alzheimer's when he first called Sellers more than two years earlier, he had made an astounding recovery. Sanderson's mother Nellie, by now well into her nineties, also testified. She was, she told the court, a little deaf, but her own, unprompted account of the burglary was extremely vivid.

Perhaps it was Sellers's memory that was at fault. As will later become apparent, its reliability is a matter of no small importance.

Back at the end of October 1977, after the strangler had killed four times, the CPD's Ronnie Jones had travelled to Quantico, Virginia, and asked the FBI's Behavioral Science Unit to produce a profile of Columbus's serial murderer. Having considered Jones's account of the crimes, the FBI's experts issued their conclusions. The strangler, they stated, would be found to be a black male aged sixteen to twenty-one, a former bed-wetter who had set fires or tortured animals at a young age. He would be cunning, displaying 'no anxiety, no remorse, no guilt'. He might have been in a mental hospital, and it was likely that the nylon in the stockings he used to strangle his victims had some fetishistic significance for him. They felt sure that his sexuality was abnormal: 'He is sexually inadequate. He can't make it with a woman normally.' According to the Quantico unit's founder, Robert Ressler, all the serial killers he had ever studied shared this trait: 'To a man, they were dysfunctional sexually; that is, they were unable to have and maintain mature, consensual sexual experiences with other adults … they resented not having them; it was this resentment that fuelled their aggressive, murderous behaviour.' If they were able to have sex at all, their 'decided preference' was for 'bondage, torture and sadomasochism'.

Accurate as the FBI profile may have been in relation to most sexual serial killers, it did not fit Carlton Gary, who though sometimes promiscuous, was neither perverted nor dysfunctional. Before his capture in South Carolina in 1979, at the time he was modelling clothes from Gene Hewell's Movin' Man store on television, Gary spent many an evening at Jo-Jo Benson's nightclub. 'I knew him there, I knew him on the street,' Benson told me. 'He was a good-looking guy. But when it came to the ladies: whew. Kind of wild.' When Gary returned to Columbus after his escape from prison in the spring of 1984, nothing much had changed, although he didn't go back to modelling clothes at the Movin' Man. 'I guess you'd say he was trying to make up for lost time.'

In the weeks following his departure from the prison at Greenville, Gary went back to the hustling that had sustained his extravagant lifestyle before his incarceration. He began dealing cocaine and robbing fast-food restaurants. He also made at least seven trips to Gainesville, Florida, to visit a long-time old girlfriend, Sheila Preston Dean, and Tony and Latwanna, the son and daughter she had borne him. He might have been on the run, but he seems to have thought that if he didn't venture into South Carolina, he was unlikely to be sent back to prison to serve the rest of his sentence for robbery. He made little effort to keep a low profile. Much of the time he chose to drive round Columbus and Phenix City in a car he had rented. It was far from inconspicuous – a pink Lincoln Continental.

Floyd Washington, then and now the proprietor of another big south Columbus nightclub, the F&W Control Tower, recalled: 'Carlton used to come here virtually every other night before he went to prison, and when he got out, he started coming back.' Washington spoke as he poured shots of bourbon for his early-evening customers clustered at the bar. A club-owner for more than thirty years, he had a long, square-cut beard, and a wry, careful way of speaking that seemed to confirm what people said about him – that he knew most of everything that had happened to the city's African-Americans for many decades.

'He was always a very sharp dresser, real neat,' Washington said. 'You never saw him in jeans and sneakers; he used to wear suits, sports coats, top-line dress shirts and sometimes a little bow tie. You might almost think he was a businessman. Let me tell you, he never had a problem with no ladies. He was a very good dancer. Sometimes he'd move to rhythm and blues or soul music and the floor would just clear because people wanted to watch him, like in a scene from that movie, *Saturday Night Fever.*'

Many things divide black and white people in Columbus, but few quite as much as their view of Carlton Gary. If they think about him at all, whites understandably see him as a monster, as a brutal killer awaiting his final punishment. But many black people knew him personally, and they still have difficulty squaring their experience with the horrors that emerged at his trial.

'Over the years I knew him, he had many girlfriends: very attractive ones, with good jobs,' Washington said. 'The idea that he would leave this club with a beautiful girl and then leave her to go and rape an old woman – it just don't add up. I always knew he was some kind of hustler. I didn't think the money he spent here had come from honest work. But he wouldn't have messed with a ninety-year-old woman at all – let alone raped her.'

At forty-five minutes after midnight on 18 April 1984, two Columbus police officers waiting in an unmarked car saw Gary with two black women and a man smoking a marijuana cigarette parked outside yet another nightclub, Smitty's Lounge on Fort Benning Drive. They approached and began to search him, but Gary pushed one of them away and ran off into some nearby woods. Detective J.R. McMichael gave chase and caught him after a brief struggle, in which the policeman sustained a broken finger. Gary said his name was Michael David, the name by which he was known in South Carolina and the real name of one of his cousins, and gave an address on Sixth Avenue. He was taken to the police station, held overnight, fingerprinted and charged with obstructing a police officer and possessing less than an ounce of marijuana. Both offences were classed as misdemeanours. This was before Michael Sellers matched the set of Gary's prints that he got from South Carolina to the latents from the stranglings. Gary was released on $250 bail, and told to come back on 10 August. He made no attempt to leave the Columbus vicinity.

Beleta Turner, an elegant, successful woman who now runs her own hairdressing business in Atlanta, had known him before his prison term, and after his escape and marijuana bust she saw him in Columbus again. 'He told me he'd been released, but something didn't feel right so I challenged him. Then he admitted he had escaped, but only because another inmate had tried to kill him. I harangued him, told him he was throwing his life away. It just didn't compute with me, that a man with so many friends, with so many women after him, was an escaped convict, and maybe I got through because he fell back on the bed and wept a little. I had never seen a man cry. He said, "I want to be normal, like everyone else: have children, be normal." '

A year or two earlier, Beleta had visited Gary when he was in a high-security prison in Columbia, South Carolina. She didn't tell her bosses at work: at the time she was employed as a clerk in the Columbus District Attorney's office.

'He stepped out to see me in starched pants and snakeskin shoes,' she said. 'He'd told me on the phone that he had a good job in prison, but he didn't look like a convict at all.' According to Beleta, he never had. 'He just stood out from the other men in the city. He was always so stylish, gregarious and well-groomed. He'd walk into a room and heads would turn and people would say, "Now, who is that?" Women literally used to beg him for sex. They'd come by his house and wait for him, come and hang out in the hope of being the one he'd take upstairs. He was that attractive that women were falling out with each other over him.'

Sellers and his colleagues wasted no time in following Chief Wetherington's order to put their investigation into overdrive. On 30 April they talked to Boyd Battles, a detective from Phenix City, whose informants among local criminals had told him that a man who called himself Michael David was hustling cocaine and driving a pink Lincoln. 'Michael David', said Sellers, was wanted for something much bigger than dealing drugs. At 1.30 a.m. that night, the police found the car parked outside the Coweta Apartments in Phenix City. Carlton Gary was in a bedroom inside, naked, with one of his girlfriends, Anita Hill.* Later she told the police that as soon as he noticed a flashlight being shone from outside, he peered through a gap in the curtains, spotted the police car and fled by a fire escape at the back of the building, clutching his clothes in his hand.

Gary spent the night of 1 May 1984 in a Holiday Inn on Victory Drive, Columbus, with another woman he had known for years – Ruby Miles, the owner of the angelic voice I would hear singing in Jo-Jo Benson's car many years later when he played me his new CD. Twenty years after the manhunt for Gary, she and I met for Sunday breakfast in a chain restaurant on Highway 280, on the outskirts of Phenix City. Ruby was dark-skinned and petite, and her voice had a melodic timbre even when she spoke. For years she had sung every night at a club she ran with her ex-husband in Columbus, and she was still performing. Her own life had given her too

---

* No relation to the Anita Hill who in 1991 alleged that she had been sexually harassed by Supreme Court nominee Clarence Thomas.

many reasons to know how to interpret the blues. A nephew she had raised had turned schizophrenic, shot four people dead and was now on death row. A beloved niece had been killed with her children in a head-on car crash – with a vehicle driven, in a terrible coincidence, by her own husband.

In common with most of Carlton Gary's friends, Ruby referred to him as 'Mike', his middle name. 'I guess we must have met at the beginning of 1978,' she said. 'I was singing in a club in Phenix City and Mike came in one night. We started hanging out, and he'd come to the club and send me drinks and stuff. I started going back to his house on Dawson Estates in Columbus. There'd just be a few people: Mike, his friend we called little Mike, one or two other guys, three girls maybe. We'd go there at 3 a.m. when the club closed, listen to music while Mike fixed breakfast. The house he had was so nice. Perfect. He loved nice things. Everyone used to think we were going together, but we weren't. We were so tight, but he was my buddy. We had a great relationship.'

Like Beleta Turner, Ruby couldn't help but notice Gary's smooth public persona. 'He and little Mike were very cool, always dressed to the max. Very free with everything; they would set up the whole club with drinks, and the club would be packed. And they were the two best dancers. There was that song by Barry White, "Your Sweetness is My Weakness", and when that came on, the two Mikes would do this thing together …' Ruby paused, got up from the restaurant's leatherette seat, and began to sway as she sang *a capella*, showing me the way Carlton Gary was impressing his associates around the time of the night of the terrors.

She might have been largely immune to it herself, but she also noticed his effect on women. 'And they were well-dressed, fine women,' she said. 'I'm not talking about skanky types. If a skanky woman did try to talk to him, he'd be polite, maybe buy her a drink, but that would be it.'

Ruby said she also saw another side to him. 'I still care a lot for Mike, because he took a lot of care over people himself. He always had time for my children. One time he bought them Easter baskets, dresses, shoes. My mother just loved him because he was so respectable, such a nice, sweet man.'

When they met at the hotel on 1 May 1984, Ruby saw that Gary seemed unusually tense. At one stage she left the room to go in search of food, and when she came back he was standing behind the door, holding a .357

Magnum. 'I said, "Mike, what are you doing?" He just shrugged and said, "You can't be too careful." '

That night, they had sex together for the first and only time. 'It was normal, just, you know, plain Jane sex,' Ruby said. 'But it was also so relaxed: sex wasn't a big deal between us because we'd known each other so long. It was there for us if we needed it, and finally it happened. When we were making love, I remember we had Luther Vandross on in the background, "A House is Not a Home". Every time I hear that song I think of Mike.'

As we parted, Ruby sighed. 'I miss that boy. You could spot him among a thousand people: the way he dressed, the way he carried himself. As if he'd been a college boy. He might have been a stick-up man, but I know this in my heart and will take it to my grave: he didn't do the stranglings. He was not that type of man.'

Leaving the Holiday Inn on the morning of 2 May 1984, Gary took Ruby to her mother's house in Phenix City and left her there. Unaware, it would seem, just how keen the police were to find him, he phoned Anita Hill, his girlfriend who lived at Coweta Apartments, and told her that he was planning to drive to Albany, sixty miles to the south-east, in order to sell some cocaine. Unbeknown to Gary, Hill's phone was being tapped. At 8.30 a.m. on 3 May, he and a woman from Columbus, Robin Odom, checked into room 254 of another Holiday Inn, on Oglethorpe Boulevard.

By 1 p.m. the Albany police had found him, and set up surveillance posts in the rooms on either side of his. They watched while Robin Odom twice left the room and returned. Each time, she knocked and waited for Gary to open the door. On a third occasion, when she left to get some ice, Detective Joe Monzie stopped her in the corridor. The Albany SWAT team was already in position. Odom told Monzie that Gary had his Magnum. She agreed to knock again, wait while Gary came to let her in, and then stand aside to let the SWAT team overpower him.

In the event, she panicked: she knocked, but as Gary began to turn the handle, she dropped the ice bucket and ran back down the corridor. Two of the SWAT men rushed the door. Gary tried to shut it, but they were too strong. Officer James Paulk pointed his Mac-10 sub-machine gun and Gary put his hands up, muttering just one word: 'OK.' His own gun remained on the bedside table, loaded but unused. 'We snuck up on him pretty good,'

David Noel, the SWAT team leader, told reporters later. 'It was a classic situation. He had a gun, but we kept it from him.'

Mike Sellers, with Ricky Boren and Charlie Rowe, arrived at the Albany police station at 7.15 that evening. By eight they were on their way back to Columbus in a Chevrolet Impala. Boren, the future chief of the CPD, was driving, with Lieutenant Rowe in the passenger seat. Gary, in handcuffs and leg irons, sat in the back with Sellers.

'For two days I was on an adrenalin rush,' Sellers said. 'We had caught and I was sitting with a guy three hundred law-enforcement officers had been looking for for years. At one time I bumped him with my arm to make sure he wasn't a ghost. Richard Smith and Ronnie Jones would have given their right arms to have been in that position. I was very fortunate.'

Even before their return to Columbus, Chief Wetherington had been telling reporters that the police had 'the strongest lead we've ever had' on the stranglings. Gary and the detectives arrived at the CPD headquarters to the glare of cameras and TV lights, and while the police began to question their prisoner, Wetherington called a late-night press conference. Gary, he said, was an 'extremely brilliant' high school dropout with a 'genius level' IQ, and had 'played the game well' in evading arrest for the stranglings for so long. Whatever potential he might have possessed had been ruined by his crimes and convictions, which dated back to his teens: breaking into a car and arson in Gainesville, Florida, in 1968; first-degree robbery in Albany, New York, in 1970; possession of drugs and handling stolen goods in Syracuse, New York, in 1977; finally the sequence of restaurant stick-ups in Georgia and South Carolina that came to an end in February 1979, almost a year after the final strangling. The cops who dealt with those crimes had given Gary a nickname, Wetherington disclosed – the 'steak-house bandit'.

Born on 24 September 1950, Gary had spent fourteen of his thirty-three years in some form of custody. Next morning, he was pictured on the front pages of most of the newspapers in Georgia. He was wearing a zip-up sleeveless top, and looked sweaty and dishevelled. He also seemed to be grinning. Appropriately enough, the man photographed next to him, leading him by the arm in his trademark moustache and plaid shirt, was Detective Michael Sellers.

# FIVE

# The Hanging Judge

As he lived very much in the here and now except for pleasant daydreams just before he went to sleep, the judge seldom brooded over the past in which, as a judge, he had almost unlimited power – even the power of life and death. His decisions were always preceded by long cogitations; he never considered a death sentence without the aid of prayer. Not that he was religious, but it somehow siphoned the responsibility away from Fox Clane and dribbled it to God.

CARSON McCULLERS, *Clock Without Hands* (1961)

Inside the Muscogee County Jail, the guards soon noticed that their effervescent new prisoner did not conform to the standard image of the lonesome serial killer. A grand jury sat on 4 May, the day after Carlton Gary's arrest, and formally indicted him for the murders of Florence Scheible, Martha Thurmond and Kathleen Woodruff, together with the burglary in which Henry Sanderson lost his gun. District Attorney William Smith announced that he planned to seek the death penalty. Meanwhile, Gary's jailers were fielding Gary's girlfriends, who were writing him letters, pledging their love and asking to visit.

Anita Hill, from whose apartment in Phenix City Gary had fled naked four days earlier, came to the jail for the first time on 5 May, bearing gifts of a shirt and a pair of shoes. For the first five months of his renewed incarceration, Gary kept a daily diary: it records that throughout this period 'Nita baby' was there to see him every Saturday and Sunday. Almost every

106

weekend his sister Miriam and his mother Carolyn David visited too. Sheila Preston Dean, the girlfriend from his teenage years in Florida and the mother of his first two children, sent the first of many passionate letters from her home in Gainesville on 7 May. 'Dearest Carlton, I want to come there to see you,' it began. 'My wish is to be with you until death do us part this time. After all these years, I still love you, and I knew it the minute I saw your face.'

Three weeks later she wrote of her disbelief that he could have been the strangler:

> Know I don't believe anything I read. I worked for the Albany [New York] Police Department and I know what lies can be printed. Besides, I love you, and I know in my head you didn't do what they said. Don't worry baby, I know in my heart you will be free again … Keep your head high. Everyone sends their love and they are pulling for you.

On the back of her envelopes Sheila scrawled: 'I'll be there.'

He was also corresponding with Marianne Clark,* from Greenville, South Carolina, where he had escaped from the Goodman open prison. His first letter, on 6 May, provides his earliest written response to being accused of the stranglings:

> Hi Marianne! The lies, deceit and misrepresentation have all reached your ears by now. I have no real need to tell you I am innocent, but please believe me I have never done anything like that. I know you already know this for yourself, but we have FACTS to further support my innocence … I have robbed and sold dope, baby, but I have never harmed any person physically.

Much of the academic literature on sexual predators and serial killers suggests that sadistic sexual fantasy plays a crucial role in such offenders' motivation. According to often-cited American research based on lengthy prison interviews that was published in 1986, 95 per cent of repeat rapists

---

* Not her real name.

and sexual murderers had indulged in violent fantasies of this kind. 'Fantasy was critical to what motivated them to kill,' its authors concluded. A later Australian study found that these fantasies are often 'offence specific', mental re-enactments of horrifying crimes that the subject has personally committed. The FBI serial murder expert Robert Ressler wrote in his memoir:

> [Their] fantasies are characterised by strong visual components, and by themes of dominance, revenge, molestation and control ... Normal fantasies of inter-personal adventure are fused with abnormal attempts to degrade, humiliate, and dominate others. Most normal fantasies have at their centre the idea that the partner will have as much fun as the dreamer. With these deviant men, the more fantasy fun they are having, the more danger their fantasy partner is in.

By chance, Carlton Gary's own writings provide an opportunity to examine the extent to which he fits this profile. Years after his arrest, he wrote to a friend in England protesting that his sexuality was normal: 'I've enjoyed ladies of ALL shapes, colours etc. And NOT ONE of them attests to anything being "wrong" with me!!' His correspondence with Marianne Clark, which gradually became more erotic, seems to support that assertion. Gary's letters contain vivid details of his fantasies at the time – not scenes of sadism or degradation, but attempts to recreate past romantic, consensual experiences with her. I asked Ruth Mann, the psychologist in charge of sex-offender treatment programmes in more than twenty British prisons, whether it might be possible for one person to become aroused both by sadistic, violent fantasies and by loving, consensual ones. 'It might,' she said, 'although it would be rare. On the other hand, you would probably find that with a sexual offender, the normal fantasies were brief and perfunctory, as if he were going through the motions – they wouldn't be fully-realised, detailed scenes.'

However, the 'scenes' in Gary's letters were very detailed. On one occasion he wrote to Marianne after she had sent him her photograph: 'How terribly I ache to hold you. You know I've never spoken disrespectful to you, but as soon as I got my picture today, I got in privacy, got nude, reflected upon our loving, slowly stroked my beef, and let the love juice ooze out. They could cut my arm off to my elbow if only that could have been deep inside your luscious body, as often has been the case.' He recalled a time when he and Marianne made love outside in the snow, wrapped in a mink coat: 'I think about us two nuts out against the wall, in the cold, getting into a creaming situation (smile).' He wrote that he had especially enjoyed pleasuring her orally: 'And you ARE delicious. I often would look at you as you came out of your clothes, took off your bra and panties, and it felt like I wanted to devour you all over again … It's been far too long for me to be without you, and I need you desperately! I'll kiss you lovingly all over, and enjoy you in the purest manner.'

Marianne's letters were more demure, but she did her best to reply in kind: 'Often thoughts of you and I flow through my head. We have truly had some beautiful times together. I love you for that. You are a truly satisfying man and know just the right way to love me.' She had big hopes for the other aspects of their relationship. By the autumn of 1984 she was visiting him regularly, and wrote of special times in the county jail which let her 'feel the warmth of you over these miles'. His letters to her 'always make my day', and despite his predicament, his smile always melted her heart:

I am drawn by that magnetic natural charm you have. You are my sunshine in the midst of a storm. It's just the little things that you do: you don't overlook the little things that mean so much. Many men do and lose a good relationship … I cannot truly express in words the feelings of love you make me feel. Baby, there is just no other love like yours. You're the best man I have ever known and there is no way I could let you go … Yes, I will wait for you. I know we want the same things – to be happy together.

Like Sheila, Marianne could not square the man she knew with the crimes of which he was accused. 'It troubles me a great deal, these things that are going on now,' she wrote in her first letter on 7 June. 'I truly cannot believe it. It hurt me deeply. I know you would never do anything as awful as that.' She had learnt of his predicament from the television news, and her first, unprompted thought was not that he might be guilty, but that the implacable workings of the Southern courts faced with an African-American accused of crimes like these might keep them apart forever: 'There goes any hope of us doing some of the things we often spoke of. I may be a fool, but my feelings haven't changed.' In his reply, Gary sounded confident that he would prove his innocence, and she became more optimistic. 'I am sure they have no case against you,' she wrote in early September. 'I will be so glad when it is all over.'

Not every defendant facing a capital murder trial, let alone an alleged serial killer and predatory rapist, would be the object of so much affection. News of it soon spread beyond the walls of the jail, while Gary's women were seen supporting him in the public gallery every time he appeared in court. If he was the stocking strangler, he also seemed to be an enigma – in the words of the *Enquirer*'s Richard Hyatt, 'a puzzle whose pieces don't fit'.

One brilliant morning in early spring, I began to try to find some of those pieces by walking the streets where Carlton Gary spent his childhood in the company of Earnestine Flowers, who shared those years with him. As Earnestine pointed out to me, both of them now spent their time behind bars. While Gary languished on death row near Jackson, she was working as a guard at a huge state prison on Schatulga Road, on Columbus's eastern limits. There, she said, she did her best to give her charges hope that their eventual release would represent a second chance.

Most of the district where Gary and Earnestine lived as children was torn down in the 1970s, to make way for the anonymous cubic structures of the Columbus Medical Center. 'That was our playground,' Earnestine said, pointing to the shady Linwood Cemetery on Seventeenth Street. 'We used to play softball right there, where the graves stopped, on the grass by the railroad track. Where we're standing now, Sixth Avenue, was just a dirt, unpaved road. All along it were what we called shotgun houses: three rooms, one behind the other – sitting room, bedroom, kitchen, so you walked from one to the other. In each house there might be three or four kids, maybe more. The walls were made of wood and they stood on stilts, with the plumbing underneath. No hot water: you warmed the water in a pot-belly stove and took your bath in a tin tub on the floor. All the water

Kathleen Woodruff's servant Tommie Stevens looks out of the window of Mrs Woodruff's home after the discovery of her body, 28 December 1977.

Ruth Schwob, the widow of the textile magnate Simon Schwob. Trained in martial arts, she survived the strangler's attack on the 'night of the terrors', 12 February 1978.

Police Chief Curtis McClung outside Ruth Schwob's house after the night of the terrors. His force's failure to solve the murders later cost him his job.

Following the night of the terrors, the police had to deal with ghoulish onlookers after the strangler killed his sixth victim, Mildred Borom. 13 February 1978.

Janet Cofer, an elementary schoolteacher, who became the strangler's final victim in April 1978.

Carlton Gary (left), Sheila Dean and their alleged accomplices after their arrest for fire-bombing a grocery store in Gainesville, Florida, 17 March 1968.

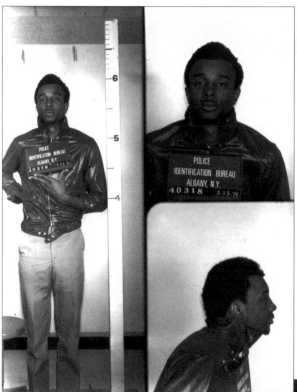

Carlton Gary after his arrest in Albany, New York, in 1970.

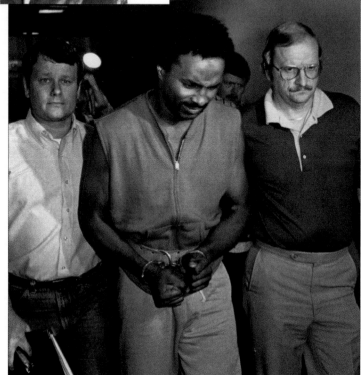

Gary arriving in Columbus on the night of his arrest, 3 May 1984. Detective Ricky Boren (who later became Chief of Police) is on the left, his colleague Charlie Rowe on the right.

came off the same pipe. If someone was running the water higher up the line, yours would be shut off.'

Conditions in the city's black neighbourhoods had not improved much since the Columbus writer Carson McCullers described them in fictionalised form in her great novel *The Heart is a Lonely Hunter*, published in 1940. There she wrote of a Negro doctor, Benedict Mady Copeland, whose patients lived in 'cold and narrow passages smelling of dirt and sickness and fried fatback', twelve or fourteen of them occupying a single shack. When five of them die of pneumonia in the space of a few days, Copeland muses: '[They] had not been lost because of any negligence on his part. The blame was in the long years of want which lay behind. The diets of cornbread and sowbelly and syrup, the crowding of four and five persons to a single room. The death of poverty.'

Earnestine's family home was unusual, because it had two storeys, and her parents made good money. Her father, Earnest, had a job in Golden's Foundry, but also ran businesses with her mother, Doris – the Nineteenth Street Grill, and later the Del Morocco nightclub. He also worked as a chef at the Big Eddy Club. Earnestine was the only child on her block to have a bicycle, and her house had a flushing lavatory at a time when most black families were still using outhouse earth closets, whose contents were collected regularly by a horse-drawn 'honey wagon'. Her family was generous with its relative wealth. 'When my Daddy cooked, he'd never cook just for the four of us,' Earnestine said. 'We'd go out in the street and say, "Daddy's cooking. Bring pots, bring pans, come and get some." We always had plenty of food.'

Carlton and Earnestine attended the Claflin Elementary School, established for 'coloured children' by the Freedmen's Bureau in 1868. On the way to school in the morning, they had to cross the railway line that ran along Fifth Avenue: 'Carlton would crawl under the trains. He'd urge me to follow, saying, "Are we late? Are we late? Come on, Earnestine, don't go round, crawl beneath the train." He was never scared of anything. If we passed a barking dog in some yard, he'd just laugh. But I was a tomboy. Usually boys and girls of that age hate each other. We were friends.'

The two children lived close to Columbus's racial boundary, and the shadow of the Jim Crow segregation laws loomed large. Claflin school –

now used as city school system offices – was housed in a low, utilitarian building with draughts and thin walls. Just two blocks away was McIlhenny, the school for white children, an imposing neo-baroque edifice with columns and stucco medallions.

'It wasn't just Fourth Avenue separating us,' Earnestine said as we strolled through what had been forbidden territory. 'What you see there was a world apart. Our books were McIlhenny's rejects, ten years old. And you'd get your ass whipped just walking down this street. They'd come out, spit at you, throw things at you. This was a part of town I knew nothing about – four hundred yards from where I lived. We had a sense of community, felt we were kindred, for a very practical reason: up on the hill in our little enclave, there were very few places we could go.'

When Carlton was thirteen, his mother Carolyn decided to leave Columbus, and took him and his sister Miriam to Florida. Earnestine would not see him again for fourteen years, until his return to the city around the time of Ferne Jackson's murder in September 1977.

The rules black children needed to learn about dealing with white people in the Columbus of the 1950s had been forged decades earlier, in the years before the First World War, when Georgia's lawyers were blaming lynching on the courts' legal technicalities instead of the lynch mobs. Murders by crowds made front-page headlines, but the law's repeated failure to punish their perpetrators created a background of less spectacular killings and attacks. For example, on 18 January 1903, the Columbus *Ledger* recorded the death of a black customer stabbed by a white butcher for complaining he had been short-changed. Next day, the paper carried the story of a black man who was shot in the head when he was mistakenly identified as a burglar. The next day, 20 January, a judge praised a white man who shot a black wagon-driver for accidentally forcing his carriage off a Columbus road, saying his actions were a 'lesson to impudent and insolent Negroes', and the 'best thing to have happened in Muscogee County in the past twenty years'. That there were three such incidents in such a short period may have been exceptional, but it was also symptomatic.

Eugene Bullard, the black son of a worker at a warehouse owned by the Columbus magnate W.C. Bradley, was born in the city in 1895. He set down much of his extraordinary life in his unpublished autobiography, *All Blood Runs Red*, describing how he joined the French Foreign Legion and was the Great War's only black fighter pilot, a feat which earned him the Légion d'Honneur. He later became the proprietor of jazz clubs in Montmartre, where he mingled with F. Scott Fitzgerald, Ernest Hemingway, Picasso and Fred Astaire. The start of this trajectory was not propitious. Bullard left Columbus at the age of eleven after his father, William, narrowly escaped from a lynch mob which was organised when he retaliated against a white foreman after months of physical abuse.

According to Eugene, his father had anticipated what was likely to happen, and even before the confrontation with his boss, gave his children a poignant, chilling warning: 'If I have to hit Stevens, I want you all to be good children. Always show respect to each and every one, white and black, and make them respect you. Go to school as long as you can. Never look for a fight. I mean never. But if you are attacked, or your honour is attacked unjust[ly], fight, fight, keep on fighting even if you die for your rights. It will be a glorious death.'

Equal protection under the law may be an abstract concept, but its denial had material consequences. Criminal justice and the right to due process had been forced into a corner, and it was the judges and the sheriffs, not the lynch mobs, who were expected to compromise. In and around Columbus, the rule of law and the rule of the mob were to confront each other very publicly twice in a single year, 1912.

The first case unfolded in the market town of Hamilton in Harris County, twenty miles north of the city. According to the *Enquirer-Sun*, a young white farmer named Norman Hadley, the nephew of the Harris County Sheriff, was killed on 13 January at the home of a Negro, Jim Crutchfield. He was shot three or four times by at least two different weapons, the paper went on, and four people were arrested – Burrell Hardaway, John Moore, Gene Harrington and Dusky Crutchfield, a woman – presumably Jim Crutchfield's wife. The *Sun* reported, 'It was known that [Hadley] had had some trouble with these negroes.'

The four prisoners were almost lynched on the night of their arrest, but Sheriff Hadley managed to evade a gathering mob and get them to his jail. This was not a high-security facility. Its guard, E.M. Robinson, used to leave the premises at night and go to his lodgings at the home of a local physician, Dr Riley.

Then as now, the prosecution of serious cases in Harris County was organised in Columbus. The judge of the Superior Court at the time was Sterling Price Gilbert, the later Georgia Supreme Court Justice. As white sentiment against the suspects in the Hamilton jail mounted, a delegation of the town's officials and citizens went to Columbus on 17 January to see Gilbert in his chambers at the courthouse. They told him 'that unless the accused persons were given a speedy trial there would be a lynching. It was stated that the jail was being watched, and it would be a matter of impossibility to get them out and carry them to another jail for safe keeping.' Gilbert agreed to hold a special sitting of his court in Hamilton as soon as possible. According to the law, he had to give twenty days' notice.

This was not soon enough for the whites of Harris County. On the night of 22 January a crowd of 'determined men' first called on Jailer Robinson at his digs, and persuaded him to hand over his keys. At 11.30 p.m. they opened the doors of the jail. There followed what the *Sun*, with striking indelicacy, described as 'exciting times'. The mob, the newspaper reported, 'took the prisoners into a piece of woods just west of Hamilton, and only about a one-quarter of a mile from the corporate limits, and, hanging them to trees, riddled their bodies with bullets.'

Five months later, news broke of another killing of a white person by a black, this time even closer to the city, at the junction of Double Churches Road and River Road in Muscogee County. (Today the site lies well within Columbus's much-expanded limits.) The victim was a child from a large and powerful family, Cedron 'Cleo' Land. His supposed assailant was a black boy who was probably fourteen, T.Z. 'Teasy' McElhaney.

Cleo had been sent into the fields on the broiling afternoon of 30 June 1912 in order to pasture a mule, and when he failed to return at nightfall, his family began a search. 'It was kept up until two o'clock this morning,' the Columbus evening *Ledger* reported the following day, 'when he was found in an out-of-way place with [a] wound in his left eye.' He had taken a shotgun blast in the face, and almost the whole load of shot had lodged in his brain; he must have died instantly. Tracks led to the McElhaney family's cabin.

Although they were of different races, Cleo and Teasy were known to be frequent playmates, and Teasy was confronted by John Beahn, a Columbus bailiff. At first, said the *Ledger*, the Negro boy denied any knowledge of what had happened, and claimed that he had not used the shotgun found at his home for some time. However, 'Mr Beahn examined the shotgun and found it had recently been fired.' Worse, he found some bloody clothing and sacks, which appeared to have been hidden – presumably by Teasy. Beahn decided to arrest him on a charge of murder, and he was taken in chains to the Muscogee County Jail. On the way there, Teasy 'admitted that he was with the Land boy when he was killed, but claims [sic] that the killing was accidental'.

Cleo was buried beside his late mother, Lula Land, at the Mount Moriah Primitive Baptist Church later that same day: in the heat of summer, his family could not afford to wait. Hundreds of the Land clan members and friends were in attendance. Afterwards, reported the *Enquirer-Sun*, 'Rumours were afloat to the effect that the negro would be taken and lynched if he was brought to the courthouse for a hearing.' The County Sheriff, Jesse Beard, deputised seven extra men to guard the jail.

Judge W.H. McCrory, a junior colleague of Judge Price Gilbert, was assigned to deal with Teasy's pre-trial hearing on 5 July. Fearful that the prisoner might be murdered if he were taken to the courthouse, he decided to convene his court at the jail. There he heard a summary of Teasy's all-too-plausible account of what had happened. Cleo and he had been 'projecting [playing] with the gun, and the gun went off and killed the boy ... The defendant said he came back home, tried to wash up the blood, and didn't tell anyone it was an accident, [because] he was afraid.' Teasy's trial was fixed for August. Blanketed by the summer heat and humidity, Columbus remained calm.

The Superior Court grand jury that indicted Teasy McElhaney for murder sat before Judge Gilbert on 5 August. Its members included Cleo Land's uncles R.E.L. ('Ed') and Aaron Brewster Land, who had helped to murder Simon Adams in 1900, and who since 1905 had been serving as a Deputy Sheriff. In May 1911 he had even stood for election as Sheriff of Muscogee County, though he lost the Democratic primary.

The grand jury having returned their 'true bill', thus indicting Teasy for murder, his trial began on 13 August. Judge Gilbert had appointed three lawyers to defend him. In distinct contrast to the rural, farming families of both the victim and the defendant, most of the jurors were drawn from the ranks of the city's prosperous bourgeoisie, who tended to be a little more progressive than their white counterparts in the countryside. They included an engineer, four businessmen, two salesmen, a bookkeeper and a tailor. They were, of course, all white. The heat inside Gilbert's ornate second-floor Victorian courtroom must have been almost unbearable. The trial's participants did not have to endure it for very long.

The main testimony came from Cleo's father, Will Land, who told how his son had gone missing, and of his body's discovery. It was plain enough that Teasy had had something to do with Cleo's death. But the evidence that it had been anything more than an accident was weak, consisting mainly of Teasy's vain attempt to conceal what had happened. The defendant sat with his lawyers in the well of the court, barefoot in shorts and a blue short-sleeved shirt. Having heard the prosecution case, he got to his feet, a lone black boy in a room of huge white adults. 'I am just a little black nigger,' Teasy said in a voice that had not broken, 'and I knew that if I went to Mr Land and told him I had killed his boy, he would kill me. I was afraid to tell him, so hid the body.'

All the evidence was heard before lunchtime, and afterwards the jurors retired to consider their verdict. Their foreman, the proprietor of a down-town hardware store, read their decision to the court at five o'clock. Teasy was, as his attorneys had argued, innocent of murder, and guilty only of manslaughter 'in the commission of an unlawful act'. Gilbert's sentence was the harshest the law allowed: three years' hard labour in the penitentiary. Assuming the day's business was over, he and the lawyers, followed by the women in the public gallery, got up and left the court.

It had been a brave verdict, and while they made no outburst as it was being delivered, the three Land cousins present – Cleo's uncles Brewster and Ed, and his father Will – seem to have been icily clear before its delivery that they would not allow such an outcome to stand. After the trial it was learned that weeks earlier Cleo's father had visited Sheriff Beard, warning him that 'should the verdict be less than murder, there might be trouble'. The *Enquirer-Sun* reporter was a witness to its sudden unfolding:

The trouble began when Bailiffs R.L. Willis and J.T. Darby started to take the negro from the courtroom into the sheriff's office. Gathered in the aisles were numbers of relatives and friends of the dead boy, perhaps twenty-five in all. Suddenly the men closed around the officers and demanded the prisoner. Neither of the bailiffs were armed. They refused to surrender McElhaney and one man struck Willis in the face. Another dealt him a heavy blow and he turned the negro loose to defend himself, a strenuous fisticuff following. The negro was torn from Darby and a powerful man hurled the officer bodily several feet into the courthouse rotunda where the struggle had shifted by that time. Deputy sheriff Gibson came running and was temporarily disabled by being kicked in the stomach.

As the running fight continued, little by little Teasy's abductors were easing him down the courthouse stairs, towards the front door. Aware of what was happening, he began to scream for protection, but none came. While the vanguard of the mob bustled him outside, another detachment, with pistols drawn, blocked the courthouse door, preventing Sheriff Beard and his deputies from following. 'The negro was hurried across the lawn of the courthouse by eight or ten men,' the newspaper said. By the time Beard and his men were able to struggle their way outside, Teasy and his abductors had gone.

The mob did not want to commit its intended crime inside the city, because its members knew that once across its limits, they would be beyond the reach of the Columbus police. Interference with their enterprise would then be most unlikely. The *Sun* report continued:

A streetcar, No. 18 ... was going east on Tenth Street. Just as it reached the west side of Second Avenue, a pistol is said to have been pointed at the motorman and he was ordered to stop the car, which he did, and several passengers who were in the car at the time got off. One of the men with the negro is said to have held a pistol on the motorman while the another did the same with the conductor. The car was not allowed to stop again until it reached the city limits where it stopped, and all the passengers ordered off.

117

It had reached the stretch of woods and just beyond the prisoner was taken off, pleading and screaming for mercy. The car was ordered to move on. Then several of the men in the crowd pulled out pistols, and the negro was taken off and riddled with bullets. He uttered a cry as the first shots hit him, then fell dead.

By the time the men with the negro had gotten but a few blocks out on Tenth Street, the street was alive with excited persons – many of them not knowing exactly what the trouble was. Automobiles, motorcycles, buggies and every other form of vehicle filled the street … Many persons followed on foot.

The Muscogee County Coroner, J.S. Tefry, accompanied by his six-man coroner's jury, went to the scene of the shooting soon afterwards, examined Teasy's tattered body and held an immediate, on-the-spot inquest. According to the *Sun*, 'it was impossible to tell how many bullets had been fired into the negro's body', although the *Ledger* later estimated that it contained between twenty-five and fifty holes. No one, it added, was found at the scene 'who would state whether they knew any of the men engaged in the killing, or at least, they had refused to state names'. It was, however, possible to say how many men had bundled Teasy into the streetcar, because they bought themselves eighteen tickets from the conductor, and another for their victim. As in thousands of lynchings across the South, the coroner's verdict was that Teasy met his death 'at the hands of persons unknown'.

I first read about Teasy McElhaney's murder in the newspaper reference section of the fine stucco library on Wynnton Road named after W.C. Bradley. I was sitting very close to the spot where Teasy was killed. The library was built on what was once a railway line, by a set of points known as the Wynnton switch: this was where Teasy's terrifying streetcar ride came to an end. In the woods above the library grounds lay the homes where the stocking strangler later did his own murderous work. As I pored over the clippings, it began to be apparent that the ties that bound these very different killings sixty-five years apart amounted to more than the coincidence of location.

*　*　*

Carlton Gary had left Columbus in 1963 as a gangly adolescent. When he came back as an adult in the late summer of 1977, one of the first things he did was to phone Earnestine Flowers. A few weeks after our tour of the city twenty-five years later, Earnestine, her mother Doris and I were sitting in a catfish restaurant on the slopes of Wynn's Hill, surrounded by families in their Sunday best who were lunching after church.

'I just knew it was him as soon as I heard his voice, though he didn't give his name,' Earnestine said. 'He'd disappeared, and suddenly he was back. Somehow, it didn't seem surprising.'

By then Earnestine was married to a military officer and was working as a Sheriff's Deputy. But she took Carlton home to meet her family, and Doris cooked him Southern delicacies – barbecue meat and collard greens.

'We were all glad to see him,' Doris said. 'Of course he was older, but he looked much the same. 'Cept for the cast on his leg.'

Gary didn't say how he got his injury, and as he talked to his childhood friend, there were gaps in his life story. Earnestine guessed he had probably been in prison. Years later, at Gary's trial, she would learn that he had broken his leg the previous month while escaping from the Onandaga correctional facility in Syracuse, New York, where he had been serving a sentence for handling stolen property. Having sawed through the bars of his cell, he jumped twenty feet from the prison wall, breaking his left ankle when he landed. In considerable pain, he made his getaway on a stolen bicycle. But if he was less than forthcoming about the source of his injury, there was no disguising its effects.

'It was a proper, big old plaster cast. It ran from halfway up his calf to his foot,' Earnestine said. 'It had a rubber heel, so he could kind of walk. But he certainly couldn't run. I mean, he was lopsided. He could only get about with a limp. I can't be sure now how long he wore it, but I think it was about two weeks. When they took it off, the muscle was all withered. His leg looked like a child's.'

Doris and Earnestine couldn't be certain of the date that Gary reappeared. But they thought it was early September, or at the very earliest, the last days of August. The strangler's first victim, Ferne Jackson, died on 16 September; even if Gary had not then been in plaster, he would not have had his normal mobility. It seems very likely that he was still wearing the cast on 11 September, when Gertrude Miller, who survived the strangler's first attack, was raped.

As he picked up the threads of life in Columbus, Gary told Earnestine a little about his missing years. His mother Carolyn had taken him from Columbus to Fort Myers, on Florida's west coast; later they had lived further north in the same state, in Gainesville. After leaving home, Carlton had spent time living in the North-East, working as a musician.

Carlton's high-rolling, womanising side was very visible in the autumn of 1977. But Earnestine saw other aspects of his character, too. Carlton's mother was back in Columbus, living in straitened circumstances, and at once he resolved to take care of her. 'He borrowed my car so he could go buy his mother groceries,' Earnestine said. 'At first, he borrowed a little money, too. He always paid it back.' He arranged a lease on a house on Old Buena Vista Road in south Columbus. In 2001, Earnestine took me to see it: a cramped, draughty building made of cinder blocks, plastered in a seal of crumbling grey cement. He also borrowed Earnestine's phone to call another girlfriend, Tula Jones,* who lived in Syracuse, New York, and had borne him a daughter, Coco, earlier that year. 'When he got the place on Old Buena Vista Road he asked Tula to bring the baby down to Columbus so they could all live together. Around the same time he asked me if I could ask my daddy to help him get a job.'

In mid-November Carlton started work with Earnestine's father Earnest on the late shift at Golden's Foundry. On his application form, he filled in his version of some of the gaps that Earnestine had noticed in his verbal accounts of his life – he said he had worked as a musician for ten years, and then as a heavy-equipment operator in Gary, Indiana. No one took steps to verify these statements. In any event, the work at the foundry was not to his taste, and he lasted barely a month. Easier ways of making money – such as modelling clothes for the Movin' Man – beckoned.

Although it went through stormy weather, Gary's relationship with Tula was relatively durable. Once, after a row at the end of October, she stormed back to Syracuse, taking their daughter with her. On 5 November Gary left

---

* At her request, I have changed her name and that of her daughter. After Gary's trial they experienced severe harassment.

the poky house on Old Buena Vista Road and rented a bigger, more comfortable place on Ninth Street. Tula and Coco rejoined him, and later, in August 1978 – four months after the final strangling – they all moved to a modern, luxury dwelling in Dawson Estates, an upscale black subdivision in the south-east part of Columbus. Even after Gary's arrest in South Carolina the following May, Tula and Coco continued to live in the city for several months, until the pressure of staying with Carlton's mother and his sister Miriam became too great.

Gary had male friends, too. J.T. Frazier, now an auto-dealer in Opelika, Alabama, used to manage the Movin' Man when Gary was both its best customer and its advertisement model. 'We were selling totally high-fashion merchandise, and our job was to get people to part with their money,' he remembered. 'I first got to know Carlton because he was such a big spender, and gradually he started helping out at busy times, like Saturday mornings. The ads came about because he was tall, handsome and good-looking, just naturally the guy you'd want to do your TV spots. While he modelled the suits, I recorded the voice-over. He was good company, a very cool, well-dressed guy, so I started hanging with him. We'd go for a beer in a club in Phenix City, or sometimes to the Control Tower. I visited his house [in Dawson Estates] and my wife came too: it was immaculate, with white carpets and beautiful furniture. I even met his mother.'

Like most African-Americans who knew him, Frazier reacted to the news of Gary's arrest for the stranglings with astonishment. 'I just thought, "How could this be?" This man was always so clean, so popular; he knew how to talk to folks and he had a lot of confidence. As for the rapes, it just seemed crazy. This guy did *not* have a problem with the ladies.'

Many of those who knew Carlton Gary best at the time of the stranglings are now dead, including his mother, his sister, many of his former girlfriends and other close relatives. But in a freezing Syracuse in the winter of 2001, when the snow lay piled six feet thick on the sidewalks, I found Tula and Coco, now an attractive, college-educated woman who works in local government, her features cast in the image of her father – whom both women knew by his middle name, Mike. They still used the last name Gary.

'When I was living with Mike, I was happy,' Tula said as we ate dinner in her apartment. 'I was on welfare but he got me back to school, enabled me to get a job. Without Mike I would have been on the street, getting into trouble. He showed me I was special.'

Tula had worked for a time in a nursing home, and when I met her in 2001 she had a job with the US Postal Service. For a long time after Gary's trial she had concealed the reason for his absence from her daughter: 'I lied to protect my baby. I told her he was in the service.' At the same time, she had kept a folder of clippings about the case, together with Gary's letters and the rings he had once given her. Like so many of the women he had known, she still carried a torch for him.

Coco, twenty-three when I met her in 2001, talked about her father with passionate, seemingly hopeless loyalty, tears forming in the corners of her eyes when she pondered his likely fate. 'I knew nothing of what he's supposed to have done until I was nine,' she said. 'When I was younger, I wasn't allowed to play outside with the other kids, and sometimes the police would come and sit outside in their cars and stare at us, rubber-necking. I never knew why. It was like being an animal in a zoo. Nothing can bring back what's been taken away from our family. My aunt died when he had his last execution date; my grandmother, Carolyn, the time before that.'

Coco made the thousand-mile journey from Syracuse to the Jackson prison as often as she could. 'I know he doesn't have so much time left. I just want them to let the truth come out, to let him go.'

Before the mob killed Teasy McElhaney in August 1912, no white person had ever stood trial for murdering an African-American in Columbus. Judge Price Gilbert's fury at the abduction from his courtroom meant that this was about to change. Though he was facing imminent re-election, he found the inner resources necessary to act.

He was not alone in his revulsion. Within a few days of McElhaney's death, women from some of the city's charitable clubs and ministers of religion began to canvass for signatures on petitions against the lynching. Published by the *Enquirer-Sun* on 21 August, the women's petition registered a 'solemn protest in the name of humanity, religion and the law, against the brutality of mob violence which has ... stained the record of our courts and put to shame the authority of our officers of the law ...

Cruel retaliations without the sanction of the law can accomplish nothing save the moral degradation of the individual and the community.' It was signed by the wives and daughters of some of the wealthiest businessmen in Columbus. A second petition, drawn up by deacons and ministers from many of the white churches, the synagogue and the Young Men's Christian Association, was published the same day.

Gilbert's speech to the Muscogee County grand jury six days earlier, on 15 August, revealed impressive courage. Preliminary inquiries had indicated that Teasy's abduction was led by the late Cleo Land's father, Will Land, and his cousins Brewster and Ed Land. Now, as Gilbert asked the grand jury to conduct a thorough inquiry into the lynching, the first obstacle he faced was that both Ed and Brewster Land were sitting grand jury members. As he began to speak to a packed courtroom, its occupants rapt despite the crushing August heat, he went straight to the symbolic magnitude of what was at stake: 'Since the convening of the last grand jury, a most momentous event has occurred, one that brings into question the power of the government itself. The question that now arises is not the guilt or innocence of any one person, but whether the American is strong enough and patriotic enough to govern himself.'

The mob's actions had killed not only Teasy, Gilbert went on: in lynchings, 'it is the law that is assassinated'. He concluded with an appeal of unusual eloquence:

I am fully aware that this investigation which I shall ask you to undertake will be seized upon by some to turn into a partisan contention that it is for the protection of the Negro, but those who say so are either fired by passion or are wilfully misstating a fact ... The question is whether any body of men may take a man from the confines of the courthouse and visit a death sentence upon him when a jury of their peers have said that such was not just and right ...

God, in his infinite wisdom, created this earth and all that is in it and upon it and man, and imbued in his breast the necessity to restrain the passions of men. And God directed in his infinite wisdom that whenever man was incapable of living up to that government he lapses into savagery: then there is no protection for the innocent, no protection for anyone, but the question is, who has the strongest arm and the boldest heart ...

It is currently reported that they made the trip from here to the suburbs on a streetcar on which were women and children. It must pale the face and shame the cheek of every American to suppose that such a thing was possible in this enlightened community. I ask you, gentlemen, to leave no stone unturned.

Sheriff Beard and his deputies, Gilbert made clear, would have the power to issue warrants for the arrest of anyone the grand jury deemed appropriate to detain.

Grand jury proceedings took place in secret, so the details of what transpired in their special room within the courthouse remain obscure. It is known that they met four times over the succeeding three weeks, that they subpoenaed numerous witnesses, and that after their first session Brewster and Ed Land were excused from attendance. The grand jurors rose to the challenge posed by their judge. On 30 August they issued three 'true bills' (indictments). These charged Ed and Brewster Land, together with a millworker, Lee Lynn, with the murder of T.Z. McElhaney. A week later they added the name of Cleo's father, Will Land, who also faced a charge of unlawfully using a firearm.

It looked like a great and historic triumph in the struggle against mob rule. Through the force of his rhetoric and personality, Judge Gilbert had managed to persuade a white grand jury to overlook the essential matter of race which underlay so many transactions between the state and the individual within the South's criminal justice system. In his closing comments he had reaffirmed the meaning of the frayed and decrepit Fourteenth Amendment, with its prescription of equal protection under the law.

It was to be a Pyrrhic victory. When Lynn and the Lands came to trial, Dixie's norms were swiftly reasserted. The four accused displayed their contempt for the proceedings they faced by quietly disappearing for almost three months after the indictments were issued – with the collusion, if not the active assistance, of Muscogee County's Sheriff Jesse Beard and his deputies, who made little attempt to arrest them. When they finally deigned to rematerialise in an automobile outside the Columbus courthouse on 5 November, Brewster Land made a short statement to the press: 'We have not been running away from justice. The only thing was that we did not wish to lie in jail until the next term of the court.' Such privileges were not commonly afforded to accused murderers.

Their trial began on 20 November. Much of it – more than two days – was devoted to choosing a jury supposedly free from bias. When the prosecution, in the shape of solicitor George Palmer, opened its case, it was immediately apparent that the law's procedural requirements – those irritating 'technicalities' that Georgia's jurists claimed fostered lynch mobs – were likely to hamper his chances of getting convictions. The problem was that while there were witnesses able to describe how the Lands and Lynn had led Teasy's abduction, this was not the same thing as the homicide with which they were charged. Many people had seen the shooting, but none of them had come forward to testify. It was therefore uncertain whether the accused had actually shot McElhaney, and for the murder charges to stick, the prosecution had to prove that the Lands and Lynn had been engaged in a 'conspiracy' to kill Teasy from the outset – no easy task.

Palmer's job was made still harder by the fact that his witnesses were far from cooperative. Sheriff Beard's testimony was chilling enough: he described seeing Brewster Land fighting with men at the courthouse door to stop them going after McElhaney and the men who had abducted him, adding that Brewster warned him not to follow, 'or I might get hurt'. But as to how the abduction began, or who were its main perpetrators, there were curious gaps in Beard's memory. Deputy Sheriff C.A. Gibson, who had been in charge of the courtroom, recalled seeing the Lands at the end of the trial, and told of receiving a mighty kick in the stomach at the moment when Teasy was taken. But as to its donor, he was vague: 'I know the defendants well, but I don't know if it was some of them who kicked me.' The other deputies and bailiffs who testified turned out to have equally selective memories, or in one case, defective eyesight for which he wore no spectacles. Some of the streetcar passengers gave harrowing evidence. They had heard Teasy's last, plaintive words: 'Oh, Lordy, don't kill me.' None, however, was able to name the objects of this pathetic appeal.

The three Lands did not give testimony under oath, but as was their right, made unsworn statements. The longest was the first, from Brewster.

Having insisted that the reason he had not surrendered when first charged was 'I knew it would be hot in jail at that time of year, so I did not want to give myself up,' Brewster asserted: 'I had nothing to do with the lynching, and I never went out to the scene until afterwards. I am innocent of any connection with it at all.'

Will Land spoke more forcefully. He described Teasy as a 'Negro brute' who deserved to die, and while he admitted warning Beard that there might be trouble if he were not condemned for murder, he had done so 'in the interests of the county'. Had he wanted to lynch Teasy, he would have done so sooner: 'Why, gentlemen, if I had wanted to kill the Negro, I could have done it after I found my boy.'

The jurors retired at 11 a.m. on 23 November. They filed back into court at 11.29. The foreman, S.W. Dudley, read the verdict – which had been reached without discussion, on a vote taken as soon as they reached the jury room: 'We the jury find the defendants not guilty.' There was little reaction from the defendants or their huge extended family, who filled the public benches. No one had expected the jury to convict. After a bizarre and unexpected detour, normality had been restored. Will Land made a statement on the courthouse steps on behalf of all of them: 'I knew they would turn us loose. I want to thank the people for the kind words said about us in the trial. We are now going home to our families.'

Price Gilbert was to become not only a justice of Georgia's Supreme Court, but a leading member of a State Commission which sat in the early 1930s to reform its criminal code. In 1912 he had passed through what must have been the most intense weeks of his long career, in which his own personal safety may well have been at risk. The principles that sustained him had been tested almost to destruction, and having at first appeared to triumph, he had then gone down to wretched, nullifying defeat. Yet in his memoir he left no word of this tumultuous period, and the word 'lynching' does not appear. Perhaps he still found it too painful; or perhaps, as he approached the end of his life, he merely wished to be remembered with warmth in all quarters of the society he had served.

By the time Brewster Land's son John – the deceased Cleo Land's first cousin – began to handle the case of Carlton Gary, he had been a judge for twenty years, and was the chief jurist of the Chattahoochee circuit Superior Court where Price Gilbert had once presided. His influence extended well beyond his courtroom, and he was widely regarded as one of the most powerful men in Georgia. For more than fifty years he ran a dining circle, a private Freemasonry known as the 'Fish House Gang' which met (and at the time of writing in 2006 continues to meet) every three or four months for liquor and catfish suppers – initially, in the days of its inception in the early 1950s, at a now-defunct restaurant known as Pritchett's Fish Camp, and later at the Rose Hill restaurant just to the north of Wynnton. Long after retiring from the bench, Land controlled the shifting list of two hundred men invited to these gatherings: businessmen, attorneys, state officials and legislators. On the rare occasions that the media asked him about it, he always insisted that the gang was merely a way of getting congenial people from different walks of life together, and that its meetings had no political content. Others claimed that an invitation to catfish with John Land was a sign of approval from Georgia's behind-the-scenes leadership, and perhaps a shortcut to high public office. In 2002, when Sonny Perdue was elected Georgia's first Republican Governor for more than a century, he told one of his neighbours: 'Now at last I'll be asked to the Fish House.'

Back in the winter of 1978, a few days after the night of the terrors, as Columbus's chief judge, Land had expressed his disgust at the failure to capture the killer in typically trenchant terms. 'I don't have too much confidence in the investigative ability of the Columbus Police Department,' he told the *Washington Post*. 'The real emphasis here is on traffic enforcement. I heard one policeman say the other day that they'll get the strangler the first time he runs a red light.'

A few months later, *Chic* magazine named Land one of America's top four 'hanging judges', and published a caricature depicting him holding a noose. He told the Columbus media that the article had made him laugh, pointing out indignantly that since 1976 he had presided over only four trials in which the defendant had been sentenced to death.

There was more to Land's palpable toughness than capital statistics. Sentencing an armed bandit at a time in the 1970s when such crimes appeared to be increasing, he suggested that the best way to handle them might be to ask the police 'to shoot some of these robbers'. When the State

Assembly passed a law allowing young, first-time offenders to avoid imprisonment, Land made clear that there would be no 'one free crime philosophy' in his court: 'This business of first offenders being entitled to leniency and probation to me is a bunch of hogwash.' *Chic*'s label stuck.

Born in 1918, six years after his cousin Cleo's almost certainly accidental death at the hands of T.Z. McElhaney, John Land had nine older siblings. By this time, cotton cultivation in Georgia was in irreversible decline, and his father Brewster was devoting most of his farm to a dairy herd.

A tall, balding, bulky man, physically not unlike his father, John smoked heavily, and despite the rigours of his strict Baptist upbringing, was known to enjoy alcoholic beverages. As a high school student, he was prevented by his father from dating. He later managed to make up some of the lost ground, and in the spring of 1984 was about to make the painful transition from his second marriage to his third. Having lived at the centre of state and local politics for three decades, he had made many enemies, which at times included the Columbus newspapers, but he revelled in their criticism. 'I'm never timid about saying what I think,' he told an interviewer in 1988, adding that he saw nothing wrong with a judge trying to exercise direct influence with state politicians and legislators: 'I've never hesitated to speak up when I saw something that needed to be corrected. I thought they'd appreciate it.' In another interview ten years earlier, he repeatedly adapted that singular phrase first uttered by J.F. De Lacy in 1899, in his address to the Georgia Bar Association. In his court, Land told the *Chattahoochee Magazine*, 'I believe in the certainty of punishment.'

As chief judge of the legal circuit, it was natural in 1984 for Land to take charge of the stranglings case. The decisions he would make in pre-trial hearings over the following year would do much to determine its outcome.

# SIX

# *Under Colour of Law*

It was an old brick jail, three storeys high, and surrounded by a cyclone fence topped with barbed wire. Inside were thieves, robbers and murderers. The criminals were caged in stone cells with iron bars before the windows, and though they might beat on the stone walls or wrench at the iron bars, they could never get out ... F. Jasmine knew some people who had been locked up in the jail, all of them coloured.

CARSON McCULLERS, *The Member of the Wedding* (1946)

A few days after the arrest of Carlton Gary, the three policemen who had brought him back to Columbus from Albany – Michael Sellers, Ricky Boren and Charlie Rowe – moved into new accommodation, not at the Columbus Police Department, but in the District Attorney's office on the third floor of the Government Center tower. Removed entirely from ordinary police work, they had been assigned to work full time on preparing for trial the biggest case in the city's history. There they would be supervised by lawyers – District Attorney William Smith and his hefty assistant Douglas Pullen, the ardent advocate of capital punishment who had fought so hard to send the retarded Jerome Bowden to his death in the electric chair. Told they could draw on any resources they might happen to need, they would be working together for the next twenty-seven months. The five men knew that much would depend on the outcome – not least, their own careers.

The strangler's trail had long grown cold when Sellers picked it up, but as he had already demonstrated with his inquiries about Henry Sanderson's stolen weapon, he and his detective colleagues were prepared to push hard. Their natural leader was Ricky Boren, a skilled department politician who seemed to know most of the families in Columbus. When I contacted him by telephone in the spring of 2001 he was amiable and courteous, and readily agreed to an interview the following morning. Burly but dapper, he came down the stairs to meet me in the spacious atrium of the new CPD building, a few blocks from the Government Center. When we met, it was apparent immediately that his attitude had changed.

He grasped my hand in a painful, bone-crushing grip that went well beyond a mere display of manliness. 'I'm sorry, buddy,' he drawled, squeezing still harder. 'I'm going to have to decline this interview until this pending litigation is finished.'

'That could take years,' I pointed out, retrieving my mangled paw. 'Are you saying that you won't talk to me until Carlton Gary has exhausted all his appeals?'

'Yes. Well, I'll be happy to sit down with you then for as long as you like.'

'Is this something that's likely to apply to everyone who took part in the investigation?' I asked.

Boren simply shrugged.

'Who told you that you can't discuss it?' I asked.

Further words began to form in my mouth, but Boren's heels were already halfway up the stairs. 'Like I said, I have nothing to say until this litigation is finished,' he replied over his shoulder. Boren's caution stood him in good stead. By 2002 he was head of the Detective Division; two years later he became chief of the CPD, in charge of 389 sworn officers and ninety-five civilian support staff. 'The Department is one of the most modern in the south-east,' Boren boasted on the force recruitment website. 'Its reputation as a forward-thinking, creative Department is known nationwide.'

As their inquiries unfolded over the spring and summer of 1984, the police tried to rewind Gary's life, tracking down his friends, associates and lovers in states the length of the Atlantic seaboard. They were looking for evidence that his serial killings in Columbus were part of a pattern, established years earlier, and were trying hard to squeeze possible testimony from his friends and relatives. One reason may have been that unexpected gaps were beginning to appear in the prosecution's case.

In Georgia, 'indigent defendants' – those unable to afford to choose and pay their own lawyers – have them assigned and funded by the court. Six days after Gary's arrest, Judge Land assigned him a local attorney who had been born and raised in Wynnton, William Kirby. The history of Southern capital trials is littered with cases where defendants have been sentenced to die not for having committed the worst crimes, but for having the worst lawyers. Kirby, however, was a determined and able fighter. At high school, many of his friends' parents had been in the military, and when he went to college at the University of North Carolina in 1965, it seemed a natural step to join a navy scholarship programme that paid for his books, tuition and living costs. In return, he was supposed to attend regular training and serve for most of each summer, and for an additional four years after graduation. But during his second summer, Kirby realised he loathed military disci- pline, a feeling that was only intensified by his growing disenchantment with the Vietnam War. In October 1967 he was one of seventy thousand protesters who went to Washington for the 'March on the Pentagon', the biggest demonstration against the war to date. Not long afterwards, he was told that his naval career was over. He had been photographed taking part in the march, and his presence among other officer cadets was now deemed 'subversive'. He was no redneck.

I met Kirby for the first time in 2001, at a bar on Veterans' Parkway, Columbus's north–south artery, where we had to shout against a live blues band to make ourselves understood. A big man with a grey goatee and a booming laugh, he took a pull of his drink and shook his head ruefully.

'From an early stage, I formed a view about Carlton Gary,' he said. 'I thought there was a pretty good chance he was telling the truth – that he really was innocent.'

For weeks after being assigned, Kirby visited Gary almost every morn- ing, as bewildered as anyone by the puzzling discrepancy between his gregarious, attractive personality and the crimes of which he stood accused. Working with an experienced legal investigator and former police detective, Don Snow, he began to expose surprising areas of weakness in the prosecution's case. At several hearings before Judge Land, Kirby complained that he was not being given proper access to the prosecution's witness lists, its forensic science files and crime scene samples. But Snow travelled to Atlanta and managed to speak to Byron Dawson, the Senior Forensic Investigator at the Georgia Bureau of Investigation Crime Laboratory. Dawson told him that two labs – his own, and another run by the FBI – had tested the pubic hairs left by the strangler around his victims' bodies with samples plucked from Carlton Gary after his arrest, and found they did not match.

Twenty-one years after Snow's visit to Dawson, in the summer of 2005, I tracked Dawson down at his retirement home in White Plains, by Georgia's Lake Oconee. He still recalled the case vividly: it had one been of the biggest he handled. I asked him what these differences were. 'It was pretty simple,' Dawson said. 'The hairs were a different colour.'

There also appeared to be problems over matching Gary's blood serology with the killer's. According to the tests carried out on his semen after the murders, the strangler was a relatively rare group O non-secretor: there were only tiny traces of the blood-group chemical marker in his other bodily fluids. After his arrest, the police had taken a saliva sample from Carlton Gary. It revealed that, together with some 40 per cent of the population, he was an O secretor.

Meanwhile, Kirby's young assistant attorney, Stephen Hyles, was told by contacts at Fort Benning that the military police Criminal Investigation Department had begun an inquiry into a soldier as a suspect for the stranglings. Hyles and Kirby could not help wondering if the CPD and the prosecution lawyers were really as confident as they seemed that they had charged the right man. By the end of August 1984, Kirby was looking forward to the trial with something like enthusiasm.

Gary probably wouldn't have entirely trusted anyone assigned by Judge Land, and to his own eventual detriment, he did not trust Kirby. He was also worried about Kirby's relative inexperience. Although he had been involved in three previous capital cases and several other murders, he had never fought a death penalty trial from start to finish as lead counsel. Instead, Gary decided that he wanted the lead counsel position to pass to a lawyer from Atlanta, August F. 'Bud' Siemon III.

Siemon, a tall, well-built man with startling blue eyes, was a leading member of a small, closely-knit group of Atlanta capital defence specialists: attorneys who dedicated their professional lives to acting for prisoners on death row or facing the prospect of going there, because they believed that the death penalty was wrong, and the legal system that enforced it unjust. Their doyen was Steve Bright, Director of Atlanta's Southern Center for Human Rights, who managed to combine trials and appeals with writing a long series of academic papers about the death penalty and annual spells teaching at Yale University Law School. Bright always warned that those who took on a career in capital defence would never be rich, but many of the younger lawyers who ended up at the centre or doing similar work in Georgia and elsewhere across the South had first been inspired as his students.

By the time Siemon first met Gary, he had fought a dozen capital trials, and his client had avoided a death sentence each time. He had also been involved in more than fifty capital appeals, not all of them so successful. There was no doubting his personal resilience. The son of an air force officer, Siemon joined the army in 1969 and served with distinction in Vietnam, winning two Bronze Star medals and ending his tour with Special Forces. He told an interviewer soon after taking on Gary's case that his childhood had been spent moving from base to base, a background that had made him careless of popularity and instinctively in sympathy with the underdog: 'You were always the new kid on the block, the outsider, sort of ostracised. So I always sided with the people in trouble, people who aren't part of the in crowd.' Vietnam, Siemon said, had prepared him for capital defence work: 'In combat, you make decisions and people die. I've functioned under this kind of pressure, and I know I can do it. When things go wrong in a trial, and they do, I have a frame of reference that allows me to keep control.' The war had also cemented his abhorrence of the death penalty by convincing him that 'Whenever our government goes into the business of killing people, it does it poorly.'

There was another reason for his wanting to accept the case of Carlton Gary. A few years earlier, he had fought and lost appeals on behalf of Jerome Bowden, the mentally retarded teenager executed in 1986 with the help of Columbus's Assistant District Attorney, Doug Pullen. 'I had seen what they did to Bowden,' Siemon told me in his Spartan office in January

2001. 'It was monstrous. His trial attorneys barely raised his mental incapacity. He was railroaded, and I didn't want to let that happen to Carlton Gary.'

On 28 August 1984, after a meeting with Gary in jail, Siemon appeared in Judge Land's court, saying he had been asked to take over the defence. Land was happy to agree. But the conditions he set were severe. First, Siemon would have to work for nothing, for as long as the case might take. The laws of Georgia and the United States said the courts must give men on trial for their lives a lawyer, Land said, but there was no stipulation that public funds had to be provided for a defendant's counsel of choice.

That was onerous enough. Land's next ruling was even tougher. While Siemon had always expected that he would have to work *pro bono* himself, he also assumed that Land would agree to reappoint and fund Bill Kirby as his co-counsel, together with his investigator, Don Snow, men he held in high respect, and whose help he considered essential. At a special hearing on 25 September, Siemon set out the reasons: Kirby and Snow's extensive local knowledge, and the hundreds of hours of work they had already done on the case, including interviews with more than thirty witnesses. There were at least ten times as many still to get through, while there was the additional difficulty that the crimes were already seven years old. Siemon said there was simply no way the defence could fight on an equal footing without adequate funding.

The US Constitution imposed a right to due process, Siemon reminded the court. Its definition was somewhat nebulous. 'But when the interest is life, there's an enhanced due process, if you will ... When we are no longer talking about the defendant's liberty but we're talking about his life, the balance changes to require more stringent procedures and more stringent guarantees to ensure that the defendant's due process rights are being protected.'

Land, however, was implacable. 'I take the position in this instance at this time that Mr Gary has exercised [his] alternative of procuring counsel of his choice,' he said. Gary had been given the opportunity to have a court-appointed lawyer, but he had rejected him. Now he wanted to have his cake and eat it by taking Kirby back, but it was up to the judge to choose a publicly funded lawyer, not the defendant. 'I cannot at this time allow him to name indigent counsel of his choice,' Land said, 'and I decline to reappoint Mr Kirby.' Nor could he have Don Snow: 'I don't think [the defendant] could name an investigator any more than [he] could name the counsel.' The consequences, it was soon clear, were devastating.

In May 1985, when Land was reminded of the critical comments he had made to the *Washington Post* in 1978 about the CPD's investigation, he 'recused' himself from the trial, to be replaced by another Columbus judge, Kenneth Followill. He took Land's original ruling and applied it even more severely, deciding that because Gary had changed his lawyer, the state could not give the defence a single cent for any purpose in any conceivable circumstance. In a series of 160 separate motions, Siemon asked Followill for money to meet the costs of finding witnesses, to pay their expenses so that they could testify, and to employ a variety of independent experts to examine the state's scientific evidence. Each time, from the moment he took over the case until the end of the trial, Judge Followill refused. Siemon, he said, had volunteered to represent Gary, saying that he had the resources to do this *pro bono*, and that meant that he had undertaken to meet all that job's costs.

For a while, two of Siemon's colleagues tried, *pro bono*, to assist him: Gary Parker, the African-American lawyer I had met on my first trip to Georgia, and Bruce Harvey from Atlanta. Months before the trial started in the summer of 1986, all three were facing personal bankruptcy. Eventually, first Parker, then Harvey, were forced to withdraw from the case altogether, leaving Siemon alone. Meanwhile, Pullen and the cops were trawling for witnesses across the United States. The defence, Siemon told me, 'couldn't even make long-distance phone calls'.

In 1996 I interviewed Michael Bowers, then Georgia's Attorney General. In Europe, and in other advanced countries that have signed the legal conventions on human rights developed after World War II, there is a well-developed principle: for a trial to be fair, it has to be even, with what lawyers call 'equality of arms' between the defence and prosecution. I asked Bowers how Georgia could square this idea with cases such as Gary's. Bowers, who was then planning to run for State Governor and still carried himself with the West Point rigidity he'd learned more than twenty years earlier, snorted. 'Equality of arms? If we had equality of arms, half these critters would get away.'*

By denying Gary funding, John Land had begun to load his trial, so that it was likely to produce only one outcome. As we shall see shortly, this was not the only occasion in his long career that his actions in a racially charged *cause célèbre* seem questionable. There were times when the justice dispensed by John Land, the man of the law, did not seem very different from the lynchings participated in by his father, Brewster. Both, however, were men of their times and place.

In post-World War I Columbus, the period of John Land's childhood, the rule of law edged close to collapse. African-Americans had already experienced the results of its shallow rooting. Now, however, white people were also victims. The climacteric came in 1919, when the city's fledgling trade union movement achieved its highest point with a city-wide strike over pay. Late one May evening, a pro-union rally was held in an open yard next to the giant Bibb textile factory, overlooking the Chattahoochee close to the spot where Simon Adams had been lynched in 1900. On a sudden signal from some unknown hand, the lights were extinguished, and hired armed thugs fired repeatedly into the defenceless crowd. Miraculously, only one man was killed, but many more were injured, some seriously. That night marked the end of trade unionism as an effective force in Columbus. In its place, the textile magnates tried to substitute racial hatred, its vehicle the Ku Klux Klan.

Passionately devoted to Protestant, white supremacy, the Klan had been re-established in 1915 and was once again a national organisation. In towns such as Columbus, with its large population of economically straitened, 'linthead' white millworkers, it found support across the social classes. For the legal, business and political elites, the Klan was a means of exercising social control. For their impoverished workers, it was a way of channelling insecurities and aspirations whose other possible outlet – the organised labour movement – had been bloodily stifled. By 1920 the Klan in

---

* Bowers's electoral prospects later suffered a fatal blow when it emerged that though a family-values Republican, he had been involved in an extra-marital relationship for many years.

Columbus had five hundred members and was expanding rapidly, publicly endorsed by the city's civic leaders. In February 1921 the Klan press bureau in Atlanta released a statement signed jointly by Columbus's Mayor, Joseph T. Crouch, and the Police Chief, J.T. Moore, in which they openly avowed and defended their Ku Klux Klan connections. The *Enquirer-Sun*, owned and edited by Julian Harris, the son of the famous Atlanta journalist and writer Joel Chandler Harris, had been publishing articles that were highly critical of the Klan, accusing it of sponsoring violence. Crouch and Moore responded by saying that its Columbus chapter was made up of 'citizens whose integrity is above reproach, and law abiding in every respect'.

Julian Harris would eventually win a Pulitzer Prize for his campaigns against the Klan, which were published despite a stream of murderous threats. In the spring of 1921 he realised that the Klan was also surveilling him. Late one evening he was working alone at the office. A man entered, raised a pistol and threatened to kill him. According to the story passed down among his family, Harris remembered something his father had once told him: that if a would-be assassin begins to speak instead of firing immediately, it may be possible to talk him out of killing you. That is exactly what Harris did. It was only after the man had left that he noticed that the blotter on which his arms had been resting while the intruder threatened him was soaked through from his sweat.

In January 1922, Columbus's local government was reformed, and a new Mayor, J. Homer Dimon, took office, together with a Yankee city manager – H. Gordon Hinkle, who came from Pennsylvania. To the Klan, and the alcohol bootleggers with which it had become allied, the new regime seemed to constitute a challenge. Both men began to receive death threats, and on the evening of 21 April Hinkle was ambushed in the street and savagely beaten. While Harris editorialised against 'Ku Kluxism, boot-leggers, gangsters and terrorists', the police made little effort to find Hinkle's assailants. Not only was their police chief a Klan member, the Columbus chapter was holding its regular meetings in the armoury at police headquarters. A month after the attack on Hinkle, Mayor Dimon's home was bombed. No one was injured, but his front porch was reduced to rubble. A few days later, Hinkle left Columbus, never to return. His replacement was a grandson of the Confederate attorney and General,

Henry Louis Benning. With his appointment, equilibrium was restored.

By the end of the decade the Klan's strength had begun to ebb, although it was far from extinct. In the 1930s, the years of the Great Depression, there were few signs of challenge to Columbus's established order, especially in race relations. But in 1945, as African-American servicemen returned to Dixie from fighting the racism of the Nazis in World War II, they began to find this ossified society and their place within it intolerable.

On the brow of the hill above the house where Carlton Gary passed his childhood, Primus King's barber shop acted as the grapevine for black Columbus. 'King cut my father's and my brother's hair,' Earnestine Flowers told me. 'It would surprise me if he hadn't cut Carlton's, too.' Many of King's customers were members of the National Association for the Advancement of Colored People (NAACP), whose Columbus branch, swelled by the soldiers at Fort Benning, numbered more than two thousand. Its leader was an African-American physician, Dr Thomas H. Brewer. 'My whole family knew him well. He was always very talkative, opinionated,' Earnestine said. It is likely that he helped Gary's mother through her pregnancies, and treated his infant ailments.

Like Carson McCullers's heroic black doctor Benedict Mady Copeland in *The Heart is a Lonely Hunter*, Brewer was imbued by a vision of change. One of a small group of Columbus black professionals, in 1929 he helped found the Social-Civic 25 Club. It stood for the transforming powers of education and self-help, and among the city's African-Americans it rapidly acquired prestige. Brewer, however, was first among equals, and the force of his personality earned him the nickname 'Chief'. His community work soon developed a harder political edge. In 1939 he was one of twenty-one African-Americans who applied to register the Columbus chapter of the NAACP.

In the NAACP's hall of fame in Atlanta, Brewer's portrait hangs alongside that of Dr Martin Luther King Junior. Brewer was one of the first to see the slumbering potential of the US Constitution as a vehicle for achieving social change, by using the courts to enforce the Fourteenth Amendment's promise of equal protection under the law. From 1944 on, Brewer organised a series of federal lawsuits. The first was probably the most important – a challenge to Georgia's effective disenfranchisement of

African-Americans. The Republicans' position as the party of Lincoln meant that in this era, and for decades still to come, their candidates stood no chance: to all intents and purposes, Democratic primaries were the real elections throughout the South, and in Georgia, blacks were prohibited from voting in them. On the symbolic date of 4 July 1944, the barber Primus King sought to register to vote in that year's primary at the Muscogee County courthouse. Having been removed by a Deputy, he went to a nearby attorney's office which had been told to expect him. The case took two years to reach the US Supreme Court, and ended in resounding victory. The path had been opened for the eventual transformation of Georgia politics.

As the fight for the vote gave way to further struggles over black civil rights, Columbus's whites had no intention of ceding their supremacy. In 1978 Ruth Schwob, the widow of the textile baron Simon Schwob, would try to fight off the stocking strangler, and would survive by pressing her panic button during the night of the terrors. In the 1940s and fifties, Simon Schwob was one of several Columbus magnates who funded a racist Baptist preacher, Parson Jack Johnston. (His other donors included the W.C. Bradley company and the Bibb mill, which claimed at the time to be the biggest in America.) Besides running the Baptist Tabernacle in the heart of the factory district at Eighteenth Street and Second Avenue, a church that regularly attracted a congregation of more than a thousand, Parson Jack edited and published a virulent scandal sheet aimed at the city's workers. Originally known as the *Trumpet*, it later evolved into the state-wide *Georgia Tribune*, and boasted a circulation of thirty thousand. It maintained continuous attacks on two evils that Johnston claimed were closely related – racial miscegenation and organised labour. According to one contemporary account, 'every time a union organiser showed up around Columbus's textile mills, copies of the *Trumpet* mysteriously appeared in workers' mailboxes. The message was that the Congress of Industrial Organisations was communistic and un-American and that "no man could join a labour union and remain a Christian".'

In 1946, Johnston related a meeting with Schwob to two young interviewers, Calvin Kytle and James A. Mackay. 'You know, it's always a mistake to take on the Jews,' Johnston said. 'Year or two ago I said something about 'em [in the *Trumpet*] and first thing I knew old Simon Schwob had me on the carpet ... Schwob told me, polite like, to lay off the kikes ... I didn't argue.' Johnston's relationship with Schwob did not prevent him from employing as his head printer Homer Loomis, the leader of the Atlanta-based neo-Nazi blue-shirt Columbians, who was later imprisoned for assaults on black people, illegal possession of dynamite, and a plot to blow up Atlanta's city hall.

The two reporters described Johnston's office: 'A stack of cartoon art lay atop a small table. The top one showed a spotlight labelled "The South" turned on a monkey labelled "Rape" that cast a terrible shadow on a servile Negro.' Johnston told them: 'Niggers say they want to vote. What they really want is to mix the blood. They want to have our women and wipe out the white race ... we aren't going to have peace in Georgia till niggers stop raping white women.' He claimed that although he had been a member of the Ku Klux Klan in the twenties, 'I haven't joined this new one.' However, he seemed to know a lot about its activities: 'Chapters are starting up all over Georgia. The boys have the idea that if they can't keep niggers from votin' any other way, they'll have to use force.'

Johnston's visceral appeal to the deep-seated Southern rape complex resonated on the streets and among police patrols. In 1951, black soldiers at Fort Benning complained that they were being harassed without cause and subjected to police brutality. One African-American veteran wrote: 'Soldiers are being beaten, their money taken ... We do not appreciate this after fighting in Korea.' In one typical incident that May, four black soldiers who were told they were under arrest during a weekend evening retaliated by destroying the cops' squad car – with hand grenades. As the police sought to restore order, the NAACP organised a petition claiming that police, 'motivated as if by mob instincts, roved through Negro sections of the city, indiscriminately beating, cursing, molesting ... and intimidating almost every Negro they saw'.

When the US Supreme Court issued its landmark decision in *Brown vs Board of Education* in May 1954, and decreed that segregated schools were unconstitutional, the temperature of Georgia's race relations rose by many degrees. At the state level, stoked by the rhetoric of Governor Marvin Griffin, the legislature passed new laws in contemptuous defiance of all attempts to desegregate. Under the rubric of the campaign known as 'massive resistance', it became a criminal offence for a public official to permit desegregated teaching, and any teacher who took such a class would have his or her salary revoked. The Assembly prohibited expenditure on desegregated schools, and passed an amendment to the state constitution that effectively privatised the entire educational system: its logic was that if the Fourteenth Amendment required a state to grant equal protection, this would have no consequence if schools no longer counted as state institutions. Griffin declared that the Supreme Court's opinion in *Brown* was 'null, void and of no effect' in Georgia.

In Columbus, Parson Jack and his allies preached a new intensity of hatred. In the wake of the court's decision in *Brown*, Johnston founded the Christian Civic League of America, and held its inaugural meeting in his Tabernacle church. The flyers and advertisements he published beforehand left nothing to the imagination. 'Are You White People Interested in the Unborn Generations?' their headline asked. 'Are You Willing to Sacrifice Just a Little So These Unborn Children May Find the Faces of Their Parents "White" as Yours Are?' Negroes, the text explained, had 'progressed more rapidly' under segregation than any other race. 'What more could they want? ANSWER: Intermarriage with your sons and daughters, but, we say, by the grace of God, THIS SHALL NOT BE!'

In the months after *Brown*, the crude, highly sexualised pages of Johnston's weekly *Georgia Tribune* recall nothing so much as the Nazi storm-trooper paper edited by Julius Streicher from the 1920s to the end of World War II, *Der Stürmer*. In a lengthy sermon delivered from his pulpit and published in the paper on 3 June, Johnston laid out themes that he would reiterate time and again: that segregation was decreed by the Bible; that the main reason blacks sought to end it was to create opportunities to violate white women and girls in the schools; and that their project of mixing white and African-American blood was also a goal of Communism. 'It has never been God's plan, nor according to His will, that the races of men should be mixed,' Johnston wrote. 'It has long been known that it is Communism's plan to mongrelise the races in America ... The hope of America lies in the South, and what is more, in our white women, and God help you to retain your race pride! God have mercy on any community, state or nation where the white women have lost their racial pride, and have thrown down the gauntlet; have sold their bodies to the whims of passionate desires to the detriment of the greatest race of people on earth.' According to Johnston, *Brown vs Board of Education* and the campaign for black civil rights embodied the Apocalypse: 'There is no doubt in my mind that we are facing rapidly the rise of the anti-Christ.'

Johnston published photographs of black and white people together in social settings, with captions stating that they depicted unacceptable 'interracial marriage' and 'interracial friendship'.

Those who missed their *Tribune* could tune in each Sunday to the most popular Columbus radio station, WDAK, where Johnston gave a weekly half-hour talk. As the months went by, his message became even more extreme. 'Negroes Resorting to Any Eventuality', claimed the front-page editorial headline on 6 October 1955. Negroes were pushing to integrate kindergartens, so that when the children grew up, 'they will be accustomed to each other, and inter-marriage will result'. The following week, Johnston's editorial asserted: 'They Not Only Spread Red Propaganda but Gonorrhoea.' According to the accompanying article,

> the mixing of black and white children in public schools where they are compelled to use the same facilities may have some tragic consequences for the white youngsters which the do-gooders with more zeal than judgement hadn't figured on and which may cause them to hang their addled heads in shame. It develops that, in addition to spreading Moscow-inspired propaganda for 'integration', they are also preparing to spread venereal disease among the helpless victims of their misguided enthusiasm ... Sanitation and hygiene are practically unknown among large segments of Negroes in the South and gonorrhoea is largely regarded by them as little more serious than a bad cold. While Southerners are deeply sympathetic of coloured children who contract this repulsive disease from the carelessness of their elders, they don't want this unspeakable malady spread among their own little boys and girls. And they are going to the last ditch to prevent it, especially in Mississippi, Georgia, Alabama and other States of the Deep South where these horrifying conditions prevail to an even greater extent.

A *Tribune* news report claimed that teachers in Washington DC, where schools had already been desegregated, were finding that their 'hardest job was to make the coloured boys keep their trousers buttoned or zipped', while female students were so afraid of sexual assault that they would not bend to drink from water fountains. Another story said that white people in Chicago were 'literally afraid to venture into the streets at night' because of black criminals; lapsing into overtly neo-Nazi language, the paper claimed that crime was 'more prevalent among non-Aryan niggers than among Aryan people'.

Amid the reams of racist propaganda, the *Georgia Tribune* also published genuine news items, albeit with a heavy supremacist spin. In the autumn of 1955 it reported that Columbus's NAACP leader Dr Brewer had organised petitions to the Muscogee County School Board, urging it to put the *Brown* ruling into effect and end school segregation. Another was the front-page lead of 5 January 1956, 'Local Negroes Make Bid to Defy Georgia's Law', an account of an attempt by Brewer to desegregate the Columbus golf course.

Brewer had long grown accustomed to threats from the Ku Klux Klan and its allies. In 1946, after the Primus King court ruling, he told his friends at the Social-Civic 25 Club that the Klan had promised it was 'going to get him' that night. Fifty-five years later, in January 2001, one of the club's last survivors, A.J. McClung, told me what had happened. McClung, who died in 2005, had gone on to become a model of political moderation, and had served for years as Columbus's Deputy Mayor. But in the forties, he and his allies had known that the only way to protect themselves was through superior force. On the night Brewer said that the Klan was coming, his friends stockpiled an arsenal of rifles, handguns and ammunition at his home, and sat up all night waiting.

In the end, McClung said, there was no attack, and they spent the night talking and drinking coffee. 'If the Ku Klux Klan had showed up, there would have been murder. The most frightening thing was that no one knew who they were. The Columbus Police Department was extremely racist, and you couldn't identify the Klan members. To go to them for help might be to get yourself killed.' From that time on, Brewer usually carried a small pistol.

By the beginning of 1956, Brewer had gained national prestige as a passionate but lawful campaigner for civil rights. He had been a delegate to the Republican Convention that nominated Thomas Dewey as presidential candidate in 1948, and two years later was chosen to represent Georgia at a four-day White House conference on children and youth. But it was becoming apparent that the South's road to equal protection under the laws would not be a peaceful one. In Georgia, the message of the state's political officials had become indistinguishable from that of the Klan and its cheerleaders, such as the *Georgia Tribune*. In the 1850s the supporters of slavery had mobilised around the slogan 'states' rights'. A century later, the same term was a shorthand code for campaigns to preserve the Dixie version of apartheid.

On 11 January the States' Rights Council, a new body pledged to resist federally enforced desegregation by all available means, held a rally in Americus, fifty miles south of Columbus. Flanked by Governor Griffin, Georgia's highest legal official, Attorney General Eugene Cook, urged his fellow citizens to 'openly defy' the US Supreme Court. Like Parson Jack, Cook tried to tap the Southern rape complex, warning that desegregated schools would soon be followed by racial catastrophe: 'As I view it, the scope of this decision [*Brown vs Board of Education*] goes directly to our miscegenation laws,' he told the *Atlanta Journal-Constitution*. 'Carried to its ultimate effect, it means these laws, too, could be struck down by legal attack. Once they are struck down I foresee an amalgamation stampede.'

Across the South, political violence was on the rise in response to such appeals. On 30 January, in Montgomery, Alabama, a bomb exploded at the home of one of the men who had been organising a boycott of segregated buses, the then-unknown Reverend Dr Martin Luther King Junior. The following week, on 5 February, white students and the Ku Klux Klan rioted in nearby Tuscaloosa. Enraged by the local university's admission of its first black student, they attacked and beat random African-Americans in the streets, dragging some from their cars.

One day earlier, Dr Brewer had happened to be looking out of the window of his consulting rooms on First Avenue, which lay above a department store, the F&B. Outside on the street, a white police officer named R.L. Cannon was trying to arrest an African-American, Sylvester Henderson, allegedly for drunkenness. He had already handcuffed his prisoner. Then, under Brewer's horrified gaze, Cannon took out his heavy wooden truncheon and brought it down on Henderson's head with such force that he broke the weapon in two. As a doctor, Brewer's awareness of the damage such a blow might do can only have increased his sense of outrage. That day, he wrote to Columbus's Police Chief, E.S. Moncrief, demanding an investigation. Brewer knew that there was another witness to the incident. Standing on the pavement watching the arrest of Henderson had been Brewer's landlord, the owner of the F&B store, a white man named Luico Flowers.

On several occasions over the following fortnight, Brewer tried to persuade Flowers to support the complaint; repeatedly, Flowers refused. He claimed that Henderson had still been struggling, and was 'trying to smash his cuffed hands on [officer] Cannon's head'. Brewer tried one last time at about 7 p.m. on Saturday, 18 February. He was on his way to visit a patient, and leaving his office with his doctor's bag, he went downstairs and entered the F&B. As well as the staff and customers, there was a police detective there, Jack Coulter. According to Coulter's later testimony, he saw Brewer, and briefly acknowledged him.

Flowers was standing towards the back of the store, by one of the cash registers. Brewer spoke to him. Then, Coulter said, 'I heard three or four gun shots in rapid succession. I turned back to see what the trouble was and as I turned I ran into a counter containing merchandise. I then ran straight for Mr Flowers who was about twenty-five or thirty feet away. I shouted, "Mr Flowers! Stop! Stop!" I could see him firing a gun but I couldn't see Dr Brewer ... As I got around this mirror I could see Dr Brewer in a crouched position with his left side toward Mr Flowers. At this moment I saw another bullet strike Dr Brewer's left arm. I made a lunge for Mr Flowers and said, "Mr Flowers, give that gun!" Just at this moment, Mr Flowers fired one more round from the gun and I grabbed his right hand which was holding the gun. Mr Flowers then voluntarily released his grip and told me: "You can have the gun, Jack. I'm not going to cause any more trouble."

'I said, "Mr Flowers, what have you done?" He said, "Jack, I had to do it. He was going to kill me."'

Brewer had been hit seven times by Flowers's low-calibre .25 automatic, once in the head, twice in the arm, and four times in the chest. He was dead on arrival at Columbus's City Hospital. But though Flowers had killed him in front of numerous witnesses, including a police officer, he was not arrested. Instead, Captain Clyde Adair from the Columbus Police Department ordered an ambulance. For reasons which remain unexplained, it drove Flowers across the Chattahoochee into Alabama, where he was checked into a private room at the Cobb Memorial Hospital in Phenix City under a false name, 'Mr Travers'.

News of Brewer's death spread quickly. To Columbus's African-Americans, its impact was overwhelming. 'I remember people screaming and hollering in the streets, and parents gathering their children in because they were sure it had something to do with the Ku Klux Klan, them or the Columbus police,' Ronzell Buckner, the proprietor of a beauty salon in south Columbus, told me. 'Killing Dr Brewer in this city was the equivalent of killing Martin Luther King. We knew at once that we had been set back years.' In 1990, thirty-four years after Brewer's death, Buckner set up a committee that raised funds for a granite monument to his memory. 'It brought the black community to life to be able to honour him after so much time. I remember one old lady brought the press clippings to one of our meetings. She'd kept them under her bed for all of those years.' The passage of the decades had done nothing to diminish the hatred felt by some whites, Buckner discovered. 'I had threats on my life – people who called me, saying, "Dr Brewer is dead. Let him stay dead – or join him." '

The Sunday *Ledger-Enquirer*, published on the morning after the shooting, had no doubt as to the significance of Brewer's death, which it splashed across the front page. In an editorial, published under the headline 'Order Must Prevail', the paper urged its readers not to prejudge why this 'terrible thing has happened', and expressed confidence in the officials dealing with Brewer's death: 'Law and order have and must and will prevail in Columbus; commonsense, justice, fair play and decency will not be denied.' Its news pages disclosed the identity of the man who would command the inquiry. He was the city's recently appointed chief prosecuting lawyer: John Land.

Like most white men of his generation and upbringing, Land's opinion of the new wave of political turmoil engulfing the South was straightforward:

he was a vehement segregationist. When the Supreme Court issued its opinion in the *Brown* case in 1954, he became the chairman of what the Columbus papers called 'a committee to preserve segregation in Muscogee County schools'. He had already served a term as Senator in the State Assembly, and the following year he was one of two hundred prominent Georgia figures who founded the States' Rights Council. It was Georgia's racist Governor, Marvin Griffin, who appointed Land as Chattahoochee circuit 'solicitor' – District Attorney for Columbus and the counties around it – in June 1955. This placed him in charge of every felony prosecution, and every grand jury investigation.

For a man in Land's position to make selective and controversial public statements about the early stages of a homicide inquiry was highly unusual. But in the days before the grand jury met to consider whether to issue a 'true bill' against Luico Flowers, Land briefed the press regularly, with remarks that seemed almost calculated to support the claim Flowers allegedly made to Detective Coulter – that if he had not killed Brewer, 'he was going to kill me'.

On the day after the killing, Land told the newspapers that Brewer had set down his doctor's bag in Flowers's store and 'reached toward a pocket' before the shots were fired. Brewer's own pistol had been found in one of his trouser pockets, and later that week, Land leaked the claim that Brewer had been trying to grab it when he died. He added the assertion that two hours before the shooting Brewer had 'threatened to get' Flowers, and that there had been 'a lot of bad blood' between them. Land was also determined to refute the suggestion that Brewer's death might have anything to do with politics: 'You can quote me as saying that we have not uncovered any connection between this shooting and Dr Brewer's membership in the NAACP.' He and his colleagues were 'conducting this investigation as we would in the case of any slaying, without regard to propaganda issues'. The Columbus press did not, however, report a statement by Roy Wilkins, the NAACP's National Executive Secretary, which was published by the *New York Times*. According to Wilkins, Brewer had 'received several threats during the past few days'.

Having been spared the discomfort of being confined in a jail cell, Luico Flowers came before the Muscogee County grand jury on 29 February, eleven days after the shooting. A series of white civilian and police witnesses gave evidence, building an apparently persuasive case that although Brewer's gun had not been fired, Flowers had indeed killed him in self-defence. Captain J.D. Armstrong said that Flowers had first contacted the police to say he was scared of threats from Brewer as early as 11 February, warning: 'Captain, I may have to defend myself and I wanted you to know about this and keep it in mind in case I have any further trouble with him.' Flowers himself claimed that Dr Brewer had accosted him outside the store on the afternoon of his death, and had seemed like a man beyond control, stepping on his toes, pushing him backwards and using profanities. Their conversation, Flowers said, ended with Brewer threatening to return 'at seven o'clock, or as soon as he closed his office, and get me'. As a result, he had gone inside and called the police. Two officers came to check on him shortly afterwards, and Flowers supposedly told them too that Brewer had been threatening him.

Jack Coulter, the detective who witnessed the shooting, said he found Flowers 'scared to death' when he first entered the store some time later, supposedly to protect him and prevent Brewer from carrying out his 'threat'. He said that Flowers told him: 'Jack, Dr Brewer said he was going to kill me tonight, and if he tries to kill me, I'm going to kill him.' Finally, two white customers who said they witnessed the incident testified that they had noticed Brewer's hand moving towards his pocket. No one had actually seen Brewer's gun while he was still alive.

The grand jury did not consider the question of whether it would have been in character for Thomas H. Brewer, a physician of sixty-one who had devoted himself to saving lives and pursuing change through legal, constitutional means, to have threatened or tried to kill Flowers because he would not back a complaint of police brutality. The reason for this was simple: John Land did not raise it. Plausible or not, Flowers's claim that he shot Brewer in self-defence was believed. The grand jury refused to indict him, and he walked free.

Almost a year later, early in the morning of 11 February 1957, Flowers's body was found slumped against the office door of the Dixie Theater, on the same street as his store. The chief of detectives, H.T. Whitley, told the Columbus *Ledger*: 'We are looking for an unknown assailant. We do not believe at this time that it was a suicide.' A handkerchief had been stuffed into his mouth and his pockets turned out, while two guns, both of which had been fired, were discovered nearby – a .25 automatic of the same type used to kill Dr Brewer, and a .45, a bullet from which passed through Flowers's skull from his left to right temple. Bullet holes caused by both weapons were found in the door, one of which contained bits of Flowers's flesh and flecks of his blood.

The *New York Times* published a photograph of Flowers under the simple caption 'Murdered'. But a few weeks later, a second Muscogee County grand jury delivered its verdict. It decided that Flowers had committed suicide.

Some of those who remember Dr Brewer and the manner of his passing believe that both verdicts were wrong: that Flowers murdered Brewer, and that he was later murdered in turn – either to stop him talking about what he knew, or as an act of revenge. Reading accounts of the grand jury hearing that considered Brewer's death, one has a sense that the evidence was somehow too pat; statements were being tailored to support each other, and to lead to a foreordained conclusion.

On a spring afternoon in 2001, I interviewed Albert Thompson, the city's first black Superior Court judge, at his home in south Columbus. (Having been appointed by a reforming Governor, George Busbee, in 1980, he lost a contested election two years later to a white woman, Rufe McCombs. Her campaign was based on a single issue – Thompson's decision not to seek the death penalty for a black youth aged sixteen who had shot and killed a white police officer.) Well into his eighties, Thompson's memory and intellect were undimmed.

'We took years and years to get over Dr Brewer's death,' he said. 'It left us without a leader. And most of the black professionals left town. We'd had a good medical community: we were left with just three older men, who weren't so well trained. The exodus left just one black lawyer – me. I remember talking to Herbert Haskins, Brewer's son-in-law and a doctor himself. He told me, "Al, I never thought they would kill someone like this." It frightened him and it frightened his wife. The day he heard the news he went home and she said, "We've got to leave." It wasn't until the sixties that a new group of people began to talk about civil rights. Even then, we had a perception of what could happen. A lot of people were fearful.'

Long after they had begun to crumble elsewhere, old South values persisted in Columbus, partly because the local black leadership was wary of confrontation. In 1963, when students organised sit-ins in the whites-only sections of buses and tried to desegregate public libraries and movie theatres, the Columbus chapter of the NAACP refused to support them, so undermining their protests. Other black community groups, fearful of retribution, actively opposed the civil rights campaigners. Jean Benton, a black real estate agent, announced his resignation from the 'Bi-Racial Committee', a local government body established to promote 'dialogue' between the communities, with the despairing comment: 'All the Negroes seem to have turned white.'

Meanwhile, after Brewer's murder, white people seemed to be closing ranks against progress and dissent. One of the more notable contemporary records is *God Wills Us Free: The Ordeal of a Southern Minister*, the memoir of a white, liberal clergyman, Robert B. McNeill. Appointed in 1952 to the First Presbyterian Church on First Avenue, a prestigious institution with seven thousand members and a weekly congregation of twelve hundred, McNeill spent years trying to nudge his flock towards accepting a greater measure of racial equality. The shooting of Brewer shocked him to the marrow, and the following Sunday he preached against the many who seemed to be rejoicing at Brewer's death: 'The issue now is beyond segregation. It is even beyond the contest between anarchy and the law. It is deeper, more fundamental, and theological. When we pray "Our Father who art in heaven," do we consider the other men of the earth, diverse in colour and origin as brothers, creatures of God, justly deserving our reverence for their personality?'

In the next week, McNeill learnt that the Klan, based at an open office in Macon Road, was planning a celebratory march past the store where Brewer was killed. He arranged a meeting with the Chief Detective in an attempt to get the police to ban the march, only to be told that the detective was personally friendly with the local Klan leadership: 'Sure, I know them all,' he told McNeill nonchalantly. Little had changed since the 1920s.

What McNeill called 'the crossroads of my life' came the following year, in April 1957, when he agreed to write an article about his work and

Southern attitudes for a New York magazine, *Look*. It was far from radical, merely advocating 'creative contact' between the races while the ongoing battles between state and federal authorities over segregation raged. But McNeill's Board of Deacons regarded it as 'anti-Southern', and he found himself ostracised, the target of threatening phone calls in the middle of the night – especially on the *Georgia Tribune*'s publication day. Finally, the church convened a 'judicial commission' to investigate his supposed neglect of his pastoral duties, and he was fired. For questioning the Dixie consensus from within, Reverend McNeill had been run out of town.

When I phoned the home of John Land for the first time at the end of November 2000, I did not expect him to agree to an interview, but he did so readily, and it was with some trepidation that I approached his house the next morning. He lived in a bungalow above the Chattahoochee in north Columbus, not far from the Big Eddy Club. The day was mild, a dazzling riot of blue and gold, and I stood in his driveway for a moment to gather my wits. He soon spotted me. Before I had time to ring the bell, Land was opening the door.

Now eighty-two, he was wearing a dark plaid shirt and corduroys. He looked well, and his big frame barely stooped; he complained of glaucoma, but his blue eyes still sparkled. He showed me into his kitchen, made coffee, and then we sat together while Land chain smoked. 'I'm afraid my memory is going,' he said. 'I won't be able to help you much.' His voice occasionally wavered, and to my unaccustomed ear his accent sounded rural: 'memory' came out as 'memra'; 'help' as 'hep'. But he was wrong. In more than one way, his recall of distant events was astounding.

'I hear a lot of politicians nowadays saying they were never segregationists,' Land began. 'I say that any white Georgia boy raised on a farm eighty years ago who says he wasn't a segregationist is lying. I was a segregationist. Our culture was the offshoot of the slavery time. Black people were still thought of as chattels. The difference between me and some you may meet is that I'm not ashamed to say that I was wrong. I have many black friends now, but fifty years ago, things were different.' That was why he had joined the States' Rights Council, he said. At that time, preserving segregation just seemed 'natural'.

Unprompted, he mentioned Dr Brewer. 'I knew him pretty well, you know. When I'd see him on the sidewalk, he would stick out his hand. I'd look up and down the street before I took it – to make sure no one was watching.'

'Did you really think that Luico Flowers killed Brewer in self-defence?' I asked. Land drew more smoke into his lungs and exhaled noisily, taking his time replying. The only sound was the tick of his kitchen clock. Then he met my eye.

'Dr Brewer had no reputation for violence. I liked him. He was a real congenial person, real friendly; a very quiet-spoken, gentle man. There was nothing in his disposition to indicate that he could have killed a man. They say that he and Flowers had been real good friends, before they became enemies. But the grand jury and the citizenry, the white citizenry, anyway, was looking for an excuse not to indict Flowers for what he, a white man, had done.'

Usually, he said, a solicitor or District Attorney would 'make a recommendation', tell a grand jury what he wanted it to do – and he had already drawn up an indictment of Flowers when the grand jury hearing began. But on this occasion, Land went on, 'I made no recommendation. I just presented the evidence. It was a very tense time, right at the start of desegregation. Back in those days, if a black man went into a white man's establishment and the white man said he'd threatened him, I don't think you could have got a jury to convict the white man at all. But no. The honest truth is that I don't think Brewer would have killed Flowers, and I don't think Flowers killed Brewer in self-defence.'

The one subject Land didn't want to discuss was his father, and the elder Land's trial for the lynching of Teasy McElhaney. It was a 'blemish', he said, which had hung over his family for years. 'My father was tried and acquitted,' he added, visibly uncomfortable. 'I asked him about it many times, but he would never talk about it. He just said he wasn't there.'

But when we turned to the stocking stranglings, Land's candour returned. 'In many of these high-profile crimes, there's a lot pressure on the police to find the guy who did it, and on occasion, they put the wrong guy in the frame. Sometimes the Police Department don't care too much whether they got the right guy – as long as they got someone. As solicitor, I never would prosecute anyone unless I was professionally convinced he was guilty. But I was never 100 per cent convinced that Carlton Gary was guilty, and I'm still not.'

Gary's death sentence troubled the old judge. He sighed. 'People believe the death penalty's a deterrent. I've always had mixed emotions: if a life sentence meant a life sentence, without possibility of parole, that might be better. Personally, if it was me on trial, I might prefer to die than to spend the rest of my days in prison. But the burden of proof is "beyond reasonable doubt". With the death penalty, it should be beyond all doubt.' I felt like pinching myself. Here was Land, repeating some of the same argument that Bud Siemon had used in his court sixteen years earlier, when he tried to persuade him to carry on funding Bill Kirby and his investigator, Don Snow. Gently, I reminded Land that his own decision to refuse this had been very damaging to Gary's defence, and that as a result of his ruling, Judge Followill had refused to grant public money for experts, witnesses and any other defence investigation costs. The pause this time was even longer, and the silence more intense.

'I don't recall that denying him money to pay the expenses for experts and all ever came up in my court,' Land said finally. 'Our practice was, that if you turned down a court-appointed lawyer, you had to get yourself one. But if they had asked for expense money, I would have given it to them, as being necessary to the defence, in order to have a fair trial. I didn't mean that he shouldn't get funding for experts, or for tracing witnesses.' He said he would hate to criticise Judge Followill directly, but he would not have done what he did.

We heard a car: Land's wife, coming home from an errand. The spell was broken, and it was time for me to go. Before I did, Land had a final surprise: a list of names and telephone numbers of others who might be ready to help me. At the top was Floyd Washington – the African-American owner of the F&W Control Tower, the nightclub in south Columbus once frequented by Gary. 'Floyd and I are buddies,' Land said. 'We have lunch together every week.'

Land's capacity for honest self-criticism astonished me. But as I stepped back into the sunlight, I couldn't help reflecting that for Carlton Michael Gary, it had come a little late.

# SEVEN

## *The Trial*

The object of all legal investigation is the discovery of truth. The rules of evidence are framed with a view to this prominent end, seeking always for pure sources and the highest evidence.

Code of Georgia (1933), Title 38, Section 38-01

After many months of procedural wrangling, preliminary hearings, false starts and delay, District Attorney William Smith rose to his feet to make his opening speech to the jury that would try Carlton Gary on Monday, 10 August 1986. Judge Kenneth Followill's court occupied much of the ninth floor of the Consolidated Government Center, the ugly white concrete tower that loomed over downtown Columbus. Its walls lined with dark wood panels, the room had recessed spotlights and a beige carpet that muffled sound: a bland, identikit public space with all the character of a chain hotel conference room. Flanking the raised judge's bench were the standards of the United States and Georgia, the Confederate Stars and Bars. There were no windows. Outside, beyond the courtroom's air-conditioning, the feverish Columbus summer burned. In the old court-house building that had formerly stood on the same site, Teasy McElhaney had gone on trial for killing Cedron Land, seventy-four years earlier to the week.

Aware of the requirement that justice ought to be seen to be done, Followill had allowed the trial to be televised. On the floor above his court, a special room had been set aside for the media. Festooned with wires, it carried a live video and audio feed, with three channels permanently on hand to record and report it. Newspaper photographers were also allowed to take still photographs. Some people preferred to watch in person. Much of the time, the hundred seats for the public at the back of the court were packed.

Aside from Gary and three members of the jury, the main *dramatis personae* were all white. Like human beings everywhere, their education and experience had helped to shape their mentality, and these in turn had been moulded by the past. The jury members bore the psychological imprint left by their community's history, and the way it had been remembered. Americans first, they were also Southerners, Georgians, and with the exception of the jurors, citizens of Columbus.

Followill, Smith and Assistant District Attorney Doug Pullen were too young to have played active roles in the white South's resistance to desegregation and the battle for civil rights. But the historical memories that they had absorbed, through their families, schooling and wider socialisation, were little different from those handed down to members of an older generation, such as Judge John Land and his erstwhile comrades in the Georgia States' Rights Council. Their knowledge of the region and city in which they lived had been formed by accounts such as those in the local history books by Nancy Telfair and Etta Blanchard Worsley, and as lawyers, not revisionist historians, they would have seen no reason to question these writers' ideological starting point, the Lost Cause legend of the wronged and wounded South.

In Columbus, even as recently as the 1980s, the murder of the Republican leader George W. Ashburn in 1868 was still being remembered as the well-deserved dispatch of a scalawag who got his comeuppance, not the assassination of a martyr to the cause of racial equality. In the books taught in Columbus's schools and on the shelves of its public libraries, his alleged killers were remembered as they were first described in the white supremacist pamphlet *Radical Rule* – as oppressed and innocent victims of Yankee intolerance.

At least Ashburn's death was recorded, albeit in a warped and slanderous fashion. Recollections of the unpunished reprisal murders of freed slaves at the end of the Civil War, and the lynchings in the decades that followed, had all been suppressed. When Carlton Gary's trial opened in August 1986, the local writer Billy Winn had yet to disinter and publish his story of the killing of Teasy McElhaney in 1912 and the subsequent acquittal of his killers, and it played no part in the discourse of white Columbus. As for the 1956 assassination of the black civil rights leader Dr Thomas H. Brewer by Luico Flowers, the official version put out at the time of his death, that the two men had been in fierce dispute and that Flowers had acted in self-defence, still stood unchallenged. The evasions, distortions and acts of outright concealment that characterised Columbus's approach to its past meant that in 1986 the connections between the cases of McElhaney, Brewer and Carlton Gary – not least the presence of the Land family – were invisible.

Embodied within this selective process of forgetting and remembering violent incidents was an interpretation of the rule of law that had been shared widely for more than a century. The Constitution, especially the Fourteenth Amendment's guarantees of due process and equal legal protection, envisaged the law as an outward expression of higher principles, something that must stand above a community's contingent needs and passions. In Columbus, however, it had sometimes been used in a more relative, instrumental way, in order to achieve particular ends. Lynchings, as the leaders of the Georgia Bar used to say at their annual conferences, were not necessarily wrong *per se*, but merely demonstrated that the law was too slow and cumbersome, and that defendants had too many rights. The remedy was not decisive, punitive action against lynchings' perpetrators, but to make the ordinary legal process swifter and more summary. The men who took the life of Teasy McElhaney, a helpless teenage boy, believed they were right because his acquittal for murdering Cedron Land meant that justice in court had failed, and had to be restored by extra-legal means. Later, despite Judge Gilbert's eloquent plea, it could only be maintained by finding McElhaney's own killers, Brewster Land included, not guilty. Now, in 1986, as District Attorney William Smith and his assistant Doug Pullen prepared to try the African-American accused of what, from a white perspective, were the most heinous crimes in Columbus's history, they sought the same end as their predecessors had a century earlier – the 'certainty of punishment'. Anything else would have seemed unbearable.

William Smith was a dapper, clean-cut man of forty-three, his plump, baby face still youthful. In court he was often seen in shirtsleeves and khaki trousers, rather than a formal suit. Born in Overlook, the southern annexe of Wynnton, he still lived across the street from the house where he grew up. Although he did not begin his studies at Columbus High School until 1956, two years after *Brown vs Board of Education*, the continuing struggle for 'states' rights' ensured that desegregation had yet to make the least impact there. The 1959 issue of the *Cohiscan*, Smith's school yearbook, reveals that both the faculty and the student body were entirely white: the only photograph of a black person is that of a mechanic, seen changing an automobile tyre. In this cultural milieu, images that would now be seen as racist were regarded as unexceptional. The yearbook's page 224 consists of a photograph of four white students blacked up as 'minstrels', with a caption written in a crude pastiche of African-American speech: 'Mr Bones you kno' dat was a gr'at show. Yea it sho' were!'

Smith went on to study at Auburn University in Alabama from 1960 to 1964, and throughout his time there the faculty and students also remained all-white. The photographs in Auburn's yearbook, *Glomerata*, depict the norms of its student social life in this period. The Confederate battle flag flew over the varsity football field when Auburn played at home. At the end of each summer semester, Smith and his fraternity brothers dressed up in grey Confederate uniforms to escort their dates to the university's annual Old South Ball, an attempt to re-enact the glamorous – and largely fictitious – world of *Gone With the Wind*, when Dixie meant hooped satin gowns, chivalrous passion, and wealth derived from slavery. Smith went on to Tulane Law School in New Orleans, where the faculty and students were once again all white.

Before coming home to Columbus to join the DA's office as an Assistant District Attorney in 1970, Smith spent three years in Washington DC as an FBI agent. Having been elected District Attorney in 1978, he had been working full-time on the stranglings case ever since Carlton Gary became a suspect in April 1984, and he often described the case as 'the most important in Columbus's 160-year history'. Before Gary's trial, Smith had already sought the death penalty successfully seven previous times. He had never employed an African-American as an assistant attorney.

I would eventually meet Doug Pullen, Smith's pugnacious co-counsel and assistant, ten years after the trial, in May 1996, when he took me to Fort Benning and later to dinner. Not only had Pullen and Smith worked together for many years, they both often worshipped at the First Baptist Church on Twelfth Street. Originally from West Point, Georgia, a village on the Chattahoochee about twenty miles north of Columbus, Pullen was three years younger than Smith, and by 1986 he had been working as a prosecutor for thirteen years. His background was strictly blue-collar: his father worked in the weaving room of a mill. Like Smith, Pullen's years at school were spent among white students only, but by the time he entered the Baptist Mercer University in Macon in 1963 it was becoming racially integrated, thanks to a daring campaign of civil disobedience led by a visionary professor, G. Mcleod Bryan. Pullen loved to play on his working-class, 'cracker' origins, and reveled in being called a redneck. Six weeks before the Gary trial began, Jerome Bowden, the mentally retarded African-American whom Pullen had prosecuted for the murder of Kay Stryker, had died in the electric chair, and despite international protests, Pullen had expressed his voluble approval. Several years after my first meeting with him, I talked to Pullen about the case again. The US Supreme Court had just declared it unconstitutional to put the mentally retarded to death, and I asked him if he'd had any more thoughts about Bowden. He said he had no regrets. As for his critics, they were 'a bunch of egg-sucking Commie liberals'.

The background of Judge Kenneth Followill was more privileged than those of the two prosecutors. He was born into wealth: his parents owned a savings and loan corporation. But like Smith, he was also an alumnus of Columbus High School, four years ahead of him. He studied for his first degree between 1952 and 1956 at a private, all-white college, the University of the South in Sewanee, Tennessee, where he was President of the Kappa Alpha fraternity. This was founded in 1865 with the help of the Confederate General Robert E. Lee, in order to foster 'the ideals of Christian manhood as demonstrated by the chivalrous knights of old England and the true gentlemen of the South'. Kappa Alpha held its own annual Old South Ball, and in addition, according to the *Sewanee Purple* student newspaper, it hosted regular tea dances, cocktail parties and banquets with the Kirby-Smith chapter of the United Daughters of the

Confederacy: 'Attired in grey uniforms or coats and tails, the brothers escort their lovely Southern belles.' The fraternity, the report went on, 'is Southern in this sense: that its essential teaching is that its members shall cherish the ideal of character and perpetuate the ideal of the gentleman, of which Robert E. Lee is the perfect expression'. The Lost Cause legend had never been so decorous.

Followill was a *Sewanee Purple* editor, but the paper's treatment of African-Americans did not conform to this gentlemanly ideal. One issue in May 1954 (published just as the Supreme Court was handing down its opinion in *Brown*) carried a photograph of some African tribespeople, its caption claiming that they were members of a rival (white) fraternity with their dates. The following year, as the political crisis over desegregation moved towards its climax, it published a spoof article claiming that a senior university administrative post was about to go to a black man, along with a photograph of a white student in blackface make-up with a bone through his nose, describing him as a 'cannibal'.

Followill went on to study at the then all-white Emory University School of Law in Atlanta. During his time there, the Student Bar Association, to which he belonged, voted unanimously to 'unalterably oppose the admission of Negroes to any graduate division of the university'. An editorial in the *Emory Wheel* published during Followill's last year, 1959, claimed that to accede to integration would 'violate the duty the University owed its students, alumni and the South', and prevent it from 'providing an atmosphere for the development of good leaders for the Southern community'.

Like most judges in Columbus, Followill's career before he joined the bench had been spent as a prosecutor, although in his case this had been as Solicitor at the State Court, where lesser crimes were tried, rather than handling felonies as a District Attorney. He was a convivial man who was known to enjoy a drink, and his black judicial robes hid an unexpected talent – for playing blues guitar.

On the one hand, Smith and Followill could be said simply to be men of their time and place. If white boys from comfortable backgrounds wanted to be educated in the South of the 1950s, they went to white schools: there was no choice. Membership of a fraternity such as Kappa Alpha did not, in the era before the victories won by the civil rights movement, indicate that a student was a diehard racist. However, like other prominent white citizens, Followill and Smith had also elected to prolong the segregated social life of their youths into adulthood, by spending their leisure in expensive all-white clubs. Followill belonged to the Columbus Country Club, and through his mother's membership, frequently dined at the Big Eddy Club overlooking the Chattahoochee, where Smith was also a member. As Marcel Carles, the former chef and chief steward, told me in his French accent, still heavy after forty years in America, 'We had the successful people, good people, the best people in the world. It was mainly the older families, of course. But you have to be asked. You could win the lottery and you couldn't join if the members did not think you were the right kind of family. Now there are second- and third-generation members there, people whose parents and grandparents were members and introduced them to the club's ways when they were still children.'

The three lawyers may well have had black friends elsewhere, but the ways of the club were very firmly segregated. 'Let's face it, we didn't serve their kind of food,' Carles said, echoing the stereotypes he had perhaps heard expressed at the club. 'The members used to joke about it with me. They'd put on a kind of Louis Armstrong voice and ask me, "Hey, Marcel, when you gonna start serving fries and catfish and black eyed peas?" It was just their history, their attitudes. It was hard for them to change.'

The first time, he said, that a black person came to the club as the guest of a member was in 1986, the year of Gary's trial. The host was John Amos, the multi-millionaire chairman and chief executive of Columbus's biggest corporation, the American Family Life Assurance Corporation (AFLAC), an early backer and close friend of Jimmy Carter. Amos, a liberal who worked for many years to achieve a greater measure of racial equality in Georgia, brought the newly-appointed black Superior Court judge Albert Thompson for lunch.

Amos had phoned ahead to say that he would be bringing Thompson. But there was another, white, Judge Thompson in the city, Carles said, and 'everyone assumed that he was the one who was coming'. When the pair entered the great oak dining room, 'it fell completely silent. You could almost smell the shock. Then the whispering started. I clearly remember one guy indicating Amos and saying, "Well what do you expect? He's not from here."' The only other time Carles could recall a black person entering the club before his retirement at the end of the 1990s was during the Carter administration in 1978, when the President's wayward brother Billy brought a delegation of Libyans with whom he was trying to negotiate business deals. But that was on a Monday, when the club was closed for ordinary business.

The audience for the trial's forthcoming drama, the jury, were not from Columbus at all. Followill had granted a motion from the defence, ruling that there was a risk of possible prejudice from local jurors, who would have both lived through the stranglings and absorbed huge amounts of local media coverage after Gary's arrest. Instead, they had been recruited from Spalding County, about forty miles south-east of Atlanta, safely beyond the reach of the Columbus papers and TV stations. Most of them lived in the county seat, Griffin. Like Columbus, it was an old textile mill town, although its population of twenty thousand was only a tenth as big.

Like all American jurors faced with trying a death case, they had to be 'death qualified'. That meant that before the proceedings began in Columbus, Followill had moved his court to Griffin, where a large pool of prospective jurors was required to fill in a questionnaire and submit to examination by counsel for each side. Part of the purpose was to discover if a juror had some connection with the victims or the defendant. But Smith and Followill also wanted to be certain that no juror objected on principle to capital punishment, and that if he or she thought it appropriate, they would not hesitate to impose it in the trial's second, penalty phase.

Prosecutors had the legal right to 'strike' jurors without giving reasons, and those in Columbus had used this power on numerous occasions to remove all African-Americans from the juries who tried black defendants. When Pullen prosecuted Jerome Bowden in 1976, and when Smith's predecessor as District Attorney, Mullins Whisnant, tried William Brooks for killing Jeannine Galloway the following year, they made sure that the juries were all white. But four months before Carlton Gary's trial began, the US Supreme Court had decreed in the case of *Batson vs Kentucky* that prosecutors could no longer dismiss jurors on grounds of their race. Smith and Pullen knew they had to be careful. They struck five potential African-

Americans from the jury pool on the grounds, Pullen said later, that they were 'weak on the death penalty', but the rest remained. Gary's jury included three black men, while among the four 'alternates', chosen in case one or more jurors had to withdraw, was an African-American woman.

For all the jurors, trying Carlton Gary was going to be arduous and inconvenient. Their selection finished in Griffin by the middle of Thursday, 6 August. Each was given just a couple of hours to pack a suitcase for what they were told might easily be a three-month absence, then driven to Columbus. There they were sequestered in the Hilton Hotel, much of it built inside a converted Victorian mill, and told they could not watch television or look at a newspaper until the end of the trial, nor leave the building or receive a visitor except in the company of a Deputy Sheriff. Their phone calls were monitored. 'We were prisoners,' Eleanor Childers told me at her home in Griffin. 'Once I'd been chosen, I only had time to make one phone call, and then I just left my life behind. I'd even left some vegetables out on the kitchen counter.'

'I got just a few minutes to say goodbye to my wife and baby son,' David Glanton said at the huge Pentecostal church where he had worked as a technician and junior minister for more than twenty years. 'When I left, he was crawling, and when I got back, he could walk. We had a floor of the hotel all to ourselves, but it was pretty rigorous. If we went out to eat and you needed to use the rest room, a deputy would follow you right in.'

Childers, who looked much younger than her eighty-five years when I met her in 2003, had kept herself in shape by tending her huge and beautiful garden. Her memories of the trial itself were undimmed. 'Smith came across in court as very deliberate, careful, well prepared. That was a big contrast with Carlton Gary's attorney. It seemed he was constantly complaining about the fact that the state had not given him public funds.'

He had good reason to. The state, meanwhile, was determined to maintain its financial advantage. One afternoon during jury selection, a black juror was struck after admitting that she had donated $5 to a community group that was trying to raise funds for Gary's defence. She had no opinion about his guilt or innocence, she said, but believed he was entitled to a fair trial. Smith pounced on her words and demanded an investigation. 'For two years we have heard "Funds, funds, funds." That they have no funds.

Now we hear that they do!' His raised, aggressive voice, the Columbus *Enquirer* reported, startled the reporters and spectators, who had been lulled by an otherwise low-key afternoon. 'If they have received any money they have misled the court for two years!' Smith shouted.

Wearily, Siemon rebutted his claim. 'We haven't had one cent to spend on this case, where the prosecution has spent tens of thousands of dollars.' His co-counsel, Bruce Harvey, offered to produce his bank statements, adding: 'I want the record to show I had to get a loan to eat.'

Gary Parker, the African-American lawyer from Columbus, who had two young children, had already retired from the case because he could not carry such a financial burden. A week before the trial proper opened, while jury selection was still going on, another defence team member was forced to withdraw. Bruce Harvey told Followill that after working on the case for almost two years without remuneration, he could no longer afford to continue. 'Up until the time of the trial, throughout the extensive pre-trial hearings, Mr Siemon and I slept on the floor in sleeping bags in the transient housing for Fort Benning,' Harvey stated some years later in a legal affidavit. 'I can recall my secretary from Atlanta driving to Columbus to bring us boxes of macaroni cheese to eat. I was sued by a number of legal supplies companies, a direct result of my spending all of my time on Mr Gary's case and not having any income.' The trial, he said, had originally been due to begin in March 1986, and he had managed to get a personal loan to keep abreast of his mortgage payments and continue to feed his family. But the further delay meant that this money simply ran out. 'The issue was not that I was not making any money on the case. The issue was that I was forced to spend my own personal resources, and was now at risk of losing the home I shared with my family and of not being able to put food on the table.'

Siemon set out the costs of representing Gary in his own affidavit. 'From the moment I got involved in the case, it was apparent to me that I was going to need help in preparing a defence for Carlton Gary. There are few, if any, more notorious crimes in the annals of Georgia history.' Denied resources, he and Harvey had 'investigated the only way we could think of' – sending letters to 250 potential witnesses. The attorneys were so impoverished that they could not take collect calls: they had to ask the letters' recipients to phone them. Not surprisingly, only ten did. Unable to travel, the lawyers were forced 'into the untenable position of going to trial without having interviewed the witnesses'. Siemon, his affidavit said, ended up thousands of dollars in debt: 'My wife left me and we eventually divorced, in no small part because of what this case did to me emotionally and financially.'

The consequences for Siemon's trial strategy were equally devastating. 'Having no money meant that all I could really do was preserve a proper record for future appeals,' he told me in 2001. 'From a due process standpoint, what was happening was a travesty. It also meant I couldn't take the risk of calling Carlton as a witness. Having no money to put on a proper defence and uncover the real facts, it would have been madness to put him on the stand in the hope that somehow he could persuade the jury not to convict him. It would have been like making him a sacrificial lamb. It made much more sense to protect him, in the hope that some court in the future would recognise this trial as a total denial of justice.'

As Bruce Harvey left the court, Judge Followill gave him a warning. Before he departed, he had better reimburse the Columbus courthouse some money he owed for phone calls, or he would face severe consequences.

With Harvey gone, Followill insisted he was trying his best to help the penniless defence: one of the reasons he had picked Griffin for choosing the jury was the fact that it was not far from Atlanta or Columbus, and had some good hotels. 'Forget about hotels,' Siemon retorted. He had been commuting from Atlanta, he told the judge, and one morning the previous week he had arrived in Griffin late. 'I wasn't late on purpose. The fact is I had to borrow a truck to come down, and I had to bum a ride to get to the truck.' The Sunday *Ledger-Enquirer* reported: 'The defence has argued for money as often as a sales clerk says "Have a nice day." Lately, the argument has seemed almost as stale … Followill repeatedly has denied the request for money and clearly has no patience left for the subject.'

Since the early days of his incarceration more than two years earlier, Gary's morale had plummeted. For almost all of this time he had been held in what the Columbus authorities euphemistically termed 'administrative segregation', solitary confinement. His cell in the Muscogee County Jail measured seven feet by ten, slightly larger than a king-size bed. It contained a television with a five-inch screen, a combined toilet and washstand, a metal bunk and little else. Throughout his stay there he was given no outdoor exercise, on the grounds that the jail's yard bordered a railroad line. Although there were two high walls topped with razor wire, Sheriff Jack Ruttledge claimed it was too risky to allow this prisoner out in the open air. Most weeks, Gary left his cell only for weekend visits from his family and friends, or in order to see his lawyer.

The only natural light in his cell came from a small pane of frosted glass high on one wall, and sometimes the electric light did not function. By the time his trial began his eyes had suffered irreversible damage, becoming over-sensitive to light; he would have to wear dark glasses for the rest of his life. He complained that the jail's staple food was pork, which he had not eaten for many years. Never a fat man, he lost about sixty pounds. On his first day in front of the jury he found that the suit he had planned to wear in court no longer fitted, forcing him to appear in his prisoner's uniform, white slacks and a polo shirt stamped with the county jail logo.

Under this pressure, his mental health began to deteriorate. He was normally fastidious about personal cleanliness and hygiene, but although he was entitled to shower twice a week, sometimes he preferred to stay in his cell, unwashed. By March 1986 his lawyers were finding him withdrawn and uncommunicative, and argued in a preliminary hearing that he had become unfit to face trial. Bruce Harvey told Followill that when he first met Gary in October 1984, he had been 'very fixed in reality'. Now, however, 'He rambles – he is not fixed in reality with regard to the present proceeding. The bottom line is I don't think he understands what I recommend.' Followill decided that Gary should undergo psychological tests, and then there would be a short 'competency hearing' at which a jury would have to decide whether his sanity was really failing, or whether his symptoms were feigned.

After Gary had spent a few days at the Georgia State Mental Hospital in Milledgeville, the competency hearing took place in April 1986, four months before the main trial. Most of the time he sat bowed, ignoring the proceedings, his head resting on the defence attorneys' table. His former lawyer, Gary Parker, who still paid him regular visits, testified that he had changed almost beyond recognition, becoming 'withdrawn and very paranoid'. Parker had the impression that Gary 'didn't give a damn any more'. In order to rebut this testimony, Smith produced a Milledgeville psychologist, who said that although Gary had refused to answer his questions, he had played an alert and active role in a game of volleyball. He was 'playing very skilfully, bouncing up and down ... I saw him go over to a player next to him who had made a good play and pat him on the arm.' The psychologist added that Gary had spoken to other inmates, but did not react to loud noises in his vicinity, apparently deliberately. In his opinion, this meant he was fit to be tried.

According to his usual policy, Followill refused to grant funds for the defence to introduce its own mental health expert. The jury decided that if Gary could play volleyball, he was well enough to go on trial for his life.

While the impending contest was terrifyingly unequal, it seemed to Siemon that the state's case was weak. Gary's hair and serology type did not appear to match the samples left at the crime scenes, and the two strongest pieces of prosecution evidence looked open to challenge. The fingerprints the prosecution had produced proved, it claimed, that Gary had been at the victims' homes, but not that he had murdered them. He had, allegedly, made self-incriminating statements to the police. But as we shall see, they had been produced in extremely questionable circumstances.

At a pre-trial hearing on 8 August, as the jurors settled themselves in the Hilton, Smith laid out his strategy for dealing with these deficiencies. Gary was charged with only three of the seven rapes and murders, those of Florence Scheible, Martha Thurmond and Kathleen Woodruff, at whose homes the police were said to have found his fingerprints. In Georgia, as in other jurisdictions based on the English common law, it was an ancient principle that in order to avoid insuperable prejudice, defendants were tried on the facts of the case of which they were accused, not on their past convictions, nor on other crimes for which they might have been suspected. Now, however, Smith told the judge that he also wanted to present evidence about the other four stranglings; the rape of Gertrude Miller, the victim who survived; the attempted assault on Ruth Schwob; and several burglaries in Wynnton. All these crimes, Smith insisted, were the work of the same man.

In addition, Smith said, he was also asking for permission to tell the jury that Gary was responsible for two crimes, a rape/murder and a sexual assault, that had taken place long before the stranglings, not in Georgia but a thousand miles away, in upstate New York. Gary had never been tried for, much less convicted of, either of these offences. But Smith said that he had committed them, and that they were the start of his pattern of sexually driven, murderous behaviour. Citing a legal precedent from the case of Wayne Williams, the Atlanta serial killer who murdered twenty-one children in the early 1980s, Smith accepted that there was nothing approaching 'proof beyond reasonable doubt' that Gary had committed these 'uncharged crimes'. But it was enough, he argued, that there was 'some evidence' to connect him with them, because they were 'logically relevant to establish the defendant's motive, intent, plan, scheme, bent of mind and identity'. Both these New York attacks were on white women of mature years who lived alone, and they were, Smith said, 'so nearly identical in method ... as to earmark them as the handiwork of the accused'.

Smith took four hours to make his pitch. Bud Siemon's appalled and disbelieving reaction leaps from the bald, typed words of the transcript. 'Your honour,' he began, 'I know that I have talked about the funds issue, which I am going to start off with, many times, and I'll do it briefly this time so as not to tax your honour's patience and the patience of Mr Smith. But for over two years, your honour, I've been arguing to the court for the necessity of us having funds to adequately investigate this case. Now, on the eve of the trial, we see that the state themselves have admitted that what in fact we've got is sixteen separate crimes.' Once again he implored Followill to reconsider his appeal for public funding. Followill shot back with a two-word answer: 'Motion denied.'

After so many months of anticipation, the tension in court in these last pre-trial hearings was palpable. The next day, Followill ruled that all the uncharged crimes were admissible as evidence. Smith suggested that since Siemon had not been able to travel to interview out-of-state witnesses, he would be willing to make them available for interview in his office before they testified. This would not be sufficient at all, Siemon said: 'Mr Smith misapprehends a defendant's right. We don't have just to talk to the cops that are making cases against the person and take their word for what happened. We've got a right to do an independent investigation.'

'Every journey starts with the first step, Mr Siemon,' Judge Followill said tartly. 'It's a good time to start.'

'Maybe you haven't read our affidavits, your honour,' said Siemon, visibly needled. 'I've interviewed over two hundred witnesses. It's not the first step.'

The colour rose in Followill's face. 'Maybe you'd better not holler at me any more,' he said quietly.

'It's not the first step,' Siemon said again.

Now it was Followill who was doing the hollering. 'Sit down,' he ordered. 'Sit down right this minute. I'm not going to put up with that kind of hollering and carrying on in this courtroom. I've warned you before, and I'm going to warn you one more time, any more of that kind of outburst and I'm going to put you in jail.'

The next day was Sunday. The morning after that, the jurors filed into Followill's Columbus courtroom for the first time. After a few preliminary remarks – the judge thanked them profusely for their service, and, bizarrely, told them not to make any notes – the trial of Carlton Gary began.

For the whole of that first day, Smith was on his feet, outlining his case in his opening statement. His delivery was measured and evenly paced, like that of a surgeon recommending a course of treatment, rather than a courtroom fighter. 'He made it all sound logical, relentless, overwhelming,' one of the jurors recalled. 'He'd just planned it all out, and then he executed his strategy.' To assist him in his presentation, Smith placed two large easels at the front of the court. One displayed a map of part of Columbus, with the scenes of each murder and Carlton Gary's various residences marked. The other held a chart listing all the crimes for which Smith claimed Gary had been responsible, going back to 1970, setting out their salient details and alleged 'signature' features.

Most of what Smith said consisted of a careful, factual summary, but towards the end he built to a modest climax: 'Based on this evidence, which we expect to be presented from the witness stand during the course of this trial, the state intends to ask you at the conclusion of the trial to return a verdict of guilty on all counts.'

Smith's address contained just one puzzling discrepancy with stories that had already been told about the stranglings and the police investigation, although it would have taken a close student of the case to notice it. When he came to describe how Gary had become a suspect, he repeated the story of how Henry Sanderson's gun had been stolen in the burglary at the home of his aunt, Callye East; how the police had always thought this might be linked to the murders; and how, years later, Detective Michael Sellers had traced it to Carlton Gary's uncle Jim in Phenix City.

There was, however, one significant difference between the account Smith gave in his speech and what he and Sellers said on other occasions. Smith told the jury that the trail began when Sanderson had phoned the Columbus Police Department in April 1984 with 'a simple request: "Has anyone found my pistol that was stolen back in 1977?"' The claim that Sanderson had only made this call because he was responding to some mysterious, untraceable message was missing. There was, therefore, no talk of any 'phone call from God'. Smith's simpler version avoided an awkward problem, and left the jury with a story that was easier to believe.

Before the trial began, the court had agreed to provide the defence with a small office inside the Government Center, a place to store files and statements and, in those days before mobile telephones, make phone calls. The next morning, Siemon arrived at the room he had been given on the tenth floor to find that its lock had been removed, rendering it effectively useless. To store sensitive documents, he needed a place with security, Siemon told the judge, and to be deprived of it was yet another obstacle to his fighting the case successfully.

'I have provided you with a closet to keep your records in,' Followill said. The office, he added, would be revoked 'until you pay your phone bill. Now, I understand about your funds problem and all that, but if you recall, [we] stipulated that the telephone would be provided for local calls only, and the record shows that in excess of $100-worth of long-distance calls has been run up on that telephone. Mr Harvey has paid me for approximately half of it, and when you're able to pay me for the rest of it, I'll get a little more serious about trying to find you a room.'

Siemon had already fought ten capital trials and numerous appeals in far-flung parts of Georgia, but not for the first or last time in this case, he found it hard to believe his ears. 'Are you saying we forfeited our office in the courthouse because I owe approximately $50-worth of telephone calls?'

'Yes, sir,' Followill said.

'I'm in a situation where if I pay the phone bill right now, I won't have money to eat, I won't have any gasoline money to get back and forth to the courthouse,' Siemon said. 'I mean, your honour, I mean it's incredible to me that because I owe $54 in long-distance telephone bills, a bill that I acknowledge and a bill that I'm informing the court that I'll pay at the earliest possible time, that because of that I forfeited the office in the courthouse. If that's the court's ruling, of course, I can't argue with it.'

Followill remained adamant. 'The office is yours to use. The lock comes with the payment of the bill. All right, are we ready? Seat the jury.'

The first trial witnesses gave accounts of the murder of Florence Scheible, the almost blind eighty-nine-year-old woman who was the strangler's third victim. One of her neighbours told the court how she used to hobble about her yard on autumn mornings, enjoying the sunshine and raking leaves; she had seen her thus at eleven o'clock on 21 October 1977, probably less than three hours before she died. In stiff, dispassionate policeman's language, Ed Gibson, the patrolman who came to Mrs Scheible's home in answer to the emergency call from her son, related the horror of discovering her body: 'I went on inside and I went through the living room, back to my left where the bedroom was. And once I got in there, the bed was to the left and I could see that there was a person lying on the bed, and the person was covered up with the bed covers and so forth, and there was a pillow laying over the head of the body that was laying, and just to the right of it was a walker. So that would indicate to me it was an older person ...'

Later, at the mortuary, Detective Richard Smith had to use a pair of scissors to remove the cause of Mrs Scheible's death from her bruised and bloodied body – a knotted nylon stocking.

Joe Webber, Columbus's medical examiner, was a veteran pathologist. Originally from Dayton, Ohio, he had been practising in the city since 1958. He had testified in court in at least a hundred previous cases, and it had fallen to him to conduct the post-mortem examination of Mrs

Scheible, just as it had with the first two victims. As he gave his evidence in his even, Midwest accent, the court was absolutely silent.

'Beneath the scalp and skull there was a massive haemorrhage, typically caused by trauma, or a blow to that area. The examination of the neck region, after removal of the ligature, revealed the classic signs of strangulation … Further examination of the neck revealed a fracture of the hyoid bone. The hyoid bone is a bone involved in swallowing, it's the little bone that rides up and down as the swallowing cycle proceeds … there was a deep groove left in the neck, which exactly fit and was due to the tightened ligature around the neck.'

Webber concluded that the cause of death was anoxia, the absence of oxygen to the brain. But before she was strangled, Mrs Scheible had also suffered a blow to her head, from either a 'strong fist' or a heavy, flat instrument, such as an iron. Either way, it was so powerful that 'the first cervical vertebra and the second cervical vertebra were loose, and there was dislocation and fracture to the first vertebra'. The killer had struck her head so hard that he had broken her neck just below the point where it joined her skull. The evidence that she had been raped was equally gruesome. 'The vaginal area showed a massive laceration of the posterior portion, which is called the fourchette,' Webber said. 'A good deal of bleeding had occurred from this area. We retrieved secretions from the vaginal canal, and microscopic examination revealed a number of spermatozoa.' These lacerations were not clean-cut, as if by a knife, but were 'an irregular, ragged, pulling apart of the tissues, such as in overstretching or severe trauma'.

The brutality of Florence Scheible's murder was not a matter for doubt. But had Carlton Gary committed it? Smith's case depended on a right-hand thumbprint allegedly found and then lifted by tape from the frame of her bedroom door – what police officers call a 'latent' mark, because until they are dusted with a special powder or treated chemically, they are invisible. Sergeant Harold Harris, a CPD fingerprint officer, said he later identified ten 'points' – characteristics such as forks and ridge-ends in the lines of the latent's pattern – that matched features from the police ink-rolled prints taken from Carlton Gary. While the jury took a recess, Siemon argued that the FBI usually required at least twelve points of comparison to make a positive identification, and in his view, there were also differences:

'There's an obvious streak down the middle of the latent print that's not on the rolled print – it looks to me like it could be a scar ... I've seen plenty of latent prints myself, and that's an extremely poor-quality print.'

Siemon cited several legal precedents which he believed meant that the defence 'should be entitled to have an expert of our own to look at the prints and tell us first off whether they match'. Where scientific issues were in dispute, even in cases in which the defence had been denied public funding, the law contained a special requirement that money should be made available, he said. Followill disagreed. He could see nothing questionable about the print's quality. The jury could make up their minds perfectly well without hearing from any more experts.

In addition to the fingerprint, Smith presented two identification witnesses – women who said they had seen Gary near Mrs Scheible's home close to the time she died. The first was Doris Laufenberg, a widow who lived at the top of Wynn's Hill on Twelfth Street, three blocks from Mrs Scheible. At around midday on 21 October, she said she was unloading groceries from her car 'when I saw this man coming around the corner from Owsley Avenue. He was travelling at quite a fast pace, and he kept looking behind him.' The man was tall, black, in his early twenties, and sported an Afro hairstyle, a light beard and moustache, a black turtleneck sweater, a dark green suit and a black knitted cap, which was rolled up on his head. 'Everyone was pretty edgy back in those days,' Laufenberg said. 'We noticed things that we didn't ordinarily notice.' As the man passed, she got a good look at his face.

'Mrs Laufenberg,' said Smith, 'I ask you to look around the courtroom and I ask you whether or not you can identify anyone as being the individual whom you saw on the date at the time in question that you've testified to?'

'Yes, I can,' she replied. 'He's sitting right there at the table.'

'Right here?'

'Yes.'

'OK, let the record show, your honour, that she pointed out the defendant.'

Mrs Laufenberg said she heard about Florence Scheible's murder from the television news. At that time, however, she did not say anything to the police. It was only after the 'night of the terrors' four months later that she phoned them and mentioned the mysterious African-American. Six and a half years after that, in October 1984, Detective Michael Sellers came to see her and showed her an array of photographs. One of them, she told the court, depicted Carlton Gary, and she quickly picked it out.

Cross-examined by Siemon, Mrs Laufenberg agreed that by this time she had seen numerous pictures of Gary on television and in the newspapers. Five months had passed since his arrest by the time of her visit from Sellers, and Gary's photo had, she accepted, been published frequently. But she insisted that the man she had seen in 1977 was him, because of his 'very high forehead' and 'unusual nose'.

The next morning, 13 August, Smith called a second identification witness, Sue Nelson, a young military wife. Like Doris Laufenberg, in 1977 she had been living three blocks from Mrs Scheible, on Dimon Street. One evening early that September, just as night was falling, she had been walking with a friend in Lakebottom Park, a green and shady open space at the foot of Wynn's Hill. She had left her friend and was strolling towards her bicycle when she saw two black men. One of them was running towards her in jogging gear: 'I looked him straight in the eye, and he scared me very much, and I turned round and I saw my friend hadn't gotten to his car yet, and I ran across the park, yelling for my friend, "Please stop!" I asked him to take me home and please take the long way home because someone was following me.'

Her friend did not see the African-American, and she did not call the police. This had happened around Labour Day, right at the start of September, and weeks before the Scheible murder – when Carlton Gary, it may be recalled, was still wearing a plaster cast on his leg. But just two days before Mrs Scheible died, said Nelson, she saw the man again. This time she was sitting on her porch when he came jogging by, dressed as before in a tracksuit and cap. She 'backed up', keen to ensure he did not see her. After that, nearly nine years passed. But shortly before the trial, Nelson returned to Georgia after living overseas in Germany, and saw a photo of Gary in the *Atlanta Journal-Constitution*. 'I thought it was the same man,' she said. After watching a tape of the TV news, she was certain. 'I thought about it for a few days, and I thought it was time to call the District Attorney.'

Like Mrs Laufenberg, Nelson remembered the man's nose. It wasn't, she said, 'dark and flattened … he didn't have the typical black man's nose'. Cross-examining her, Siemon tried to find out more.

'Did the man have a beard or was he clean-shaven?'

'I looked him in the eye. I'm not certain.'

'You don't know whether he had a beard or whether he was clean-shaven?'

'He didn't have a full beard. He could have had a moustache. Like I said, I was looking him in the eye, just like I'm looking you in the eye.'

'Well, you looked at his nose, didn't you?'

'Yes. I saw this part of his face very distinctly.'

Like many Wynnton residents, Nelson had been interviewed by the police at the time of the murders and asked if she might have any relevant information. Back then, in 1977, she had failed to mention the man in the park. It was only several months later that she realised he might have been the killer, she said. But she had not told anyone, because by then she was no longer living in Columbus.

After her testimony, Siemon asked Followill to have it struck from the record, and to tell the jury to disregard it. Her identification was 'inherently unreliable', he argued. Followill refused. The jury could decide, and Siemon's motion was denied.

By the summer of 1986 there was a substantial body of scientific research that suggested that identification evidence might be very risky in a criminal trial unless it was handled carefully. Since that time, the amount of research on its unreliability has grown much larger. According to Professor Gary Wells, a psychologist at Iowa State University and one of America's leading experts in the field, in more than 80 per cent of cases where DNA tests have proven that persons jailed for rape or murder were victims of miscarriages of justice, mistaken identifications were originally used to convict them. In one case, a person who turned out to be innocent was wrongly identified by five separate witnesses. Psychologists' experiments have shown that the apparent confidence a witness displays in court is no guide at all to the reliability of his or her evidence, Wells told me. Often this confidence will increase dramatically as a result of 'positive feedback' from detectives who confirm an identification's accuracy. Half of all witnesses who identified the wrong person in controlled conditions said they were 'positive' or 'nearly positive' they had made the right choice.

I asked Wells – who for more than a decade has worked designing police training programmes and national US guidelines – to review the testimony given by Laufenberg and Nelson. 'These identifications are both basically worthless,' he said. The length of time that had elapsed, the basic difficulty that people have in recognising strangers, the poor lighting when Nelson saw the man in the park, and the fact that Gary's face had been widely shown by the news media made them even weaker than the identifications Wells had come across when defendants were later exonerated by DNA tests. Moreover, although Laufenberg had picked out Gary from among several photographs, they had been shown to her by a detective who knew he was the suspect, and who had an interest in getting him convicted – Michael Sellers. To stand any chance of being reliable, Wells said, line-ups should be 'double-blind' tests, where the police officer has no idea who the suspect is: 'The need for double-blind testing is particularly critical for photo line-ups. There are innumerable ways that an investigator can influence an eyewitness when administering a line-up' – not only verbal hints but cues such as smiling, frowning or leaning, which are 'particularly difficult for the tester to inhibit, and yet which affect the respondent'.

Already the trial was moving much more quickly than anyone had expected. Over the rest of that day, 13 August, Smith produced a series of witnesses who swiftly dealt with both of the other two murders with which Gary was charged, the killings of Martha Thurmond and Kathleen Woodruff.

Mrs Thurmond's son, William, told how he had seen her the day before she died, and had fitted her door with a new deadbolt lock that later failed to function. The pathologist, Dr Webber, disclosed that the attack on Mrs Thurmond was, if anything, still more violent than that endured by Mrs Scheible: 'There was bleeding from both ears ... [that] would usually indicate severe injury or fracture of the base of the skull, and this fracture usually requires a considerable amount of trauma or energy delivered to the head. It's often seen in head injuries associated with automobile impact, aircraft crashes and so forth.' The stocking around her neck had been pulled so tight that it had burnt her skin, leaving a hard, reddish-brown groove. The evidence suggested that her ordeal may have lasted for a considerable time. The heavy swelling to Mrs Thurmond's tongue indicated that 'several minutes, maybe half an hour' had elapsed between the blow that fractured her skull and her eventual asphyxiation.

As before, fingerprint officers from the CPD and the Georgia Crime Lab in Atlanta testified that an inked, rolled impression taken from Gary's right middle finger matched a latent left at the crime scene, this time on the frame of a window screen by Martha Thurmond's front door. (In Georgia, as in much of the southern portion of the United States, almost every window has a detachable, fine mesh screen, so that the glass can be opened in warm weather without letting insects in.) The Columbus print technician, David Rice, said he had listed nine points of identification, emphasising his testimony by showing the jury photographic enlargements of the latent and of the print from Gary's finger. In Columbus, there was no rule as to how many points were required to make a positive fingerprint identification, he said. It was more 'a matter of what the examiner feels comfortable [with] to base an opinion'.

The evidence from the scene of the killing of Kathleen Woodruff also came down to a fingerprint – the clearest of all the print identifications during Gary's trial. Bruce Sanborn, a former police evidence collector, testified that he went to Mrs Woodruff's house on Buena Vista Road after her servant had found her body at about one o'clock on 28 December 1977. Several cops were already there. From the room where she lay dead, 'one of the officers took me to the back bedroom, where he pointed out where they had found a latent fingerprint there on the window, and they said they felt very confident that it was a valid print in that area they had found it'.

In fact, the print was not on the window, but the aluminium frame of its screen – apparently the killer's point of entry. Sergeant Harris said that although the screen was still attached at the top, it had come away at the bottom, where there were two little holes, as if someone had pried open the latches that should have held it shut. Harris had dusted the screen with black powder, and found the latent on the frame's left side, about twelve inches up from the bottom. As with the other crime scene latents, his colleague George Keller had lifted it with tape and stuck it to the back of a white card, which he later signed and dated.

Harris said he also found another latent, of a palm, on the wooden sill inside. He admitted that the similarities between this latent and Gary's hand were weak: the latent was smudged, there were only seven identification points, and at first the Crime Lab experts in Atlanta had said that no comparison was possible. The latent from the screen, however, was unusually clear. When compared with Gary's right little finger, no fewer than sixteen points matched. The first time he made the comparison with the Woodruff latent, Harris said, it was with a set of Gary's prints that Detective Sellers had been sent from South Carolina, after Gary had absconded from prison. The second was with the ink-rolled prints made in Columbus after his arrest. 'All three were the same person,' Harris said.

The last of the murders from which the police claimed to have matched a crime scene latent with a print taken from Carlton Gary was the first of the stocking stranglings, the attack on Ferne Jackson. (Gary was not formally charged with this crime, but as with all the 'uncharged' stranglings, evidence about it was allowed at his trial.) Once again, the court heard harrowing details of the finding of Mrs Jackson's body and of the injuries inflicted on her. Dr Webber said that the deep, livid bruising seen on the wall of her vagina initially led him to believe 'that an implement, such as the handle of a large screwdriver, may have been forcibly rammed into this area'. Later, however, 'it became apparent that this was bruising of tissue that had not been subjected to sexual intercourse for a long period of time. The lining of the vagina in older women, fifty-nine years of age and older, tends to be quite delicate.' Ordinary rape would have been enough to cause these injuries. Mrs Jackson's perimetrium, the tissue supporting the vagina, uterus, fallopian tubes and ovaries, had bled profusely, Dr Webber added.

Sergeant Harris testified again, this time about a left palm print latent lifted from Mrs Jackson's dining-room door. On 11 October 1984 he had compared it with Gary's ink-rolled prints, and made 'no positive ID'. Nine months later – fourteen months after Gary's arrest – another prints expert, Charles A. Moss from the Georgia Bureau of Investigation, came down to Columbus from his base in Atlanta and looked at the samples again. He determined that they did match, with nine points of identification. Moss could not explain why he had been called in only after this long delay, and told the court that he was unaware when Gary was arrested.

Citing this difference of view between the two experts, Siemon yet again asked the judge for funding, to allow the defence to commission tests of its own: 'Why should they be able to bring in multiple experts to testify about these things when we can't even have one? It's just not fair.'

'I overrule your objection again,' Followill said.

Until now, the trial had had its share of the gruesome. Confronted with the crime scene photos, some of the jurors had visibly grimaced. But there had been little drama. On the morning of Friday, 15 August, all that changed, with the testimony of Gertrude B. Miller, who had survived the strangler's first attack. If the case had a tipping point, this was it.

Aged seventy-three, Gertrude Miller shuffled stiffly towards the witness stand, helped by a deputy as she climbed its steps. 'Mrs Miller, I call your attention to the early morning hours of 11 September 1977. Do you remember that?' Smith asked. 'Would you tell the jury what happened shortly after midnight the morning of that day?'

Her reply began hesitantly, but it rapidly swelled until her words seemed to gush in a torrential stream of consciousness: 'When I came to enough to know what had happened, he had come in and had gotten the door open, came in through the window, because then you didn't lock windows or anything else ... I didn't even hear him because I was keeping children for mothers who were working and because their dads were overseas in the army, and so, they left, and I was in bed by 11.30. And then I was – had gone sound asleep. And it was then that I realised that someone was right there on top of me, and I said, "Who are you?" And he began – he had gone over, and I hadn't noticed, I hadn't even awakened enough for that, to my dresser, and had pulled out stockings, and he had three pair of them, and he had intended to wrap them round my throat.'

Siemon objected: at the time, Mrs Miller could not have known her assailant's intentions. 'You might just tell Mrs Miller to tell what she knows and what she remembers, not what she figures must have happened,' Followill told Smith.

Then she went on: 'He came over to the bed, this individual did, and he turned me over on my back, and he pulled my stockings down – the clothes that I had on, my night clothes, and I said, "Don't do that." And he put me – he raped me on front and back, both, and he – and I kept fussing at him, and he hit me on the head with a board, that the day before I had thrown out of the yard … later on, when he was raping me, he had turned the light on so he could see better. He started to rape me with the light on. The light at the head of the bed. I had a small light there so that I could see if I woke up and anything had happened.'

'Was this person black or white?' asked Smith.

'He was black,' said Mrs Miller. She could not give his height because she had been lying on her bed while he leaned over her. His age, she said, was eighteen to twenty, 'and his hair was not too long'. He wasn't very dark: 'He had a light colour of brown and the black' – a reasonable description of Gary's own complexion.

'All right,' said Smith. 'Mrs Miller, I ask you to look around the courtroom and state whether you recognise the person who attacked you that night?'

More than a hundred pairs of eyes followed her as she pointed at Carlton Gary. 'That guy right there.'

'This man?'

'Yes.'

'Let the record show that she pointed out the defendant.'

Years later, Mrs Miller went on, she had been watching television with her family when the screen was filled by an image of Gary being led into the police station after his arrest. She said that in the years following her attack the police had come to her home on numerous occasions, had taken her to the station and shown her hundreds, even thousands, of pictures of possible suspects. But on each and every occasion she had told them, 'No, uh-uh, that wasn't him.' This time, from the moment she saw Gary on TV, it was different. 'I said, "That's the man, that's the man, that's the man … that is him, that is him, that is him." ' She had seen him clearly both from the front and in profile in the light of her bedside lamp as he raped her, and she had no doubt in her mind. 'He's all dressed up today, and got longer hair; got a moustache, which he didn't have then.' But he was the same man.

Bud Siemon did what he could to repair the damage to his client's case in his cross-examination. The day before Mrs Miller gave her testimony, Siemon had been told for the first time that about six weeks after she was attacked, the police had had her hypnotised in the hope of eliciting more information. A tape had been made of her hypnosis session, and although its poor quality meant that a third of it was indecipherable, it appeared to reveal significant differences between her story in 1977 and what she was saying in 1986. Siemon put these discrepancies to Mrs Miller. For example, in a statement she made to the police a few months before the trial, she said that the man who raped her had tied her hands with her stockings. In October 1977, the hypnotist, a Dr Wiggins, had asked if she had ever been tied or strangled, and her reply to both of these questions was negative. Did she recall saying this? Mrs Miller seemed to avoid an answer: 'Well, he used his hands on my throat, see, and when you take two hands like this [here she raised her hands to her neck to demonstrate], a throat is not that big.'

Her descriptions of her assailant in 1977 also differed from Gary's appearance. 'Do you remember telling [the hypnotist] that the person had eyebrows that came all the way around?' Siemon asked. 'Do you recall telling anybody that the individual who attacked you had dimples in his cheek?'

'The thing is, he was dressed like they did then, and now he's dressed like they do now,' Mrs Miller said. ('They', of course, referred to African-Americans.) Siemon asked Gary to stand and remove his glasses. His eyebrows, it was plain, were no more extensive than normal. Nor did he have dimples, or, as Mrs Miller had claimed in 1977, a cleft in his chin.

Siemon had exposed some inconsistencies in Mrs Miller's recollection of the details. But after such a long lapse of years, a juror might well have thought this inevitable, and on her main allegations, that she recognised Gary as the man who had raped her and, as a headline in the next day's *Ledger* put it, 'left her for dead', her testimony looked unshaken. It would not be for many years that its true value would become apparent.

# EIGHT

# *A Benchmark for Justice*

The security of civil life, which is essential to the value and the enjoyment of every blessing it contains, and the interruption of which is followed by universal misery and confusion, is protected chiefly by the dread of punishment. The misfortune of an individual (for such may the sufferings, or even the death, of an innocent person be called) ... cannot be placed in competition with this object.

WILLIAM PALEY, *Principles of Moral and Political Philosophy* (1785)

Carlton Gary's trial appeared to act on him as a tonic. By the end of the first week, the gaunt and shuffling figure in prison overalls, who had sat with his head on the defence attorneys' table during his competency trial in the spring, was but a memory. In his place was what looked like the Gary of old: alert, seemingly confident, and above all well-groomed, dressed each day in a suit, silk tie and steam-pressed shirt. As he entered court each morning, he flashed a smile and a thumbs-up sign to his family. 'I'll be the first to admit I've seen a marked improvement,' Bud Siemon told Judge Followill, pointing out that for the time being his client was no longer subject to what amounted to sensory deprivation. During recesses in the evidence, Gary conversed animatedly with his lawyer, his mother Carolyn, his sister Miriam and her son Anthony, who were all in almost constant attendance. The restaurant food that they were able to bring him for lunch was helping him to put on weight. Siemon, however, looked haunted. During the proceedings he stood erect in a pale linen suit, his eyes blazing beneath his mop of strawberry-blond hair, addressing the judge and jury with controlled passion. More than anyone, he knew how poor his client's chances were.

Having presented the devastating testimony of Gertrude Miller, District Attorney Smith turned his attention to burglaries at the homes of two of Columbus's oldest and richest families, the Swifts and the Illges. There was no physical evidence to connect Gary with these crimes, and no witnesses had seen him commit them. Nor was there any proof that the man responsible was a murderous sexual predator, and unlike the stocking strangler, this intruder – if he was one man – had taken portable valuables such as jewellery and money.

The Illges burglary took place on 10–11 February 1978, the 'night of the terrors', when the strangler attacked Ruth Schwob, who pressed a panic button and survived, and then, almost immediately afterwards, his penultimate murder victim, Mildred Borom. By the time of the trial Mrs Schwob had died from cancer, and it was left to her neighbour, Fred Burdette, to describe how he had fixed a simple alarm between her house and his, and heard its buzzer at 5.45 a.m. The testimony of Burdette and others allows us to recreate some of what happened. First, as the strangler began to tighten the ligature around Ruth Schwob's neck, she groped for the panic button. Hearing the alarm, Burdette called her number; the killer must still have been in her bedroom when the phone beside her bed started ringing. Perhaps he realised that whoever was on the other end of the line was likely to call the police. As the patrol cars raced to Schwob's residence, he ran.

The fear of capture gave him no time to effect his usual silent and delicate entry when he got to Mildred Borom's home two blocks away. He simply ripped a screen from the downstairs window to the left of the front door and smashed the glass behind it. The noise may well have woken her; perhaps she was already on her feet, terrified and ready to defend herself, when she came face to face with the strangler. In any event, the officers who entered the house later that day found signs of a fierce struggle, and their photographs depict a scene of disarray. One of Mrs Borom's bedside lamps lay broken on the hallway floor. Her rugs, normally set out neatly, were in crumpled heaps. Inside her bedroom, another lamp, her bedding and several books had been hurled to the floor. The little cupboard on which the lamp had stood was open, its contents strewn across the carpet. Mildred Borom's body appeared to have been dragged from her bedroom into the front guest room, where she lay on her back, with her clothing, a nightgown and housecoat, pulled up over her face. Her purse, which had been turned upside down, was beside her. It still contained cash and credit cards.

Dr Webber, the medical examiner, also found evidence that Mrs Borom had fought her attacker. As well as the now-familiar signs of strangulation, caused in her case by a cord from a Venetian blind, he described 'a broken fingernail of the left thumb, possibly indicating or consistent with a struggle, a hand-to-hand struggle with her assailant'. There were 'severe bruising and scratches all over the body'. Her resistance, however, had been in vain. Like the other victims, Mrs Borom was raped before she died, and her vagina contained 'abundant spermatozoa'.

There were no identifiable fingerprints at Mrs Borom's house, and nothing else, given the state of scientific knowledge in 1978, that might have helped the police to identify her killer. The body of the strangler's final victim, Janet Cofer, murdered on the night of 19–20 April 1978, was a different matter.

Mrs Cofer's son Mike testified that he had been staying at her bungalow on Steam Mill Road most nights during the working week because he had taken a job at a building supply company near Columbus, and it was too far to commute every day from his own house in Dallas, Georgia, a few miles north-east of Atlanta. That Wednesday, however, he went home to get more clothes, and next morning, he went straight into work from Dallas. There he was told of his mother's death by telephone. The police asked him to come to her house to see if he noticed anything unusual. He thought, he said, that a coffee canister she kept on the kitchen counter was not in its usual place. Its contents, it transpired, had been scattered across her garden – apparently in an effort to confuse tracker dogs. Otherwise, 'everything looked completely normal'. Mrs Cofer, it seemed, had been given no chance to struggle. The last person, other than the killer, to see her alive was her friend Vivian Tyler. On the eve of her death they sat next to each other in their usual pew at choir practice at Wynnton Methodist Church. Afterwards, they walked to their cars. 'We discussed the fact that she had given tests to her kindergarten children that day, and she had to go home and grade them,' Mrs Tyler said. 'Then we said goodbye and got in our separate cars and went to our homes.' It was no later than 9.20 p.m.

Like Ferne Jackson, the first of the strangler's victims eight months earlier, Janet Cofer was known as a very reliable woman, and the alarm was raised when she failed to turn up for work at Dimon Elementary School next morning. The principal, Jack W. Hendrix, first tried to phone her, and then, when she failed to answer, drove the four or five blocks to her house. Even as he knocked on her door, he could see that the screen on one of her front windows was damaged.

Inside the house, the jury heard, was a scene that had become depressingly familiar. Former patrolman Bruce Sanborn told the court that Mrs Cofer was lying on one of twin single beds, naked except for an undergarment that had been pulled up, with a pillow over her face. Her pyjama bottoms were balled up in a corner of the room, where the killer appeared to have thrown them. A stocking was tied round her neck. As with the earlier killings, Joe Webber described her injuries. Like the other victims, Cofer displayed 'the usual findings of throttling', although in her case the hyoid bone was still intact, while her cricoid cartilage, the protective ring around the bottom of the larynx, had been crushed. There was bruising at the top of her vagina, though no sign of spermatozoa. However, there was one potentially significant difference between Janet Cofer's body and those of the other victims. On her left breast, Dr Webber told the court, were 'tooth marks'.

As soon as he mentioned this, Smith interrupted him. 'You say there appeared to be tooth marks on the left breast. Could they be positively identified without a saliva sampling being taken?'

'No,' Webber began. 'We consulted some odontology experts and they …'

Siemon rose to object, saying that under the rules of evidence, Webber could not testify as to what other experts had said. But a little later, Siemon came back to the subject. He could see the bite marks clearly on the police photograph of Mrs Cofer's body, and just as he had so many times before, he asked Judge Followill to grant him funds so that an expert could compare the photo with Carlton Gary's teeth.

Smith objected. 'We don't have any comparisons to make.'

'I don't believe that's a critical piece of evidence in the case,' Followill added.

Gamely, Siemon kept up the pressure. 'Well, it could be, your honour. If the teeth marks don't match Carlton Gary, it could be extremely critical.' If the teeth marks did match Gary, the state would have used them against him, Siemon said. 'If they don't match him, then it could clear him. It's an extremely critical piece of evidence because we know that whoever murdered that woman, left those teeth marks.'

Gary, Smith said, had had some dental work done between the murder and his arrest for the stranglings, 'and therefore any comparison, we felt like, would have been invalid'.

'Maybe that's what they feel like, your honour, but we don't necessarily feel like that,' Siemon retorted. 'Unless we have an expert to tell us that the comparison wouldn't do any good, we're entitled to have funds to get this kind of expert that could potentially prove that this man wasn't the murderer. It's incredible to me that we've got this evidence here that can potentially clear a person on a capital charge, and to save a couple of thousand dollars we aren't going to be able to get somebody qualified to compare it to this man and see if he's the one that did it.'

Followill's response was characteristically laconic. 'Motion denied. Seat the jury.'

However, the story of the tooth marks on Janet Cofer's breast wasn't over. There would come a day when Siemon's words would come to seem prescient.

Towards the end of the same afternoon – 18 August 1986 – the court began to hear from one of the trial's most important witnesses: Detective Sergeant Michael Sellers, the man who had traced Henry Sanderson's stolen Ruger automatic to Jim Gary in Phenix City and thence to his nephew Carlton. Without Sellers, there would have been no trial at all. Now, as he began to give his evidence, it became clear how central he was not merely to Carlton Gary's becoming a suspect, but to his possible conviction. Sellers would be the jury's only source for some of the most crucial testimony of all – Gary's response to being accused of the murders, and what the prosecution claimed were some highly damaging admissions.

Eight months before the trial, on 16 December 1985, Judge Followill had conducted a special, sequestered 'Jackson-Denno'* hearing, closed to the public and media, to determine whether Gary's alleged confessions ought to be admissible as evidence. On that occasion, not only Sellers, but Ricky Boren and Charlie Rowe, the other two detectives who participated in Gary's interrogation, testified about the circumstances in which his statements had been produced. According to Sellers, by the time the cops loaded Gary into their car and began the drive back to Columbus at 8 p.m. on 3 May 1984 after arresting him in Albany, they were extremely tired, having been up without sleep 'for just days'. Running on adrenalin, Rowe told the suspect of his right to be questioned in the presence of his lawyer, according to the rules established by the Supreme Court in the case of *Miranda vs Arizona*. But Gary, Sellers said, had declined, saying the 'last thing he needed' was a lawyer. Once they were on the road, they began to ask him about the stranglings.

It had been raining heavily, and they did not get back to Columbus until 9.40 p.m. According to Sellers, Gary was wearing handcuffs and leg irons, but chatted happily to the police. He carried on doing so later that night, after he had been photographed and given his fingerprints and footprints, as well as samples of hair and saliva. Sellers claimed that they talked in an interrogation room until half past midnight on 4 May, went on a drive around Wynnton, then resumed their conversation back in the police station, talking continuously until 3.30 a.m. 'We had suggested that we were tired and were ready to go home, but he continued to want to talk,' Sellers said. 'We finally just cut it off.' Throughout this period, Gary was given only some water and crackers; nothing resembling a meal. But when the police finally insisted they were just too tired to continue, 'He was totally against it. He wanted us to stay right on so he could talk.' His general demeanour was 'excited, happy, caught up in what he was talking about'.

At the Jackson-Denno hearing, Sellers confirmed that the CPD often used tape machines to record interviews with suspects, but not in this case, because the machines were 'not available'. Nor did anyone take any kind of

* Named for the 1964 Supreme Court case that set the precedent requiring hearings of this type.

notes while the interrogation proceeded. Fighting off sleep, Sellers only began to create a written record of what Gary had said after getting home from the police station. Starting at 4.30 in the morning, he said, he sat down at his kitchen table and began to scribble notes of everything he could remember. 'To the best of my human ability', the notes were an 'accurate reflection' of Gary's words. Sellers said he used the notes to produce a typed report several days later, though he couldn't be sure how many. Gary had not signed it, nor confirmed in any other way that he considered it to be accurate.

However, even this typed statement by Sellers was not the record of Gary's interviews presented to the jury as a legal exhibit at his trial. The only document to be used in court was a different, closely-typed twelve-page memorandum that was neither signed nor dated. This document, Sellers explained at the Jackson-Denno hearing, was even further removed from the events of 3–4 May. It was a 'conglomerate', composed some time later still, when he sat down with Ricky Boren and Charlie Rowe and combined his record of the first interrogation session with a separate note made by Boren, also from memory, of a further six hours of interviews that took place the following night, 4–5 May.

Bruce Harvey, who was still working on the case at the time of the Jackson-Denno hearing, had cross-examined Sellers on behalf of the defence. 'So, you had advised him of his rights and apparently he was willing to give you statements, but you had not thought it wise to write down what he said ... I'm asking you as a fourteen-year veteran whether ... you did not feel it wise to write down what he said, have him initial it and have him sign it?'

'We didn't do that, no sir,' Sellers replied.

'Did you ever go over with him what your notes reflected was your conversation and asking if it accurately reflected the conversation?' Harvey asked. Once again, Sellers replied in the negative.

The testimony from Rowe and Boren at the Jackson-Denno hearing only deepened the murk. Sellers had claimed that no tape recorder had been available, but Rowe volunteered that he had been in possession of one during the interrogations, but that it 'was not turned on'. Strangely enough, Gary's girlfriend, Robin Odom, who was arrested with him in Albany and driven back to Columbus in a separate police car, *was* taped while she was being questioned. (She said nothing of any consequence, and was soon released.) Rowe confirmed that he had been involved in writing the twelve-page 'conglomerate' statement, but could not recall when it was composed. It was not, he admitted, a 'word-for-word description' of the many hours' conversation Gary had had with the detectives. Nevertheless, he insisted it was a 'true and correct representation of the events surrounding the arrest and interrogation of Carlton Gary'.

When it came to his turn, Boren added that throughout their interviews Gary had been 'very nice, very cordial; within, say, an hour to two hours we were on a first-name basis, no hostilities, no anything'. He confirmed Sellers's claim that there were no contemporaneous notes or tapes.

At Gary's trial the following August, Smith decided not to call Boren and Rowe to give evidence. This was a tactical decision, he explained to the jury, and they ought not to wonder why the two detectives had not testified – it was his prerogative as a prosecutor. Of course, it meant that possible discrepancies which might have arisen had the court heard from all three detectives would be avoided. As Sellers stepped up to the witness stand, Boren and Rowe sat on a bench outside, silent.

Sellers testified that it didn't take long for Gary to begin to open up. Once he started, 'he didn't shut up, and we weren't going to stop him … He was just continually bubbling with information and just rattling it off faster than you could almost comprehend it. He amazed me at things that he could tell about the Wynnton area and places that he could tell from memory.' This time, Sellers did not assert that tape recorders had been unavailable, as he had at the Jackson-Denno hearing. Instead, he claimed that despite Gary's volubility, he did not want to be taped, and 'we didn't push it'. But like Jerome Livas six and a half years earlier, the mentally retarded odd-job man who was wrongly suspected of the first two murders, Gary began to tell the police things about the stranglings that 'only the killer could have known'.

According to Sellers, Gary's admissions followed a pattern. Each time he was asked about a particular crime he would admit to being present, but insist that someone else had been the main perpetrator. In the car back from Albany, for example, he supposedly recalled the burglary at Callye

East's house and the theft of Henry Sanderson's gun. But Gary, Sellers said, denied entering the house himself: 'He said that he had gone there with a friend of his named Theophilis Joe Preston, and that they had gone over there in a truck. And he said that Theophilis Joe had actually burglarised the house and he had stayed outside.' According to Sellers, Gary told the cops that Preston later gave him the gun.

By the time the police were done with fingerprinting and photographing Gary, and taking samples of his hair and saliva, it was 11.25 in the evening, Sellers said, and he and Boren recommenced their interrogation. They had already told Gary during the journey from Albany that his prints had been found at some of the houses where women had been murdered. Now, he testified, Gary told them: 'I'm ready to tell you the truth. I did go into some of the houses where you have my fingerprints.' The cops had not specified which homes they were referring to, but according to Sellers, 'The first thing he said was that he had gone into a house on Buena Vista Road, and he believed the lady's name was Mrs Woodruff.'

'All right,' Bill Smith asked. 'Now, did he say that first, or did one of you use it to him?'

'No, sir, he used her name, and he called her by name, Mrs Woodruff.'

'Neither of you had ever mentioned her name in his presence?'

'That's right.'

'Go ahead,' Smith told Sellers.

'And then after that he said that he had also gone into a house where there was an old lady in the front yard on a walker. And we started to ask him about it and to elaborate about it, and then he started to shake, and he started to rock back and forth in the chair, and he said, "I was not alone."

'And we told him, we said, "What are you talking about, what do you mean?" And it took him about five minutes, and then he blurted out that there was somebody else that was with him. And we asked him who, can you tell us who, and he just looked like it was a big labour for him to finally push this name out and he finally said, he really seemed that he was tormented with it, rocking back and forth, but finally he said that "A friend of mine went in," and we said, "What's his name?" and he said Malvin Alamichael Crittenden. And I was kind of stunned at the name, you know, I thought he might come up with somebody like Joe Smith or John Doe or something like this, but he came out with this guy's name.'

Sellers added that neither he nor Boren had ever heard of Malvin Alamichael Crittenden until Gary mentioned him. But just as Gary had blamed Theophilis Joe Preston for stealing Sanderson's gun, he went on to accuse Crittenden of being the stocking strangler: 'He said, "I did the burglaries, and Michael killed the old ladies."'

According to Sellers, Gary told the police that at the time of the stranglings he had been living with his childhood playmate Earnestine Flowers, and riding around in her Datsun 280Z. On the day that Florence Scheible, the lady with the walker, was murdered, Gary supposedly said, he and Crittenden had been driving in the car together through Wynnton, when they saw her raking leaves in her yard. Then, according to Sellers's account, the telling details proliferated:

'When they came up from behind the house they saw that there was an apartment below it. And they came up and he [Gary] said they slipped in the side door, that the door was open, that the screen door was shut, but it was not locked.' Talking to Sellers and Boren seven and a half years after Mrs Scheible's murder, Gary had allegedly said that he entered Mrs Schieble's home, stole $1,200 that he found in cash in an envelope, and noticed that she had a 'real nice TV'. Leaving Crittenden inside, he went outside to get the car in order to drive it to the back of the house so that he and Crittenden could load the television into the boot. According to Sellers, Gary had even remembered coming across a woman with groceries, who gave him directions to Mrs Scheible's back driveway – a reference, apparently, to the evidence given by Doris Laufenberg, who had identified Gary in court the previous week.

'He was telling us that he drove around to the back in the car, that he got out and he opened up the hatchback, and I asked him why and he said they were going to put the TV in it,' Sellers said. 'And when he opened it up he looked up, thinking that Michael was going to be coming down the hill with the TV, and he saw Michael jogging down the hill toward him without the TV. And he said that Michael got in the car and they drove off and he never said anything about the old lady being hurt.'

'Now, had you ever been to Mrs Scheible's apartment on Dimon Street prior to this night?' Smith asked Sellers.

'No, sir.'

'Did you know what he was describing or the accuracy of what he was describing at the time?'

'No, sir. I had seen some old files [stating that] the door that you went in was on the side, but as far as the way the house was constructed and the apartment in the back, no.' In fact, Gary's alleged description was very accurate indeed. According to Sellers, he went on to tell the cops that he had gone into other houses that he could also describe, 'but he could show us better, because he couldn't tell us where they were at, but he could show us'.

So it was that at 12.30 in the morning on 4 May 1984 Sellers and Boren collected their colleague Charlie Rowe, who had been having a snack, got back in their car with Gary and headed out to Wynnton. One by one, they visited the crime scenes: often, although it was dark, Gary was able to give them directions, Sellers said, while coming out with detail after detail. Some were architectural, others related to the murders: all were later corroborated. At one house, Sellers said that Gary recalled: 'Michael [Crittenden] told me that he had trouble with the woman, he said she was big and strong, but everything came out right' – the home of Mildred Borom, who had seemingly fought so fiercely. At another (Ruth Schwob's), Gary allegedly said: 'This is the house where Michael almost got caught by an alarm going off.' At the home of Kathleen Woodruff in Buena Vista Road, Gary 'pointed, and he said, "Right there, there's the screen porch," and told us that this is the house where he and Michael had gone in through the back. And he pointed at it, right there, said, "There's a window on the right back side," and he said, "The first time I saw the lady she was sitting in a chair in the living room, or the den area, and the next time that I saw her, Michael had her by the neck or around the neck, and he was pulling her." And he said that "I remember something about a scarf or a pillow used on the woman." '

They returned to the Police Department at around 2.45 a.m. and talked for another forty-five minutes. It was only then, said Sellers, that he went home to begin writing his kitchen table notes.

Taken at face value, this was devastating testimony. No one had ever suggested that two intruders had been involved in the stocking stranglings, so Gary's apparent admission that he had entered the victims' homes, coupled with his 'accurate' recall of their layout, implied that he must have been the killer. He might have tried to lay the blame on Malvin Crittenden, but as the jury was about to discover, there was no evidence that Crittenden had been involved at all.

Crittenden's own testimony was brief. A diminutive man with a goatee, in a chalk-striped suit, he spoke almost inaudibly, describing spells working for a railroad company and tending the bar at the Columbus Country Club, the venerable all-white institution on the edge of Wynnton. Asked by Smith about Gary, he said he had known him on and off all his life. They had played together as children, and then in 1978, while Gary was living with his girlfriend Tula and their baby in Dawson Estates, they started 'running together', making out-of-town trips to Albany and Macon, Georgia; to Florida and South Carolina; even to Syracuse, New York, where Gary first lived with Tula.

'Mr Crittenden, did you ever commit any house burglaries with the defendant during 1978?' Smith asked.

'No, sir.'

'Did you ever commit a rape or a murder during the course of a burglary in 1977 or 1978 with or without the defendant?'

'No, sir.'

Smith went through the names of the strangler's victims, asking if Crittenden had broken into any of their homes, raped or killed them. He said that he had not.

It was left to Bud Siemon to delve a little deeper into the real nature of Crittenden's relationship with Gary. They had, Crittenden said, stayed friends, but when they stopped 'running together' in October 1978, 'I wanted to stop what we were doing.'

'And what you were doing was robberies, right?' said Siemon.

'Yes, sir. He was robbing; I was driving.'

'Y'all were robbing like fast-food places?'

'Fast-food places.'

Crittenden said that after pulling out of the robbery business, he continued to see Gary regularly in Columbus's African-American nightclubs for at least eight months after the last of the stranglings. He had not, he added, ever been prosecuted for his part in the robberies, but neither had he been offered any kind of immunity. By 1986 he was earning a living shining soldiers' boots at Fort Benning.

Sometimes criminal trials are like a seesaw, their outcome in doubt till the last, as first the prosecution, then the defence, appears to gain the upper hand in the courtroom duel. In Carlton Gary's case, the repeated decisions by Judges Land and Followill to refuse all funding to the defence were keeping the seesaw firmly weighted on the side of the state. As the court turned to consider the testimony of forensic scientists, what Siemon saw as the trial's inherent unfairness once again became manifest.

Next up after Sellers's testimony about Gary's confession was the serology evidence, which the prosecution claimed would demonstrate that the semen found at the crime scenes was compatible with Carton Gary's bodily fluid. Siemon asked the judge to send the jury out while he made yet another impassioned appeal.

'They are talking about proteins and enzymes and the interactions of these different genetic markers,' he said, 'and the different types of testing. And it's just an extremely complex subject. I mean, they are going to call their witnesses, and I am going to make an attempt to cross-examine them, but I am not nearly qualified, without some kind of expert assistance I am not nearly qualified to cross-examine these people.' If Gary were convicted he would be entitled to appeal, Siemon warned, and then, 'It's going to be an issue that this court has passed up the opportunity to have a full and fair hearing.'

'Well, you can cross-examine,' Followill said. 'I at this point would deny the motion for funds.'

The state's main expert was a forensic serologist named John C. Wegel, who worked at the Georgia Bureau of Investigation Crime Lab in Atlanta. He testified first about a sample of semen recovered from Florence Scheible's bed sheet. His tests indicated that it came from 'a person who is a non-secretor or possibly a weak secretor, type O'. The killer was secreting only minute quantities of the blood group O chemical marker, an antigen known as 'H-reactive substance', into his other bodily fluids. Seminal fluid had also been found on Ferne Jackson's bed sheet, Wegel went on. This too appeared to come from a non-secretor, as did the semen recovered on swabs from Mildred Borom's vagina.

After his arrest, the police had taken samples of Gary's saliva. Tests on it demonstrated that along with 80 per cent of the population, he was a regular, strong secretor, also from blood group O, producing much higher levels of the H-reactive substance in his own bodily fluids. Despite this apparent discrepancy, Wegel insisted that Gary could not be eliminated. His wiggle room came from his professed uncertainty as to whether the victims had been raped by a non- or a weak secretor. If the killer were truly a non-secretor, then Gary would have been ruled out. But if he was merely a weak secretor, then, Wegel argued, he could have produced the semen found at the murders.

Bud Siemon was no scientist. Nevertheless, Wegel still had to explain how it was that Gary seemed to be secreting much higher levels of the H-reactive substance into his saliva when he was arrested in 1984 than the killer had in his semen at the time of the murders. When Siemon pressed him on this point, Wegel's normally clear and articulate syntax disintegrated. His answer was that Gary might have been secreting higher levels into his saliva than his semen. The killer might have been 'weak in the seminal fluid'. It was also possible, he went on, that the level of antigen secreted by an individual might vary over time: 'Periodically, if you would test someone over a given amount of time, you will see that the titre [concentration] can in fact fluctuate.'

Wegel had reached the limits of Siemon's scientific knowledge. His explanations went unchallenged.

Later, two hair and fibre experts testified about their attempts to compare pubic hairs found at the crime scenes or on the bodies of the victims with samples plucked from Gary. The first, Benny Blankenship from the GBI, said he was sure that hairs from six of the murders came from the same person, and that they were 'Negroid'. But he could not conclude that they were Gary's, because 'they did not reveal sufficient similarities to me to conclude that they could have had a common origin'. Yet this, Blankenship insisted, did not exclude Gary, either. The hairs 'did not reveal sufficient dissimilarities to say they don't have a common origin'.

Myron T. Scholberg, a consultant who had formerly worked at the FBI, expressed the same opinion: 'Because of the slight differences involved in the microscopic characteristics, I could reach no conclusion whether or not these hairs could have originated from this particular individual. However, the differences in my opinion were not sufficient to eliminate this individual as a possible source of the hairs.' As Wegel had said of Gary's semen, Scholberg thought his hair might also have changed over time. Byron Dawson, the GBI Atlanta laboratory boss who back in 1984 had told Gary's former investigator Don Snow that he was sure the hairs didn't match, and who later told me that they were a different colour, was not called to testify.

A pattern had emerged. Neither the serology nor the hair evidence could confirm that Gary was the strangler. It did not provide a positive match. But neither, according to the state's experts, did it 'exclude' him, or help his claim that he was innocent.

William Smith was nothing if not a shrewd courtroom strategist. If he was aware that the forensic science was his case's weakest area, he must also have known that any doubts it might have provoked within the minds of the jurors would soon be overwhelmed by the testimony he planned to adduce next. In his opening statement, Smith had spoken of various 'uncharged crimes' that he believed had been committed by Carlton Gary. As the trial resumed on 20 August, his witnesses revealed the details of these crimes.

The first was Robert Westervelt, a former cop turned security guard. The principal elements of the scene he described had already been related numerous times during the trial: a room in disarray; the body of a brutalised, sexually assaulted, elderly female. This time, however, there was a difference. Westervelt was not speaking about an old lady's home in Georgia, but what he had seen more than seven years before the first stocking strangling, in a long-stay hotel room in Albany, in upstate New York.

Westervelt said that at eight o'clock on the morning of 14 April 1970 he was sent to room 604 of the Wellington, a large, run-down building not far from the state capitol. Two of his colleagues were already there. 'Laying on the floor, maybe four or five foot out from the bed, was an elderly woman later identified as eighty-five-year-old Nellie Farmer. She was lying basically face down on the floor. She was covered partially. She had a slip and some other clothing over the rear portion of her body, and something else up around her neck covering her on the floor. The room basically in general was ransacked. It was all messed up, stuff laying all over the place, and on the foot of the bed was a large steamer trunk, open, some of the stuff was pulled out of that and thrown around.'

Westervelt displayed some of the photos he had taken that morning. One of them conveyed the nature of the violence inflicted on Nellie Farmer very vividly. It needed no elaboration, but Westervelt explained: 'This is another photograph that I took, showing some bloodstains and faeces stains on the rectum, on the rear of the woman laying on the floor.' Another image showed bloodstains on her legs. Leon Feldman, the pathologist who examined her, would later find injuries to both her rectum and vagina, together with spermatozoa.

One of Westervelt's colleagues dusted the room for latent fingerprints. As well as several smudges, he found one unusually clear one on the side of the trunk by the bottom of Nellie Farmer's bed, and before he 'lifted' it onto a signed and dated card with special adhesive tape, Westervelt photographed it *in situ*. The next witness to testify, the Atlanta print technician Charles Moss, had compared the print with Carlton Gary's. It was, he said, an unusually clear match, with no fewer than sixteen points of identification.

Under the precedent established by Georgia law in the case of the Atlanta serial killer Wayne Williams, in order to adduce evidence of an 'uncharged crime', the prosecution had to show that it revealed a clear behaviourial pattern on the part of the defendant. There were some obvious similarities between the murders of Nellie Farmer and the victims in Columbus: like them, she was an elderly white woman who lived alone, and she too was raped and strangled – albeit not with a ligature, Dr Feldman said, but manually. It was, however, when Smith came to deal with Gary's statements to the Albany police that the murder there assumed its deepest relevance. Questioned in Columbus in 1984, Gary had allegedly admitted a peripheral involvement in burgling the victims' homes, but blamed someone else for the murders. Fourteen years earlier, interrogated at the Albany County Jail about the killing of Nellie Farmer by Detective Anthony Sidoti, he had apparently done much the same thing.

Sidoti testified that he questioned Gary – who at that time, was using the name 'Carl Michaels' – on 21 July 1970. On this occasion, Michaels/Carlton Gary showed no reluctance about having his words recorded contemporaneously. Sidoti said that one of his colleagues sat in the room, typing all that was said. Afterwards, Gary read through the transcript and signed it.

Speaking in his heavy Yankee accent, Sidoti read Gary's 1970 statement to the court. It said that he had been playing the bass in a local band, The Intruders, performing at a downtown club called the Down Beat. There he had befriended a man he knew as 'Pop', whose real first name was John. 'Now, because I was hard pressed for money, this man, Pop, or John, and I started to pull a few jobs, mostly television sets and radio and stuff out of cars,' the statement said. 'My job was to keep chickie, or watch out for the police or anyone who could identify us.'

John, the statement continued, had a propensity for violence. Around midnight one evening, Gary met John again at the Down Beat, and they agreed to 'hit a few places'. On a side street at the back of the Wellington Hotel, they climbed a fire escape onto a parapet from which it was just possible to reach a sloping roof. Then, Gary's statement said, 'I boosted John up onto the slanted roof and I stayed there … I seen him slide open this window and slip inside. John was gone all of ten minutes when he came back to the window and told me to come up, but he just knew I couldn't make it from where I stood near the fire escape. Then he told me to come around the front way.'

Gary's statement said that he went back to the street and walked through the Wellington's front door, where he found John by the elevator. Together they went up to the sixth floor, John leading the way. They went into Ms Farmer's darkened apartment, and John went into the bedroom and looked through drawers, holding a flashlight. Then, 'I seen John with the flashlight go over towards the door, and I seen the beam hit a trunk. I saw John pick up this head of a human being and throw it to one side. It was then that I knew that there was a human being lying on the floor. John told me to give him a hand, as the trunk was heavy … I stayed away from the body and reached down and helped John pick up the trunk and we put it on the bed. John forced a lock on the trunk while it was on the bed. We searched the trunk for money.'

Gary's statement said that he was scared, so he went back down to the street and waited for John, who joined him twenty minutes later. 'As we started down Howard [Street] I noticed the front of John's pants. They were wet, and had some blood and some stuff that stunk. And I thought it was shit … I asked John what had happened and he started to talk crazy like, and said, "Man, I did a job on that bitch." '

Sidoti told the court that he had shown Gary some photographs, from which he had identified his friend as an African-American named John Lee Mitchell.

Mitchell himself was the next prosecution witness. Six feet four inches tall, he wore a dark brushed-cotton suit and a pale silk shirt with cufflinks and a tie. His features furrowed with old acne scars, he described himself as a businessman. In 1970 he had had a job as a maintenance man, but now 'I own real estate, I own convenience marts, and I own a heating and plumbing firm.' He said that he had known Gary slightly from the Down Beat, and had shared a few drinks with him. But he denied having anything to do with burglary or the killing of Nellie Farmer. Gary's testimony had, he claimed, caused him to spend a year in jail awaiting trial for her murder, a crime he did not commit, until a jury acquitted him.

'If you did not commit this crime, do you have any idea why the defendant would make a statement to the police, and would testify in court, as a witness for the prosecution, that you in fact committed this crime, and that he simply acted as a lookout for you?' asked Bill Smith.

'He wanted to shift the weight,' said Mitchell. Gary had pleaded guilty to robbing Nellie Farmer, though not, of course, to killing her; sentenced to ten years, he was paroled after just five. Mitchell admitted that he had attacked Gary while they were both in the Albany jail awaiting trial. Now, however, he said he bore him 'no personal animosity'.

Afterwards, while the jury waited in their room, Siemon asked Smith for further information about the Farmer murder. If the only evidence against John Mitchell was Carlton Gary's statement, it seemed baffling that he had ever been charged. After all, Gary had been the original suspect, because of the discovery of his fingerprint. 'In no state in the union is the uncorroborated testimony of a co-defendant sufficient to put a person on trial and to convict him,' Siemon said. The law recognised that the risk of a guilty person trying to save his own skin through a malicious allegation was simply too great.

Smith disclosed that he had a copy of the whole Albany case file, which Siemon had never seen, and the court recessed while Judge Followill examined it. Smith was right, the judge announced: the file contained no other evidence against Mitchell, and nothing that might have undermined Smith's claim that Gary, rather than Mitchell, had murdered Nellie Farmer. Siemon asked to read the file for himself, but Followill refused. His assertions would have to be taken on trust.

The Farmer murder was not the only 'uncharged crime' of sexual violence that Smith suggested Gary had committed in upstate New York. Next on the stand was Jean Frost, a slim, bespectacled white woman of sixty-four from Syracuse, New York. She told the court that on the night of 2 January 1977, her fifty-fifth birthday, an intruder had ransacked her apartment and attacked her. He stuffed her nightgown down her throat when she began to scream, then strangled her to the point where she lost consciousness. When she awoke, her bedsheets were soaked with blood and she was still bleeding from her vagina. (There was no evidence of spermatozoa, and it was not clear whether she had technically been raped.) Later she would need surgery in order to repair her injuries. Among the items stolen that night was a Kelbert watch that she had left on her dining table. Frost could not identify her attacker. She could only say he was male. Having come to, she called the police, who found her bedroom window open, and a line of footprints leading across the newly fallen snow towards a cemetery.

The crucial evidence came from a Syracuse police Sergeant, Daniel Grinnals. He told the court that he had arrested Carlton Gary on 4 January 1977, two days after the attack on Jean Frost, when he was caught by a bank teller trying to convert some stolen coins into paper money. Arrested with him was an African-American from Syracuse named Dudley Harris. Grinnals said that in the police interrogation room he asked Gary to turn out his pockets. They contained two watches – one of them the Kelbert stolen from Jean Frost.

The evidence linking Gary with the attack on Frost was weak, and he was charged only with possessing stolen property and jailed for a year. But when he was questioned by the Syracuse cops, here too he admitted a peripheral involvement, but put the principal blame on someone else. Moreover, Frost was attacked less than ten months before the first Columbus strangling.

Gary's statement said that on the night of 2 January 1977 he went to the movies to see *King Kong* with Dudley Harris and two women. 'We dropped the women off and Dudley told me to come ride with him, so I did.' Having driven up a back road through the cemetery, they parked near Jean Frost's apartment building. 'Dudley told me to keep an eye on the car while he went into the apartment to cop some stuff. He told me to make noise, then hide if anyone came. He left and walked towards the apartments. I hid behind a gravestone so that I could see the road. About fifteen or twenty minutes later Dudley came back. He was carrying something small in his hands. He said he got some chump change and that there was nothing else worth taking. We then walked back down to the car and drove off.'

Smith went on to call further witnesses from Syracuse, who revealed that Gary had escaped that August from the local Onandaga County correctional facility. That was why he was wearing a cast and limping when he first showed up in Columbus: he had broken his leg jumping down from a high wall after sawing through the bars of his cell.

There wasn't much more of substance in Bill Smith's case for the prosecution. A series of policemen testified about Gary's arrest in Gaffney, South Carolina, in February 1979, after a botched attempt to rob a Po' Folks restaurant there. At first he had tried to blame even this crime on someone else – none other than his Columbus associate Malvin Alamichael Crittenden. This time the police did not believe him. Having run his fingerprints through the FBI's National Identification System, they swiftly learnt his real name and his criminal record. Gary, they realised, was wanted for some similar restaurant robberies in Greenville, the work of an unknown criminal who had been dubbed 'the steakhouse bandit'.

Confronted with this allegation, Gary told the truth, and agreed to 'clear the books' of the unsolved Greenville stick-ups. A few weeks later, as we have seen, the Columbus detective Richard Smith visited him in jail, where he readily admitted yet more robberies in Columbus. Strangely enough, although Gary *had* committed many of them with the help of Malvin Crittenden, once he decided to come clean about his own role he did not mention Crittenden again. Gary had been armed with a .357 Magnum, but in none of these robberies had anyone been physically injured.

Bill Smith closed his case by calling some witnesses who told the court a little about Gary's life, including his girlfriend from Gainesville, Florida, Sheila Preston Dean. As she left the witness stand, she beamed a big smile at Gary, promising in a stage whisper to 'See you later.' Gary grinned right back.

In all, Smith had produced 139 witnesses in just over a fortnight. Bud Siemon called only five. The first was Ronnie Jones, the one-time director of the stranglings task force. By now the Chief of Police in Americus, about fifty miles to the south, he described the intense operation that the police and other agencies had organised in their futile attempts to prevent further murders, and the consequent difficulty that an unknown black man would have had in moving through Wynnton at night: 'If [an] individual was out of the ordinary, anything that didn't belong in the neighbourhood, if it was an odd hour – he was stopped and questioned. We wanted to know what they was doing in that area, because of what was going on there.' After midnight the police were stopping anyone they encountered, he said, and his officers did not neglect the side streets and alleys: 'I wouldn't really say you had front roads and back roads of Wynnton, you know. The streets are well marked. The neighbourhood is an elite-type neighbourhood, well kept-up. If there was any alleys or anything, we went in, whether it was on foot or whether it was on [sic] patrol car.'

Siemon's most important witness was the ponderous, shambling figure of Jerome Livas, resident, in August 1986, at the Terrell County Correctional Institute, where he was serving his sentence for the murder of his former girlfriend Beatrice Brier. As Siemon discovered when he asked him to look at some legal documents, Livas was still illiterate. He told the court that he remembered being interrogated in October 1977 by three Columbus detectives, and signing his statement page by page as it was typed in front of him.

'Did you rape and murder and strangle Ferne Jackson?' Siemon asked.

'They say I did.'

'Did you do it?'

'The statement I gave.'

'But did you do it?'

'No, sir.'

'Did you break into her house with a screwdriver?'

'They say I had a screwdriver, but I didn't break in.'

'How did you know that her house was broken into with a screwdriver?'

'Well, they took me there and said a screwdriver had been placed there.'

'Did you rip her gown off?'

'They say I did.'

'How would you know that she had a gown ripped off her?'

'They said she had one on.'

Siemon went through all the details in Livas's confession: he said that every one of them had been suggested by the police. Of course, suspects who make admissions often make such claims. In this case, however, there was proof that Livas was telling the truth, in the shape of the stranglings committed after his arrest, to say nothing of his jailhouse interview with the journalist Carl Cannon, in which he claimed he had murdered two US Presidents and kidnapped the Lindbergh baby. His other confession – to killing Beatrice Brier – was equally false, Livas insisted: 'I was scared and upset and I didn't know what was going on, you know, and somebody else did it, but, now, they say I did it, they looked for me for it. And I asked them, "Why are you looking for me for it? I didn't kill nobody."' There was no other evidence that he committed this crime. Convicted and sentenced to life, the mentally retarded Livas was released on parole after fifteen years in prison in December 1992. As of September 2006, he has not been accused of any further crimes.

Siemon also called Ronald Lynn, one of the detectives who questioned Livas. Unrepentant, he denied suggesting anything to him, insisting that all the details in Livas's confessions had come from Livas's memory. Some of them, such as the fact that the strangler used a screwdriver to enter the home of Ferne Jackson, had not even been known to the police at the time. In Lynn's opinion, the wrong man was on trial.

The trial's last witness was former detective Richard Smith, who testified about his visit to Carlton Gary in South Carolina in March 1979. He said that once Gary had agreed to clear the CPD's books, he had spoken 'freely' about the Columbus robberies, and insisted on answering Smith's questions, although this was against his own attorney's advice. Once again, in distinct contrast to his statement about the stranglings, Gary's confession to robberies in Columbus was recorded contemporaneously, dated and signed.

With the testimony finished, it was time for first Siemon, then Smith, to make their closing summations. Siemon began by discussing Livas's statement, suggesting that the cops had arrested him because they 'decided that he was a good suspect', and that having done so, they 'moulded the evidence to fit him'. Had the killings not continued, he said, Livas would have stood trial for his life. It was 'an extremely difficult proposition to stand up in front of a jury of good citizens and convince them that the police, the people they rely on for their safety ... should be capable of doing this kind of thing'. But the alternatives were stark: 'Either that Jerome Livas committed these crimes, or that the police in Columbus, Georgia, were trying to frame this man for those crimes.'

Michael Sellers's testimony about taking Gary for a drive and his directing the police to the victims' homes sounded all too familiar, Siemon said; like another version of the tale of Livas's confession. Moreover, Sellers had changed his story as to why the interview was not taped: at the Jackson-Denno hearing in December, he had said that no tape machine had been available, but now he had claimed that Gary had refused to let the cops turn it on. 'None of the so-called insider information that was allegedly told to the police, that is supposedly contained in those statements, proves that Carlton Gary committed any crime. Because we know that the Columbus Police Department will tell people what they need to know when they take a statement from them.'

Gary, Siemon said, was 'not a Boy Scout ... there's no question that the man commits crimes. But what I'm trying to tell you, and what I think the evidence shows, is that the state hasn't proved that's he's committed any murders.' The identification evidence was worthless. The two witnesses who had said they could identify him near the scenes of murders – Doris Laufenberg and Sue Nelson – were recalling the events of seven years earlier when they first contacted the police, by which time they had seen Gary's photograph in the media. Nelson had testified that she saw him jogging six weeks before Florence Scheible's murder – when his leg was in a cast. Gertrude Miller, his first alleged victim, had not come forward for more than a year after his arrest. Meanwhile, at the very time of the murders, Gary had been appearing on TV: 'Does it make any sense to think that somebody who was committing those crimes, and knew that he had left survivors around, would get on television to model clothes, to take the chance that somebody's watching their TV, and they look and they say, "That's the person that attacked me, that's the person that raped me, that's the person that tried to strangle me?"'

Siemon argued that the case 'basically boils down to fingerprints'. Although the defence had been unable to call its own experts, there were, said Siemon, grounds for doubt – especially the fourteen months that it had taken to identify the palm print from the window used by the killer to enter the home of Mrs Woodruff. Could the jury be sure that the prints had not been 'planted'? 'All you know about the fingerprints is that Columbus police officers have come in and told you that they lifted his fingerprints from the scenes of those crimes.' The CPD had apparently tried to frame Jerome Livas: 'Can you find, beyond a reasonable doubt, that the same Police Department ... didn't try to frame Carlton Gary?'

The police knew what cars Gary had been driving at the time of the murders, Siemon went on, but none had ever been logged in or near Wynnton, despite the huge security operation and police computer data-base. 'How did he get into this neighbourhood and commit these crimes? How did he escape the dragnet of the GBI, the State Patrol, the Patrol Division of the Columbus Police Department, the Columbus Task Force, the stake-outs, the officers in unmarked cars patrolling the back roads?' As for the scientific evidence, the police had been 'trying to explain the hair evidence' ever since Gary's arrest, relying on Benny Blankenship's claim that even though the crime scene hairs did not match Carlton Gary's, this was not enough to exclude him. There was, of course, no defence expert who might have rebutted this claim, nor one who might have refuted the state's assertions about the serology.

'I think if you look at the evidence in this case objectively, ladies and gentlemen, you're going to see that from the very beginning the state has been trying to prove Carlton guilty,' Siemon concluded. The judge, he said, would shortly tell the jury that the case was circumstantial: that meant in law that in order to convict, the jury must be satisfied that there were no other reasonable hypotheses. 'This case doesn't exclude any hypothesis, ladies and gentlemen. All they've got on Carlton Gary is fingerprints, maybe. I would suggest to you that in a circumstantial evidence case, that the evidence is insufficient to convict Carlton Gary.'

When Siemon finished, the court recessed for lunch before Smith began his own summation at one o'clock. Opening the case, he had been factual, clinical, almost detached. His closing appeal, however, was visceral, bravura, and at times heavily sarcastic. In many places it rested on little more than the excellent character of his witnesses – so different, he was at pains to emphasise, from that of the defendant.

Siemon's argument, he said, had come down to one point: 'That the defendant was framed by the Columbus Police Department.' Sellers, the print identification specialists, the women who had said they recognised Carlton Gary – all, 'delicately phrasing it', had committed perjury. 'Well, members of the jury,' Smith said, fixing them with a level gaze, 'if there was a frame-up in this case, I submit to you, if there's a frame in this case, they did a mighty poor job.' Had the cops really been trying to frame Gary, the evidence would have been far stronger: his fingerprints would have been all over every murder scene, and there would have been a 'drawer full' of eye-witness evidence putting him near the victims' homes. This was not, however, a circumstantial case. There was a very important piece of 'direct evidence' – Gary's own confession.

Granted, Smith went on, it had not been recorded. But nowhere did the law require that such a statement should be. 'And whose fault is it that you don't have a tape recording or contemporaneous notes? The defendant, the defendant.' It was true that he had not called Boren or Rowe to testify, Smith said. However, 'I have to make such tactical decisions during the course of the trial. Defence counsel made tactical decisions during the course of the trial … if you want to hold that against someone, hold it against me.' If the jury wished, let them disbelieve Detective Sellers. But if so, 'What you'll be saying to him is we give you police officers a badge and a gun and we pay you half what you're worth, and we expect you to go out

206

and put yourself on the line for us. But when you come into court, and you swear a solemn oath to tell the truth, we're not sure whether we're going to believe you or not. The decision is yours. It's that clear. Either he's telling the truth or he's committing perjury. By your verdict you so find.'

Intensifying the emotional impact, Smith deployed the crime scene photographs. Gary, he said, pointing to a grisly photo of the deceased Florence Scheible, 'turned this lady, at age eighty-nine, after a life to age eighty-nine, into *this*'. Gary's fingerprint had been found in her house, and he confessed to the cops that he burgled her. Doris Laufenberg had seen Gary as she unloaded her groceries. 'Does she look like the kind of lady who would come into court and swear under oath and tell anything but the truth?' asked Smith. 'The important thing is when she swore that solemn oath, she sat there in this witness stand, she looked at him, and she pointed him out, and she said, "That's the man." ' Was Mrs Laufenberg not the kind of person the jurors would happily invite to their homes for a chat over coffee? Did they really think that a woman like that could lie? Could not the same be said of Sue Nelson, who had said she had seen Gary looking so menacing as he jogged through the park?

Gertrude Miller, the survivor of the strangler's first attack, was equally virtuous, and hence, Smith implied, credible. The defence had suggested that her memory might not be reliable. 'Members of the jury, let me express it to you a different way. Do you think Mrs Miller could ever forget? Instead of thinking, "Can she remember?", ask yourselves, "Can she ever forget?" Don't you know, the evidence was that she looked at hundreds, she looked at thousands of pictures and she never identified one, until she saw this man on television. It wasn't her fault that that's the first time she saw him.

'Don't you know that every night Mrs Miller has laid her head on her pillow and closed her eyes to go to sleep, that she has seen the face of this man? It's burned into her memory, it's forged into her memory, she can't put it out of her mind if she wants to.' She had been raised before the 'sexual revolution', and for an old lady of her generation, to come to court in order to talk about 'the most intimate things' was a deeply traumatic event: 'I'm confident you'll reward her courage for doing what must have been an awfully courageous act, for her or anyone else, but especially for her.'

Smith went through the other murders in a similar way, his syntax and grammar lapsing at times into the atavistic rhythms of the preachers he had heard so often at the First Baptist Church of Columbus. Gary, he said, holding up the photograph of Martha Thurmond's body, 'turned this lovely lady into *this* with a stocking'. The jury had seen Mrs Thurmond's son, who had stayed at her home with his family until the night that she was killed. 'Don't you know the guilt and remorse he must feel? "If I had just stayed one more night with Mother this would not have happened." Blames himself. Feel it.'

As the jury took a short break, Smith brought in the charts he had used in his opening speech, which purported to reveal the similarities between the three murders of which Gary had been formally accused and the various 'uncharged crimes' in Georgia and New York. This time he made just a few theatrical comments. 'Literally you could hold that photograph up,' he said of the murder of Nellie Farmer in Albany, 'and you could hold a photograph up, members of the jury, of any one of the seven stocking strangling victims, and I ask you to do this when you're back in the jury room, you couldn't tell which one she was. It was identical. Counsel says no similarities. It was identical. Obviously the method of attack was by strangulation – manual strangulation, but still strangulation.' Jean Frost in Syracuse might have been mistaken for Columbus's Gertrude Miller: 'Weren't they so much alike on the stand? Didn't you feel like saying, "I've heard this before?" Like Mrs Gertrude Miller, Jean Frost lived by the Grace of God, and that alone.'

Overwhelmed by the rising tide of Bill Smith's rhetoric, hard fact sank to the bottom. No matter that there wasn't a shred of evidence to connect the theft of Henry Sanderson's pistol with the stocking stranglings. Such difficulties were being swept away: 'No similarity? Forced entry. There was no rape, there was no murder or attempted murder … But it was in the Wynnton area, three blocks, you remember, three houses from the next one, the Scheible case, that occurred two weeks later to the day. Is it logical that the one who did the East case did the Scheible case?'

Finally, Smith said, there was the damning pattern of Gary's statements to the police, starting with the day he was accused of murdering Nellie Farmer in 1970: 'He said, "All right," he said it in four pages, but he said, "All right, you've got me, I'll admit, I was there, but I just acted as a lookout." And he told the name of a friend and you saw that man come in here.' One by one, he went through Gary's reactions to being questioned about the attack on Jean Frost, about being caught for robbery in Gaffney, South Carolina, and about the stranglings themselves, repeating the same form of words: 'All right, you've got me, I'll admit, I was there, but I just acted as a lookout.'

For a few minutes, Smith turned to the case made by the defence. There might, he allowed, have been 'some over-zealousness' in regard to Jerome Livas, 'but the important thing is that he wasn't charged. The system almost failed, but it worked.' He mentioned Detective Richard Smith's meeting with Gary in jail in Greenville, South Carolina: Smith, he said, was 'obviously a good detective ... and it's just unfortunate, members of the jury, that he didn't come back and have [Gary's] fingerprints compared with the stocking strangler's latent prints on file in the Columbus Police Department'.

Smith concluded by stating that it was true that some of the evidence was circumstantial. But that didn't mean it was weak: the evidence against a four-year-old with crumbs all over his face standing next to an empty cookie jar would be circumstantial too. But Carlton Gary hadn't been caught with crumbs: 'In this case, he's been caught with the blood on his hands.' Smith sat down, glowing with sweat. It had been a virtuoso performance.

After a short tutorial on the law from Judge Followill, the jury began to deliberate at 4.20 p.m. They had been lucky. Told when they were chosen that they might be away from their homes for three months, the trial was over after barely a sixth of that time. Each night they had been taken to eat at the best restaurants the city had to offer, among them, the *Ledger* reported, the Rankin Deli, Ryan's Steak House and Prichett's Fish Camp, running up a tab to the city, when added to their hotel bill, of $59,000. 'They tried pretty hard to make it tolerable, and they gave us things like movie cassettes,' Eleanor Childers told me when I visited her at her home in Griffin in 2003.

'For me, the trial had no defining moment of drama,' said Ginny Mobely, a young office-worker at the time she was a member of the jury, now married with children, in Griffin in 2003. 'It was just the sheer weight of evidence, piling up day after day, with almost nothing to refute it.' 'Afterwards, you tend to block out the unpleasant memories,' her friend and fellow juror Eleanor Childers told me. 'But I remember most the victims, and those terrible pictures.' None of the jurors had much doubt in this first, guilt phase of the trial. 'That Carlton Gary, he had an arrogant look about him,' juror David Glanton told me at his Pentecostal Church. 'He wouldn't look at the jury. The testimony that persuaded me was the fingerprints, and what he said to the police; his alibi – "I was there, but I didn't do it." I remember the lady who survived his attack. The defence tried to confuse her; said she was old and couldn't remember. But that was the horrific thing – that she was so old. Overall, the evidence was overwhelming.'

Exactly an hour after they retired to consider their verdict, a member of the jury knocked on the door of their deliberations room to indicate that they had reached a decision. Before they filed back into court and took their seats, Followill warned the courtroom that he would not tolerate any outbursts. Gary and his sister Miriam were staring at each other, the *Ledger* reported. Silently she mouthed the words, 'I love you.' He seemed to know what was coming: 'Sitting down and turning round in one smooth motion, he held out his right hand with those sculpted, expressive fingers, flipped out his thumb and pointed it to the ground.' Then, according to the formula required by Georgia law, the court clerk read aloud the verdicts on each of the nine counts with which Gary had been charged. 'We the jury find the defendant guilty of the murder of Florence Gerche Scheible, Count One, indictment 48,573; guilty of the rape of Florence Gerche Scheible; guilty of the burglary of Florence Gerche Scheible,' he began. The jury had reached the same unanimous decision on each of the other counts, which related to the murders, rapes and burglaries of Martha Thurmond and Kathleen Woodruff.

A photograph taken at the moment that the first verdicts were pronounced was published in the newspapers next day. It shows a close-up, side view of Gary, who holds his right hand against his face, and Bud Siemon; both look goggle-eyed, dazed. The tears began to roll down Miriam's cheeks, the paper said, 'into a neck adorned with a string of pearls'. Each of the jurors was 'polled' individually, asked to stand and confirm that the clerk had read the correct verdicts. Then, said the *Ledger*, Judge Followill told the deputies to take the prisoner away. 'Gary calmly picked up the notebooks under his chair, stood up tall and looked again at his sister. "I'm all right," he said softly, his hands working the air, his feet not missing a step. "You wait. I'm on. The next time. Don't worry." Then he was gone.'

Carlton Gary stood convicted as the Columbus stocking strangler, but the question of punishment remained to be settled. The following morning, 27 August, the same cast was back in court for the trial's sentencing phase, when the jury would have to decide whether he should spend the rest of his natural life in prison, or be executed. Before the jurors were brought back into court, Siemon made yet another request for funds. The only way he could prevent his client from facing death in the electric chair was to present evidence about his life that would somehow mitigate the severity of his crimes, he told Followill. 'The testimony has been crystal clear that Carlton Gary's life has been one of travelling round the country. In order to tell the life story of this person, it would be required ... that we be given just the basic funds to go out and travel.' His appeal takes up three pages of the court transcript. The judge's response requires less than a line: 'Motion is denied.'

Georgia's role in the recent history of the American death penalty is central. In *Furman vs Georgia*, the state produced the case that persuaded the US Supreme Court to halt all executions in 1972, on the grounds that the application of death sentences had become capricious and arbitrary, and hence a violation of the Eighth Amendment's prohibition on cruel and unusual punishment. Four years later, with *Gregg vs Georgia*, the court effectively reversed itself, and judicial killing was re-legitimised. In the interim, the Georgia State Assembly had enacted a new capital punishment statute, an attempt to codify the circumstances in which a convict might be sentenced to death, and so to eliminate the capriciousness that the court had objected to in *Furman*. In the penalty phase of a trial, the new law said, juries would have to find that there had been one or more 'aggravating factors' that made the crime still worse than an 'ordinary' first-degree murder, such as extreme cruelty, or a murder committed in pursuit of other crimes, including rape or burglary. The jury would also have to decide whether these aggravating factors outweighed any possible mitigation advanced by the defence.

In this phase of the trial, it fell to Smith to make his summation first. As with his speech at the end of the guilt phase, he did not spend long on legal technicalities, but appealed instead to the jurors' emotions. He began by saying that although they were not from Columbus, they should think of themselves as 'the conscience of the community'. Others would look to their decision 'as a statement of how our state deals with individuals who commit particularly horrible crimes'. It seemed clear, he went on, that the aggravating circumstances that the law required were present: Carlton Gary had raped and burgled his victims. In arguing that he deserved to die, Smith focused on three main factors.

The first was Gary's personality. This was not a case of a young or inexperienced defendant, for whom there might still be some hope of redemption, but of a mature and intelligent 'career criminal'. Even in the course of committing a crime where defence counsel had argued that no one was injured, the Po' Folks robbery in Gaffney, Gary had put a gun to the head of a teenage girl. 'Can you imagine what it did to her?' Gary had spent much of his adult life in prison, Smith said, and the jurors should create an imaginary ledger in their minds, in order to record 'how much misery this man has wreaked in the lives of other individuals'. There was some evidence that Gary's early life had been unstable. However, if the jury decided that this was enough to mitigate his crimes, that would be 'an absolute insult to the hundreds and thousands of other people who have been through similar, if not more difficult, circumstances', but who had emerged nonetheless as 'stronger people, productive citizens, contributing citizens to society'. To allow Gary to live would be to allow the risks he posed, even if serving life in prison, to persist.

Secondly, Smith turned to the horror of Gary's crimes. A society could be judged by the way it treated its children and older people, its defenceless members: 'Let's be judged by this in this case.' Gary's victims had been raped before they were strangled, 'so they knew what was happening to them before they died … They were already in fear. And for that instant, whether it's thirty seconds before this man strangled her or whether it's two minutes or five minutes, fifteen minutes, whatever it was: it was an eternity.'

The third factor, he said, was the 'overwhelming proof' of Gary's guilt. He did not dwell on this. By reaching their previous verdict so quickly, he said, the jury appeared to share this view.

Sometimes, Smith said, laying the foundations for his speech's climax, defence counsel asked juries to consider the purpose of punishment. 'I submit to you that the mark of a civilised society is that the primary purpose of punishment, no matter what else we might want to accomplish, is retribution.' Allowing the punishment to fit the crime was a 'thousand-year-old axiom' that 'separates civilisation from savagery, that separates civilisation from barbarism'. Perhaps the jury shrank from the responsibility of sending a man to his death. But if they did send Gary to the electric chair, who would have been responsible? Was it 'the officers who tracked down the gun through their excellent police work'? Or the brave SWAT team who had arrested Gary in Albany? 'How about the three detectives that he confessed to, are they responsible for his death sentence?' Was it the judge, or the prosecuting lawyers? The jury could no doubt guess which way his argument was heading, Smith said. 'I don't want to diminish the importance of your act and the soul-searching nature of it.' But the fact was, 'Carlton Gary is responsible for it. He imposed the death sentence on himself, when after burglarising the home of Mrs Scheible, he strangled the life out of her with one of her stockings.'

Perhaps Bud Siemon intended to invoke the Bible, and the Ten Commandments' instruction 'Thou shalt not kill,' Smith said. Maybe he planned to quote the Sermon on the Mount: 'Blessed are the merciful.' If so, the jury must not be swayed. 'How much mercy did this man show an eighty-nine-year-old blind woman who used a walker to get around? How much mercy, at least in this life, is he entitled to?' If there was a crime or series of crimes that the Georgia law of capital punishment had been written for, 'I submit to you that this is it'.

Thus far, dramatic as it sounded, Smith's address had mainly consisted of some well-worn tropes. The prosecutors who delivered summations in the penalty phases of earlier capital trials in Columbus, such as those of Jerome Bowden and William Anthony Brooks, also argued that the defendants had effectively sentenced themselves to death by their actions; had shown no mercy to their victims; might well kill again, even in prison; and needed to be condemned as a mark of the collective revulsion that society felt for their crimes.

Then, however, as he brought his speech to a conclusion, Smith departed from the familiar script, and cited a document of intense, totemic power – Abraham Lincoln's Address at the Dedication of the Gettysburg National Cemetery in November 1863, the *ur*-text of American democracy, its exceptionalist global mission, and of national reconciliation after the Civil War. He can have expected that many of the jurors would have known it by heart, and as schoolchildren absorbed its message – America's 'dedication to the principle that all men are created equal', along with its promise to provide 'government of the people, by the people, for the people'.

That an official of a state of the former Confederacy should choose the Gettysburg Address, delivered by the Union's President after the bloodiest battle of the war, had additional implied meanings. At a subliminal, sub-conscious level, Smith seemed to be suggesting that the stranglings' impact far transcended the races of their perpetrator and victims; had nothing to do, in other words, with any Southern rape complex or racial hang-ups, and that these crimes would have been just as egregiously terrible had they been committed in Ohio or Vermont. He must have been aware that in the necessary myths of post-war reconciliation, the acts of remembrance that made possible the emergence of the United States as a great, ideologically motivated power, the Gettysburg Address had opened the way for the Civil War to be venerated as a wound that hurt both sides equally, as a national sacrifice that, in Lincoln's words, obliged the living 'to be dedicated here to the unfinished work which they who fought here have thus far so nobly advanced'. By citing Gettysburg, Smith was suggesting that the stranglings were likewise an outrage that had wounded the entire American nation, female and male, black and white, not just Southern white womanhood. As Muscogee County District Attorney, he could formally claim to represent only the state of Georgia, but by invoking this text he was making the claim that Carlton Gary's execution could be carried out in the name of the United States and its universal, civilising mission.

'In dedicating a cemetery at Gettysburg after the battle there, President

Lincoln gave an address,' Smith said. 'A part of that address comes to my mind at this time. It is that "The world will little note, nor long remember what we say here, but it can never forget what they did here." And let me take that and apply that analogy to you: the world will little note nor long remember what I say here or what Mr Siemon says here or even what the judge says in his charge. It'll be a dusty transcript only a very few years from now, but the world will not forget what you do here. You will set the benchmark, you will set the tone for justice in our state, in our county. And again, you notice I said justice, I didn't say vengeance or revenge … You don't see any family members sitting out here on the front row demanding vengeance, demanding their pound of flesh. All they want, all I ask you for on behalf of the state of Georgia, is justice.'

For the last time, the court recessed for lunch. Afterwards, Siemon's plea for his client's life seemed weak and lacklustre. Dutifully he worked through the areas where the state's evidence had appeared less than certain, especially the doubts over the hair and the serology. But as he tried to draw the threads of his argument together, he rambled, barely coherent, as if reeling from the force of Bill Smith's eloquence. 'I wish I knew the Bible well enough to give you chapter and verse on this,' he said, 'and I know that some of you have experience, much more experience than I do with the Bible. And if I misquote anything, if I've misquoted anything, I know that there are those of you on the jury who know what – who can – who know what words I've used wrong and who know what I've misquoted, and I will rely on you, those of you, to express what the true word is. But the passage in the Bible that I'm always reminded of when I'm doing this, when I'm at this stage of the trial or when I'm preparing for this stage of the trial or when I'm actually up here talking, is when Jesus was talking at the judgement day about how he was in prison, and he was sick and he was hungry and nothing was done for him, and the people that were listening said, "When were you going through all these things, when did we – when did we forsake you, when did we not give you this type of consideration?"'

He concluded his summation by saying that only the merciful deserved mercy, a point that didn't seem to have much relevance, given that none of the jurors had been convicted of heinous crimes. 'If we're confronted with someone who is not merciful and then we aren't merciful to them, well, then, how do we deserve that kind of mercy? And that's what I want to ask you for on behalf of Carlton Gary, is mercy. Thank you.'

This time, the jurors deliberated for more than three hours. Deciding whether Gary ought to be executed had not been easy, jury member David Glanton told me in 2003. 'I favour the death penalty, simply because if I read my Bible right, it's justifiable, that if you take someone's life, you forfeit your own life. I don't think life without parole would have been just, because it would have meant he was getting away with murder, really. We knew in our hearts he was guilty – I certainly did. But to put a man to death is still a hard thing, to come to the conclusion that he did it beyond a shadow of a doubt. You've got a man's life in your hands, and the evidence *was* all circumstantial.'

'You've no idea how hard it is to cast your vote for the death penalty,' Eleanor Childers said. 'None of us were saying, "Let's get him." Afterwards, I had the worst headache I've ever had. My whole body was in that head-ache.' 'Myself and several others were near to tears,' Ginny Mobely told me. 'We got back to Griffin late at night. I went to work the next day, but I couldn't stay more than hour. I was just too exhausted.'

Despite the jury's confidence in Gary's guilt, Eleanor Childers told me that he came quite close to avoiding the ultimate punishment. That required a unanimous jury, and until relatively late, one elderly African-American man, T.H. Askins, who had once worked as a gardener for Childers's husband, was still holding out for life imprisonment. Childers said: 'This guy, he just couldn't stand to do it – he'd told the judge when he was picked that he could vote for electrocution, but now he felt that he couldn't. He and I went over to the window together. He said to me: "What would Mr Reid have done?" Reid was my late husband. I said, "He'd vote for death."' After that, Childers said, Askins agreed to vote to execute Gary.

With the jury back in their usual seats, the clerk stood ready to read their verdicts in the penalty phase at 6.15 p.m. on 27 August. Some of the jurors looked as if they had been crying, Richard Hyatt wrote in the *Ledger*, while others held their hands to their lips. 'The offence of murder was committed while the defendant was engaged in the commission of another felony, to wit: rape,' the clerk began, speaking of the death of Florence Scheible. 'The offence of murder was committed while the defendant was engaged in the commission of a burglary ... We the jury recommend the death penalty.' The verdicts in respect of the murders of Kathleen Woodruff and Martha Thurmond were the same. After each juror had been polled individually, Followill told Gary to come forward for him to formally pass sentence. 'Surrounded by officers, Gary stood there,' wrote Hyatt, 'hand on either hip, his mouth chewing gum at an uneven clip.' Followill asked him if there was anything he wished to say. Gary opened his mouth as if to speak, then appeared to change his mind. Followill went on: 'Mr Gary, the jury has found you guilty in this case, with a recommendation of punishment to be inflicted as death by electrocution. Therefore it becomes mandatory on this court, as a matter of law, to impose sentence in this case.' Gary, Hyatt wrote, shifted from foot to foot as the judge told him he would 'be electrocuted no sooner than noon on 3 October and no later than noon on 10 October'. He thus became the ninth person sentenced to death in Columbus after the penalty was restored.

As the guards led him away from the courtroom, Gary managed a smile and a wave to his family. His sister Miriam was more emotional. Hyatt's article recorded: 'She had braced herself before the sentence was read, holding the hand of her son, Anthony White. "Don't cry, Mama, don't cry," her son said. As the death sentence was read, the muscles in her face tightened, her eyes shut tight and then opened again, red and watery, as her legs pumped up and down uncontrollably. Caught in the bottleneck of spectators leaving the courtroom, she pushed forward, gasping for air ..."Get out of my face," she snapped at an Atlanta reporter who sought her reaction as she and other family members squirmed into the elevator.'

Afterwards, Bill Smith held a news conference, praising his staff and the three detectives, Sellers, Boren and Rowe. 'If anybody deserved the death penalty, it was this man,' Smith said. He realised that, inevitably, there would be years of appeals. But he had no worries over future litigation: 'Only God knows what the Eleventh Circuit [US Court of Appeals] will do. If they say so, we just try them again. That doesn't scare us. Ten years from now, those who survive may be talking about an execution. But we're used to that.'

When the media reporters had gone, the three cops joined Smith, Pullen and Followill in the judge's chambers. The mood was celebratory, Sellers told me when we met in 2001. According to him, the judge asked: 'Anyone got a birthday or anything special coming up? We'll make that the execution date.' Later that evening, Gary Parker, the African-American defence attorney who had continued to visit Carlton Gary regularly since coming off the case, went to see his former client once again. It was Gary's last night in his dark, insanitary cell in the Columbus County Jail: the next day he would be moved to death row at the Jackson state prison. 'Carlton didn't want me to be downhearted. He wanted to crack jokes,' Parker told me. 'Part of it was he still didn't believe this was happening. He still wasn't taking it seriously. But he didn't want anyone to feel bad on his account, so I told him: "Carlton, my friend, you'd better be getting yourself a pair of rubber underpants."'

With the lawyer, Gary kept up a bluff façade. But later that night he wrote an anguished letter to his family. It thanked them for being there throughout his trial, and ended with a protestation of his innocence: 'Mom, Sis, I did not kill. This I swear.'

# NINE

## *To the Death House*

House catch on fire, ain't no water 'round
If your house catch on fire, and ain't no water 'round
Throw your trunk out the window, buildin' burn on down.

MA RAINEY, 'Southern Blues' (1923)

The gatehouse stood opposite a dusty truckstop, at the top of a long, sloping drive. To the right, along a narrow, winding road through woods and red-dirt fields, lay the little town of Jackson, Georgia; to the left, amid a tangle of restaurants and gas stations, were the exit ramps from I-75, the highway to Atlanta. As I slowed to a crawl and drove ahead, the razor wire atop the distant walls seemed to pulse and shimmer, like a desert mirage. A stone sign confirmed that this was the entrance to the Georgia Diagnostic and Classification Prison.

Inside the perimeter fence I found myself in a lush, incongruous parkland, with picnic tables, wandering ducks and peacocks, tended shrubs and a lake. Despite the season, it was still warm in Georgia. On either side of the driveway, trusted inmates from the 'general population', dressed in white polo shirts and slacks, were cutting the grass with rotary mowers, their heads bowed. Their guards were armed with rifles with telescopic sights. Half a mile from the public road I reached the parking lot, and as previously instructed, left everything I had with me in my car except my keys and passport, before yelling my name and the purpose of my visit to a guard in a high concrete tower. His records must have shown that I was expected: he said I could go in.

It was almost nine on the morning of Saturday, 7 November 1998, more than twelve years after Carlton Gary had been sentenced to death. He was somewhere inside the prison, still alive. It had taken me weeks of bureaucratic correspondence, including a letter from my local police chief in Oxford advising the Georgia authorities that I had no criminal record, to get permission to make the first of many visits. I joined a clump of other inmate visitors, lining up to have my hand marked with a stamp that glowed in ultraviolet light; before I left it would be checked to ensure that I had not changed places with a prisoner. Beyond a metal detector and a reinforced glass electronic door was a long, straight gallery that seemed to lead into the heart of the prison, decorated with photographs of the great outdoors: the cliffs of Yosemite, sunsets on empty coasts. The only sound was the jingle of the keys of the guard who accompanied us, a bulky middle-aged woman who panted a little as she walked.

At the far end was a flight of stairs, and at the top of these, another identity check. Behind another double set of electronic gates lay a big, airy room with foam chairs and vending machines, where inmates who did not face execution were already embracing their loved ones. I told a guard who I had come to see. After a short wait I was ushered through yet more gates to the junction of three huge corridors that stretched into the distance, dotted here and there with prisoners and guards, ringing with the clangs and ululations of the jailhouse. The death row visitation facilities lay to my left and right. A guard unlocked a door, took me inside a long, thin room, then left and locked me in again. Carlton Gary rose from a stool that was bolted to the floor and shook my hand.

His voice was deep, with the rich timbre and elongated vowels that typify the African-American variant of the Georgia drawl. Like all the prisoners, he was wearing the same uniform as the lawn-cutters outside; as well as the slacks and polo shirt, white rubber-soled shoes. Well over six feet tall, he was freshly groomed, his hair, beard and moustache trimmed. His eyes, which he said had been damaged by being deprived of light in jail in Columbus before his trial, were protected by dark glasses, but I could see them well enough. They met mine and held my gaze. He was forty-eight, but looked younger, a little thickset, but muscular, in visibly good shape.

The prison rules stated that death row visits began at nine in the morning, and continued till three in the afternoon: a long time to be locked in a room listening to the life story of a convicted serial killer, with no prospect of a break other than to go to the bathroom. Gary, I soon discovered, had a way of waking his visitors up when their attention, blunted by the prison's warm, stale air, began to wander. Long ago he had been a professional musician. At appropriate moments he started to sing, illustrating his story in a pure gospel tenor.

Georgia does not allow journalists to interview men on death row, and as a private visitor, registered as an approved 'friend', I could not carry writing materials. Later that day, in the prison parking lot and then at a motel in Columbus, I scribbled furiously from memory, trying to recall the blizzard of details that Carlton Gary had related. My first impressions were that he was 'intelligent and articulate', a man from whom ideas and stories tumbled with little need for prompting. His grasp and recall of his case seemed impressive. As to his status as a serial murderer, he made no secret of his criminal past, nor tried to explain it away. 'I'm not Prince Valiant,' he said. 'But I'm not Satan, either.'

One of the first things he told me about was the Big Eddy Club. 'All those crackers who run Columbus and its legal system belong to it,' he said, going on to list the families of most of the strangling victims, together with the members of the city's legal establishment who had helped to convict him, and who, he claimed, were members or regular visitors – William Smith, Doug Pullen, Kenneth Followill and Robert Elliott, the federal judge who by 1998 was responsible for his appeals. With the exception of Pullen, his information was accurate. As well as his case, he talked about his life. There had been some heady, picaresque interludes: playing with a touring revue on the stage of the Apollo in Harlem; escaping from the cops, naked and clutching his clothes, from his girlfriend's bed in Phenix City; nightclubs and relationships with women. Gleaming nuggets of his life's narrative, he described them vividly and at length. Between them were the long, grey, wasted years in prison.

Now, in the autumn of 1998, Gary seemed optimistic that the innocence that he had long protested would soon be legally recognised. After our meeting he wrote to me regularly, referring confidently to 'our coming victory' and the 'crackers' lies' that would soon be officially exposed. Parts of his letters concerned his case, with detailed analyses of the evidence and advice about who I should contact. A keen consumer of news, he also sent reflections on world affairs and politics, and gifts for my children at Christmas: dolls he crocheted in his cell, and beautifully painted cards, together with line-drawn cartoons that he suggested they colour in.

'They do know that my case is going to come back to haunt them,' he wrote in one letter, referring to the officials who had worked to convict him. 'This case is a test case, because coupled with all the garbage, I'm the only death row defendant declared a pauper by the court, yet given not one cent to defend myself.' The time was coming, he felt sure, when 'exposure will take place in abundance'. At the same time, he expressed remorse for the crimes he had always admitted. 'I do not own a patent on a criminal lifestyle,' he wrote. 'In my time on the streets, I had gone against God, gone against how I was raised: I chose to indulge myself in doings of negativity.'

Over time I would learn how he tried to compensate for these failings. For many years, the next cell to his was occupied by José High, an illiterate on the border of mental retardation who had been just seventeen when he was convicted and sentenced to death – on the sole basis of his confession – for a murder committed during a robbery in 1976. Gary taught him to read and spent years trying to pull him out of his periodic depressions: as High wrote in a letter to a friend, 'He watches my back and looks out for me when I need it, which is a lot.' Gary carried on some long correspondences: for several years, he and a man with terminal cancer who lived in England supported each other with their letters, until the man's death in 2005. Gary was an avid student of the legal textbooks available from the prison law library, and filed several suits on behalf of himself and other inmates in an effort to improve conditions in the prison. When he considered himself to have been the victim of some petty injustice he could be impressively stubborn, preferring to endure punishment – such as weeks in the dark and vermin-ridden segregation block known as 'the hole' – rather than submission.

He did what he could to maintain his family and other relationships. His daughter Coco, Tula's child who lived in faraway Syracuse, New York, wrote

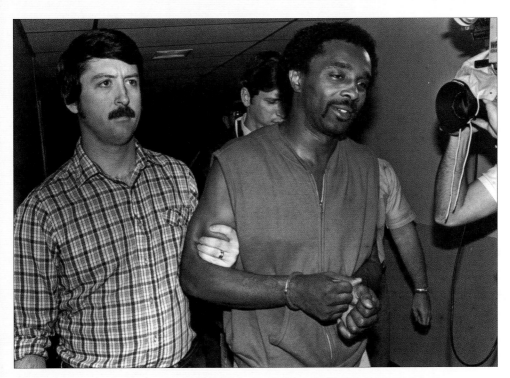

ABOVE: Gary on the night of his arrest with Detective Michael Sellers, who was the only cop to testify about his alleged confession.

BELOW: Police Chief Jim Wetherington (elected Mayor of Columbus in November 2006) gives a press conference on the night of Gary's arrest.

ABOVE: Judge John Land, who handled Gary's case pre-trial. The furled Confederate Stars and Bars, at that time the Georgia state flag, is at right.

BELOW: Bill Kirby, Gary's defence attorney May–September 1984.

NEW MACON ROAD

Gary Parker, a member of Gary's defence team 1984–86, and later a state Senator. He left Columbus because he said he found its pervasive racism oppressive.

August 'Bud' Siemon, Gary's trial attorney. Deprived of funds, he almost went bankrupt as a result of the case.

ABOVE: Bud Siemon (left) and Assistant District Attorney Doug Pullen approach Judge Kenneth Followill's bench during Gary's trial.

BELOW: District Attorney William Smith addresses the jury about Gary's movements at the time of the murders.

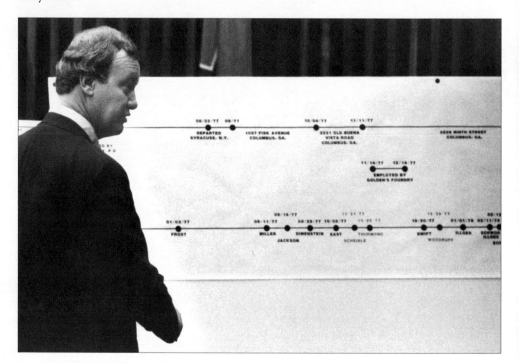

and visited. In 1996 a church group brought him into contact with Sara,* a nurse-practitioner who lived near the Georgia–Alabama border. After a few months they married, and Gary adopted Sara's daughter Virginia, then aged seven. As of September 2006, they still visit most weekends. Virginia, now a student at college, told me that Gary had been an invaluable source of help and advice about her upbringing and education.

Gary had made similar efforts to keep such bonds alive during earlier periods of incarceration. Among the documents in his prison file from the sentence he served in South Carolina from 1979 is a letter to the warden of the Kirkland Correctional Institution in Greenville, imploring him to grant a special dispensation to allow four of his current and former girlfriends and wives to visit him with their children. His sole aim, he wrote, was to 'maintain family ties', and he promised that 'there will never be one single disruption or incident because of this situation, should you approve … I further assure that the mothers will fully comply to all visiting rules and regulations. I took care of my children while free and I find it impossible to simply omit, delete or choose which of my children to visit with, which to forget. My sentence is lengthy, I'm just beginning, and I do love my children. Sir, they are all under 12, and needless to say, unable to bring themselves.' The mothers, he added, would each write to the prison stating they knew about the others. Subject to this condition, the warden agreed. How many children had he fathered, I asked Gary one day. He did a swift mental calculation: 'Er … fourteen.'

On death row, Gary told me early on that his refusing to yield to the arbitrary exercise of prison bureaucracy, and staying involved with the outside world, had the same psychological origin: his determination that he not become institutionalised, and would be able to adjust to freedom after his eventual release. His optimism was partly a reflection of the fact that the autumn of 1998 was by no means the worst of times for prisoners on Georgia's death row. There had been an execution that September, but that was the first for two years. Afterwards the state was plunged into a prolonged judicial and legislative debate about replacing the electric chair

---

* As with Coco and Tula, to protect Sara and her daughter from harassment, I have used pseudonyms.

with lethal injection, and while this unfolded, no executions took place at all. (In the event, the first execution using the new method would not be carried out until October 2001, nearly three years after my first conversation with Gary.) For the first time since executions had resumed as a result of the Supreme Court's reinstatement of the death penalty in 1976, inmates were not regularly losing men with whom they might have been housed for many years. Illusory as it was, they felt a sense of security.

At the same time, the death row regime of the late 1990s was relatively relaxed. Most days, even when he had no visitors, Gary would be allowed out of his cell for several hours. He had ready access to artists' materials, with which he had created a striking body of work, examples of which had been exhibited in a prisoners' show in Atlanta. Gary Parker, his one-time lawyer, later gave me one: a pastel drawing of Tina Turner, whom Gary had met many years earlier, when she and her then-husband Ike were at the start of their careers. Others hung on Parker's walls. One was a painting, in a distinctive and original style, of African-Americans in 'the hood'. Another was a stylised drawing of an electric chair, behind which stood an image of Christ weeping.

Like every personal visit to death row, my first ended at a minute before 3 p.m., when a guard unlocked the door of the strange, narrow room. Gary and I shook hands again. Our escorts arrived: he went left, along one of the corridors back to his cell, and I went right, back through the series of gates and electronic doors. At last I emerged, dazed and a little hungry, into the daylight.

My journey to death row began with a letter at the end of 1997 from Wendy Murphy, an English dental hygienist who had been visiting and corresponding with Carlton Gary for several years. I already knew a little about the stocking stranglings from my trip to Columbus on behalf of the *Observer* the previous year, and enough about the circumstances of Gary's trial to want to know more – to say nothing of my strange and disquieting encounters with lawmen like Doug Pullen. I asked Wendy to send me copies of some of the legal papers that she had amassed about the case, and as I worked my way through them I began to think it possible that her passionate insistence that Gary was innocent might have some foundation.

I had been writing about crime and the law in Britain since the beginning of the 1980s, and had uncovered fresh evidence in several high-profile murder cases the convictions in which were eventually reversed by the Court of Appeal. The more I read about Carlton Gary, the more it seemed that the evidence that convicted him bore little resemblance to the standard shared by jurisdictions on both sides of the Atlantic – 'proof beyond reasonable doubt'.

Wendy lived at the bottom of a windswept, sloping barley field in the far east of Norfolk, a few miles from the Saxon village of North Walsham and the bracing North Sea coast. She shared her isolated, ramshackle cottage with her dogs and Tony, her teacher son. Warmed by an Aga range, the house was filled with diverse signs of her long relationship with Carlton Gary. It was obvious that it was one of the most important things in her life.

A tall, determined white woman in early middle age, Wendy had been introduced to Gary by Lifelines, a British organisation that exists to find penfriends for death row prisoners, founded by a Quaker from Cambridge, Jan Arriens. A hundred and fifty years earlier, British Quakers and evangelists had been at the forefront of campaigns to abolish slavery, their efforts fuelled by their unshakeable belief that the American South's 'peculiar institution' was a fundamental outrage, an affront to the laws of God and man. Their fervour helped sustain men such as the freed slave Frederick Douglass, whose speaking tours of the United Kingdom saw him addressing huge crowds, and treated with reverence. Now, in an era imbued with ideas about anti-racism and human rights, European agitation against capital punishment in America occupies an analogous cultural space. Its contemporary stars are not former slaves but prisoners released from death row, speaking in person at the meetings of bodies such as Lifelines, or indirectly in television documentaries and plays such as the international hit by Jessica Blank and Erik Jensen, *The Exonerated* (2002).

Early in their association, Gary sent Wendy a drawing of his death row cell: a concrete shell eight feet by seven, furnished with a cabinet, a metal cot, a small sink and a toilet. 'I can lie in bed and touch the sink and toilet,' he had written on the sketch. There was also a socket for headphones and a dial, offering him a choice between rock, soul or country music, or the sound for a small TV set. Gary passed some of the 150 hours he spent locked in this space each week with embroidery, and he had sent Wendy cushion covers, quilts and framed needlepoint pictures. He liked to sew pastoral scenes and flowers – working, of course, from memory: death row prisoners exercised outside in an asphalt yard, from which the verdant park around the prison was invisible. In his letters to Wendy he maintained the unyielding persona of cheerfulness and hope that he also displayed to me, asserting his innocence and his confident belief that the evidence which had put him on death row would soon be shown to be worthless.

Drawn in ever deeper, Wendy began to visit Gary regularly, sometimes as many as five or six times a year. When he needed money to buy copies of his legal documents, art supplies or food from the prison commissary, Wendy supplied it, a burden that, coupled with her mounting travel costs, required her to take a second, evening job. In the autumn of 1997 she had to provide him with a different, more urgent kind of support. After many vicissitudes, Gary had reached the end of his state court appeals, and although he was legally entitled to launch a fresh petition in federal court, Georgia set an execution date. As the weeks went by and the date crept closer, without any sign of a stay from J. Robert Elliott, the elderly federal judge who was responsible for dealing with his case, Wendy flew to Georgia. 'We both genuinely thought he was about to die,' she said, 'whatever the lawyers were telling us.' She laughed. 'I had one piece of luck. Delta gave me a half-price ticket – they said it was a special "pending bereavement" flight.'

Three days before his scheduled execution, Gary was moved from his cell on death row to H5, the death house, a small block on its own that contained a single cell and the room with the electric chair. Each time he was taken back to the cell after visits or a shower, the guards made sure that the door to the execution room was left open, the chair in plain sight. At night he lay in his bed listening to the hum of the generator used to produce the necessary 2,200 volts being tested. On Monday, 3 November 1997, the day he was scheduled to die, Wendy's visit was due to end at 11 a.m. – eight hours before his execution. 'We were just getting ready to say our farewells. At 10.30, a guard came in with a piece of paper.' Having been legally obliged for months to issue a stay pending the outcome of

Gary's federal appeals, Judge Elliott had finally done so. It was this apparent brush with death that prompted Gary to ask Wendy to find a writer who might look at his case with an unprejudiced eye, and thus, a few weeks later, her first letter to me.

Robert Elliott, America's longest-serving federal judge, sat on the bench in a white, neo-classical 1930s courthouse in downtown Columbus, presiding over the Middle District of Georgia. At the time of my first meeting with Gary in 1998, his next appeal was still in Elliott's in-tray, although by then the judge was in his late eighties. Lately, it was said in Columbus, Elliott's health had started to fail: he had stopped playing tennis. He had not, however, retired.

Like so many others in the saga of the stranglings, Elliott, as Gary informed me, had long been a member of the Big Eddy Club, and like Judge John Land he had started his career as an avowed segregationist. In the late 1940s he was a lawyer and a state politician, the architect of a series of notorious machinations on the floor of the Georgia Assembly aimed at installing the deeply reactionary Herman Talmadge as Governor. The central plank of his campaign was a blatantly unconstitutional Bill to ensure that only whites could vote in Democratic primaries. 'This will certainly eliminate the coloured people,' Elliott said when he introduced it as a member of the Georgia House of Representatives in January 1947. A few months later he promised two interviewers who came to see him at his Columbus office that if the measure fell, his friend Talmadge would 'think up something else to keep the niggers from the polls, and if two years later the Supreme Court decides that's unconstitutional, then he'll think of something else'. The following year, Elliott was a state delegate to the Democratic Party National Convention in Philadelphia. The proposed party platform for the 1948 presidential election included pledges against lynching and racially discriminatory employment hiring. He spoke eloquently against these proposals, describing such ideas as 'a slap in the face to the South'.

Unlike Land, Elliott did not change his opinions much over time. He was appointed to the bench by John F. Kennedy in 1962, one of six segregationist judges Kennedy chose as part of a pact to placate the 'Dixiecrats', right-wing Southern Democrats, after they threatened to form a breakaway party. In the ensuing thirty-nine years he spent as a judge, Elliott granted just one criminal appeal – that of Lieutenant William Calley, convicted and sentenced to life by a Fort Benning court martial in 1971 for the massacre of 102 Vietnamese men, women and children at the village of My Lai. Justifying his ruling from the bench, Elliott said that Calley had been denied a fair trial by the intensity of media coverage, going on to add a biblical allusion: 'Joshua did not have charges brought against him for the slaughter of the civilian population of Jericho. But then the Lord was with Joshua, we are told.' Although the US Appeals Court later reversed Elliott's decision, Calley was not re-incarcerated, and at the time of writing, in 2006, he still lives in Columbus, running his jewellery store on Macon Road.

Elliott did his paperwork beneath the painted gaze of a portrait of the Confederate General, Robert E. Lee – 'One of my greatest heroes,' Elliott said in a newspaper interview just after his retirement. As Columbus's federal judge throughout much of the civil rights era, he issued injunctions against planned marches due to be led by Martin Luther King, did what he could to dilute the effect of *Brown vs Board of Education* in desegregating the city's schools, and stymied the lawsuit brought in 1971 by the former Columbus policemen who had cut the US flag from their uniforms in protest at the racism they had experienced inside the CPD. In one judicial opinion that he issued about school desegregation in 1963 in response to a suit brought by the NAACP, Elliott claimed that Southern whites had been 'abused by agitators, castigated by commentators, and larruped by litigators', and 'the last thing they need is a precipitate rake of the judicial claw'. He endorsed the testimony of Columbus's Schools Superintendent, William Henry Shaw, who told his court that segregation was a 'long and universal custom', and that to abandon it suddenly would 'injure the feelings and physical well-being of the children'. Educators, said Elliott in another case, had no business trying to effect 'social revolution'.

At the end of January 2001, a month after his retirement on the eve of his ninety-first birthday, I made an appointment to see Robert Elliott at his house on Hilton Avenue, Wynnton, less than a block from the home of Ferne Jackson, the strangler's first victim. He shuffled to meet me at the door in a striped dressing gown and slippers. He was visibly frail, but behind his eyes the embers of a fierce and active mind still glowed. The house was huge, arranged along five sides of an octagon, and stuffed with exquisite Chinese prints, rugs and antiques. We sat down on a sofa while his wife brought tea.

'Well, you've come a long way now,' Elliott began. 'So what can I do for you?'

'Judge, I'm from a different country,' I began, trying to seem ingenuous. 'We've had a very different history, and when I look at some of the events of long ago I find it hard to make much sense of them. One of the reasons I want to talk to you is to try to understand the mentality you had when you were active in politics. Why were you a segregationist? How did you come to hold the views that you had then, way back in the forties and fifties?'

Elliott paused for a very long time, so long that the winter sky seemed to be darkening. At last he sighed. 'I don't feel I can talk about any of it. I'm sorry, Mr Rose. I just can't do that, because if I ever get started, I'd never stop. And because I spent so long as a judge, that might get me into trouble.'

Vainly, I tired to persuade him that I wasn't asking him to explain his courtroom decisions, just his opinions on race. It was still no-go. The tea came and I took a sip, reflecting ruefully that I'd played this interview wrong. We made small talk for a while about my journey to the United States and my home in Oxford. Then there was another pause, while Elliott appeared to marshal his inner forces.

'I'm going to tell you just one thing,' he said. 'I went to Europe and I heard Adolf Hitler speak. It was 1935, a little town in Germany, I think it was the place where they invented the bicycle. A huge crowd had gathered, and there was a terrible storm. There was thunder and lightning, but the crowd did not leave. Hitler just carried right on. Yes, I heard Hitler speak. You make of that what you will.'

Elliott died in 2006.

In Georgia, as in other death penalty states, the appeals of the condemned follow procedures so complex and prolonged that they seem to leave little room for error: unless an inmate chooses to waive his rights, even the simplest capital case will have been reviewed by at least six higher courts.

First comes 'direct review' by the state Supreme Court, whose judges will read the transcript of the trial and take argument from defence and prosecution lawyers about its conduct. If that fails, the prisoner's next chance is to lodge a claim of *habeas corpus*, an ancient writ whose origins lie in England before the Magna Carta of 1215. A *habeas* claim asserts that the inmate's continued detention is unlawful, because one or more of his constitutional rights have been violated. In most capital cases, a defendant will file two successive *habeas* claims: the first with the courts of the state that convicted him, and the second in the US federal system. Federal *habeas* claims usually end up being appealed up the judicial ladder to the United States Supreme Court, and if they fail there, there is often a desperate flurry of eleventh-hour petitions, lodged with any court that a defence attorney can get to accept them. In Georgia, usually by that stage the only hope of reprieve lies with the state Board of Pardons and Parole, which has the power to grant clemency. Since the death penalty was reinstated in 1976, the Board had exercised it just six times up to the end of 2006. In the same period, thirty-nine inmates have been executed.

From his point of view, Carlton Gary's direct review to the Georgia Supreme Court appeared to start unexpectedly well. Bud Siemon filed an appellate brief on his behalf that raised twenty separate issues. Among them was a claim which, if granted, would have invalidated the entire trial: that the repeated decisions by Judges Land and Followill to refuse him public money had made the proceedings unfair. According to the brief, 'the total absence of any assistance made it impossible to construct any meaningful defence'.

The six judges who considered the case thought about it for almost six months before issuing an order in June 1987. In this they agreed that the lack of funds might well have prevented a fair trial. But they did so on a somewhat curious basis. The obvious thing for them to have done would have been to decide the funds issue in the light of Gary's right to basic procedural fairness, to 'due process' under the Fourteenth Amendment of the US Constitution, and thus to have ordered a new trial. Instead, they dealt with it more obliquely.

Under the Constitution's Sixth Amendment, criminal defendants have a right to 'the assistance of counsel'. A line of decisions by the US Supreme

Court dating back over half a century had established that such assistance has to be *effective*, and by the early 1980s the claim that the trial defence attorney had been ineffective was one of the commonest grounds in death penalty appeals. The Georgia Supreme Court's handling of Carlton Gary's case arose from this tradition. The judges said that they wanted to discover whether 'for any reason, including the lack of funds, the defendant failed to receive effective assistance of counsel'.

Meanwhile, rather than trying to answer this question for themselves, the judges decided to 'remand' it. They passed the buck back down – to the place where Gary had been tried, the Muscogee County Superior Court in Columbus. The result was that the very same judge whose decisions were supposedly being scrutinised, Kenneth B. Followill, would be the one doing the scrutinising. No judge likes to be reversed. Thankfully for Followill, the Supreme Court had given him the chance to affirm his own wisdom.

The question Followill had to answer created immediate potential for conflict. As far as Siemon and Gary were concerned, if counsel had been ineffective, the only reason was the denial of funds. But Bill Smith and Doug Pullen interpreted the order rather differently. In their view, the wording of the question – with its vague reference to 'any other reason' – had given them a chance to examine other matters as well, such as Bud Siemon's personal competence and his strategy at the trial.

Judge Followill appeared to share their interpretation. The State Supreme Court had asked him to make sure that Gary had a lawyer, who this time would be paid from public funds. Bud Siemon, who knew the case better than anyone, should have been the obvious choice. But because Followill also thought that Siemon's performance was now under review, he decided against this, on the grounds that it would amount to a conflict of interest. He announced that Gary was to get a new attorney – Haywood Turner III, the son of a doctor from an old Columbus family.

Turner had never handled a death penalty trial, and his experience of capital appeals was very limited. Regarded in the city as somewhat eccentric, he had an obsessive interest in the Second World War, and had been known to attend social functions dressed in period military uniform. Eventually he became a municipal court judge, responsible for trying misdemeanours. In August 2006 he was arrested and charged with pointing a gun at a woman driver who overtook him in his car a few blocks from his courtroom.

I met Turner at his office in 2001. A tall, bald and palpably earnest figure, he told me early in our interview that his deepest interest was the study of evil, and two of the worst examples that he knew of it were Adolf Hitler and the death penalty. His unusual manner did not seem to have damaged his social standing. Like William Smith, Kenneth Followill, Robert Elliott and a number of the strangling victims' families, he belonged to the Big Eddy Club. 'I was a member through my father,' he told me. 'It's a clique, a place where people gather, and I suppose that wherever that happens, deals get made. One of the things that was said about me was that because I was part of that group, my loyalties were with them, not with Carlton Gary. I reject that and I'm horrified by it.'

Turner may not have approved of capital punishment, but Carlton Gary did not approve of him. 'The remand hearing seems to be an effort by judges to deny me the lawyer of my choice,' he wrote from prison a few days after Turner was assigned, 'especially one free from the political control and dominance of judges from Muscogee County. Under NO circumstances do I want to be represented by any lawyer appointed by Followill.' In October 1987 he asked Bud Siemon to file a motion asking Followill to remove Turner and restore Siemon himself.

The remand hearing started in Followill's court on 12 November. Still hoping to persuade the judge to let him stay, Siemon had travelled down to Columbus, bringing with him an Atlanta friend and colleague, Frank Derrickson. As the hearing began, Assistant District Attorney Doug Pullen got to his feet before either of them could open their mouths, and asked Followill to have Siemon thrown out of the courtroom.

Siemon tried to resist. 'Mr Gary has never alleged that his trial attorney, me, ever committed any professional errors,' he said. Gary's complaints were confined to the consequences of having no funds: 'There is no conflict between me and Mr Gary. If there's a conflict of interest in this case [it] exists between Mr Gary and Mr Turner.' But Followill had made his mind up. At the end of Siemon's impassioned address, he told him simply: 'I will not permit you to remain in the case at this point, Mr Siemon. If you'll kindly remove yourself from the counsel table I would appreciate it.'

Derrickson asked if Siemon could at least remain in court, in order to provide factual assistance from his compendious knowledge. But Pullen again objected, arguing that if the court were about to review Siemon's conduct of the trial, he himself might be called to testify. Under normal courtroom rules, that meant he had to leave.

'All witnesses who are going to testify in this matter will be required to leave the courtroom,' said Followill. 'Mr Siemon, I'll ask you to leave the courtroom.' That left Gary with Haywood Turner, a man he did not trust and would not talk to, and Derrickson, whom the judge had not yet accepted as counsel. Although Derrickson was independent, he barely knew the case at all. Gary's own preference soon became clear.

'Mr Gary, do you want Mr Derrickson as your lawyer?' Followill asked.

'Yes, I do.'

'And do you have confidence in him? Do you feel he will properly represent you?'

'I feel that he's independent of this political power that is here in Columbus, Georgia, and I think that would be a whole lot better.'

This time, Followill had no choice. 'All right,' he told Derrickson, 'you are permitted to enter the case.' But he would postpone his decision as to whether Turner should be removed until the following Monday, 16 November. For the time being, Gary would be represented by both of them.

When the hearing reconvened, Turner made an opening statement. It was true, he admitted, that in his three previous capital appeals, the only ones he had ever handled, he had been forced to ask other, more experienced lawyers to write his legal briefs, but in this his only goal had been 'to get the best possible help that I could for the people I was appointed to represent'.

Then the British death penalty specialist Clive Stafford Smith testified that he had worked unpaid for ten days writing a brief in one of Turner's cases in 1985. The only thing Turner had given him for his efforts was a disused parking meter, and even for this he later sent him a bill for $10. He had done all the work, Stafford Smith said, but Turner, the official court-appointed attorney, had been paid $6,400. Here, complained Derrickson, was 'Alice world' justice: Siemon, who had spent thousands of hours working on Gary's case for nothing, had been expelled from the court-room, while Turner, who was being paid thousands of dollars for doing nothing, was being allowed to remain.

At times the hearing degenerated into farce. Turner's grasp of what had happened at the trial was extremely weak. For example, he said he had phoned someone called 'Melvin Gary'. No one of that name had ever appeared in connection with the case. But in trying to disentangle this mess, Derrickson – who, after all, knew little more about the trial than Turner – only made it worse.

'Do you know what Mr Melvin Gary had to say about this case?' asked Derrickson.

'I don't have it in my memory,' Turner replied.

'Well, I'll tell you. He testified that Mr Gary gave him a gun which turned out to be the murder weapon in this case.'

'Right. I couldn't remember if it was that Gary or another one.'

These were fundamental errors. The Columbus murders were, of course, stranglings, in which no gun was ever used. As for 'Melvin Gary', pre-sumably Turner meant Carlton Gary's uncle Jim, the supposed recipient of the weapon stolen from Henry Sanderson. It was obvious, as Pullen glee-fully pointed out, that 'neither one of them has read the transcript'.

At last, Followill made his less than epochal decision. Derrickson would conduct the hearing, but Turner could stay 'to fill in any chinks'. That afternoon, the proceedings turned more serious. As the session began, Derrickson revealed that all Carlton Gary's previous attorneys had been subpoenaed to appear as witnesses, apparently because the prosecution lawyers intended to explore their effectiveness. Convinced that this had nothing to do with the question of funds, Derrickson was determined to stop this happening. He was walking into a fateful legal trap.

The subpoenas, said Derrickson, were 'a naked power play to try to get these lawyers up and cross-examine them about their innermost secrets and conversations with Carlton Gary'. Not only had Gary made no com-plaint about his counsel, Derrickson went on, he wished to preserve his legal right to attorney–client privilege, the confidentiality of everything that had passed between him and his lawyers. Questioning them on the stand about their conduct would surely breach this.

He turned towards his client. 'Mr Gary, do you wish to waive your attorney–client privilege or your work product privilege* here today?'

'No, sir,' Gary replied.

'Do you wish your attorneys to testify in these proceedings?'

'No, I do not.'

Followill was unmoved. 'I suggest to you that we are not going to get one inch closer to deciding the effectiveness of counsel until we have an opportunity to hear from counsel,' he said.

Pullen drove home his advantage. Deficiencies in Gary's defence *might* have been caused by a lack of money, he said, but there could have been other reasons. It was up to the defendant to prove the reason, and for that, the lawyers would have to testify. 'This is his opportunity to make the record now and forever more. If he is going to avail himself of that opportunity, he does it now: speak now or forever hold his peace.'

Now the threat was laid bare. Death penalty appeals may be lengthy and numerous, but they are bound by rigid procedural rules. Pullen was arguing that unless Gary waived his attorney–client privilege now, he would be relinquishing any future right to complain that lack of money had deprived him of an effective defence, throughout the rest of his appeals. Followill agreed.

The trap was already almost shut, and later that afternoon it closed completely. The first of the former defence lawyers to testify was Bud Siemon. Cross-examining him, Pullen got straight to the point. Siemon, he said, had not called any mitigating evidence on Gary's behalf in the trial's penalty phase. Surely, he continued, Siemon would agree that carrying out a thorough investigation in order to present such mitigation ought to begin as soon as an attorney took on a client who faced the death penalty. 'Did you do that or attempt to do that in this case?'

'Your honour, we object at this time,' said Derrickson. 'We think it violates Mr Gary's attorney–client privilege.'

Once again, Followill warned Gary that if he did not waive his

---

* Work product privilege is an American term that refers to any paperwork or other material generated by the process of legal representation. Like the conversations between an attorney and a client, it is strictly 'privileged', i.e. exempt from legal 'discovery' or compelled disclosure.

attorney–client privilege, he would be abandoning all chance of claiming that his counsel had been ineffective in future.

'I'm not waiving anything,' Gary said, 'and I don't have any question about Mr Siemon's representation of me. I think the whole crux of the matter is the fact we don't have any money and you've been constantly denying that.'

Pullen posed a few more questions, seeking to probe the details of how Siemon had prepared for the trial: each time, Derrickson and Gary invoked his privilege again. Between the two of them, Followill and Pullen had managed to transform a hearing ordered by the Georgia Supreme Court to ascertain whether the denial of funds had harmed a capital defendant into an investigation of his trial attorney. As Siemon's testimony sputtered to its end, Pullen started reading from a long list of possible witnesses, asking him whether he had ever interviewed them, and whether he had considered asking them to testify at the trial. At first he asked about each one individually; later, he listed up to fourteen names at the same time. By then, of course, Pullen knew he would get no response. He also knew that over the question of funding, he and the state had won.

It was not until 12 June 1989, nineteen months after the hearing, that Followill issued his 'order on remand', and thus returned the case to the Georgia Supreme Court. In a document that ran to twenty-nine pages, he stated his conclusions. The first was somewhat surprising: that having no money to pay for experts had not harmed Carlton Gary's case at all, because the scientific evidence given at his trial had not in fact been very important.

Followill wrote that the dozens of motions asking for funds failed to 'define areas of inquiry', and that the defence had never said in sufficient detail how it would have used the money if it were granted. As a judge, he had to 'balance the necessity for providing the criminal defendant with adequate tools for his defence on the one hand and the proper stewardship of public monies on the other'. He could not allow mere 'fishing expeditions'. As for Gary's insistence on attorney–client privilege, he had been clearly warned of the consequences. It had rendered scrutiny of the possible disadvantage he might have suffered impossible. There was, therefore, 'no suggestion that the failure to provide public monies in any way undermines the reliability of the verdicts ... The defendant has completely and totally failed to demonstrate any harm or prejudice to him to any degree.'

Worse, in Followill's eyes, the entire funding issue was an irrelevant diversion concocted by Gary's lawyers, 'a deliberately planned attempt to create an impression of ineffective assistance, laying the blame solely upon the court's failure to provide funding, and to pave the way for that issue to be raised by way of appeal'. In ordinary circumstances, a disastrous strategy such as this might in itself be evidence that counsel had indeed been ineffective. But in this case, Followill went on, 'There is no doubt that such a course received Carlton Gary's full acquiescence.' He was equally to blame. Asked to review his own decisions by the Georgia Supreme Court, Followill had not merely found them just, he had censured the defence for questioning them in the first place. As for Gary, he would pay the price for his attorney's impertinence.

From Columbus, the case went back to the state Supreme Court in Atlanta. From Gary's perspective, Followill's order had been damaging enough, but the opinion issued by the Georgia Supreme Court in March 1990 was catastrophic. It dealt with the funds issue in a few crisp sentences, finding that Pullen and his colleagues had bent over backwards to give Gary the chance to show how lack of money might have harmed him: 'The defendant was given an opportunity to prove he was denied effective assistance of counsel. He declined to do so. We agree with the trial court that he knowingly, voluntarily and intelligently has waived any issue of effectiveness of trial counsel.' All the other areas of possible doubt were swept aside. For example, although Gary had never been charged with the crimes in upstate New York, let alone tried and convicted, the Supreme Court reported as fact that 'he committed them'. Overall, the evidence was sufficient, the court said, and the sentence appropriate.

Aghast at how the funds issue had been turned against them, Siemon and Derrickson exercised their right of a further appeal to the United States Supreme Court. On 1 October the highest court in the nation decided that Gary's case contained no constitutional questions worthy of consideration, and as it always does in such circumstances, issued an unsigned, two-word ruling: 'Certiorari denied.'

It was not the end of Gary's appeals. But on every legal front, the outcome of his direct review had been total defeat.

Having met Carlton Gary for the first time in November 1998, I took a winding back road from the prison west to Columbus, a pleasant drive through undulating farmland and autumnal forests. For most of the next two days I sat in the W.C. Bradley Public Library, reading what I could of the history of the city, and of the mountain of newspaper clippings about the stranglings and Gary's trial. Early the following week I went to Atlanta to meet his current attorneys. Eight years after the end of his direct review, Gary's case had reached the federal courts, and he had two specialists in federal capital defence work to represent him – Jack Martin and Michael McIntyre.

Most of the death penalty defence lawyers in Atlanta work in a pleasant, breezy quarter downtown, within walking distance of the state and federal courts. It has some striking eighty-storey towers built in the 1990s, as well as some older ones that might have rated as skyscrapers seventy years earlier, most of them adorned with ornate art-nouveau façades. The firm that Martin ran with his brother, a Democrat member of the Georgia Assembly, was located inside the Grant Building, one of the finest. The previous year, Jack Martin had come to national attention for his successful defence of Richard Jewell, the security man falsely accused of planting a bomb at the 1996 Atlanta Olympics.

Wendy Murphy had sent me a copy of the federal brief that Martin and McIntyre had recently filed on behalf of Gary. It seemed to cast doubt on numerous aspects of the prosecution case, providing strong support for Gary's claim of innocence.

Both lawyers were born and raised as Southerners, and neither had met a reporter from England before. As we sat around the table in an oak-panelled conference room, I told them that I had been to see their client and – at that time – was thinking of writing an article or making a television documentary about him. I described some of the criminal cases I had covered in England; like Carlton Gary, the defendants in those cases had been demonised, but their convictions had still been quashed by the Court of Appeal. I said the arguments they were making for Gary seemed to be equally compelling.

McIntyre, a tall man with a high forehead who wore braces over an immaculate starched white shirt, spoke first. 'David, we appreciate your interest. But I don't think you quite understand what death penalty litigation is like. Our job is to try to save our client's life, and I'm not sure that you wouldn't be more of a hindrance than a help. We may be able to get the federal courts to look again at his sentence. But to persuade them to vacate his conviction would be extremely difficult, and sitting where I do, it doesn't look very likely.'

There was, he went on, a fundamental difference between a capital case and the kind I was used to in England, where the death penalty had been abolished in 1965. 'Sometimes these things go to sleep. Carlton's case is huge and very complicated, and right now nothing much is happening. Neither the judge nor the state are pushing it. [At this point, the judge responsible for dealing with Gary was the ageing Robert Elliott.] But if you go ahead and give it some publicity, it might just suddenly wake up. The state might decide it wants to get on with Carlton's last appeals and get him executed quickly. I don't think that your involvement is in his best interests.'

As to the possibility of overturning Gary's conviction, McIntyre gave me a quick lesson in American constitutional law. From time to time, striking fresh evidence emerges in a death case, and in one where the trial defence lawyers originally had no money, this might be more likely. The problem, however, was to get the courts to consider it. Usually this could be done only if the defence could prove that the new evidence could not have been found at the time of the trial, or demonstrate conclusively that the prosecution had taken steps to conceal it, thus violating the defendant's constitutional rights.

Martin, a tousled figure with big, owlish spectacles, seemed more relaxed. Maybe, he said, McIntyre was being a little hasty, and they should at least give me a chance: 'It can't do much harm to let him go away for a while and see if he comes up with anything.' Finally we agreed on a compromise. I would continue to make inquiries into the case, but only on the condition that I reported any new findings to them. Then we would talk again, and at that stage they would consider giving me their full cooperation, and access to all the case papers.

It was, I knew, unusual for a reporter to make such an agreement, although once or twice in England, investigating doubtful convictions for murder, I had done so. Some take the view that the requirements of journalistic objectivity ought to preclude a close relationship with people who would, inevitably, be important sources of information. I thought the counter-argument more powerful. I did not know whether Carlton Gary was innocent or guilty, although I believed that he had not had a fair trial. But if I found genuine reasons for suspecting that he was not the stocking strangler, then it seemed to me that the normal ethical equations would change. It could not be right to keep such evidence to myself until the vagaries of print or TV schedules allowed it to be brought into the public domain. There might, at worst, be circumstances in which my failure to cooperate with Martin and McIntyre led them to miss a crucial filing deadline, ensuring that the possible new testimony could not be used. Thus, according to the inflexible rules of death penalty litigation, my insistence on 'objectivity' might help to cause the execution of an innocent man.

I agreed to Martin's proposal. We stood and shook hands.

TEN

# *Violation*

The criminal process itself must afford remedies for its abuse and deterrents against the misuse of official power ... The reversal of a criminal conviction is small price to pay for an affirmation of proper values and a deterrent example of what will happen when those values are slighted.

HERBERT PACKER, *The Limits of the Criminal Sanction* (1968)

For detectives and journalists alike, it is the cold cases that are the hardest to crack. At Scotland Yard in London, cops talk of the 'golden hour', the immediate aftermath of a serious crime when the prospects of gathering 'best evidence' are at their highest. Confronted with events that happened in the distant past, one has to follow one's instincts, and sometimes, apparently tangential details play a large part in forming them. When Detective Michael Sellers looked at the stranglings in 1984, six years after the final murder, Carlton Gary's record in upstate New York made him feel confident that he had the right suspect. For my part, when I began to probe Gary's conviction, it wasn't the trial's core evidence that first made me feel uneasy about whether Columbus's law enforcers had the right man. It was when I noticed a troubling pattern: several witnesses who told me that they had faced strong persuasion to provide testimony that they did not consider true.

It seemed that the police were perplexed by the same question that worried many people who had known Gary in Columbus: why would a popular, sexually active ladies' man who was so attractive that he had

241

worked as a TV model have been raping and murdering elderly women in his spare time? Perhaps the cops believed that if they could show that Gary was some kind of pervert, even in his relationships with African-American women from his own age group, this question would not arise. In any event, early in my researches I tracked down some of Gary's former girl-friends, and all of them said similar things: first, that they did not believe that he could have been the strangler; and secondly, that they had come under heavy pressure from detectives before the trial to give testimony that suggested he was.

Tula Jones, Gary's sometime partner from Syracuse, New York, who had lived with him in Columbus at the height of the strangler's rampage, told me in 2001 that after his arrest in 1984, CPD detectives visited her several times: 'They wanted me to say he was abusive. They wanted me to say he forced me to have sex in the rectum. They wanted me to say he'd get violent when I wouldn't have sex with him. They wanted me to say he beat me. Sure, we had rows, like any couple, but he never did anything to hurt me.'

The officers, Tula said, 'tried to make me angry with him' by telling her about other women they claimed Gary had slept with. She said she moved home in an attempt to avoid them, but still the Columbus detectives continued to harass her, accompanied by local cops from Syracuse. But despite the passage of years, Gary still had a place in her heart: 'I have no remorse whatsoever about those times, and I had no abuse from him. The only abuse I ever had was from the police, after he was arrested. Sure, one time I left him. But he called, apologised, was sweet and loving and then I came right back. Now I just want him out of there [death row], because he deserves better, even though I know I'm not the one he'd be coming back to.'

Of course, it would have been easy for Tula to have made such claims so many years after the event. But later, in Gary's lawyer's office, I found a file with several letters that she had sent Gary in jail before the trial. They were still in their dated, postmarked envelopes, and they told the same story. 'Baby, I miss you and I do love you,' she began one on 20 June 1984, seven weeks after his arrest.

Those policemen came here and they are saying there are another side of you … I am hoping that the one in love with me don't love all of the

242

other women they told me about. They asked me did you ever beat me, and I told them the truth, and then they wanted to know have you ever choked me or knocked me out. I told them no. Why they want to know that? Are they trying to make me say that? They say that's how you killed those people. I don't know what they want.

The pressure on Tula continued. 'Mike, the police came here *again*,' she wrote on 28 February 1985. 'They even talked to Kim [another woman Gary knew who lived in Syracuse]. She told them that you fucked her one night in Rochester. What in the hell you and Kim done in Rochester?' The police, she went on, had told her that Gary had made Kim pregnant, and she urged him to write to their daughter Coco and assure her that their claim was untrue.

But her fury at his alleged infidelity would not, she added, make her insinuate that he might have been the stocking strangler:

I hoped they would leave me alone. I even told them, *please*, just leave me alone. I can't tell them anything because I don't know anything. They asked me, had you stayed away from me a couple of days [in Columbus]. Mike, I can't recall you staying away for so long, you always returned home. *You never choked me.* We just had our ups and downs like any other family. Mike, they want me to come down there and testify against you. How in the hell can I do this when I don't even know what they are talking about?

Tula was not the only one to make such assertions. Gary's jail journal for 3 June 1984 records a visit from his Phenix City girlfriend Anita Hill: '[Cops] attempting to get her to lie and say I "hated old white women".' Beleta Turner, the Atlanta hair-salon owner who had dated Gary while working for the Columbus District Attorney's office, told me that a few days before his arrest in Albany, Georgia, when the cops were hunting for him, she had come home from a party to find a SWAT team at her apartment. Next day, she said, she was told to report to the CPD for questioning. 'They put it to me that he was the stocking strangler, and they tried to make me say I thought he was. All I would say was, "The man I know is *not* the strangler."'

In Phenix City, a long-time platonic friend of Gary named Ruby James claimed that in an attempt to get her to provide damaging testimony, a detective told her that Gary had killed people by locking them in the deep-freeze rooms of restaurants.

The roughest treatment was reserved for Gary's childhood playmate and former Sheriff's Deputy Earnestine Flowers. At the end of the trial in 1986, William Smith had planned to call her as a witness. But there was an unexplained hiccup. Earnestine had been due to testify on 22 August, but for some reason failed to show up. The following Sunday, 24 August, acting on a subpoena from Judge Followill, the Sheriff's Department arrested her, and when she did testify next morning, it was after a night in jail. Her evidence only added to the mystery. All she said was that she had seen Gary, complete with leg in plaster, back in Columbus after a long absence at the end of the summer of 1977, and that her father later got him a short-lived job at Golden's Foundry. When she finished, Followill gave her an angry lecture. 'I find that you have obstructed justice, upset the orderly process of this court, and I am going to find you in wilful contempt ... [you] should have had at least more regard for your duty.' He sentenced her to twenty-four hours in jail – the time she had already served.

It was only when I interviewed Earnestine in January 2000 that the real reason for her reluctance to appear in court became clear. Gary's apparently normal sexuality was not the only difficulty that the prosecution had faced. They also had to explain how he could have known where elderly women lived alone in a wealthy, all-white neighbourhood, and how he had managed to evade intense police patrols each time he struck. According to Earnestine, the police had leant on her heavily in an effort to fill these gaps: 'They were trying to make me say that I provided Carlton with information, because I was working out in the field as a Deputy. It wasn't true. Then they tried to make me say that I'd lent Carlton my car, a Datsun 280Z. They said it had been seen in the area. The truth was I lent him the car twice – once to take some groceries over to his mother, and once to pick up his girlfriend from the bus station. It was the daytime on both occasions, and both times he ran his errand and brought it straight back.'

Why was the 280Z so important? Not because anyone had seen it in Wynnton – at least, no one ever testified that they had. But according to

Gary's alleged confession, the document based on the notes that Sellers had written out from memory at his kitchen table at 4.30 a.m. after the marathon interrogation, he had been riding round in it regularly during the time of the stranglings, and had used it to drive to Florence Scheible's house on the day that she was killed. Had Earnestine agreed that he had indeed borrowed her car often, this would have been important corroboration for the cops' unsigned and undated 'confession'.

As my fascination with the case deepened, I made further trips to Columbus and death row, making the time to travel to Georgia for long weekends during other assignments. Gradually, I learnt more about Gary's life and upbringing. His mother, Carolyn David, bore him when she was seventeen. By then Carlton's father, Willie Frank Gary, was no longer living with her, although they went on to have a daughter, Miriam, eighteen months later. Carolyn had been abandoned by her own mother when she was still an infant, and her straitened economic circumstances forced her to take a succession of irregular and part-time jobs. There were times when the bond she felt with her own children seems to have been weak. However, Carlton had a large extended family, which he remembered as giving him both love and material support. Usually he stayed with his great-grandfather and grandfather, both named Clarence David, his aunt Lillian, and her husband Thurmond, who owned furniture removal and dry-cleaning businesses. Years later, before her death in 1997, Carlton's sister Miriam swore an affidavit about their childhood for use in one of his appeals, claiming that their aunt had been an abusive alcoholic. Interviewed on death row, Gary vehemently denied her allegation. Lillian's home, he said, was large and well-equipped, and his upbringing happy and secure. 'Everyone in that house was working,' Gary said. 'I never wanted for nothing. We used to have the proverbial white Christmases – I mean, they were like a Caucasian family's Christmas, with roaring fires, Christmas cake, nuts, presents and everything you could eat.'

Slowly, the condition of Columbus's African-American districts was improving a little. 'When I was first growing up, the surface of the roads where we all lived was dirt,' Gary said. 'When it rained – man, you should have seen the mud! Later, they put in tarmac.' When he was a little older he stayed at the home of another aunt, Alma Williams, who lived in the middle-class black neighbourhood of Carver Heights, across the main road from Wynnton.

One summer, when Carlton was aged about twelve, his father took him for several weeks to the place where he was living, Gary, Indiana, a tough industrial city near Chicago that specialised in making steel. Willie Gary had been feeling his way towards developing his relationship with Carlton for a while, sending letters, gifts and money. But it soon became clear that Carlton did not get on with his wife. 'She was talking about spanking me for something, and I said there weren't no way that was going to happen,' Gary said. 'I told them they could put me back on the train.' He would not see his father again, and by the time of Carlton's arrest for the stranglings, Willie Gary was deceased. The official cause of his death was a construction site accident. According to his brother, Carlton's uncle Jim from Phenix City, he was murdered.

The following summer, Carolyn's brother William David and his wife Suzie, who had recently moved from Columbus to Maryland, invited Carlton to their new home for an extended visit. Their son, Rudolph, was a little younger than Carlton, and later the Davids took the boys on a road trip. 'All I can say is that when he was with us, he was a totally normal teenage boy,' Suzie David told me at her retirement apartment in south Columbus. 'He was polite and did what he was told, and was a pleasure to be with.' She said that she considered him her 'second son', and that she and her husband discussed adopting him. In a statement to Gary's lawyers, Rudolph David recalled that when he was a child, 'I looked up to Carlton as the kind of boy I wanted to be. We would play together, go see movies, roller-skate and ride our bikes. I was very proud to be Carlton's friend because he was well-liked by everyone.'

In the autumn of 1964 Carlton enrolled at Carver High School, a few blocks from Aunt Alma's house. *Brown vs Board of Education* notwithstanding, its student body remained entirely black. He was not there long. The following year he started classes at another black Columbus high school, Spencer. The school records listed Aunt Lillian as his mother and Carolyn as his legal guardian.

By now Carlton's sister Miriam and his mother were living with his mother's new partner, a man named Julius Parker, in Fort Myers, Florida, a naval port on the state's west coast. Miriam stated in the affidavit she swore before her death that Carlton was 'devastated' when Carolyn moved there without him, although he finally joined the rest of the family in 1966, and enrolled in another school, Dunbar High. It was a difficult period, fraught with emotional upheaval. There was high tension between Carlton and his stepfather, and according both to Gary and to Miriam's affidavit, Julius Parker's relationship with Carolyn was becoming violently abusive. On one occasion, Miriam said, her mother was forced to seek protection from him by taking out a restraining order. Trying to make light of what must have been a traumatic situation, Gary told me of one especially bewildering detail he recalled from his new school: 'It was the time of Beatlemania. In Florida, even the black kids were wearing Beatle haircuts. I looked out of place and I asked someone: "How come all these guys are wearing wigs?" '

Carlton already felt unwanted, but worse was to come. After some months he got home from school to find that Carolyn, Miriam and Julius Parker had simply 'disappeared', leaving no word of their whereabouts. He was just fifteen. 'That,' said Gary, 'was when the bad things in my life really began.'

For a while he slept rough, in cars and at a church. Some days he got a little work, picking vegetables and selling them at a farmers' market; when that was unavailable, he stole in order to eat. Eventually, he said, an evangelical preacher with eleven children of his own took him in, and in return for this hospitality Gary, already an accomplished musician, played drums and keyboards in the church band. 'It was in his house that I had sex for the first time,' said Gary. 'It was with the preacher's sister. She just came into my room one night and crawled into my bunk.'

Carlton still had no idea of his mother's whereabouts, but he set off on the Greyhound with a few dollars in his pocket for Washington DC, the home of one his grandmothers, Carolyn's mother Lucille. He only got as far as Gainesville, Florida, an inland city about two hundred miles north of Fort Myers. 'That was where my money ran out. All I had with me was an old, rusty suitcase. I went into an electronics shop and stole ten or twelve pocket radios, planning on selling them. I was standing at the bus station, thinking about stealing a car, when I met this black cat. I still don't know what made me do it, but I asked him, "Do you know a woman named Carolyn, who has a daughter called Miriam?" He said, "Sure I do, they live right there." They were one block away. I just walked into the building and up the stairs and there she was.' It was an emotional reunion. 'We hugged and kissed. Julius Parker was out of the picture and I took over a bedroom.' The University of Florida campus was nearby. Carlton started work there as a short-order cook.

Richard Hyatt described the neighbourhood where the Gary family was living in the *Ledger-Enquirer* in 1986. A far cry from the relative affluence of his aunts' homes in Columbus, the Gainesville ghetto, Porters Quarters, was 'twenty-five blocks of misery. Four blocks away from a university frat house and a couple more from the main campus, it is light years away in reality. One world wears Izod [the American designer leisure-wear label]. The other wears anger. It is a trip into a time warp. The streets are narrow; cats, dogs and chickens scratch in the sandy dirt. So do wide-eyed children. Old cars are left for dead.'

Carolyn was working at the Blue Rose Café, an establishment owned by a woman named Dee-Dee Preston; Carlton and Preston's son Joe became friends. Joe had a sister, Sheila, who was seventeen, a year older than Carlton. She was a former high school track star, but when Gary first arrived in Gainesville she was coming to the end of a spell at a state reformatory in the nearby town of Ocala. A little before Christmas 1966, when the time came to bring Sheila home, Dee-Dee asked Carlton if he would like to join her for the ride.

'Sheila was older than me and a little wiser,' Gary said. 'She had been raised on the street, and I was only just learning. So there we were in the waiting room at the reformatory. I had a green cap on with a shiny silver pin, and thought I was the coolest thing going. The rest of her family went to get her, and then we all walked out together along this cinder-block corridor. As we were walking she looked up at me and asked, "Do you have a girlfriend?" I said that I didn't. She said: "Well, you got one now." She was just a little bitty thing. Not so pretty really, but to me, she was the most beautiful thing on earth – this amazing, mature woman, with a big butt and skinny legs, like a horse's. She had accumulated some money, savings from work in the reformatory, and on the way home we went shopping. That night we went back to her house and Dee-Dee showed us a bed. She said: "This is where you're sleeping." I thought, "Who's she talking about?" It was me and Sheila. I was shocked: I was like in another world. I got this woman, sex, and she got money; and I'm in a house, eating good. I just thought: "Wow."' Before long Sheila was pregnant by Gary. Their daughter, Latwanna, was born on 7 August 1967.

In the late 1960s, Gainesville was in ferment. Dubbed 'the Berkeley of the South' because of its campus political activism, it was one of the first places where the moderate civil rights movement typified by the leader-ship of the Reverend Dr Martin Luther King Junior began to make way for more radical successors, such as the Student Non-Violent Coordinating Committee (SNCC) and the Black Panthers. These groups were prepared to use force to defend themselves. They had their white supremacist coun-terparts in the Young Men's Democratic Club, an institution that went back to Reconstruction, and the Ku Klux Klan. Some in Gainesville still remem-bered how the Klan had cemented its influence in January 1923 with a massacre at Rosewood, fifty miles to the south-east. When a white woman claimed that she had been raped there by an African-American, the Klan marched through Gainesville, bearing placards that read: 'First And Always – Protect Womanhood'. This was followed by six days of terror. A mob burned down the entire Rosewood township, murdering and maiming an unknown number of its black inhabitants. Afterwards, an editorial in the *Gainesville Daily Sun* commented that while it was unfortunate that people had died, this was only to be expected. After all, 'a brutish negro made a criminal assault on an unprotected white girl ... In whatever state it may be, law or no law, courts or no courts – as long as criminal assaults on innocent women continue, lynch law will prevail, and blood will be shed'. In cases of murder and arson, the paper added, the law could take its course. But the violation of white women was different: 'Preach and admonish and warn as you may, the crime of rape will never be tolerated for one single moment ... the time will never come when a Southern white man will not avenge a crime against innocent womanhood.'

By 1967, as race riots, triggered by claims of oppression by white-dominated police forces, broke out in cities such as Newark, New Jersey, and Detroit, tensions in Gainesville were running high, fuelled additionally by the burgeoning movement against the Vietnam War. Even before meeting Sheila, Gary was involved with SNCC. 'There were a lot of white people in it as well as black, especially academics,' Gary said. 'There was one couple who lived down a dirt road in an orange grove. You'd have guessed the guy was a red-necked bubba, but he was fighting injustice, same as we all were.' SNCC and the anti-war activists saw the police and the FBI as the enemy, and their campaigns took on some of the character of an underground resistance.

Sometimes politics segued into crime. In the autumn of 1967 Gary was arrested for breaking into cars, and like Sheila before him served a short spell in the reformatory. 'The night before I had to report for jail, I was crying like a baby: I was going to be separated from Sheila and my little girl. I said to her, "Let's run," but Sheila said, "No, let's get it over."' In the event Gary served three months, and although he was locked up at night, by day he studied music and art at a community college.

The Gainesville SNCC was already used to physical confrontations. On 17 March 1968, Gary made the front page of a newspaper for the first time, when with five others – Sheila included – he fire-bombed a white-owned Porters Quarters grocery store. No one was hurt, but the building was razed to the ground. In his 1986 profile, Richard Hyatt wrote that the reason for the attack was that the owner had called the cops when Gary's mother tried to cash a bad cheque. Talking to me in prison, Gary denied this: 'It wasn't personal, it was political. I had no idea that he had refused my mom's cheque, and I never heard about it until years afterwards. We bombed him because we thought he was racist.' Either way, Gary, Sheila and their alleged accomplices were arrested four days later. Once again, Sheila was pregnant.

With the city approaching boiling point, there were several cases in Gainesville during this period in which black suspects were mysteriously sprung from custody, only to be found shot dead: the evidence suggests that law-enforcement bodies had deliberately set them up.* According to

---

* Four years later, in 1972, the 'Gainesville Eight' trial would reveal the lengths to which the Florida authorities were prepared to go in order to stifle dissent. The eight anti-war activists arrested while preparing a protest at the Republican National Convention in Miami managed to prove that the state government had planned to have someone killed and to blame it on the demonstrators, then to trap them on a beach where more would have been shot by police. The eight were acquitted of conspiracy after arguing that their own weapons were only for self-defence.

Gary, he learnt from a friendly guard in jail that he was being lined up as their next victim. Security, however, was lax, and somehow he and another SNCC comrade he called 'Homeboy' managed to escape. Having spent the night in an empty house surrounded by farmland, they were picked up by members of the local SNCC underground and driven north across the Georgia state line. On the run for the first time, Gary and Homeboy travelled by bus to Homeboy's grandparents, who lived in rural seclusion in Pinewood, South Carolina. There Gary learnt a little about country life: 'One day Homeboy's grandmother asked me to hold a hog while she took its balls off for food. They call them "mountain oysters" – you crush them, and eat them with egg.' Gary took a job at an agricultural processing plant, but left after getting his first week's pay – $8, not a lot of money, even in 1968. 'Homeboy's grandfather said, "That good!" To me, he had the typical slave mentality.'

It was not a life to which Gary was ideally suited. At the beginning of May 1968 he and Homeboy burgled a general store, forcing entry with a crowbar and stealing jewellery and cash. 'I told Homeboy that the police were going to know we did it, because the other black folks in the area had been living there all that time but had never stolen anything. As we got back home I could see that the yard was full of police.' Homeboy was arrested, but Gary fled, leaping over fences and then hiding at the home of a local girl he had been seeing. 'This old black cat took me through the woods and we walked I don't know how far.' Gary found a car, hot-wired the ignition, and drove away. Once again, he was on the run.

In the autumn of 1991, having lost his direct review in the Georgia Supreme Court, Carlton Gary took his case to the next stage of the capital appeals process – a claim of *habeas corpus*, a petition asserting that his continued detention was unlawful, because his constitutional rights had been violated. Like all such claims in Georgia, it was lodged with the court nearest to death row – the Butts County Superior Court in Jackson. So many *habeas* petitions find their way to Butts County that it has to draft in extra judges from other parts of Georgia in order to cope. Gary's case was assigned to Judge Daniel Coursey from DeKalb County, a region of suburbs just to the east of Atlanta, around the base of Stone Mountain. Like many lawyers in the South, Coursey, who had been on the bench for almost ten years, took his religion seriously. A lay preacher in the United Methodist Church, he once told an interviewer that if he were to allow his faith to govern his professional judgements, 'I probably wouldn't punish anybody for anything. Basically, you're supposed to forgive people.' However, he also believed in the separation of Church and state, and had found that this principle made it possible for him to send defendants to the electric chair with a clear conscience: 'Our society believes you should be punished for your crimes. The ultimate punishment is the death penalty.'

Having given so much, Bud Siemon was off the case at last. Representing Gary for his state *habeas* appeal was the Georgia Death Penalty Resource Center, a not-for-profit organisation funded, not very generously, by the state and federal courts. In the autumn of 1992 the centre's director, Michael Mears, asked his newest lawyer, Jeff Ertel, to take Gary's case on. A rugged, down-to-earth figure with sandy hair and an open, easy manner, Ertel was happier wearing jeans and a leather jacket than the standard attorney's suit. Born and raised on the Canadian border in Buffalo, New York, he had come late to the legal profession, having spent eleven years in his home town working as a Deputy Sheriff. 'I just happened to be in the office and didn't have many other cases,' Ertel said, 'so Mike Mears called me over and said he had an opportunity for me – to work on the most notorious case in Georgia. I was three or four months out of law school.'

One of the peculiarities of Georgia law is that while the prosecution has wide powers to keep documents and other evidence secret when a case goes before a jury, later, after conviction and the first, 'direct review', appeal, it can be compelled to hand over almost everything to the defence – by which time, owing to the strict rules of procedure, it may be too late for them to use it. Under the state Open Records Act, a local freedom of information law, defence lawyers can demand to see the sealed files held by District Attorneys and police. This Ertel did. He had already spent weeks poring over the enormous public record: the thousands of pages of pre-trial, trial and direct review transcripts, together with the statements and reports that had been turned over earlier. Now, as a result of his Open Records Act filings, he was told that he and an investigator, Mallikah Rollins, could go to Columbus and read the rest of the state's hidden paper trail – taking both the District Attorney's and police files together, around thirty thousand pages. They sat for weeks in the DA's office, going through the files and having them copied, while Doug Pullen came in and out – a seething, resentful presence. In a later court hearing, Pullen would describe Ertel's persistent enquiries as 'sheer harassment'.

'A lot of this work was just mind-numbing,' Ertel recalled in an interview in 2006, 'especially some of the police files. We knew we had to read them all, but most of them contained nothing that was going to help us. I've never dreaded a day's hard work in my life, but there were times when I came pretty close to it.' Meanwhile, he was visiting the prison in Jackson, getting to know Carlton Gary. 'When I first got the case I thought it was going to be brutal,' Ertel said. 'I remember thinking, "I just don't know how we can possibly win it. Here I am, months out of law school – what have I got myself into?" I went back to Buffalo to see my mom and she asked me what kind of work I was doing, and I said, "I'm fighting an appeal for a black guy on death row who was convicted for raping and murdering a bunch of white women who were about your age." After that she didn't ask me about my work too much. But when I met Carlton I began to think about it differently. I liked him immediately, and when I got to know him better, I liked him a lot.'

Some of Ertel's discoveries lay in the vast documentary record. Others he made as he began to do what Siemon could never afford – to travel the length of America's eastern seaboard, retracing Gary's own journeys and interviewing many of those who had known him. One early meeting was in Syracuse, New York, where he talked with Tula Jones, Gary's live-in lover in Columbus during the time of the murders. She told him that she had gone to see Gary and spent several days with him in the early autumn of 1977 in Rochester, on the shore of Lake Ontario, before he travelled south for the first time since 1968. She was certain she could not have gone to Rochester until after 16 September 1977, she told Ertel – and, some years later, me – because that was the day she got her welfare cheque, and without it she could not have made the journey from Syracuse. 'That was when I really started to take Carlton's innocence seriously,' Ertel said. 'She seemed utterly convinced. And if Carlton had been in New York on or after 16 September, he could not have raped Gertrude Miller [who was attacked on

11 September] or killed Ferne Jackson [murdered in the early hours of 16 September itself].'

To be considered in a *habeas* appeal, new testimony has to be 'pegged' to some constitutional violation. One of the commonest means of doing so is for the defence to claim that the prosecution failed to fulfil its duty before the trial to disclose all the evidence in its possession that might have favoured the defence. As the US Supreme Court first ruled in the 1963 case of *Brady vs Maryland*, a failure to meet this obligation breaches the Fourteenth Amendment's 'due process' guarantee. Subsequent Supreme Court opinions have extended this duty's scope: the prosecution must disclose not only direct evidence that might suggest innocence, but also facts that might 'impeach' – i.e. call into question – the reliability or truth of other prosecution testimony. This applies both to the prosecution lawyers and to any government agencies working with them, including the police. Faced with a *Brady* claim, a court has to decide whether there is a 'reasonable probability' that the undisclosed evidence might have affected the verdict; if so, it must vacate the conviction and order a new trial. In a 1995 case, *Kyles vs Whiteley*, the Supreme Court tried to explain what 'reasonable probability' meant: 'The adjective is important ... the question is not whether the defendant would more likely than not have received a different verdict with the evidence, but whether in its absence he received a fair trial.' A reasonable probability had to be 'sufficient to undermine confidence in the outcome'.

Under English law, the principle is essentially the same. The nondisclosure of exculpatory evidence has featured in many of the miscarriages of justice exposed in the Court of Appeal in London since 1989, when the Guildford Four – three men and a woman convicted of killing five people by planting a bomb in a public house in Guildford, Surrey, in October 1974 – were released after almost fifteen years' wrongful imprisonment. In their case, the new evidence consisted of formerly hidden documents that showed that their supposed confessions had been fabricated by the police, instead of being made spontaneously, as the prosecution claimed at their trial. The documents revealed that the police had slowly concocted and polished them from a series of rough drafts. In other English cases it was the emergence of concealed scientific evidence that eventually demonstrated a prisoner's innocence. One of the saddest was that of Stefan Kiszko, who spent more than sixteen years in prison for raping and murdering an eleven-year-old girl. His conviction was overturned in 1992, when the Court of Appeal heard that the prosecution had hidden laboratory test results that showed that unlike the killer, Kiszko had a zero sperm count. Although he was freed, the hellish life in prison of a child sex killer had taken its toll, and he died a broken man less than two years later.

Working through the paper mountain, Ertel came across evidence in former District Attorney William Smith's files that had never been 'turned over' to Carlton Gary's defence counsel, and that seemed to him to meet the requirements of *Brady vs Maryland* exactly. Some of this unseen material concerned the testimony of Gertrude Miller – the rape survivor whom Smith, at a press conference after the trial, had described as his 'star witness'. In the words of the brief that Ertel would eventually file in Butts County on Gary's behalf, 'The devastating impact of Mrs Miller's testimony and in-court identification of Mr Gary as the man who broke into her house, hit her in the head with a board, tied her up and attempted to choke her with her stockings, raped her vaginally and anally and left her for dead, cannot be overstated.' Smith, of course, had laid heavy emphasis on Mrs Miller in his closing speech to the jury, claiming that there was no way she could have got her identification wrong: 'Don't you know that every night Mrs Miller has laid her head on her pillow and closed her eyes to go to sleep, that she has seen the face of this man? It's burned into her memory, it's forged into her memory, she can't put it out of her mind if she wants to.' Smith said that she had managed to look at her attacker closely, because while he was trying to kill her, he had turned on a light in order to see what he was doing.

Mrs Miller was particularly important because hers was the only evidence at Gary's trial that was not circumstantial: only she could implicate Gary directly as the man who had attacked elderly women in Columbus. But Gary, Ertel discovered, was by no means the first man she had identified. In Smith's file were no fewer than nine separate documents that cast grave doubt on Mrs Miller's testimony in court.

The first was a police statement from an Elizabeth D. Bell, who had called the police after she learnt that her neighbour, Mrs Miller, had been attacked. That same day, 11 September 1977, she told the cops what Mrs Miller had said to her when she asked if the man had been black or white: 'I don't know what it was.' Also on 11 September, the police interviewed Mrs Miller, who told them, they wrote, that 'she would not be able to identify the subject and she wasn't able to describe him'.

Five weeks later, on 17 October, after the arrest of the confession-addict Jerome Livas, the cops went back to see Mrs Miller and showed her a line-up of photographs. Without hesitation she picked out Livas as the man who had attacked her. 'Mrs Miller stated that the picture of Livas was the closest to the suspect in her case,' the formerly secret police report said, 'and he had the right features.' He looked nothing like Carlton Gary. Two weeks after that, the police went to her home again. This time she showed them the lamp that the rapist had switched on, and said that he was a short man, not much more than five feet tall. Gary stands six feet three inches in his socks.

By 17 January 1978, the day of the cops' next visit to Mrs Miller, three more women had been murdered, and Livas, having told a reporter that he had also killed two US Presidents and Charles Lindbergh's baby, had been cleared. This time Miller sat down with a police artist who produced a 'composite' sketch of the attacker. When it was finished, she said the result was 'very accurate and very similar to the perpetrator'. It depicted an African-American with thin, triangular cheeks and a sharp, pointed chin. Gary's cheeks and chin are round. In yet another hidden document, Detective Richard Smith reported that Mrs Miller had changed her mind about the rapist's height. Now she said that he was five feet eight to five feet ten inches tall, in his early twenties and 'very slender'. Gary has always been a big man with a strong, muscular build.

That spring, the murders stopped. Another few months went by, and then a Mr Mitsopoulos, a Columbus businessman, told the police that the women in his office had encountered a black man 'acting strangely'. It was not much of a lead, but once again the police artist went to work, and with the help of Mitsopoulos and his staff produced another 'composite' drawing. It looked very different from the earlier picture. On 13 July, agents from the Georgia Bureau of Investigation showed the sketch to Gertrude Miller. Special Agent Webb recorded her reactions: 'When Mrs Miller first observed the drawing, she immediately lost her composure and exhibited a shock attitude [sic]. Her action upon seeing the drawing indicated that the individual that attacked her is the same individual seen by Mr Mitsopoulos.' It was, she told Agent Webb, 'a very good likeness of the man that raped her'.

There were two more police reports that were not disclosed to the defence before the trial, recording meetings between Detective Ricky Boren and Mrs Miller after Carlton Gary's arrest – the first on 30 May 1984, the second nine months later, on 6 March 1985. It was only during these interviews, years after her attack, that she claimed for the first time that her attacker had attempted to strangle her. Previously she had described only her rape and sexual assault. It seems that Boren knew about her previous identifications and felt uneasy, because he asked her how she felt about the two composite drawings. Now, her previous certainty forgotten, she told him that she 'never believed the first drawing was accurate', while the second one, though closer, was 'not exact'.

Ertel's brief to the *habeas* court pointed out that anything that might have undermined Mrs Miller's evidence would have been critical to Gary's defence. It is plain that if Siemon had been given copies of the nine concealed reports, the force of her testimony would have been seriously weakened. I asked Professor Gary Wells, the Iowa State University psychologist and advisor to law-enforcement agencies on identification procedures across the US, what he thought the implications were for Mrs Miller's testimony. He said: 'When a witness has made a prior identification of another individual, we know that makes their testimony very unreliable. Studies show that people who do that are simply displaying their willingness to help the investigators, and they don't have enough data in their memories to reject other plausible suspects. And if a witness can't give a reasonable description in her original police report [as, of course, Mrs Miller could not], that speaks volumes about her basic inability to make any kind of identification subsequently.'

The information from the hidden reports is not only notable for the light it sheds on Mrs Miller. It also raises serious questions about the professional ethics of William Smith, who stepped down as DA in 1989 in order to sit as a judge in Columbus's Superior Court. His own files contained the details of Miller's prior identifications – of Jerome Livas from his photograph, and of the two mysterious faces in the composite drawings. Yet when he examined her at the trial, he seems to have forgotten this, and so misled the court.

'Now,' he asked her, 'so, you looked at literally hundreds or thousands of pictures of individuals and told them [the police] "No" on every one of them until you saw this man on television, is that right?' Smith asked.

'Yes,' Mrs Miller replied. An elderly, vulnerable witness, her mistakes can be forgiven. But it was not William Smith's job to elicit them.

From the first day that Bud Siemon began to represent him, Carlton Gary had always maintained that the police version of his interrogation – that he was happy to talk, but only on condition that they neither made contemporaneous notes nor taped him – was a lie. In fact, he said, there was a tape running wherever they spoke – in the car back to Columbus from Albany; inside the police station; in the car again during their drive round Wynnton. His story seemed plausible. By the 1980s, using tapes to record interviews with suspects, especially in murder investigations, was common throughout the United States. One of several examples from Columbus was the case of Jerome Bowden, the mentally retarded youth who went to the electric chair in 1986. Had he not confessed on tape to detectives, he would never have been convicted, let alone executed: there was no other material evidence against him.

Cross-examining Detectives Sellers, Boren and Rowe in the pre-trial hearings, and Sellers at the trial itself, Siemon tried repeatedly to get the officers to admit that Gary's interrogation had also been taped. They always denied it. But according to Gary, if only the purported missing tapes could be rediscovered, they would expose his police statement as a fabrication. He claimed he had not made even the partial confession alleged by the prosecution, had never admitted being at any of the homes where the victims were murdered, and had never accused Malvin Crittenden of perpetrating the killings. Working through the files in Columbus, Jeff Ertel found evidence that suggested that his client might well be telling the truth.

Most significant was what looked like an early version of parts of the eventual twelve-page statement that the state disclosed to Siemon. It consisted of various blocks of text, some of them whole paragraphs, others only a sentence or two, separated by wide gaps. Among them were denials that Gary had been involved in the killings, and assertions that he 'did not know why his prints were in the houses where the ladies were killed'.

The curious thing was that next to some of these remarks were annotations in ink, each one a Roman numeral followed by a number. By the sentence quoted above, for example, was a note reading 'V 415'. Next to the line 'Carlton told Robin Odom that he was sorry for her being involved in the arrest and embarrassment it had caused her,' the note said 'II 865'. The Roman numerals, Ertel suggested in his *habeas* brief, identified which of a series of tapes each quoted comment came from, and the numbers referred to the tape recorder meter reading. This disjointed document did contain some of Gary's more damaging supposed admissions, such as having been present at Florence Scheible's house while Malvin Crittenden murdered her. Next to them, however, there were no numerical markings, suggesting that they may not, unlike other parts of the document, have been transcribed from a recording.

Other documents in William Smith's files in Columbus also suggested that the interviews with Gary had been taped. One was a police report of the car journey from Albany. This too was annotated with Roman and Arabic numerals. Another was something close to the final, public version of Gary's twelve-page statement, with highlighted sections and, once again, the numbers. 'Eventually,' Ertel's court brief said, 'all the notations, highlighting and spaces were deleted,' so leaving the clean document that William Smith gave to Bud Siemon. 'The logical progression of the notations and revisions indicates exactly what defence counsel suspected,' the *habeas* brief stated. 'A tape had been made and what was represented on that tape was not the same as what was testified to by the police at [the] trial. The series of documents shows that the way the state told the jury the interrogation took place was not the way it actually happened. The state had to make revision after revision until the final, highly prejudicial, and factually inaccurate version of the interrogation process was complete.' If Ertel was right, the hidden documents undermined Gary's supposed confession in the same way as the papers discovered in police files in England had undermined those made by the Guildford Four.

There was only one man who might illuminate this and other mysteries – William Smith. Intending to ask him to explain it, I spoke to him by telephone in March 2001. He refused either to meet me or to answer any questions: 'I don't give interviews about the stocking stranglings. The case is still under appeal. I've made it my practice not to talk about it until it's finished.'

Talking to me in prison, Gary repeated his assertion that his conversations with the cops had been taped. During the trip from Albany on the day of his arrest, and later on the drive round Wynnton, 'the tape machine was right there on the seat'. He also claimed that during the night of 3 May 1984, the time when Detective Sellers said he had made his incriminating statements, the police barely asked about the stranglings at all. 'I talked to them about the Columbus robberies I'd confessed to in South Carolina,' Gary said. 'The deal I did then meant I couldn't do time for them. That was the reason I was smiling in those photographs taken when I got to Columbus – I was thinking, "Why are they tripping on like this about those robberies which are over and done with?" ' He said it was not until the early hours of 4 May that he realised he was under arrest for murder – although he admitted that having taken a lot of cocaine in Albany the previous night, he was in a somewhat befuddled state.

There is support for Gary's account of the night of his arrest from two surprising sources. The first is John Allen, now a judge of the Chattahoochee Circuit Superior Court in Columbus, where Gary himself was tried. A tall, quiet African-American with a reputation for integrity, Allen flew more than fifty combat missions as a pilot in Vietnam. In May 1984, it was Allen who spent more than a week as the first of Gary's defence attorneys.

Allen was retained to represent Gary by his mother, Carolyn, on Saturday, 5 May 1984, his second full day in custody. By this time, of course, according to the prosecution story presented at Gary's trial, he had already made his alleged confession, and his interrogation was complete. But as Allen recalled in an interview with me in 2001, two or three times that first weekend the detectives went down to the county jail and tried to question Gary again. Now that he had a lawyer, Allen said, Gary insisted on his right to consult him. Allen's advice was unequivocal: he would be wise not to speak to the cops at all, and under no circumstances should he do so without his attorney being present. 'I went down each time Carlton phoned. He listened to me and no interrogation took place.'

The police, apparently, were far from happy. The jail journal kept by Gary states that at 6 p.m. on 5 May, 'Sellers and Boren came into my cell (number 147) to talk about firing lawyer.' Allen supported this allegation, saying that the cops had indeed put Gary under pressure both to talk to them and to fire his lawyer, promising that if he did, they would 'help' him. They had even told Gary that Allen had recently 'screwed up' another suspect's case by advising her not to talk to detectives. It was true, Allen said, that a few days earlier he had given a woman such advice, but the incident had had no publicity. The only way that Gary could have heard about it was from one of the policemen.

Allen decided to take a gamble: an appeal to none other than the chief judge of the Chattahoochee Circuit Superior Court, John Land. Both men described their meeting at a pre-trial hearing in 1985, and both recalled it in their interviews with me. Allen said: 'After Carlton told me about the incident involving one of my earlier cases I walked over to Judge Land's office right away and I said, "Judge, I'd like to stop the detectives from talking to my client without first contacting me." While I was sitting in his office the judge picked up the phone and he called the Chief of Police. And he said, "Jim [Wetherington], John Allen's in my office and he says that your detectives are going down talking to his client without him."'

Following Land's call to Wetherington, all attempts to interrogate the prisoner stopped. 'After that,' said Allen in his chambers at the top of the Government Center, 'there was no further conversation between the police and Carlton Gary.' Judge Allen added that he was sure that when he first met Gary over the weekend of 5–6 May, 'he had not yet made any incriminating statements. Before that date, they did not have a confession, and after it, the police did not speak to him.'

It was left to John Land to draw the obvious inference. If the police had really obtained their confession by the weekend of 5 May 1984, they would have had no need to try to talk to Gary again: 'It would seem to me that if he had made the statement the police wanted him to make, if he'd said what they wanted him to say, it stands to reason that they wouldn't need to press him to make another one. It would be unusual for the police to pressure someone to make another statement if he'd said what they wanted him to say.' To be sure, Land added, 'there was a tremendous amount of pressure on the Police Department, a lot of pressure to solve the crimes'. But at no other time in his fifty-odd years as a lawman had he ever come across a confession recorded in circumstances quite like Carlton Gary's – by a detective sitting at his kitchen table, writing from memory in the middle of the night. 'It doesn't sound to me like the proper way to do it. I can't recall any other case where that happened.'

Meanwhile, what of Malvin Crittenden, Gary's one-time partner in restaurant robberies and high living, the man accused of the stranglings in the disputed confession? One sleety evening in January 2001, I persuaded him to meet me at his home, a shotgun house in one of the poorest parts of south Columbus, and then we drove to Floyd Washington's nightclub, the F&W Control Tower. Crittenden, a slim, stooped figure with a drawn face and a moustache, was dressed immaculately, in a brown tweed suit, a cream V-neck sweater and a matching silk cravat. Yet he looked haunted: 'This case can still hurt me a lot. I don't know why I'm speaking to you at all,' he said. 'I'm an independent paint contractor. I ain't been in no trouble for more than twenty years. I make my living now by working in ladies' homes – you know what I'm saying?'

It was a Tuesday night, and the club was quiet. Washington, flamboyant in a scarlet baseball cap and matching dungarees, poured us brandies. 'You guys [Crittenden and Gary] were here all the time,' he said. 'You two were like Robin Hoods – stealing from the rich and spending your money on the poor folks in here. Man, I was jealous of the way the chicks used to flock!'

'As I recall, you had plenty opportunities yourself,' Crittenden said.

He started to relax, and told me a little about his life. 'Carlton and I spent our childhoods getting stomped and spat on,' he said. 'That was part of the reason we done what we did. The places we hit was owned by white people. We were getting something back.' He said he hadn't spoken to Gary since his arrest in February 1979 in Gaffney, South Carolina, the day Gary tried to rob a restaurant on his own. 'I felt it was time to stop. Carlton disagreed. And so he went to Gaffney by himself and fucked it up.'

Gary, he said, had been 'closer to me than anyone. Often we slept, back to back, in the same bed, in the best hotels, at least eight floors up, so we could see the police coming.' Did he think that Gary could have been the strangler? Crittenden shook his head. 'He *loved* women, all kinds. He was *into* women.'

As Ertel worked through the documents in 1992, he made further discoveries. For example, Smith had claimed at the trial that none of the officers who interrogated Gary had played more than a peripheral role in the original investigation. Thus, he argued, they would not have known their way to the crime scenes. When they took Gary for a drive round Wynnton, their ignorance about the murders meant that it must have been Gary who gave them directions. Only he could have supplied those telling details 'only the killer would have known'. In fact, as Ertel now learnt from another document, one of the three detectives, Charles Rowe, had worked for many months on the stocking strangler 'task force', starting from the time it was formed at the beginning of 1978. To him at least, the location and circumstances of each murder should have been only too familiar.

Yet more formerly hidden documents raised new questions about the evidence that had led to Gary's arrest – the right-hand little-finger print allegedly lifted from the aluminium screen on Kathleen Woodruff's bedroom window, the point where the strangler had got into her house. In Smith's files, Ertel found police reports of the crime scene investigations after Mrs Woodruff's body was discovered. They made no mention of any latent prints being found on the window screen at all – although they *did* refer to other prints, that were never matched to Carlton Gary, being lifted from other places close by. One report, dated 29 December 1977, the day after Mrs Woodruff's murder, stated that both the 'window and window sill at point of entry [were processed] with iodine'. There were, however, 'no legible latents developed'.

Years later, I found another puzzling discrepancy between the trial evidence about fingerprints and what had been the normal practice of the CPD – and, indeed, police forces throughout America. All the prints, not just those lifted from Mrs Woodruff's house, were preserved on small pieces of cardboard, stuck down with transparent adhesive tape. On the front of each card, a short note recorded the date and location of the print's discovery. In other words, there was no independent evidence of the source of the prints. The reliability of the fingerprint evidence from all four homes where the state said prints had been found depended entirely on the officers who had made up the cards.

At the beginning of 2001, at his church-cum-real-estate-office in south Columbus, I talked through the fingerprint evidence with Eddie Florence, the African-American former cop turned preacher. His eighteen years in the print identification section covered the entire period from before the first murder until after Carlton Gary's arrest. First, he thought that the absence of a report recording the print on Kathleen Woodruff's window screen was strange: 'None of us would have left that crime scene on the day they found the body until we were done. Then we would go back to the Police Department and write a report. Sometimes that would overrun the end of your shift. But you had to finish the job in case they got a suspect.'

However, Florence found something else much more troubling. As the CPD crime scene team went through a house where someone had been murdered, they would always make a photographic record as they worked. Indeed, dozens of photos of all the murder scenes were exhibits in Gary's trial. If a latent print was found, it would invariably be photographed *in situ*, in order to provide incontrovertible evidence that it was genuine. Only then, with the record complete, would the print be lifted onto tape and transferred to cardboard. 'Stamped on the back of every photo was the date, together with the name and signature of who took the photo and who lifted the print,' Florence said. 'It would stop a lawyer in his tracks, take the breath out of him.'

When the police found Carlton Gary's print on a trunk in the Albany, New York, hotel room where Nellie Farmer was murdered in 1970, they photographed it *in situ*. Yet there were no photographs at all of any of the latent prints said to match Gary's in Columbus – not at Mrs Woodruff's house, nor at the homes of Florence Scheible, Ferne Jackson or Martha Thurmond. There were photos of the rooms where the prints were found, but none that included them. Florence found this inexplicable. 'You wouldn't only do it for a murder. You'd do it for a regular burglary. I just can't understand how they didn't photograph the latents at the scenes of the worst crimes this city had ever experienced.'

A couple of months after our first meeting I went to see Florence again. In the meantime, he had remembered something else – that Detective Richard Smith and a colleague had been to see Carlton Gary in jail in Greenville, South Carolina, in 1979, after his arrest for restaurant robbery. 'Any black guy from Columbus who was picked up in this period anywhere would have their prints checked against the strangling latents,' Florence said. 'That went on for years. They weren't even checking just felons: they were running the prints of guys stopped at random on the street. It's absolutely certain that when they went to South Carolina they would have brought back his prints and had them checked, and they would have identified him then and there if they really had those latents on file. The identification of Gary as the strangler would have been made in 1979, not 1984.'

Adding to Florence's certainty was the fact that one of the cops who talked to Gary in Greenville was Richard Smith. 'I mean, he was practically running the stocking strangling task force. If a task force officer had gone to South Carolina, I or a colleague would have been waiting up to make a match when he returned.'

Not only did William Smith fail to tell the jury at Gary's trial that his prints had been compared to the crime scene latents back in 1979, he positively asserted that this did not happen. Richard Smith, he told the jury in his closing summation, was 'obviously a good detective … and it's just unfortunate, members of the jury, that he didn't come back and have his [Gary's] fingerprints compared with the stocking strangler's latent prints on file in the Columbus Police Department'. When Richard Smith testified – as a witness for the defence – he made no mention of it either.

Sitting in his grand office overlooking Central Park in New York, I asked Smith whether he had in fact brought Gary's prints back to Columbus. He readily confirmed that he had, as well as samples of his saliva and pubic hair. This, he said, had been one of the main reasons for going to Greenville in the first place. He told me that back at the CPD headquarters he gave Gary's prints to one of Eddie Florence's colleagues in the print ID section, George Keller (since deceased), and asked him to make the comparisons. No match was found. 'I don't know how they missed that one,' Smith told me calmly. 'They should have caught it if there were prints which could have been identified. To this day, no one knows why they didn't.'

During our evening together in Gwinnett County, I also explored this mystery with the man who first made Gary a suspect after ordering a copy of his prints – Detective Michael Sellers. He knew all about Smith's unsuccessful mission. 'Richard told me that he gave them to Keller, and I believe him. I know they checked the latents against hundreds and hundreds of prints.' Perhaps, he mused, the print section had simply been disorganised, and somehow comparing Gary's prints with the latents was a job that never got done.

There are some problems with that explanation. First, Richard Smith wasn't just any Columbus detective: he was a leading investigator in robbery-homicide and the effective operational leader of the stocking stranglings task force. Secondly, when he set off for South Carolina, the cops there already knew about Gary's criminal record – about his alleged role in the two cases in upstate New York in which elderly women, Nellie Farmer and Jean Frost, had been robbed and sexually assaulted, and in Farmer's case murdered. According to the Greenville cops' testimony in Columbus, they had uncovered Gary's true name and record when they ran his fingerprints through the national system at the FBI in Washington DC. It seems unlikely that they would not have told Richard Smith about this. Keen as he may have been to clear up the restaurant robberies in Columbus, the events in New York must have made him see that comparing Gary's prints with the strangling latents might be quite important.

I was about to move on to a different subject when Sellers came up with an alternative explanation that I found still harder to swallow: that the fingerprints *had* been matched, but the person who did the matching had kept this fact to themself. 'During the time of the murders, you could have written your own ticket if you had solved them. Some officers guarded their titbits of information. One wouldn't tell another. It wouldn't have surprised me if one of those officers held on to those files in case they got a big lead.'

At Gary's trial, the fingerprint testimony had seemed overwhelming. But as Ertel stated in his *habeas* brief, had the defence known more of the story behind it, its effect might have been rather different.

*   *   *

David's answer seemed not to have been what Smith and Pullen wanted to hear. His affidavit went on: 'Although I was confident that I could be of assistance in determining if Mr Gary was the individual who inflicted the wound to the victim, I was never contacted by the District Attorney's office, nor was I provided with a sufficient sample from a suspect to make a comparison.' His professional advice, he concluded, had been disregarded. 'As Mr Gary's trial progressed, it became apparent that the District Attorney was not going to use the bite-mark evidence. I had strong misgivings as to why he chose not to use what I believed to be highly relevant evidence.'

It took only a short visit to Carlton Gary on death row for Ertel to confirm his recollections: far from exhibiting overcrowding, both his lower and upper teeth were well-spaced and even. Gary told him that the only dental work he had had done since the last strangling in 1978 had been performed while he was in prison in South Carolina for the restaurant robberies. However, this had been only to his upper teeth. Later, Ertel managed to find the dentist who had treated him, Dr Paul Hahn, who had kept records of what he did. Dr Hahn also swore an affidavit, saying: 'Mr Gary was brought to my office in shackles and handcuffs, and accompanied by an armed guard. I recall that the work I performed on Mr Gary focused on his upper two teeth only and that I installed a crown where the upper left front tooth would be and capped the right front tooth.' Hahn confirmed Gary's assertion. On his lower teeth, he did nothing.

The cast from the bite on Janet Cofer's breast had been made by a dentist in Columbus, Dr Carlos 'Sonny' Galbreath. Months before the trial, Dr David had spoken to him on the phone, and Galbreath told him that instead of keeping the mould in the CPD's guarded exhibits store, Smith and Pullen had given it back to him. This was an extremely strange way to treat a piece of physical evidence that might have proven a suspect's guilt. Sometime in June 1993, Ertel phoned Dr Galbreath and asked whether he still had the cast. 'I think I have it here at home,' he told him. 'Why don't you come by and have a look?' The following week, Ertel drove to Columbus with another Resource Center lawyer, Beth Wells. Galbreath said that he had recently closed his practice and retired, but he thought he had packed up the cast in one of the boxes where he had stored his old files. A few days later Galbreath phoned Ertel. He sounded apologetic, and said his earlier statements had been mistaken. The cast had been destroyed.

In the early 1990s, when Ertel was preparing Gary's *habeas* petition, a new technology was beginning to transform the landscape of criminal investigations and appeals – DNA fingerprinting, an almost foolproof method of identifying someone by the genetic blueprint carried in all human tissue and bodily fluids. The first of 180 American prisoners condemned to death who have, as of this writing in 2006, been proven innocent by a DNA test was Kirk Nobel Bloodsworth, a former Marine discus champion. He was freed from death row in Maryland in 1993 after tests on semen found in the underpants of the nine-year-old girl he had supposedly raped and killed showed that he could not have been her murderer. As long as the crime scene samples have been preserved, DNA testing can establish guilt or innocence many years after a crime. While the older method of serology typing can eliminate a suspect – if, for example, he turns out to be a secretor when the killer is not – it operates at the level of huge groups: group O secretors make up more than a third of the population. There are circumstances when the results of DNA tests can be mistaken, especially if samples are contaminated. In general, however, they provide extremely reliable evidence.

With this in mind, Ertel established that the original swabs and microscope slides from the strangler's victims had been stored at the Georgia State Crime Lab in Atlanta. Normal practice in murder cases, especially those still under appeal, was to preserve such samples indefinitely. Ertel went to court in an effort to obtain them, and on 26 March 1994 Judge Coursey issued an order. The state, it said, must immediately produce all 'actual blood, semen and/or saliva samples', as well as 'impressions or other evidence pertaining to any bite marks found on the victim, Ms Cofer'.

However, the state could only produce this evidence if it was still in existence. On 26 May, the lab's Deputy Assistant Director Gary G. Theisen wrote a letter to Ertel, stating: 'As of this date, we are not in possession of any biologicals on the cases you are interested in.'

Worse was to come. The following month, on 20 June, Judge Coursey convened an 'evidentiary hearing' in the Butts County courthouse to find out what had happened to the missing bite and semen evidence. Representing the state, as was and is still usual in *habeas corpus* hearings, was Susan Boleyn, Georgia's Assistant Attorney General, the head of a team of lawyers who spend their entire working lives resisting capital appeals – known without affection among Georgia's capital defence bar as 'the death squad'. Boleyn had been doing the job for fourteen years, and had a well-earned reputation for toughness, for seldom being willing to concede a legal or evidentiary point. Representing Gary, Ertel was joined by Algernon L. Marbley and James A. Wilson, seasoned attorneys from Vorys, Sater, Seymour & Pease, a big private firm with branches in Ohio and Washington DC. Both men – who had been recruited by an American Bar Association scheme for death penalty appeals – have since become federal judges. On the stand to answer their questions was William Smith's successor as Columbus's District Attorney, Doug Pullen.

Ten days earlier, Pullen had written to Ertel, making the extraordinary claim that all of the samples of bodily fluid had been destroyed on the grounds that they constituted a 'bio-hazard'. Now he gave sworn testimony that as far as he could recall, they had already ceased to exist before Gary's trial in 1986: 'It is considered, if I follow correctly, by the Crime Lab to be a bio-hazard at the time it was taken. There was nothing that could have been done with it, and it was not maintained.'

Pullen was cross-examined by Algernon Marbley, a tall African-American. 'I want to turn for a moment to the serological evidence, the blood, semen, et cetera,' Marbley said. 'Am I to understand that at some point the Georgia Crime Lab destroyed that evidence?'

'I was not there,' Pullen replied. 'That is my recollection, that it is their policy to take the evidence and destroy it as a bio-hazard.'

'When you refer to it as being their policy, is it a written policy, Mr Pullen?'

'I couldn't tell you. All I know is, I asked about the vials and swabs and that kind of thing, and they tell me that they are routinely destroyed as bio-hazards as part of their policy.'

If this was true, it was a very peculiar policy, which put Georgia out of step with every other state in the union, and it was difficult to see precisely what hazard sealed vials or microscope slides might represent. But as Gary's lawyers were well aware, under Georgia and US law, non-existent evidence had no value, however significant it might, hypothetically, have been.

Marbley also asked about the bite cast. Pullen confirmed that he had taken it to Atlanta in the company of William Smith and one of the detectives, and that Dr David had examined it. But he had 'no earthly idea' what had happened to it later: 'I never saw it again.' He admitted that he knew the dentist who had made the cast, Dr Galbreath. But although they had spoken on several occasions after Ertel started digging, they had not discussed the bite: 'I have talked with Dr Galbreath about his health and that kind of thing, but I have no recollection of talking with him about the bite marks at all.'

Beginning six months later, over two days in January and one in March 1995, Judge Coursey held a second oral hearing. This time the star witness was William Smith, the former District Attorney who had become a Columbus judge. Piece by piece, Marbley asked him about the hidden evidence that Ertel had found in the files in Columbus – about the documents that shed new light on the courtroom identification by Gertrude Miller, on the fingerprints and Gary's supposed confession, and the fact there had been a bite cast.

It soon became clear that Smith had a standard answer prepared to every difficult question, and nothing that Marbley said would persuade him to deviate from it. Asked about the hidden evidence, including the earlier statements of Gertrude Miller and the bite cast, Smith said he had not disclosed it because he did not think it 'relevant or exculpatory'. Thus, he implied, he had not breached the rules of disclosure set out in *Brady vs Maryland*, and Gary's rights had not been violated. He added that he had shown the entire prosecution file to Judge Followill, who had supported almost all Smith's decisions about what ought to be turned over, adding just two short documents of minor importance.

However, when it came to explaining the multiple versions of Gary's alleged confession with their handwritten tape meter marks, Smith's explanation was rather different. As often happens when a witness in court feels under pressure, his language – normally so clear, concise and eloquent – became distinctly frayed.

'What happened was,' said Smith, 'the statement [the twelve-page confession document that the cops wrote up from memory] was so critical and
so important to us, and I considered it so critical that every detail of it be
afforded to the defence, so that I would not be subject to an objection ... I
was so concerned perhaps to the point of overkill or – well, I was very
concerned about it. And so, in final trial preparation, I got in my office the
three detectives mentioned here, Mr Rowe, Mr Sellers and Mr Boren, in my
office. I took my tape recorder, my Dictaphone, set it in the middle of my
desk and set it on conference and we stayed there for, I'm guessing, about
two days, and I said, "I want it taken from day one."'

Smith admitted that the handwritten numbers on the versions of Gary's
confession did refer to a tape. But this, he said, covered only the meeting
between him and the police. According to Smith, his assistant Al Miller
had then compared the recordings of this meeting with Gary's typed
confession, writing in the meter readings where the cops had spoken of
supposed statements by Gary that were also set out in the confession
document drawn up two years earlier.

Missing entirely from Smith's account was some explanation of the
purpose of this intensely laborious exercise – especially, as Smith had
described it, as part of his 'final trial preparation'. Still, as Algernon Marbley
realised, there would have been an easy way for Smith to demonstrate that
he was telling the truth: to produce the tapes in Butts County.

'Now, you say that you had a meeting with the detectives, and you
turned on your tape recorder, and you discussed the statement that Carlton
allegedly gave to these detectives,' Marbley asked in cross-examination. 'Is
that right?'

'That's correct,' said Smith.

'Did you transcribe that session that you had with the detectives?'

'No.'

'Do you still have those tapes?'

'No.'

Marbley had already guessed the reason. 'You erased those tapes, didn't
you?'

'I erased them.'

'You erased them personally; is that right?'

'That's right.'

This would also have been a lengthy process, and a curious use of such an important official's time. Using the technology commonly available in 1986, erasing tapes took as long as it did to record them. Smith could not remember when he had performed this task: it might have been before the trial, or it might have been afterwards.

After the evidentiary hearings, Ertel, Marbley and Wilson submitted their final *habeas corpus* brief. It raised other issues, including racial discrimination and the old, vexatious question of Followill's denial of funds. The pressure, it said, to catch the stocking strangler had always been enormous: 'So intense was the pressure, the state took affirmative steps to ensure petitioner was afforded no funds at trial. So bent on convicting petitioner was the state that they failed to disclose innumerable pieces of exculpatory evidence. So intent on conviction, the state by wilful omission allowed exculpatory evidence to be destroyed. So bent on conviction, the prosecutor deliberately mis-stated facts to the jury … This court must now look upon the entire record and determine if justice will finally be done. This court must determine if petitioner will go to the electric chair in clear violation of the State and Federal Constitutions.'

The brief also set out the curious fact that Smith, Followill, Haywood Turner, the federal judge Robert Elliott and many of the victims' families were members or regular users of the all-white Big Eddy Club. 'There could be no more powerful evidence of bias than to show that Judge Followill and District Attorney Smith belonged to racist clubs and were close friends with a number of the victims or their family members,' the *habeas* brief stated. Had the defence been told this before the trial, it might have succeeded in getting Followill recused from the trial.

In her much shorter reply, Susan Boleyn took the same position as Smith had in his testimony. None of the documents disclosed to Ertel fell within the scope of *Brady vs Maryland*, because they were not truly exculpatory: there was no 'reasonable probability' that allowing the jury to see them would have affected the outcome.

Gary's case might have been one of Ertel's first capital appeals, but it was, he told me in 2006, about the strongest he had seen: 'I think with any case other than Carlton's, we would have got a new trial at state *habeas*. But no one wants to give a new trial to a serial killer, especially a black man convicted of killing and raping white women in the Deep South.' Even as he filed the brief, he warned Gary to expect the worst.

Judge Coursey dealt with the procedural matters first, ruling that the denial of funds and ineffective counsel issues were, indeed, barred – just as Followill had warned they would be back in 1987. So were any arguments about racism, unreliable identification and the use of hypnosis. He issued his final order, just ten pages long, on 13 November 1995, dismissing everything else. Throughout it, Coursey adopted the prosecution's reasoning. Hence, referring to Gary's confession, he stated baldly, without further elaboration: 'The police stated that this statement was not taped, and Judge Smith confirmed this at the *habeas* hearing. At this time, there is no credible evidence to show that Gary's statement was taped.'

As for all the other fresh evidence unearthed by Jeff Ertel, 'none of the documents which petitioner now points to are exculpatory, and they do not fall within the purview of *Brady*. Furthermore, the combined effect of these documents does not undermine confidence in the verdict.'

Finally, although he had refused to consider whether the denial of funds had caused Gary's trial counsel to be ineffective, he did review the bigger question of whether this had violated his Fourteenth Amendment due process rights. In Coursey's view, it had not. Judges Land and Followill had not 'abused their discretion', Coursey said, adding: 'The defence stated that it should be given at least equal resources for the defence as the state had for the prosecution. Clearly, under the law, the defence is not entitled to the same funding as the state might have.' Or in Gary's case, any funding at all.

Thus Carlton Gary lost his second round of appeals.

ELEVEN

# *Due Process*

Justice, justice shall you pursue, in order that you may live.

Deuteronomy, 16:20

A day or two after stealing a car in the course of his flight from the rural discomforts of Pinewood, South Carolina, in May 1968, Carlton Gary found himself in Raleigh, North Carolina, where he knew no one. Still only seventeen, with Sheila doing jail time for burning down the grocery store back in Gainesville, Florida, and pregnant with their second child, his only plan was to keep on moving north. 'I was looking for a ride,' he told me, 'and something drew me to a Western Union office. In walked this guy, dressed in black, a musician. He and his band were playing at a local club, The Cave. We got talking and I went to the show and hooked up with one of the dancers. He said I could be his valet and maybe play an instrument. When they left that night they took me with them.'

Gary's benefactor was 'Wildman' Steve Gallon, a black radio disc jockey – he took his nickname from the station where he made his name, WILD Boston – who also led a musical comedy revue. In 1968 Gallon's career was on the up, and for a few heady weeks Gary became part of his entourage. In Boston he stayed at Gallon's home, a bustling artistes' colony, 'like a long-stay motel for musicians'. In the evenings Gary stood in on bass and keyboards during performances at Louie's Lounge in the neighbourhood of Roxbury, a storied crucible of jazz, blues and rock and roll. Topping the bill some nights were Ike and Tina Turner. The revue also did gigs out of Boston, in towns across the north-east and beyond, including an

276

appearance at the Apollo Theatre in Harlem. 'I was doing some cleaning, taking clothes to the laundry, sometimes the cooking, besides the music,' Gary said. Gallon and his wife Vicky were so taken with their new protégé that at one stage they even spoke of adopting him. For Gary, the results of meeting Wildman Steve were money, status and the attention of beautiful women.

'I was living the life of Riley,' Gary said. 'One time we were playing at the Golden Nugget off Washington Street in Boston. I met this white chick. At that time, most white females thought black dudes were pimps, and the dudes thought they were whores. But she wasn't. She was staying at the Sheraton and I went back to her room. Next morning her black room-mate came back. Then she takes off her clothes and we all had this threesome. It went on three or four days, and I thought I was in love with both of them. The white girl wanted me to go with her someplace in Connecticut. But the band was ready to go someplace else, and I stayed with Wildman Steve.'

The glory days did not last. One night that June, 'We were playing in a bar in Basin Street South in Boston. I looked across the room and I saw Sheila's twin, a girl who looked just like her. It tugged my heart.' Gary called Sheila in Florida. By the end of the month, he was off Wildman Steve's tour bus. Having spent two months in jail for her part in the arson, Sheila travelled with baby Latwanna by bus and train to join Gary in New Haven, Connecticut. 'I met them at the train station and I felt like a million dollars,' Gary said. They found an apartment in New London, forty miles up the Atlantic coast, where Gary took a job at the Lawrence Memorial Hospital. Their second child, a boy, was born there on 12 July 1968, but died after a few hours. Gary had gone from fugitive to family man, with a detour as a road musician, in less than three months. His own description of this phase of his life is appropriate: 'Everything was rapid-fire.'

For the next eighteen months, Gary and his family drifted around New England. Having left New London in the autumn of 1968, they lived successively in Hartford, Old Saybrook and Bridgeport in Connecticut, before settling in November 1969 in Albany, New York. The following February, Sheila fell pregnant again. Their son Tony was born in Albany on 20 November. Sometimes both Gary and Sheila took regular jobs: at a Holiday Inn in New London; at a factory in Old Saybrook. But as time went on Gary did more work as a musician, and on bass guitar he got as far as playing clubs in Greenwich Village in New York City. At the same time he was hustling, making money from petty crime, selling drugs and stolen goods. He was also spending it prodigiously. In 1986 Sheila spoke to the Columbus reporter Richard Hyatt for his profile of Gary, published in the *Sunday Ledger-Enquirer* a few months before the stranglings trial. 'I was nineteen years old and had a mink,' she said. 'Can you imagine that? What does a young girl need with a mink coat?'

I have three photos of Sheila Preston. In the first, a shot from the Gainesville newspaper accompanying a story about the arson in 1968, she looks slim, spirited and youthful, with a proud, defiant grin beneath a Motown beehive. In the later picture, she stands next to a sweetly beautiful teenage Latwanna in the early 1980s, stouter, in a white belted pants suit, and still smiling. The third was taken at Gary's trial, when her bloom and optimism seem to have faded. For all his other women, Sheila was the love of Carlton Gary's life. Her letters to him as he waited for his trial in 1984 provide ample evidence of the strength of her feelings, rekindled by his visits to Florida earlier that year: 'I spended [sic] a lot of years trying to hate you and thought it worked,' she wrote a month after his arrest, 'and then I saw your face … And yes, I wanted you back. I needed you, I wanted you on any terms. Nothing else mattered: you were back, and I knew I would never again lose you to nothing and no one. When I was with you, Carl, I didn't see the man you were; I only saw the sixteen-year old boy that I fell in love with so long ago … Carlton I need you, more than you'll ever know. You can always count on me.'

At that stage she was writing to Gary in jail several times a week, pledging her eternal devotion in each letter. However, of all his former girlfriends interviewed by the Columbus detectives, only Sheila agreed to testify against him. According to William Smith at a preliminary hearing just before the trial, she had told the police that Gary had beaten, choked and smothered her on several occasions, and had once even strangled her with a stocking until she passed out. Given the chance, Smith said, she would describe all this to the jury. He quoted from her police statement: 'He gave me about five good beatings, and he would always manage to choke me. Carlton would straddle you and grab you by the throat with his right hand and beat you with his left hand.' Had she given such testimony, it would have been devastating, but Judge Followill refused to allow it. In practically the only decision he ever made that was favourable to Gary's defence, he ruled that Sheila's allegations of domestic violence against her, a young African-American, were so different from the rapes and murders of elderly white women that they had to be excluded, even under the flexible laws of Georgia.

They may not have surfaced at the trial, but Sheila's claims cast a long shadow over Gary's reputation. The police made Richard Hyatt aware of them when he started to research his 1986 Gary profile, and she repeated them when he interviewed her: in one attack in New London, she told him, Gary 'squeezed her hands so tightly that her rings were crushed'. This vision of Carlton Gary as a brute who had assaulted the mother of his children still persisted in Columbus many years later, and over dinner in a local restaurant, Hyatt told me in 2003 that it had influenced his own view of Gary strongly.

Yet Sheila's letters to Gary in jail suggest that this picture may not have been accurate. After the first, relatively sunny, missives, she began to write of being under great stress, of the theft of all her furniture, of bitter rows with members of her family who, she claimed, 'hated' both her and her children and were trying to wreck her life, of Gary's son Tony running wild, of delays in getting her food stamps and bills she could not pay, of her belief that she did not have long to live. 'Baby, I'm not a strong person, I never have been,' she wrote on 25 July 1984. She felt sure that 'we belong together, it must be so, after all these years nothing's changed, you still love me and I love you with every breath I take'. But she ended this letter on a strangely discordant note. 'I might have hurt you. Well not really hurt you, but there's a greater need than you know, we must talk. Something has happened I can't write to you about, but I'll count the hours until we meet.'

The something that had happened was that Sheila had made her statement to the police. Vulnerable and lonely, she may well not have made her allegations spontaneously, but merely concurred when the detectives asked her whether Gary had ever been violent, as they did his other former partners. Having done so, she was filled with remorse. In one anguished letter dated 7 November, written on pink, children's writing paper decorated with pictures of fairies, she said that she had let him down through jealousy over his other girlfriends: 'I wanted to hurt you for all those years that I hurt and tried to forget.' She begged for his forgiveness: 'Now I have to live with the hurt and hope of being with you again. Can you ever forgive me when I can't forgive myself, will never be happy again, no never ... You know how much I love you, Carl I don't hate you, please try not to hate me too much, please let me know how you are, please tell your mother to write me a few lines and send me a phone number so I can call her.'

If nothing else, Sheila was highly volatile. Perhaps, if Followill had allowed her to testify about Gary's alleged assaults, she might have told the jury the story she gave to the cops and Richard Hyatt. It seems just as likely that she would not have. Followill's decision to exclude her allegations may have saved the prosecution from embarrassment – when she finished her much more restricted testimony, in which she merely stated when she had lived with Gary in Albany and Connecticut, she winked at him across the courtroom and smiled, promising: 'See you later, alligator.' Moreover, while victims of domestic violence are often slow to complain to the authorities, until the CPD detectives spoke to Sheila in 1984, she never had. Whatever the truth, she took it to her grave. Sheila and the children she bore Carlton Gary are all deceased – Sheila from cancer, Tony in a Thanksgiving Day shooting when he was only sixteen, and Latwanna from suspected AIDS.

Sheila's life in Albany with Carlton Gary came to an end on 21 July 1970, when he was questioned about the murder three months earlier of the eighty-five-year-old Nellie Farmer in her long-stay apartment at the Wellington Hotel. Although Gary was not tried for or convicted of this murder, it would become his life's watershed. As well as leading to his first prison sentence, it was the Farmer killing that convinced the cops in Columbus that they had the right suspect. When the stranglings jury heard that in Albany, just as later in Columbus, Gary had admitted being present at the murder, but had blamed someone else for committing it, this must have played a large part in their decision to convict him. Later, in its opinion rejecting Gary's direct review appeal, the Georgia Supreme Court would treat his supposed responsibility for killing Nellie Farmer as uncontested fact.

Yet with the Farmer murder, the murk that surrounds so much of Gary's criminal history is at its thickest. All the Columbus jury heard was that a fingerprint was found on a steamer trunk in Ms Farmer's bedroom. Gary was already in custody for stealing another woman's purse, a charge for which he would later be acquitted (according to the victim, her assailant had a beard, while Gary had been clean-shaven at the time). While he was awaiting trial for the bag snatch, one of his middle fingerprints was matched with the latent from the murder.

Sixteen years later, the Albany detective Anthony Sidoti told the court in Columbus that Gary had agreed to talk to him on two unusual conditions: that Sheila, who was pregnant with Tony, could sit on his lap as he was questioned, and that both would be given a hot meal first. After Gary had been read his rights and agreed to be interviewed without his lawyer, he and Sheila were given plates of corned beef, bread and cabbage. Supper over, as they talked in a gloomy basement, Gary told Sidoti he had gone to the Wellington with his older accomplice, John Lee Mitchell, intending only to steal cash or jewellery. It was Mitchell, Gary said in his statement, who had climbed from a fire escape at the back of the hotel across a roof to enter Ms Farmer's apartment, while he stayed outside as a lookout. Gary told Sidoti that by the time Mitchell let him in through the hotel front door in order to go through her property, Nellie Farmer was already dead.

At Gary's trial in Columbus, William Smith presented the Farmer case as the start of Gary's recurring pattern of murder, rape and attempts to blame innocent supposed accomplices. He told the strangling case jury that after talking to Sidoti, Gary did a deal with Albany's District Attorney: while he pleaded guilty to the lesser offence of robbery, he became the sole prosecution witness against John Lee Mitchell, who was charged with – and, in 1971, acquitted of – Nellie Farmer's murder. Mitchell, Smith said, was a businessman of exemplary character, who almost had his life ruined by Carlton Gary's lies.

The passage of time and the gaps in the record make it impossible to establish the whole truth. For example, because Mitchell was found not guilty, there is no transcript of his nine-day trial: such records are kept only when defendants are convicted, and so may need them for later appeals. But it is clear that here too, important evidence was withheld from the Columbus jury.

First, Gary was not the only witness who testified against Mitchell. Michael Kelly, a criminal with a long record who had been held in the Albany county jail at the same time as Gary and Mitchell, claimed that Mitchell had partially confessed to the Farmer murder while talking to him in his cell. The claims of such 'jailhouse snitches' are, of course, usually self-serving, and sometimes unreliable. Nevertheless, on 29 March 1971 Kelly testified to an Albany grand jury, and the transcript of this survives. He supported Gary's statement to Detective Sidoti: '[Mitchell] told [Gary] to wait and he said he climbed over a wall and climbed up a fire escape looking for empty rooms. And he said he came across one and he opened the window ... He seen a woman trying to reach for the phone. He wrestled with her and he figured – he said to me – that she had fainted.' Kelly also testified at Mitchell's trial.

Secondly, Mitchell was not quite the blameless young entrepreneur depicted at Gary's trial in Columbus. Both Smith and Followill reviewed the Albany case file, Followill endorsing Smith's decision that it need not be disclosed to Bud Siemon. Thus the jury was never told that Mitchell had a criminal record, with convictions before 1970 for vagrancy, drunkenness, burglary and forcible theft. He had also been arrested for possessing an offensive weapon in the shape of a 'dangerous jack knife', although this charge was dismissed.

We must assume Mitchell was innocent of the murder of Nellie Farmer. Perhaps she was killed neither by him nor by Gary, but by some unknown third party. But Smith's claim to the jury in Columbus, that Carlton Gary raped and murdered her alone, is undermined by a piece of evidence that the jurors never saw. The page numbers written in ink on the documents that describe it indicate it was included in the copy of the Albany file that Smith and Followill read and refused to show to Gary's defence. It is difficult to see how they could have failed to notice its importance.

The evidence in question is a set of reports about two fresh footprints left by Farmer's killer on the mat in her bathroom. They state that having first entered Ms Farmer's suite by the bathroom window, the murderer stood at her sink after raping and killing her, washing his genitals to remove her blood and faeces. The footprints on the mats were examined by four technicians from the New York State Crime Lab. Their sworn deposition states that by using ultraviolet light, they were able to reconstruct the size and design of the shoes that had made them. The prints, they concluded, were left by 'size eight-and-a-half to nine boot or sneaker-type footwear'. Carlton Gary's feet are US size thirteen and a half.

As for Gary, he has stuck with the story he told Detective Sidoti back in 1970. 'I helped him up onto the roof like this,' he told me in 2004, demonstrating how he had allegedly assisted Mitchell's break-in. He drew me a plan that demonstrated, he claimed, the location of the roof and Nellie Farmer's bathroom window, and their relation to the surrounding streets. I had been in Albany two days earlier, and had visited the Wellington Hotel, by then closed and set for demolition. After a lapse of thirty-four years, Gary's sketch was astonishingly accurate. He barely knew Mitchell, he said. 'When they brought me down for questioning, I only knew the guy's nickname. They brought out the mug-book and I recognised him, but I didn't know his name.'

During that visit to Albany I met Arnold Proskin, the former District Attorney responsible for the deal with Gary and the prosecution of Mitchell. Afterwards, he had gone on to serve for a decade in the New York State Assembly, and later as a county court judge; now in his seventies, he was back in private law practice. A warm, avuncular man with big bushy eyebrows, he said he was still smarting at William Smith's suggestion that he had tried the wrong man for killing Nellie Farmer, and had thus been duped by the real murderer, Carlton Gary. As for the footprints, Proskin said that at Gary's trial for the Columbus stranglings, 'evidence was unintentionally or intentionally withheld'. He added that the police had found more size nine prints on the roof that led to Farmer's bathroom window, and more than three decades later, he remained angry about the fact that he had not been told about them before Mitchell's trial. 'The footprints with that sneaker pattern were withheld from me. The fact that they didn't match Carlton Gary was further evidence that he couldn't have been the killer.'

Back in the autumn of 1998, as I sat in Atlanta at the conference table with Gary's attorneys Jack Martin and Michael McIntyre at our first, awkward meeting, I made them a promise. Having started to work my way through the voluminous documentary record, it seemed to me that the case against Gary had one unexplained and potentially significant weakness – the apparent contradiction between his serology type and the strangler's. I told the lawyers that before I saw them again I would find an expert in England prepared to examine this issue *pro bono*, to see if there might be some way to take it further.

After a search of several months, trying to make contacts through friends of friends, I found Dr David Roberts, a consultant haematologist at the John Radcliffe Hospital in Oxford, the city where I lived. A quiet, methodical man who seemed imbued with a scientist's instinctive caution, his first question when we spoke in May 1999 was why on earth I thought he might be helpful: surely DNA tests had rendered the old forensic methods based on secretor types obsolete? I told him about Doug Pullen's testimony at Gary's *habeas* appeal hearing, that the semen swabs from the victims had been destroyed on the grounds that they constituted a 'bio-hazard'. 'That was the moment I began to get interested,' Roberts said later. 'To claim such samples might be dangerous just wasn't right. It made me wonder whether they had something to hide.' He agreed to read the relevant parts of the trial transcript, together with other documents about the serology that had been given to me by Carlton Gary's lawyers.

A few days after receiving the papers, Dr Roberts called to say that he found the record not only baffling, but apparently incomplete. John Wegel, the prosecution expert, had told Gary's jury that tests on his saliva carried out after his arrest showed that he was a 'strong secretor': his spit, and presumably his other bodily fluids, contained substantial quantities of the blood group O chemical marker, H-reactive substance. The killer, on the other hand, appeared to be either a 'weak' or a non-secretor – someone whose fluids contained much lower levels. But Wegel had testified that this apparent discrepancy did not exclude Gary, as it was possible that the level of his secretions had changed in the six years between the last murder and his arrest. Alternatively, it might be the case that he secreted much less in his semen than in his saliva. There was no evidence to support these suppositions. Gary's semen had never been tested.

According to Dr Roberts, Wegel's use of the term 'weak secretor' was 'extremely odd'. Although about 2 per cent of the population could be said to fit this category, a scientist would normally be reluctant to state such a conclusion without first performing a further diagnostic test, known as 'Lewis typing'. Even non-secretors did, in fact, secrete small amounts of the marker chemicals, and without Lewis typing it was very easy to get weak secretors and the much more common non-secretors mixed up. But so far as Roberts could see from the documents, no Lewis typing had ever been carried out.

There was a further gap in the record: Wegel's original laboratory notes. Wegel had told the court that he had performed two separate tests on the crime scene semen – 'absorption-inhibition' and 'absorption-elution'. He made no distinction between them in his testimony, and did not say whether they had given different results. Without the requisite scientific knowledge or funds to pay for an expert, Bud Siemon had been in no position to challenge him. But according to Roberts, the two tests were in fact very different, and the correct one to use when trying to identify a rapist was absorption-inhibition. Because it was relatively insensitive, it would not detect the very low levels of marker chemicals left behind by a non-secretor. Absorption-elution, on the other hand, was about a hundred times more sensitive. Its danger was that its very sensitivity might give rise to 'false positives'.

Roberts wondered whether the reason Wegel had used both tests was that he had drawn a blank with absorption-inhibition, finding no trace of any marker chemicals. If so, he should have concluded that the strangler was a non-secretor – and so excluded Carlton Gary as the source of the semen. Perhaps, Roberts speculated, Wegel had then gone on to perform absorption-elution – and only then detected the very low levels of H-reactive substance that made him assert that the killer might be a 'weak secretor'. There was only one way to find out, said Roberts: he needed to examine Wegel's lab notes from 1977–78. But Gary's defence had never seen them. The state had never turned them over, and they appeared to be missing.

Returning to Atlanta in May 1999, I reported Dr Roberts's thoughts to Jack Martin and Michael McIntyre. Meanwhile, I had trawled through the scientific literature in an attempt to discover whether John Wegel's explanations – that Gary's secretion level might have changed over time, or that he might have secreted less in his semen than in his saliva – were plausible.

All the published science that I could find suggested that they were not. According to textbooks and papers in the specialist journals, a person's secretions are genetically predetermined and vary only marginally over time. Non-secretors carry a relatively rare recessive gene. Meanwhile, men invariably secrete higher concentrations of marker chemicals into their semen than into their saliva – usually about twenty times as much, but in some cases almost a hundred times. If Carlton Gary really was producing less H-reactive substance in his semen than in his saliva, according to the literature he was biologically very unusual, and possibly unique.

Before the trial and his state appeals, Gary's lawyers had asked the state for full disclosure of all the scientific documents, and each time they were assured that they already had them. But having spoken on the phone to Dr Roberts, Martin and McIntyre dutifully filed yet another request under the Georgia Open Records Act, asking to look at Wegel's laboratory work-sheets. At the end of February 2000 they were told that the worksheets of his tests on the semen from the bodies of Florence Scheible and Martha Thurmond could not be found anywhere. But Wegel's notes on the seminal fluid recovered from the bed of Ferne Jackson were still available, as, presumably, they had been all along.

The worksheets consisted of rows of figures under various headings, and meant nothing to the lawyers. But to Dr Roberts, they quickly confirmed his suspicions. On 22 April he swore an affidavit. The worksheets, it said, showed that Wegel had indeed found no trace of H-reactive substance when he tried absorption-inhibition. It was only when he used the hyper-sensitive absorption-elution method that very low levels showed up. 'Based on this new information … it is my firm opinion that Mr Gary is excluded as a possible donor of the stains believed to be semen in the Jackson case,' Roberts said. If Gary, a regular, strong secretor, had left the stain, 'the absorption-inhibition test would have been positive'. In Roberts's view, the testimony given by Wegel and his colleagues at the trial was 'scientifically incorrect and substantially misleading'. Yet again, a long-concealed document had cast doubt on prosecution testimony.

Martin and McIntyre used Roberts's declaration to apply to the Federal District Court for an evidentiary hearing, at which these scientific issues could be discussed more thoroughly. Because Wegel had testified at the trial

Carlton Gary's former girlfriend
Sheila Dean on the witness stand,
21 August 1986.

Earnestine Flowers testifies at her
childhood friend Gary's trial,
25 August 1986. Reluctant to give
evidence, she had been arrested
and spent a night in custody.

Carlton Gary in court with his lawyer, Bud Siemon.

Henry Sanderson testifies at Gary's trial about his gun, stolen from his car in Wynnton in October 1977. Detective Sellers told the author that Sanderson had Alzheimer's disease, and was 'too gone to testify' by the time the trial took place.

ABOVE: John Lee Mitchell, whom Gary falsely accused of murdering Nellie Farmer in Albany, New York, testifies in Columbus.

BELOW: Malvin Alamichael Crittenden, 'Little Mike', Carlton Gary's robbery accomplice, testifies in the stranglings trial. The police said that Gary falsely accused him of the murders.

ABOVE LEFT: A police 'composite' sketch that Gertrude Miller identified as the man who raped and tried to kill her in September 1977. She testified at Gary's trial that he had attacked her, but the jury was not told of her prior identifications.

ABOVE: Carlton Gary's mother, Carolyn, after he was given the death penalty, August 1986.

LEFT: Gary on the way to court for an appeal hearing, 14 December 1989.

that it was possible that Gary might secrete H-substance in his saliva but not his semen, they also asked the court to allow a controlled semen test. Gary was still at the first stage of his federal *habeas corpus* appeals, where his case had languished since 1997, under the nominal supervision of the ageing Judge Robert Elliott. By 2000, when Elliott was eighty-nine years old, he had been forced to take leave from the bench on medical grounds, although he was still insisting that this pause would be only temporary.

In Elliott's absence, anything to do with Carlton Gary was being handled by Judge Hugh Lawson, whose court was in Macon, a city of similar size to Columbus, eighty miles south-east of Atlanta. As a state judge before his appointment to the federal bench in 1995, Lawson had presided over several capital murder trials. One of them was in Columbus – the second trial of William Anthony Brooks, the African-American who raped and murdered the virginal white teacher Jeannine Galloway in 1977. During the case, Brooks's lawyer, Steve Bright of the Southern Center for Human Rights, asked Doug Pullen about his record of striking blacks in order to ensure all-white juries. 'These five black men were all tried by all-white juries and defended by white lawyers, prosecuted by white prosecutors, and tried by white judges. Does that offend your sense of justice?' Bright asked. Lawson interrupted him, asking: 'What does his sense of justice have to do with it?' Like Judge Coursey, who had handled Carlton Gary's state *habeas* appeal, Lawson was a devout Christian. In 1988 he allowed the retrial of Carl Isaacs, who in 1973 participated in the murders of six members of the same family, to start with a courtroom prayer, provoking claims that this represented an unacceptable blurring of the boundary between Church and state.

Gary's attorneys asked Judge Lawson to allow them to investigate another piece of evidence that might be very important. DNA tests on the semen were, of course, impossible, owing to their destruction as a 'biohazard'. But included in the inventory of exhibits preserved by the state was a single 'negroid' pubic hair that had been found between Florence Scheible's legs. The prosecution had stated at the trial that it was left by the strangler, and that although it did not positively match samples from Gary, it must nevertheless have come from him. McIntyre pointed out that DNA testing, which had not been available in 1986, could now prove Gary's innocence. If, on the other hand, his DNA matched the hair's, he would be in a worse position than before. Talking to his lawyers, Gary made clear that he wanted to take the risk.*

The state, still represented by Assistant Attorney General Susan Boleyn, was curiously reluctant to allow this to happen. To test the hair would merely be a 'fishing expedition', she argued in a written brief; and even if it turned out not to match Carlton Gary's DNA, this would undermine 'only a small portion' of the prosecution case. The fingerprints, Gertrude Miller's courtroom identification of Gary and his own confession would all still stand, and were proof enough of Gary's guilt. After all, at the trial the state had barely relied on the hairs found at the crime scenes at all.

Judge Lawson issued his decision at the end of June 2000. With regard to the serology, he was prepared to hold a hearing: the laboratory work-sheets did constitute new evidence that should have been turned over to the defence. He deferred a ruling on the semen test until he had heard expert evidence. But the DNA test on the hair was refused. Some judges might well have thought that a negative match would have undermined the entire prosecution case: after all, the state had always said that the same man com-mitted all the rapes and murders. But Lawson endorsed the state's logic, ruling that proof that the hair could not have come from Gary would cast no doubt on the rest of the incriminating testimony. He added that because DNA tests had not been invented in 1986, there were no constitutional grounds for conducting one now. According to Judge Lawson, a prisoner could not claim his rights were violated by using science that was new. 'The motion,' he ordered, 'is therefore denied.'

The serology hearing was set for Lawson's court in Macon on 21 November 2000, the Tuesday before Thanksgiving. On 17 November, the previous Friday, Jack Martin was at his desk in Atlanta, beginning to wrap up his work for the weekend. The phone rang: it was Susan Boleyn's office.

---

* DNA typing of hair, an inert biological substance, does not produce the dramatic, one-in-a-billion matches that are possible with DNA from living cells. Hairs contain only 'mitochondrial' DNA, and many individuals will share the same sequence: with any match between two samples, there is a roughly 5 per cent probability that this might be down to chance. However, if Gary's mitochondrial DNA proved to be different from the crime scene pubic hair's, this would conclusively exclude him.

The Assistant Attorney General sounded a little embarrassed. She told Martin that Wegel's worksheets for his tests on the semen from the bodies of Florence Scheible and Martha Thurmond had just been discovered at the GBI laboratory.

David Roberts was unable to travel to Georgia, so in his place Martin called another expert serologist, Rodger Morrison. Even before Roberts swore his affidavit, he had already stated his view that Wegel had performed the wrong tests. The worksheets, he said, now confirmed this. Morrison was the director of Alabama's State Crime Lab in Huntsville, and most of his five-hundred-plus courtroom appearances had been as a witness for the prosecution, not the defence. His role, he explained in Judge Lawson's court, was essentially the same in Alabama as that performed by John Wegel in Georgia.

Like Dr Roberts, Morrison stated his belief that that the correct method to ascertain a person's secretor status was to use absorption-inhibition alone, not the overly sensitive absorption-elution test. 'By being insensitive, it [absorption-inhibition] eliminates a lot of false reactions.' For that reason, he had ensured for many years that staff in his lab used only this technique. Meanwhile, Wegel's freshly-rediscovered worksheets from the Florence Scheible and Martha Thurmond murders confirmed that in these cases too, as with that of Ferne Jackson, Wegel had obtained negative reactions from absorption-inhibition, indicating that the killer was a non-secretor. Only when he used absorption-elution did he find very low levels of H-reactive substance.

According to Morrison, by the far the most significant of Wegel's tests were those on the semen recovered from Martha Thurmond. In the other two cases, Wegel had worked with stains left on bedsheets, but the two samples recovered from Thurmond's abdomen were described at Gary's trial as 'neat' undiluted semen, in which numerous spermatozoa complete with tails were seen clearly under a microscope. In a sample of that quality, 'you should see a higher concentration' of the blood group marker chemicals. The semen must have been reasonably plentiful. The semen on Thurmond's body had been plainly visible at the crime scene.

As for Carlton Gary, the saliva tests carried out after his arrest showed that he was a very strong secretor. Morrison found Wegel's suggestion that

Gary might have produced strong secretions in his saliva but been 'weak in the seminal fluid' extremely doubtful. From his reading of the scientific literature, he knew of no case where anyone had been found to be secreting less in their semen than their saliva. But the way to be sure, Morrison said, was to test Gary's semen now. That would provide a reliable guide of what Gary's semen had been like in 1977, when Martha Thurmond was killed, because 'What literature there is available indicates that there does not appear to be any significant change in secretor status over a period of time.' It was true that the longest period over which any individual had been monitored was only six years, while by now twenty-three years had elapsed since Thurmond's murder. On the other hand, secretor status was deter-mined genetically, and all the published research concluded that the small variations that might occur over time were insignificant, and of far lesser magnitude than the difference between a secretor and a non-secretor. As Morrison put it, 'Your genes don't change.' Oddly enough, Wegel had disclosed that he had conducted his own study by asking his staff to produce regular semen samples to see if they altered over time. He had, as the literature predicted, found little variance.

Martin asked Morrison what he would conclude if a new test on Gary's semen were indeed to confirm that he was a strong secretor.

'If the test results come back to show that his secreted antigens in his semen fall within the normal range,' said Morrison, 'and given that this is a neat semen sample from Mrs Thurmond, then it would be my opinion that he would be excluded as a source of that sample.'

Morrison, a prosecution scientist from a neighbouring state, was saying that a simple test could prove Gary's innocence. 'Your honour,' said Martin, 'I would renew our request to obtain from Mr Gary a sample of his semen under controlled circumstances ... We have a reputable person saying that if that test came back that he was a normal type-O secretor, he would be excluded.'

After Morrison, John Wegel, who was still working for the Georgia Crime Lab, testified at the behest of Susan Boleyn. Two internationally res-pected experts had challenged his methods and conclusions, but he refused to yield. He denied that absorption-elution was too sensitive to be an appropriate test, and though he accepted that such a phenomenon had never been observed, he still maintained that Gary might have been secreting more in saliva than in semen. However, in his view there was little point in having Gary tested now, because too much time had elapsed: 'You can vary, you can vary over time.' He admitted that this wouldn't usually be 'a big leaping jump', and there was no scientific evidence that big changes could occur. Then again, as Morrison had already testified, no one had ever carried out an experiment after an interval of more than six years. Maybe Gary's semen really had changed that much. At any rate, no one could prove that it had not.

Thus far Wegel had merely reiterated what he had said at the trial. He added just one refinement. It was possible, he said, that the reason he had detected so little H-reactive substance in the semen swabbed from Martha Thurmond was that it had been 'smeared out', taken from a layer so thin that 'you may not have enough of pure concentrated semen on there'. Martin reminded him of testimony at the trial: that the semen on Mrs Thurmond's body had been pure and uncontaminated, and visible on her naked belly, from which it had been collected by a trained technician.

At the end of the hearing, Judge Lawson said he wanted both sides to submit their arguments on paper. In due course he would issue rulings about whether the new serological evidence meant that Gary should get a new trial, and whether his lawyers could test his semen.

Carlton Gary was freed on parole on 31 March 1975, four years after being sentenced for robbing Nellie Farmer. He was twenty-five. Sheila was still living in Albany, but was gone from Gary's life. According to one of the police reports in the Farmer file, she told a detective shortly after his arrest that she was already taking steps to 'find herself a new man'. Long before Gary regained his freedom, she had done so.

In her absence Gary took up with a woman called Nancy, who had started to visit him in prison, and married her in a ceremony conducted by a Seventh Day Adventist minister nine months before his release. He moved into her house in Syracuse, New York, an industrial town close to the Canadian border, and started a job at the place where she worked as a secretary, the Southside Community Center. Later he was employed by a local construction company, and he used that experience to start his own building and decorating business. He seemed to be looking for stability, but the lure of the street stayed strong. His relationship with Nancy did not last, and he was soon dating other women: the daughter of the owner of a Syracuse nightclub; a divorcee from Alabama who had moved to New York with her two children; and eventually Tula Jones, the mother of his daughter Coco. Gary was not heavily involved in criminal activity during this period, but he could not resist making some money by selling stolen property and running gambling 'numbers' on the side.

Trouble was never far away. In July 1975, just four months after his release, he was re-arrested for a technical breach of his parole conditions – failing to keep an appointment with his parole officer, and travelling to Albany to buy a car without permission. He tried to escape and ran, only to be caught almost immediately by the Syracuse police and landed with a new criminal charge, third degree escape and resisting arrest. The incident cost him a whole further year in jail, most of it spent at the forbidding high security facility in Auburn, New York, one of America's oldest prisons, dating back to 1816. In 1890 Auburn was the site of America's first execution using Thomas Edison's patent electric chair.

Freed again in July 1976, Gary went to live with Tula, who was soon pregnant with Coco, while he and Nancy started proceedings for divorce. Then, on the icy night of 2–3 January 1977, came the burglary and violent sexual assault on Jean Frost, aged fifty-five at the time, the white woman from Syracuse who would eventually testify at Gary's trial in Columbus. Two days later, Gary was arrested with his friend Dudley Harris and charged with possessing some stolen property, including Jean Frost's watch.

Frost had passed out when the attack on her began, and she told the Columbus jury that she did not know whether her intruder had been black or white. But to William Smith, the Frost case in Syracuse bridged the gap between the murder of Nellie Farmer in Albany and the Columbus stranglings. Here too, he told the jury, Gary had attacked a white woman of mature years who lived alone, in the middle of the night, and here too he had tried to blame someone else when arrested – Dudley Harris. He had been very fortunate to be sentenced to only one year in prison, for possessing the stolen property and a small amount of marijuana. (At the end of this sentence, Gary would also have faced the revocation of his parole arising from the Farmer case: that was why he escaped in August 1977 from Syracuse's Onandaga County Prison, the place from which he made his circuitous way back to Columbus.)

'Jean Frost lived by the Grace of God, and that alone,' Smith told the stranglings jury. Seeing her testify, 'didn't you feel like saying, "I've heard this before"? What does he say when confronted? What does he say, he says, "All right, you've got me, I was there, but I was just acting as a lookout. Dudley Harris went into the house." Now hadn't we heard that before?' Smith hammered home his message: 'You've got to watch your friends, Mr Gary. They rob folks, they rape folks, and you are invariably with them.'

There was just one important difference between the way that Smith presented testimony about the Farmer murder in Albany and the attack on Jean Frost. With the case of Mrs Farmer, his star witness was John Lee Mitchell, the blameless black businessman whom Gary, Smith said, had falsely accused. About Dudley Harris the jury heard nothing, other than the fact that, like Gary, he was not charged with raping, burgling or assaulting Jean Frost. Of course, Gary's defence lawyers at the trial never had the resources to find out anything more.

Gary himself told me that as had been the case with John Lee Mitchell, he had not known Harris very well. 'He was always on the set at this small club I used to go to, Foxes' Lounge. It was never a serious hang with him. He was always drunk, or on drugs.' It had been Harris, he said, who had given him the stolen coins that had led to their both being arrested and searched when they tried to turn them into paper money at a bank. As with the Farmer case, Gary insisted that the story he gave the cops in 1977 had been true: on the night of the attack on Jean Frost, he really had been Harris's lookout. 'I didn't know nothing more about it. I only found out what had happened next day. And if it was me, why did they let me go?'

In the archives at the Syracuse Police Department and its county courthouse, I looked for more information about Dudley Harris. The Jean Frost case was by no means his only brush with the law. His first arrests came in the mid-1970s, when he was still in his teens: he was convicted of crimes including second degree assault, resisting arrest, possessing drugs and disorderly conduct. Later, after the attack on Ms Frost, his alleged offences became more serious. In 1979 he was charged with murdering a man at a pool hall, although the authorities' failure to organise a speedy trial led to the case being dropped. Three years later, he pleaded guilty to hindering the prosecution in a separate murder case when one of his associates was charged. In 1984 he was charged with breaking into the apartment of a former girlfriend and attacking her new partner, who sustained a broken cheekbone; one witness said he saw Harris jumping on the victim 'like a man jumping on a trampoline'. On this occasion Harris was acquitted at the behest of the judge, because his ex-girlfriend refused to testify.

Dudley Harris's most significant case came to court in Syracuse in February 1986, six months before Carlton Gary's trial in Columbus, when he faced charges of 'promoting prostitution', assault and endangering the welfare of a child. The transcript of the trial, which is stored in the Syracuse court archives, is horrific.

Claire Hopkins* was a white girl of sixteen whose family had moved away from Syracuse, where she had spent her childhood. On 29 August 1985 she took a bus back to the city from her new home in Binghamton after a blazing row with her parents, planning to spend a few nights at the home of a girlfriend. When she arrived, she discovered that her friend was not there. It was getting late, Binghamton was more than seventy miles away, and the last thing Claire wanted was to go home and face her parents. Unsure what to do, she walked the streets of Syracuse until she happened to pass a bar, the G & L Lounge. A tall African-American with the back of his hair dyed blond was standing outside – Dudley Harris.

He started a conversation, and when Claire explained her predicament, he took her to dinner at a seafood restaurant in his limousine, a green Lincoln town car with dark-tinted windows. Afterwards he drove her to a motel, checked her in and paid for her room, promising to pick her up next morning. Until then, Harris had been polite and charming. But the next day, Claire testified, he was very different. 'I have done some favours for you,' he told her. 'Now it's payback time. You're going to do something for me. You're going to get paid for having sex with men. You can either do that, or pay the consequences.'

Harris bought Claire some tight, revealing clothes, confiscated her old

* Not her real name.

ones and set her to work. For the next four weeks he forced her to have oral and vaginal sex, often without using condoms, with a series of men – so many that she lost count – that Harris introduced her to at the G & L and another seedy bar, the Blue Chateau. Usually they paid her about $100, all of which she had to give to Harris; sometimes he plied her with cocaine, which she had never used before. She testified that early in their relationship she saw good reason to be frightened of Harris. One night she was in his car when he caught sight of a man he knew. He reversed, got out of the car and grabbed the man. 'You fucked me and now you're going to pay,' he told him. Then, Claire said, she saw Harris stab the man, who fell to the ground. Afterwards, 'We went to the G & L bar and went in. He asked the bartender for a napkin, and he wiped off the knife.'

After Claire had been working for Harris for more than three weeks, a prospective client began to insult her in the G & L, calling her 'a white bitch'. Claire said she slapped him. Harris immediately seized her arm and dragged her to his car. There, Claire said, 'he started slapping and punching me' about the face, the start of a beating that lasted several minutes. Thinking he had finished, she managed to get out of the car, hoping that 'someone would help me'. Instead, Harris renewed his attack: 'He punched my face and I fell down. He started to kicking me in my upper chest, and in my abdomen and in my vaginal area.'

Claire finally managed to escape after four days, fleeing to a women's refuge. She was in a terrible state, and her rescuers took her straight to the hospital emergency room. The doctor who treated her, Shane Sopp, an expert in obstetrics and gynaecology, testified that Claire told him she had been 'beaten up by her pimp'. She was in 'severe pain', and he found that Harris's attack had left her vagina deeply bruised and marked with vivid lesions. It was 'excruciatingly tender', so that examining her was very difficult. Her month of enforced prostitution had also given her genital herpes and gonorrhoea. On 16 February, after a four-day trial, Dudley Harris was convicted. He was sentenced to seven years.

It is not difficult to see the relevance of this case to Carlton Gary's trial in Columbus. According to William Smith, it was Gary who had attacked Jean Frost in Syracuse, and his claim that Harris was the real perpetrator was merely a part of his pattern of lies. Yet as the Columbus jury heard, it was unclear whether Frost actually had been raped. She had been beaten and probably strangled to the point where she lost consciousness, and when she came to she was bleeding from injuries inside her vagina. Like the doctor who examined Claire Hopkins, Renate Chevli, the physician who saw Ms Frost, found examining her 'almost impossible'. But there was no evidence of spermatozoa or an attacker's pubic hairs. 'Something occurred' in Frost's vagina, Chevli said, but 'I don't know what it was.' Like Claire Hopkins, she may have been injured by a manual assault, or by kicks. The account Dr Chevli gave of Frost's wounds at Gary's trial in Columbus was very similar to that given by Dr Sopp when Dudley Harris was found guilty of causing vaginal injuries to Claire Hopkins barely six months earlier.

The trial in Columbus was told nothing of this, and nothing else about Harris's criminal history. Yet in Syracuse, Dudley Harris's treatment of Claire Hopkins was anything but low-profile, and it would have been surprising if many local cops remained unaware of it. The case was the subject of extensive news coverage, and its notoriety rose still further on the day that the jury returned its guilty verdict, when, in a surprising breach of security, Dudley Harris gathered up his coat and left the courthouse without anyone trying to stop him. It took more than a month for the Syracuse police to find and recapture him; only then was he sentenced, amid further coverage, on 21 April 1986. Even after that, Harris made the news again. On 12 May, three months before Gary's trial, the Syracuse *Star-Telegram* led its front page with a massive article under the headline: 'Prosecutor Wages War on Pimps who Enslave Women'. It consisted of an interview with Ralph Tortora III, the Assistant District Attorney who had successfully prosecuted Harris. Prominently citing that case along with several others, he declared that he and the police were going to drive the pimps of Syracuse out of business.

No fewer than five Syracuse police officers testified at Carlton Gary's trial. William Smith did not ask them anything about the sexually abusive, violent past of Dudley Harris, nor did he tell the jury or the defence about it. It is hard to believe that Smith himself, a careful, meticulous prosecutor, made no inquiries about Harris's record. Here, it appears, was yet another violation of the principles set out by the Supreme Court in *Brady vs Maryland*, the case that imposes a duty on all prosecution and law-enforcement agencies to give the defence any information that might be exculpatory, or cast doubt on the state's version of events. Had Bud Siemon known that Dudley Harris had been convicted of beating a girl and causing her vaginal injuries, Gary's claim that it was Harris who attacked Jean Frost would have seemed far more credible.

By the beginning of 2001, it was beginning to become apparent that my relationship with Gary's lawyers ought to be put on a more formal basis. I had secured a contract to write this book, but at the same time I was coming up with evidence that might prove decisive in the federal *habeas* appeal. Accordingly, Jack Martin appointed me as a paralegal investigator on behalf of his law firm, Martin Brothers PC. If that meant relinquishing a measure of journalistic independence, I considered it justified by what was at stake. My new role had one great advantage. It meant that when I visited Gary on death row, I could carry documents and writing materials, and take contemporaneous notes.

In the early months of that year I made two extended trips to Georgia, both lasting several weeks. As the second drew to a close at the end of March, almost five months after the hearing in Macon, there was still no word from Judge Lawson as to whether he would grant the semen test that might definitively prove Gary's innocence. Meanwhile, on behalf of the state, Susan Boleyn had submitted a written brief opposing the test. According to her, whatever the result, it would be of no importance, because the surviving victim Gertrude Miller had identified Gary at the trial: 'Even if the semen evidence in the Jackson, Scheible and Thurmond cases were ... to exclude petitioner as the rapist of these women, the semen evidence does not in any way undermine the testimony of the surviving victim who testified that petitioner Gary raped her and attempted to strangle her with her stockings.'

Boleyn also claimed that even if Gary were to be excluded as the rapist, he would still be guilty of murder. It was possible, she wrote, that what he had said in his alleged confession, that it had been Malvin Crittenden who had raped the women, had been true after all, and ruling out Gary on the grounds of the serology 'would not exclude petitioner as the perpetrator or the co-perpetrator of the stocking strangling murders'. This was breathtaking. Twenty-fours years after the first murder, in the face of fresh evidence that threatened to demolish her case, Boleyn had found an ingenious solution: the notion that the rapes and murders might have been the work of a team. Of course, this flew in the face of almost every aspect of the story that William Smith had presented at the trial.

Over lunch one day in Atlanta, Martin and I agreed that Boleyn's argument might seem less acceptable to Judge Lawson if we could show him that the defence experts' claims about Gary's seminal fluid were true – that he really did secrete more H-reactive substance in his semen than in his saliva, and was therefore excluded. After this conversation I devised a plan to obtain a sample of Gary's semen in order to have it tested. At the end of March I arranged visits with Gary on consecutive days. During the first, I briefed him on what would happen. At the second, we executed the plan.

Unlike meetings with their family and friends, all-day visits to death row inmates from accredited paralegals at the Georgia Diagnostic and Classification Prison include a break for lunch. In the morning, I carried in a large plastic folder. It contained various documents about Gary's case. It also contained an envelope, a sheet of plain paper and some plastic cling-wrap. I was following advice from a former President of the Royal College of Surgeons.

After the morning session, Gary took some of the documents back to his cell, together with the envelope, paper and cling-wrap. When I returned that afternoon, we were locked in a little square room just off the echoing main visitation hall, where ordinary, 'general population' inmates sat in clumps with their guests. The door had a large window just below head height. I sat with my back to it, while Gary tried to look inconspicuous as he watched for patrolling guards. We might not have been doing anything illegal, but I did not relish the prospect of being observed in the act of accepting a packet of semen. Gary slid the envelope across the table and I slipped it into the folder. Then, I gave him a second envelope. In front of me, he plucked about thirty hairs from his head, complete with roots. He placed them inside the second envelope and gave it back. By cross-matching the DNA in the hair roots and semen, I could be certain that the semen sample produced in his cell at lunchtime really was his.

Somehow I managed to think of enough questions to fill the rest of the visit, and to concentrate enough to scribble notes. At last the guards unlocked us and I bade Gary farewell, picking up the folder and tucking it under my arm as I stood. I strode out of the prison as confidently as I could, past the successive gates and electronic doors. Taking care not to hurry, I made my way past the perimeter guard tower and down the steps to the parking lot, opened my car and got in, placing the folder on the passenger seat beside me. I drove through the incongruous, manicured park and out onto the Interstate.

I was staying at a Radisson Hotel in North Druid Hills in Atlanta, just over an hour away. As soon as I got there, I went to my room, hung out the 'Do not disturb' sign and, as I had been advised, put on sterile plastic gloves. Over an unused towel on my bedroom desk top I opened the envelope. Inside, as expected, was a slightly soggy little cling-wrap parcel. Very gingerly, I undid it, and spread out the paper on the towel. The unmistakeable, pungent stink of semen filled the room. I had been told to let it dry naturally, away from artificial heat. I left it there, removed the gloves and discarded them. Unwilling to let the paper out of my presence until it was dry, I retired to the bed to watch TV.

That evening, wearing a new pair of gloves, I folded the paper and put it in a clean envelope. I had already made arrangements with one of the few people in America who still had the knowledge and equipment to do secretor testing – Brian Wraxall, the head of the Serological Research Institute in Richmond, California. As we had agreed by telephone, next day I used an overnight courier service to send him the hair, the semen-impregnated paper and copies of all the documents about the serology of the stranglings case. Wraxall, an Englishman who had once been in charge of forensic science at London's Metropolitan Police headquarters at Scotland Yard, was a teacher as well as a scientist. By coincidence, one of his former students was Georgia's own expert, John Wegel.

Wraxall – who like David Roberts and Rodger Morrison considered that the correct procedure to ascertain a person's secretor status was to conduct an absorption-inhibition test alone – first DNA-matched the hair roots to the semen and confirmed that their source was the same. Then he tested the semen. 'Utilising the semen I determined that the donor is an O secretor and that his H antigen was detected to at least a dilution of 1 in

3000,' he told me via email on 24 April 2001. 'In my opinion he is <u>not</u> [Wraxall's underlining] a low level secretor.' In a later phone conversation, and then in a legal affidavit, he gave more detail. In fact, he said, the level of H-reactive substance in Carlton Gary's semen was very high, towards the upper end of the normal range. It was inconceivable that someone secreting at such concentrations could have been classed as a 'weak secretor' earlier in his life. When Wraxall reviewed John Wegel's worksheets from his 1977 tests on the neat semen sample recovered from the body of Martha Thurmond, he concluded that Gary was secreting at least three thousand times as much as the man who raped her, and probably more. As expected, the level in his semen was many times higher than that found in his saliva back in 1984.

Judge Lawson had still not made any decision on the evidence heard in Macon the previous November. While he pondered, Martin filed a new motion, enclosing affidavits from Brian Wraxall and me, and asking the judge to take account of our tests. Predictably, Susan Boleyn opposed it. As before, she argued that none of this mattered. 'It appears that the testing of [Gary's] semen was done, not at the instigation of his attorneys, but at the instigation of a non-party journalist,' she added sniffily. She had argued strenuously against allowing a scientist to collect a sample from Gary. Now she tried to persuade Lawson not to consider the sample collected by me, on the grounds that the test had 'not been conducted in accordance with standard scientific testing procedures'.

Another two months went by. Finally, on 29 June 2001, Judge Lawson issued two orders. The first was his ruling as to whether a professional scientist should be allowed to collect Gary's semen and test it. In Lawson's view, this request was being made many years too late: Bud Siemon could have organised a test before Gary's trial. The fact that he had no funding was no excuse, and it was also too late to cite this as a reason. The funds issue had already been dealt with, Lawson said. As Gary had been warned by Followill back in 1987, any attempt to reopen it was procedurally barred.

That left the question of whether such a test ought to take place in order to prevent a 'fundamental miscarriage of justice', the execution of an innocent man. Lawson decreed that it should not. The state's expert, John Wegel, had testified unequivocally that even if Gary was secreting strongly

300

in his semen now, he might not have been twenty-three years earlier. The defence experts might disagree, but Lawson did not think it part of his job to determine who was right. It was also possible that the crime scene samples, including the swabs of neat semen from Martha Thurmond, had not been large enough to show up strongly in Wegel's tests.

Lawson's second order was concerned with whether he ought to accept Brian Wraxall's results on the sample collected by me. He agreed with Boleyn: the defence had not established that this test was scientifically valid. But even if it were, it would make no difference. Since he had already ruled that a further test by a scientist could not prove Gary's innocence, this one could not, either. 'The court refuses to receive information regarding Mr Rose's and Mr [sic] Wraxall's testing,' he concluded. 'The fact that petitioner may be a normal secretor today does not prove he is innocent of the rapes that occurred in 1977. Apparently there is a disagreement among experts as to whether Mr Gary could be excluded as the perpetrator of the rape in the Thurmond case. However, the existence of this disagreement does not prove he is innocent.' Moreover, 'Mr Wraxall does not state that petitioner could be excluded as the source of the semen in the Jackson, Scheible, Borom and Woodruff cases.' Apparently, there might have been more than one rapist. In Judge Lawson's opinion, we had been wasting our time.

That marked the end of Lawson's involvement in the stranglings case. He was about to hand over the rest of the appeal to Columbus's new federal judge, the third since Carlton Gary had embarked on his federal *habeas* petition in 1997. His surname was very familiar. Once again, the fate of Carlton Gary would be determined by a member of that sprawling clan from north Columbus, the Lands.

# TWELVE

# Southern Justice and the Stocking Stranglings

We were exposed so much to the sight of humiliation and brutality, not physical brutality, but the brutal humiliation of human
dignity, which is even worse.

CARSON McCULLERS, *Illumination and Night Glare*

When Clay D. Land was appointed to the bench of Georgia's Middle
District court by US President George W. Bush towards the end of 2001, he
was forty-one, one of the youngest federal judges in America. He had no
previous judicial experience, but his family had passed on an impressive
background of public service. John Land, the former Chief Judge of the
State Superior Court who had denied Carlton Gary funding, was Clay's
great-uncle. His father, Jack Land, was a long-time Columbus Councilman;
Clay himself was elected to the Council in 1993. Most of his childhood was
spent in a house on the ancestral Land family holding on Double Churches
Road, yards from the home that was once inhabited by John Land's father,
Aaron Brewster Land, the man who stood trial for lynching Teasy
McElhaney. From his early adulthood Clay Land had been on the list of
regulars at the exclusive fried catfish suppers that his great-uncle John
organised for more than half a century, that singular opportunity to net-
work, the Fish House Gang.

A short, anxious-looking man with dark bushy eyebrows and deep triangular furrows that ran to his mouth from the sides of his nose, for
business Clay Land wore starched white button-down collars, striped ties
and suits that betrayed few clues to his personality. His first degree, before

he attended law school at the University of Georgia, had been in accounting. He was part of a new generation of Southern conservatives, a group for whom the white supremacist rhetoric of the 1950s seemed as distant as his family's rural origins. Unlike their predecessors, Land and his peers were also Republicans. Before he contemplated becoming a judge, he had served three full terms for the GOP as a Senator in the Georgia State Assembly. Having decided to stand down in 2000 in order to spend more time with his wife and young family, Land told an interviewer he was 'totally committed to practising law for the rest of my professional life'. But once the US Supreme Court confirmed Bush's presidential victory over Al Gore after the disputed election of November 2000, 'It seemed to me it [a federal judgeship] would be a great job, so why not put my hat in the ring and see what might happen?' Having been one of several nominees put forward by a committee of state Republicans, Land was speedily selected by the White House and confirmed by the US Senate.

By no means was Land on his party's hard right. He had supported the replacement of the Confederate Stars and Bars as Georgia's state flag, and tougher gun laws. In his state Senate resignation speech, he deplored the 'partisan rancour' that had come to dominate politics, in Georgia as elsewhere. As a lawyer, he was active in a group that represented indigent clients *pro bono*. He promised that as a judge he would apply the law 'regardless of whether the outcome is perceived to be consistent with Republican or Democratic philosophy'. His down-home intention was to dispense justice with the fairness of his Columbus high school football coach, and 'the dignity, grace, courage and perspective of my mom'. After his investiture, which was followed by a party attended by several hundred friends and members of his extended family, Land moved into the white federal courthouse in downtown Columbus at the start of 2002.

The previous spring I had tracked down a man I had long been wanting to meet – Carlos 'Sonny' Galbreath, the dentist who made the mould of the bite wound left by the strangler in the breast of his final victim, Janet Cofer. This was the cast that William Smith and Doug Pullen had taken to show the forensic dentist in Atlanta, Dr Thomas David, the cast they had hidden from Gary's trial.

In 1993 Galbreath promised to find it for Gary's state *habeas* defence lawyer, Jeffrey Ertel, only to tell him later that it had been lost or destroyed. Yet there was one unanswered question that made me want to interview Galbreath. Bill Smith and Doug Pullen had claimed in the hearings that the cast was of the killer's upper teeth only, and that because Gary had had dental work on his upper jaw while he was in prison in South Carolina after the last of the stranglings, a comparison would have no relevance. But Dr David had said in his affidavit that the cast included the lower teeth as well, where the strangler displayed 'a "crowding" of the lower teeth that made them particularly distinctive'. Like Ertel before me, I had peered into Gary's mouth in the death row visitation room, and seen for myself that his lower teeth were perfectly straight and even.

I met Galbreath for coffee at the Columbus Hilton. A thin, rangy man with sandy hair and freckles, he soon showed me the reason why he had been forced to close down his practice in 1993. A devoted weekend hunter of deer, turkey and quail, he had accidentally blown the ends off several fingers with a rifle. He seemed friendly and easygoing, and was happy to recall how he had made the cast by pouring a liquid 'alginate' into Mrs Cofer's wound. Later, he said, he also made a replica of the bite itself, a negative copy of the tooth cast known as a 'cast stone' or 'exemplar'. He also remembered being contacted by Gary's lawyer Jeff Ertel. At the time, he said, Doug Pullen was still Columbus's District Attorney.

'Doug and I go way back,' Galbreath said. 'He and I go bird hunting. We still go, though not as much as we used to, with him being so busy being a judge. We used to hunt deer, until it got to the stage I'd killed so many deer it wasn't fun any more. So when the attorney called me, I called Doug. I asked him if I could show the tooth cast to the attorney.' He slapped his thigh for emphasis, unable to restrain a chuckle. 'Doug said, "You tell him any damn story you like, but on no account can he look at those models. You don't show him anything, and if he calls again, tell him that his reputation precedes him."'

This was not what Pullen had said in his testimony at the state *habeas* hearing in 1994. Although he confirmed that he and Galbreath were friends, he said they had not discussed the cast at all.

I was baffled. '*Why* did Pullen not want you to let Ertel see the cast?' I asked.

'I think the best I can remember is that he said that Ertel was not held in the highest esteem with the Bar,' Galbreath said. 'That for some reason or other, he was considered shaky by the Bar Association.' This was untrue: Ertel was highly regarded by his fellow attorneys. But this was not Dr Galbreath's real bombshell. 'I do know this: the model is still in existence.'

According to Galbreath, when he shut his practice in 1993 he had given the cast to the Columbus coroner, Donald Kilgore. Kilgore died in 2000, and then, Galbreath thought, it must have passed into the care of his successor, James Dunnavant. He promised me he would speak to Dunnavant the following week.

Over the next two months I called Galbreath at least nine times. On each occasion he was adamant that the cast could be found, and was probably with Dunnavant. On 15 May 2001 he told me he had finally managed to speak to him. The good news was that the coroner thought that the cast really was in his possession. 'He says for sure it hasn't been destroyed,' Galbreath said. The bad news was that no one could see it. The reason Galbreath gave was bizarre. Apparently, no one was allowed to look at the archive where the bite cast was kept without the permission of Columbus's City Attorney. Since this job was currently vacant, if Dunnavant went to look for the cast he would 'put his job on the line'.

When I visited Columbus in November 2002, Galbreath told me something else that sounded significant – that the cast had revealed that one of the strangler's upper front teeth was 'rotated', twisted by twenty degrees or more out of its proper alignment. Next morning I met Gary's old friend Earnestine Flowers. 'Let me ask you,' I said, 'did you ever notice anything strange about Carlton's teeth?'

Earnestine looked puzzled. 'Strange? What kind of strange?'

'Well, like, twisted, rotated out of line. Was one of his upper front teeth askew?'

'Definitely not! You'd have seen it every time the man smiled. He never had any such abnormality.' Later, her mother, Doris Layfield, who had known Gary all his life, agreed, as did Gene Hewell, Gary's one-time employer, the proprietor of the Movin' Man fashion store.

'Hey, he worked for me as a model,' Hewell said. 'Believe me, there ain't too many models with twisted front teeth.'

Later, I asked Gary himself. 'The business I was in, if I'd ever had a twisted tooth, it would have stuck out a mile,' he said. He meant stealing, not modelling clothes. 'People would have noticed. My ladies would have noticed. There must be school pictures and all that. It never happened.'

Defence attorney Jack Martin joined the hunt. One winter's morning he chatted to Dunnavant as the coroner lounged outside his office, smoking a cigarette. Dunnavant, who had worked for his predecessor, Don Kilgore, for several years, said that Kilgore kept the cast in an old plastic bag in his office desk drawer, and used to show it to visitors. But so far as he knew, Kilgore's stuff had been cleared out, though it was just possible that it had been moved to the District Attorney's office. He said he would ask. Martin kept up the pressure, but Dunnavant discovered nothing. Apparently the cast wasn't with the DA. Perhaps, he suggested, it might have been given to a member of Don Kilgore's family.

There were more frustrations ahead. In the spring of 2003 I made contact with Karen Kilgore, coroner Kilgore's widow. About to travel to Columbus, I phoned her from Detroit and arranged to meet her the following Sunday. She remembered the cast well, and told me at length about how it had been made from the wound on Janet Cofer. She was fairly certain she had it at her house. 'Just call me when you get in,' she said in a honeyed, lazy drawl. 'I'm sure it'll be fine, but just check in, then come on by.'

On Sunday, 6 June 2003 I called her from the Columbus Hilton.

'I'm so sorry, Mr Rose. I'm afraid I can't see you after all,' Mrs Kilgore said. 'You see, Ricky Boren [who by this time had risen from detective to become the Columbus Police Department's Assistant Chief] is the god-father of my little girl. He's told me not to talk to you, because this case is still under investigation. He says that if I meet you, it might be prejudicial.'

The only way forward seemed to be to enlist the help of the court, and in November 2003 Jack Martin managed to persuade Judge Clay Land to hold a hearing. One by one, the witnesses who appeared to have seen the cast during the previous decade were issued with subpoenas and testified. None of them had the remotest idea what had happened to it.

As before, there were contradictions. Karen Kilgore said she had seen the cast only in her husband's office, and was certain it was not at her home: 'I've searched everything in this house,' she said. But Henry Warden, the late coroner's grandson, told the court that some years earlier, Kilgore had shown him the cast in a bedroom at his house. Karen said it was possible that Henry's father Jack had collected the cast from the morgue after her husband's death, along with several boxes of memorabilia. But although they had the boxes, Jack and his wife Joanie said they did not contain the bite cast. Jack Martin asked Judge Land for an order to search their attic. Land refused. As for Dunnavant, he was clueless. He had seen Kilgore with the cast during the 1990s, but it was not at his office now.

The fate of the bite cast seemed murkier than ever. Jack Martin followed up the hearings with a written brief, arguing that Land's court should reconvene to put all the officials who had ever dealt with the cast on the witness stand, including Ricky Boren, William Smith and Doug Pullen, in a last attempt to ascertain the truth. In his view, the few known facts showed that the cast would have proven Gary's innocence, and that the state had deliberately concealed it through 'machinations' and 'misconduct'.

Susan Boleyn, the state's doughty Assistant Attorney General, maintained that the cast was of no significance. She doubted whether it had ever existed at all: 'I'm not sure that this isn't folklore.' Even if it did exist, it could never have proven anything except that Carlton Gary had not killed Janet Cofer – a crime for which, she reminded Judge Land, he had never been convicted. Bite or no bite, the evidence that proved he raped and strangled Florence Scheible, Kathleen Woodruff and Martha Thurmond remained unassailable. In her own brief after the hearings, she added a further, novel argument: that the failure to find the cast or prove what had happened to it many years earlier was Carlton Gary's own fault, and that of his lawyers. They had, she argued, failed to exercise 'due diligence', and any further inquiry should therefore be barred.

In 1996, the Democrat President Bill Clinton introduced a Bill into Congress designed to curb the scope of federal death penalty appeals, and to increase the speed and number of executions. Capital punishment advocates had long claimed that condemned prisoners were being kept alive for far too long by their lawyers, who would stop at nothing to exploit legal 'technicalities'. Passed in the wake of the horror and revulsion aroused by the Oklahoma City terrorist bombing of April 1995, Clinton's Antiterrorism and Effective Death Penalty Act – or AEDPA, as it is often known – achieved its ambition. Previously, death row prisoners had been allowed considerable latitude when fighting federal *habeas* cases: a second chance to argue claims about evidence and law that they had already fought and lost in their state appeals. Federal judges accepted that state courts, their judges subject to regular election, could not always be trusted to interpret the US Constitution, especially in emotionally charged murder cases. Before the AEDPA, more than 40 per cent of death sentences were overturned in federal *habeas*; by definition, since the cases had got that far, state judges had already upheld them.

The AEDPA rewrote these rules in a highly restrictive manner. Other than in exceptional circumstances, battles that had already been decided by state courts could not now be refought. New evidence could be introduced in federal *habeas* only when the defence could show that it was previously unavailable, or that it 'could not have been previously discovered through the exercise of due diligence'. In the 2000 case of *Williams vs Taylor*, the US Supreme Court defined 'due diligence': 'It depends upon whether the prisoner made a reasonable attempt, in the light of the information available at the time, to investigate and pursue claims in state court.' If these conditions were not met, the only way to get a federal court to consider such evidence was if it amounted to such overwhelming proof of innocence that 'no fact finder would have found petitioner guilty of the underlying offence'. About the only thing that might satisfy this criterion was a conclusive DNA test.

Smith and Pullen had concealed the bite cast from Gary's trial, and later, during his state *habeas* appeals, crucial facts stayed hidden; partly, it seemed, because Dr Galbreath had talked with his old shooting buddy, then-District Attorney Pullen. Yet Susan Boleyn was arguing that it was Ertel who was at fault, and that if he had been more diligent, he could have revealed the truth back in 1994. He and his colleagues had not, to use the language of *Williams vs Taylor*, 'made a reasonable attempt to investigate and present evidence concerning the bite mark'.

Her argument turned on a single detail. When Galbreath told Ertel that the cast was destroyed or lost, Ertel should not have taken him at his word, or assumed that bringing him to court would be futile. Instead, he should have issued a subpoena to make Galbreath testify during the state *habeas* hearings, and sought a court order requiring him to divulge the cast.

The defence, Boleyn claimed, had 'deliberately failed to explore the issue further'.

This might have looked like inverted logic, a case of blaming the victim, but Judge Clay Land endorsed Boleyn's argument in its entirety. In an order he issued on 2 April 2004, he said he could think of 'no legitimate reason' for not issuing Galbreath with a subpoena in 1994. The result was that Gary 'had not shown he was reasonably diligent during the state court proceedings'. Under the terms of the AEDPA, the door to conducting further investigations into the fate of the bite cast seemed to be closed once and for all.

After more than seven years, Gary's federal *habeas* appeal in Georgia's Middle District Court was rapidly approaching a conclusion. In long, final briefs, Martin and McIntyre reiterated their claim that Gary had been denied his rights under the Constitution, while Boleyn responded that he had received all his due. Land had already ruled that because of the AEDPA, many of the issues on which Gary had fought his state appeals were procedurally barred. Those that Land did agree to consider will all be familiar by now. Only two looked as if they stood any chance of success: the serology and, just possibly, the bite cast.

Land issued his final, ninety-five-page order on 28 September 2004. His last words on the bite cast ducked the issue altogether. He merely said that he was bound to defer to the judgement made seven years earlier by the state *habeas* court: that because no one knew whether the cast matched Gary or not, it was therefore irrelevant.

However, in the section that dealt with serology and Gary's secretor status, Land's order contained two surprises. Although his federal *habeas* predecessor, Judge Hugh Lawson of Macon, had refused to grant a semen test or to accept the results of mine, he had not made any decision about the ultimate significance of those newly discovered documents, the state laboratory worksheets on which John Wegel had recorded his findings. Land determined that the state's failure to give these papers to Gary's defence at the trial *did* constitute a violation of his right to due process under the Fourteenth Amendment of the US Constitution: a breach of the duty of prosecutors and law-enforcement agencies to disclose potentially exculpatory evidence to the defence. 'The fact that the worksheets were in the

GBI's possession, as opposed to that of the prosecutor, is no excuse,' Judge Land thundered. Likewise, although he endorsed almost all the decisions made by his great-uncle Judge John Land and later by Judge Followill to refuse Gary funding, there was one exception: 'Given petitioner's repeated requests for a serological expert, the court finds that the trial court was unreasonable in denying this request.' The lack of funds and advice from an expert *had* hampered Bud Siemon's cross-examination of John Wegel, Land said. It had prevented him from bringing out the difference between Wegel's two secretor tests, absorption-inhibition and the more sensitive absorption-elution. Needless to say, in Carlton Gary's twenty-year passage through the courts, these two rulings were unprecedented.

Then, however, came the 'buts'. The lack of funds may have prevented Bud Siemon from scrutinising the serological evidence properly, but on its own, this was not sufficient. To vacate Gary's conviction, Land said he would have to be convinced that if this decision had gone the other way, it would likely have led to a different verdict. Similarly, it was not enough to show that the hidden evidence should have been turned over, and would have been exculpatory. To obtain a new trial, a death row prisoner also had to show that it was 'material' – that if the jurors had known about it, they would probably have found him not guilty.

Judge Land had appeared to raise Gary's hopes. Now he set about dashing them again, more conclusively than any court had before. Falling back on the arguments used by Susan Boleyn and Judge Lawson, he said that the serological testimony had always been 'inconclusive': according to the state, it neither excluded Gary nor proved his guilt. Whatever its status, there remained a wealth of other testimony, such as the fingerprints, Gary's confession and Gertrude Miller's courtroom identification. Land repeated the claim, apparently oblivious to its dubious scientific validity, that the levels of H-reactive substance in Carlton Gary's semen might have changed radically over time. Like Judge Lawson before him, he asserted that the entire issue boiled down to an academic dispute: 'All that petitioner has shown is that a second expert may disagree with Mr Wegel's opinions and conclusions. This alone does not prove that Mr Wegel's testimony was false or misleading.' The serological component of Gary's federal *habeas* appeal was therefore dismissed.

Judge Land threw out all the other issues just as decisively. The concluding paragraph of his long order was particularly bleak: 'It has been eighteen years since twelve jurors unanimously found petitioner guilty of crimes that warrant the imposition of the death penalty under Georgia law. Petitioner has avoided the execution of this sentence by taking advantage of every legal avenue available to him. This court finds no legal obstacle standing in the way of petitioner's journey to his final destination.'

As things stood, Carlton Gary was probably two or three years away from execution. He could and would apply to reverse Land's decisions to a three-judge panel of the US Eleventh Circuit Court of Appeals in Atlanta, the federal tribunal that covers the states of Georgia, Florida and Alabama. But the scope of his petition there would be even more restricted than his *habeas* claim in Land's District Court. Under the AEDPA, it would be limited to issues for which Land was prepared to grant a 'certificate of appealability'. Here lay another conflict of interest: the Act says that it is Federal District Court judges who decide which of their own decisions ought to go to a higher court where they might be reversed. After the Eleventh Circuit there would be only the Supreme Court, a very long shot indeed: unless it decided that Gary's case raised constitutional questions applicable to other cases that had to be resolved, it was unlikely to agree to consider his petition at all. In the early years of the twenty-first century, about sixty death row prisoners will be put to death in the United States each year. Only a handful will ever get *certiorari* – a stay of execution pending an opinion from the Supreme Court. The Georgia Board of Pardons and Parole would still have the power to spare Gary's life. But this institution, reluctant as it is to commute a sentence at the best of times, was unlikely to do so for a man convicted of the serial rape and murder of old women.

Gary's morale was slipping. There were days when he was due to receive visitors but stayed in his cell, uncommunicative. His letters to me became rare events. Aside from his own legal plight, he was not short of reasons to be gloomy. In October 2001, after a long hiatus, Georgia began to kill its death row prisoners again. While the State Assembly and courts had been engineering the shift from the electric chair to lethal injection, many men had exhausted their appeals, and when executions resumed they did so with new velocity. In the twenty-two years after the restoration of capital punishment following *Gregg vs Georgia* in 1976, twenty-three Georgia men went to their deaths in the chair. In the period October 2001–December 2005 sixteen died, strapped and immobile on the execution gurney while their veins were pumped with a cocktail of chemicals that would paralyse and then kill them. Some were men that Gary had known for years. The loss he felt most deeply was that of José High, the African-American with severe learning difficulties whom Gary had taught to read, who had lived in the next cell to his for more than a decade. After a final, tearful meeting with his lawyers and his pastor, High was taken on 6 November 2001.

'They're getting ready to murder my neighbour, Tim Carr,' Gary told me during a visit at the end of November 2004 – the first that the prison had been prepared to allow since my exfiltration of his semen three and a half years earlier. 'His lawyers say he's got about ten days, and that's depressing me [Carr was eventually executed in January 2005]. He was one of my art students when we all lived downstairs.' Gary sighed. 'He was getting good.' There was little sign of Gary's old, blustery confidence, his insistence that in the end he would beat the 'crackers' who wanted him dead. He seemed easier to connect with, but also weary, almost resigned.

'It is quite depressing, you know. There are several guys who are just waiting,' Gary said. 'They don't know if they're still going to be here at Christmas. I sit in my cell and put on some classic rock or some classic jazz and try to put it from my mind.'

A recent half-baked escape attempt by another inmate had made conditions for death row inmates markedly more arduous. Most of Gary's art materials were now prohibited, while new restrictions on taking showers and making phone calls had been introduced. 'Since the escape plot they keep waking us up, shining lights at you in the middle of the night. All I got left for art is paper and coloured pencils. It's all just so silly, but I've got to deal with it every day.'

The next time I saw him, ten months later, his life was no easier. Forced to spend more time each day between the walls of his tiny, windowless cell, he had put on weight, and his face looked tired and puffy. 'They keep bringing in new rules,' he said. 'There's no TV until four. They've stopped me doing crochet and knitting.' Twice a week he was allowed outside to a yard, where there were two basketball hoops and a volleyball net. All the surfaces were concrete; it had been twenty-one years since he had touched or walked on grass. 'I try to work out in my cell every day. Every now and then I talk to the other cats, but most of the time I'm reading, doing crosswords and sudoku.' At night he watched television – '*Desperate Housewives*. I like those ladies all right! But my show is *24*.' For years Gary had been trusted as a prison cleaner, and he still took the same pride in his tier of cells as he did in his appearance: 'I come out every morning for that. I sweep the floor and I wax and polish the brass. I like to buff every day.'

Gary's appeal to the Eleventh Circuit against Land's rejection of his federal *habeas* petition was set for an oral argument in the first week of December 2005. He told me that he was still hopeful: years earlier, Jeff Ertel had warned him that he had little realistic prospect of winning an appeal before his case reached that stage, when the judges would be neither elected nor closely tied to the communities where they sat. Nevertheless, there was no getting away from the fact that Gary's date with the Eleventh Circuit was probably his final chance.

On the afternoon of 9 November, four weeks before the hearing, Gary's lawyer Michael McIntyre was poring over some paperwork in his new office, a townhouse in Virginia Highlands, an affluent neighbourhood near Emory University. Almost exactly four years earlier, Susan Boleyn had called Jack Martin to say that the state had located the missing laboratory worksheets. When she phoned McIntyre this time, her news was even more dramatic.

'Michael,' she said, 'I have something to tell you. The folks in Columbus have found the missing bite cast.'

Later that day she put more details in writing. She had been called by Gray Conger, Columbus's District Attorney; he in turn had just been contacted by the coroner James Dunnavant. Two years earlier, Dunnavant had testified that the cast was nowhere to be found. Now, it transpired, it had been in his office all along – just as the dentist Carlos Galbreath had told me back in the spring of 2001. Dunnavant told the *Ledger-Enquirer* that he had been looking for more storage space, and went into a closet next to his office to clean out some old metal cabinets. 'In the back of one of the lower drawers,' wrote the columnist Tim Chitwood, 'he found some old file

313

folders that had fallen over. He pulled them out and threw them away. Beneath them was a brown paper bag. He was about to throw that away, too. But then he felt something hard inside it.' Dunnavant looked in the bag. 'And there it was,' he told Chitwood. 'And I said, "Oh Lord." I never looked in those old cabinets, because there wasn't nothing in there, supposedly. There's nothing in there now.'

Martin and McIntyre filed a motion with the Eleventh Circuit asking for Gary's December hearing to be indefinitely postponed: the whole factual basis on which this part of the appeal had been decided was, it was clear, mistaken. The three judges agreed at once, and returned the case to Columbus without any need to state reasons. Once again, the burden of adjudicating Gary's fight for life would fall on Clay Land.

The finding of the cast produced no signs of contrition from Susan Boleyn and the state. When, in December 2005, Martin and McIntyre asked Land to allow an expert to examine the cast, and for funds to pay him, Boleyn resisted, arguing as before that the cast was irrelevant, and that it was Gary's defence that should be blamed for not finding it earlier. This time, however, Land did not buy these arguments. He no longer agreed that Gary and his lawyers had not been sufficiently diligent: 'To the contrary, it appears petitioner made a reasonable attempt to locate the bite mark impression,' and this had been thwarted by the false claims about its loss or destruction. In Land's view, the cast 'is relevant' (my italics). Gary might not have been convicted of killing Janet Cofer, but at his trial, 'the state's theory was that one person committed all the murders ... Undermining the state's evidence of the bite mark on Janet Cofer would have resulted in undermining the state's whole case.' There was only one way to find out whether it really did – to allow the bite to be compared with Gary's teeth. The defence had already chosen its expert: the same Dr Thomas David who had been shown the cast by Bill Smith, Doug Pullen and the cops more than twenty years earlier. David, said Land, would be paid with public money.

In February 2006, Dr David visited the Georgia Bureau of Investigation Crime Lab and inspected the cast by naked eye. Several things were immediately apparent. First, it was still attached to a signed and dated label, establishing that it had, as claimed, been made by Dr Galbreath in April

1978 from a bite around Mrs Cofer's nipple. Secondly, the cast found by Dunnavant was not the positive, ridged model that David was shown in 1984, but the 'cast stone' negative or 'exemplar'. Making an exemplar is the usual first step in comparing a cast with a suspect. Back in March 2001, when everyone assumed that the cast had been lost, Gary told me that an exemplar had been made from his own teeth in 1984, when he was waiting to be tried at the Columbus County Jail. It seemed possible that someone had tried to make a comparison then, and having failed to make a match, took steps to erase the cast from the record.

Prosecutors often accuse capital defence attorneys of fostering unnecessary delays, of spinning out appeals to intolerable length in order to prolong the lives of their clients. But in Carlton Gary's case in 2006 the only source of delay was Susan Boleyn, counsel for the prosecution. She forced Gary's lawyers to go back to court and fight for fresh orders every step of the way, opposing their successive requests to let Dr David examine the cast with a stereo microscope, and then to make an exemplar from Gary. Each time she lost.

Examination of the cast by microscope, Dr David wrote in an affidavit in May 2006, confirmed what he had recalled from his meeting with Pullen and Smith in 1984: 'The markings in the bite mark exemplar were of good quality, both with respect to the upper and lower teeth ... from the exemplar the size, shape and orientation of both upper and lower teeth could be determined.' There was no evidence that Gary had ever had dental work on his lower teeth. As the defence had long argued, the work that had been done in South Carolina was immaterial.

Dr David's stereo microscope photographs show that the strangler's lower teeth were, as he had always stated, crowded and uneven. The exemplar he was finally able to make from Gary confirmed that his are straight and well-spaced. It was plain, David told Jack Martin, that there was no positive match. As of this writing in October 2006, he has yet to conduct further tests in order to determine whether he will be able to testify that the bite cast excludes Carlton Gary to a level of scientific certainty.

The final act of this drama cannot yet be written. The bite cast scene has yet to be played out, and whichever way it ends in the District Court in Columbus, there will be further appeals. A victory by Gary – an order from

Land to vacate his conviction and to give him a new trial – would be appealed by the prosecution. If Gary should lose with Land, or if the cast turns out to be inconclusive, he would also still have issues to resolve in the Eleventh Circuit, principally the serology.

During the years I have worked on this book, I have been asked the same question innumerable times: do I believe that Carlton Gary is innocent? It is the wrong question to ask. Detective Michael Sellers always *believed* he was guilty, as, we must assume, did Ricky Boren, Charles Rowe, Bill Smith and Doug Pullen. In the almost two hundred cases in which DNA tests have led to the release of other death row inmates, no doubt the prosecutors' belief in their guilt was once equally strong.

Belief, however, is not enough, either to condemn or to exonerate, and writers, no more than police officers or prosecutors, do not have the power to look into someone's eyes and determine whether or not they are telling the truth. Over many centuries a method has evolved that attempts to make this distinction in a more reliable way: the adversarial criminal justice system, as practised, with many local variations, in both Britain and America. Its underlying premise is that beliefs and gut feelings should have no place in deciding whether a human being ought to be punished, let alone killed, for a crime they may have committed. What counts is evidence, fairly presented and cross-examined. At the end of the adversarial contest, a jury makes a finding of criminal guilt when it concludes that the evidence is such that it has no reasonable doubt. Even the most cursory look at recent legal history will reveal that this method is deeply imperfect. But it is the best we have.

Long before I ever travelled to Georgia, I had seen from covering miscarriages of justice in England and Wales what can happen when belief – not blind prejudice, but honest, well-founded supposition – takes precedence over evidence: the imprisonment of innocent people, perhaps for many years. I had also learned that what police officers and prosecutors sometimes call 'technicalities', breaches of the rules that govern issues such as the conduct of interrogations or the disclosure of exculpatory evidence, may not be merely 'technical' at all. Often, they just happen to be the place where a more fundamental miscarriage of justice becomes visible, the point at which the iceberg of the wrongful conviction of a 'factually innocent' person breaks the legal surface. The supposed dichotomy between 'technical' and 'factual' innocence is false: apart from anything else, it is far less likely that the police will be tempted to break the rules when dealing with factually guilty suspects, because it will generally be easier to find genuine, incriminating evidence in such cases. At the same time, if the criminal process is not to become a vehicle for the exercise of arbitrary power, its operatives, especially judges and prosecutors, must obey its internal rules. If they are found to have broken them, appeals courts must punish them by setting dishonestly obtained convictions aside. Many years ago, the Harvard legal thinker Herbert Packer described these values in detail, and taking his cue from the US Constitution, he gave them a name: the 'due process' model of criminal justice.

In a system that conforms to the due process model, when prosecutors come across evidence that weakens their case, or helps a defendant to bolster his, they must disclose it without flinching, and if they fail to do so, this must be done by the judge. If district attorneys detect flaws in the work done by detectives or forensic scientists, they must be ready to apply the brakes, and even to drop serious charges unless better evidence turns up. This is asking a lot, especially in cases involving crimes as horrifying as the stocking stranglings, when the pressure to get a conviction is at its most intense. Prosecutors are subject to a conflict of interest: when circumstances require, they must be prepared to abandon their understandable ambitions, even in places such as Georgia where they face regular public election. But their job, ultimately, is to serve justice, not the electorate. They must prosecute their cases aggressively, but with complete integrity. They must present the evidence honestly, and always tell the truth. In a death penalty case, this moral obligation is especially great.

Perhaps the most striking feature of Carlton Gary's trial is that at several points Bill Smith and his assistant Doug Pullen did not display such integrity. At several crucial points Smith made statements that he must have known were untrue, while Pullen endorsed them with his silence. For example, Smith told the jury that Gertrude Miller, the victim who survived, had never identified anyone else before she picked out Gary's as the face that was 'burned into her memory', despite being shown 'thousands' of pictures by the police. In fact, as has been seen, she had previously identified Jerome Livas and two unknown men depicted in police composite sketches. On several occasions she had also given descriptions of men who could not possibly have been Gary. Smith said that the only evidence against John Lee Mitchell, the man accused of murdering Nellie Farmer in Albany, New York, came from Carlton Gary. In fact, another man had claimed that Mitchell had confessed to the crime, while shoeprints that could not have been Gary's had been found at the scene.

In his closing summation in the trial's guilt phase, Smith said that it was 'unfortunate' that Detective Richard Smith had not brought back a set of Gary's fingerprints from South Carolina when he visited him there in 1979. In fact, as we have seen, he did, and though he gave them to the CPD print section, they were not matched to the strangling crime scenes. This must, at least, cast doubt on the matches that were made five years later – bearing in mind that there were no photos of the latent prints *in situ* at the murder scenes. Smith and Pullen had personally taken the cast from the bite mark on the breast of Janet Cofer to show Dr David in Atlanta. But when Bud Siemon noticed the mark in the photo of her body and asked for funds to investigate it, Smith insisted that we 'don't have any comparisons to make', later claiming that no such comparison would be valid because of Gary's dental work. Smith should have known that the work was confined to Gary's upper teeth. We now know that the hidden cast includes a clear impression – in Dr David's words, 'quality evidence' – of the strangler's lower teeth.

These statements to the jury were not mere sins of omission, and it does not seem likely that in a case that had taken more than two years to come to trial, Bill Smith could have made them inadvertently. Judge Followill, meanwhile, had reviewed the entire prosecution file. Either he was negligent, or he too connived in these errors. By maintaining his blanket refusal to fund any part of Gary's defence, Followill also made it much less likely that the fudges and obfuscations that so disfigured other parts of the state's case – notably the serology – would ever be properly explored.

Instead of asking whether we 'believe' that Carlton Gary is innocent, we need to put two different questions. The first is, did he get a fair trial? My answer to that is a resounding negative. He was starved of resources and was facing a prosecutor who not only hid exculpatory evidence from the defence, but lied. The second question is whether we should entertain real doubt as to Gary's guilt. Equally emphatically, my answer is yes.

We may not have the magic bullet, a piece of evidence which proves to a point beyond reasonable doubt that he did not commit the stocking stranglings, although it is possible that this may now exist in the shape of the bite cast, and the serology seems to come very close to this standard. But if we take the main areas of testimony that led to his conviction, each one is undermined by facts that were hidden from the trial. So far, however, the American appellate courts have rejected Gary's successive petitions.

As we have seen, at one stage Susan Boleyn was arguing that even if the serology conclusively proved that someone else had raped the victims, Gary would still be guilty of murder. Later she said – with Judge Clay Land's agreement – that the loss of the bite cast was the responsibility of the defence. The law was granting her an astonishing flexibility: to make a fundamental change to the state's narrative of the crimes, and to blame the defence for the prosecution's shortcomings. At the same time, the defence was hedged by dense thickets of procedural rules that prevented Gary's attorneys from raising some issues at all, or that made it impossible to revisit the decisions of lower courts – such as, most notably, about funding. For the state, there was almost unlimited latitude, and for the defence, onerous limits, made still worse by the Antiterrorism and Effective Death Penalty Act. The cumulative effect of these restrictions can be expressed in stark and simple terms. Much as prosecutors and conservative politicians like to claim that defendants in the American criminal process regularly win trials and appeals on legal technicalities, the opposite is true. In America today, it would be quite easy to be executed on a technicality, despite the existence of compelling fresh evidence that the courts, for entirely technical reasons, refused to consider.

Writing in 1968, Herbert Packer believed that with the series of landmark decisions by the liberal Supreme Court of Chief Justice Earl Warren, the values encompassed by his 'due process' model were being inculcated throughout the United States: 'No one can doubt that the norms of the criminal process have moved rapidly and spectacularly across the spectrum towards the due process model.' This trend, he was sure, would continue. In fact, it was about to go into reverse. Under Packer's model, judges would try to curb misconduct by police or prosecutors by over-turning convictions when it came to light. But in case after case, the Supreme Court of William Rehnquist, Chief Justice from 1986 to 2005, seemed to take the view that preserving the integrity of state criminal justice systems was simply not the job of federal courts of appeal. To the Rehnquist court, evidence of misconduct was not enough on its own. To get a new trial, a defendant had to demonstrate that but for this, the jury would have acquitted him. As for exculpatory evidence hidden from the trial, it was not sufficient if it merely raised doubts. A prisoner and his lawyers had to show that if the jury had known about it, it would have found him not guilty.

In the Rehnquist era, the burden of proof in appeals was effectively reversed. Fresh testimony had to amount to something close to proof of innocence 'beyond reasonable doubt', and if it did not quite reach that level, a death row inmate could be executed. Herbert Packer thought that behind the idea of legal 'due process' there ought to lie a set of substantive ethical standards to which police investigations and trials should conform. But there is nothing in the American Constitution that implies this concept: all the Fifth and Fourteenth Amendments say is that no one should be pun-ished without 'due process of law'. They are, in other words, an expression of moral relativism. If the courts decide that a prosecutor can mislead a jury or hide exculpatory evidence without a conviction being reversed, then the defendant received due process. There is no such thing as 'the spirit of the law', because the only thing that matters is its letter. 'Due process', as Packer wanted the term to mean, is not the same thing as the due process experienced thus far by Carlton Gary. At the end of the nine-teenth century, the members of the Georgia Bar Association thought that the way to prevent lynching was to restore 'the certainty of punishment'. Thanks to the evolution of American law, that goal is now nearer to fruition.

It's 6.30 on a dark and unseasonably chilly October morning. I'm sitting at a desk in the guest bedroom at the home of John Lupold and Lynn Willoughby, two dear white friends who live in the heart of the Victorian

Historic District of Columbus, Georgia – as appropriate a place as any in which to finish this book. After breakfast I'm going to hit the road in order to visit a new witness: Jim Covington, a former special agent with the Georgia Bureau of Investigation who in 1978 spent a gruelling year in Columbus working on the stocking stranglings task force. For nine months he was its co-leader. Twenty years after Carlton Gary's trial, he has contacted Jack Martin to say he has yet another piece of long-hidden evidence that casts doubt upon Gary's guilt – details of a shoeprint left by the strangler when he stood on an air-conditioning unit in order to climb through Ruth Schwob's kitchen window on the night of the terrors. Covington says it was several sizes smaller than Gary's feet, and he also has a map he made, showing a trail of the same shoeprints leading from Mrs Schwob's house to the residence of Mildred Borom, whom the strangler raped and killed.

Covington was in charge of the Schwob crime scene that day, and circulated task force members with a memo that contained her description of the man who tried to kill her. The memo states that she told the investigators that he was 'small and muscular'. Gary, of course, is big, well-built man, six feet three inches tall. His defence team has never seen this memo before. I'm already planning an epilogue: sometimes this drama seems never-ending.

Last night my friends and I took an after-dinner stroll. It was already late, and as we left their house the only sounds were our footfalls on the old brick pavement, the year's last cicadas and the rustle of autumn leaves. There was no moon. The day before yesterday, the city experienced another terrible crime: the seemingly motiveless drive-by shooting of a black teenage girl. It felt like a night for contemplation.

More than ten years ago, late on another Columbus evening, I stood near this place with Doug Pullen, and heard from him about some of the city's horrors for the first time. Now as then, I peered to the east and sensed the bulk of Wynn's Hill, with its glades and pines and antebellum mansions, the wells of shadow that hid the stocking strangler and the grounds of the old library where they shot Teasy McElhaney in the lacquered August sunlight. Much closer, the ugly concrete rectangle of the Government Center loomed. There, in 2006, Judges Followill and Pullen still preside in their courts, as, less often, does Judge Bill Smith, now officially retired. A few blocks on, in the splendid new headquarters of the CPD, Ricky Boren has turned in his detective's badge for the office of City Chief. Jim Wetherington, Chief at the time of Carlton Gary's arrest and trial, went on to be Georgia's Commissioner of Corrections and Chairman of its Pardons and Parole Board, where one of his main tasks was to decide whether or not to execute death row prisoners. Next month he faces the voters in the election for Columbus Mayor.

Most of the people who worked to convict Carlton Gary have grown grander and more prosperous. As for him, just as he did ten years ago, he rots in his cell in Jackson. Last week he needed surgery for a bowel problem; his friends are hoping it does not herald something serious. But his spirits have risen: there have been no executions in Georgia so far this year. A few days ago he sent a letter to my seven-year-old son Jacob containing a dozen jokes. He has been telling them at school, and his classmates think they're very funny.

Many years ago, Gary Parker, Carlton Gary's black former lawyer, told me at his house in Stone Mountain that he left Columbus because he found its atmosphere unbearable. Practising law there, almost always the only African-American apart from the defendant in a court full of white people, it had sometimes seemed to him that he was witnessing the playing out of a lynch-mob mentality, especially in death penalty cases: 'The crime happens. The mob gathers. All too often, the question is, which nigger's neck are we going to put the noose around?' As a black attorney fighting to save black clients' lives in the South, his impression was not unique, and death penalty abolitionists have characterised capital trials as 'legal lynchings' for many years.

Of course, there are significant differences between lynching and the modern death penalty. Lynching took place in public, sometimes in front of thousands, and lynch mobs often accomplished their murders through extended, excruciating torture. Executions in the twenty-first century are carried out in the deep seclusion of maximum-security prisons, attended by a few hand-picked witnesses, while the pseudo-clinical rituals of lethal injection mimic the procedures of hospital anaesthesia rooms, as if the executioner were merely putting the prisoner to sleep. By definition, lynchings were outside the legal system, with victims often seized from jails in order to pre-empt their trials. Contemporary American executions can only occur after protracted litigation. In some ways, suggests the penal sociologist David Garland, they are the 'inverse' of lynching.

There, are however, some deeply uncomfortable echoes, most of them focused on issues of race. 'There is a special relationship between the death penalty and African-Americans,' write the Reverend Jesse Jackson, his son Jesse Jackson Junior and Bruce Shapiro, 'a relationship going back to antebellum days, when the gallows was the principal means of punishing slaves, and on through the worst days of Jim Crow.' In the 1930s, when the era of lynching *per se* began to draw to a close, farcical, perfunctory trials became an alternative means by which Southern white society expressed its outrage at certain types of crime, and through which it enforced racial supremacy. 'Court proceedings and transcripts routinely displayed the manifest racism that prevented blacks from receiving anything that approached full justice,' writes W. Fitzhugh Brundage, the historian of lynching in Georgia and Virginia. 'There can be no doubt that proper trial procedure, rules of evidence and adequate legal representation were absent for defendants in most trials involving blacks.' As before, the deepest outrage of all was reserved for sexual crimes that allegedly breached the racial frontier, that activated the Southern rape complex. Eighty-seven per cent of the 398 executions that took place in the United States for rape – without murder – between 1935 and 1967 were of African-Americans. In Georgia, the last man to die for this crime was George Watt. A black man, he went to the electric chair on 8 November 1961 for raping a white woman in Columbus.

Since 1976 and the reinstatement of capital punishment with *Gregg vs Georgia*, expressions of overt racism in Southern courts have become much more rare. The Supreme Court has made it clear that to apply phrases such as 'coloured boy' or 'nigger' to black defendants will render their trials invalid. Thanks to *Batson vs Kentucky*, prosecutors can no longer exclude all African-Americans from a jury, as they routinely did in Columbus until the mid-1980s. Yet still the racial discrepancies in the use of the death penalty remain. The Berkeley criminologist Franklin E. Zimring has drawn attention to the fact that nearly 80 per cent of modern American executions take place in the states of the former Confederacy, and that the states with the highest density of executions are those that had the most lynchings. Throughout the thirty-eight states that retain capital statutes (some have not carried out an execution for decades), prosecutors seek the death penalty in only a tiny minority of first-degree murder cases, and fewer still ever result in an execution. In 1986, the same year as Carlton Gary's trial, the University of Iowa Law Professor David C. Baldus analysed more than two thousand murders that took place in Georgia during the 1970s. He found that defendants charged with killing white victims were sentenced to death eleven times more often than those charged with killing blacks. Twenty-two per cent of black defendants convicted of killing whites got the death penalty, but only 3 per cent of whites who killed blacks. Baldus discovered that much of this difference arose from decisions by prosecutors. Other, later surveys have obtained similar results.

In 1987 the Baldus study became the basis for another milestone US Supreme Court case from Georgia, *McCleskey vs Kemp*. The African-American Warren McCleskey had killed a white police officer during a robbery in Atlanta. His lawyers argued that the evident discrimination in the use of capital punishment revealed by Baldus meant that it was racist, arbitrary and unfair, and therefore unconstitutional, and the court should issue a moratorium, just as it had in 1972 with *Furman vs Georgia*. By 1987, however, the political balance of the court had changed, and William Rehnquist had become Chief Justice. By a five to four majority it decided that arguments about race drawn from statistics were inapplicable. To avoid electrocution, McCleskey would have to prove that the individuals who tried him had breached his Fourteenth Amendment right to equal protection, that racism was demonstrably operative in his own case. In the words of Justice Powell, 'The only question before us is whether … the law of Georgia was properly applied. We agree with the District Court and the Court of Appeals for the Eleventh Circuit that this was carefully and correctly done in this case.' Other juries might well have been motivated by racial prejudice, but that did not mean McCleskey's was.

In practice, notes the legal analyst David Cole, proving the existence of racism in a particular case is almost impossible, unless the judge or prosecutor decides to admit that they were prejudiced – an extremely unlikely event. Indeed, the standard set by *McCleskey* for reversing a conviction on the grounds of racial bias has never yet been met. I cannot prove that any of the manifest unfairness of Carlton Gary's trial and appeals has been the product of racism by its participants. I have heard Doug Pullen state his own abhorrence of such attitudes, and I have no doubt that the other white protagonists in this story would, if asked, do the same.

Yet the fact remains: this story has happened in the South, a region in whose history racism has been a constant theme, and where statistics reveal that death sentences have not always been passed equitably. However much capital trials and executions differ from lynchings, they also, as Garland suggests, exhibit some notable similarities. Like lynchings, death penalty trials are driven by local politics and politicians (a class that includes elected judges and prosecutors). Like lynching, the death penalty can claim to represent a species of popular will: death sentences are, after all, imposed by juries. 'It gives a special place to victims and "victim impact statements",' Garland notes, 'implicitly concerning itself with private vengeance as well as public order. Racial hatreds and caste distinctions, together with the passions aroused by atrocious crimes, still provide much of its energy. Its supporters still insist that regular punishment [i.e. imprisonment] is too good for "the worst of the worst" and that only death can sufficiently mark the enormity of their crimes. And of course it continues to produce false accusations (look at the faces of the exonerated) and racialised outcomes.'

Both the actual killing of the most egregious criminals and the assertion of the right to do so remain crucial ways by which the South invokes its self-proclaimed values, asserting its identity in the face of federal attempts to change them – let alone the efforts of human rights groups such as Amnesty International. Hence, on the day I first met Doug Pullen, his snorting contempt for the letters he received from Holland and Wales urging clemency for the mentally retarded Jerome Bowden: 'Folks round here don't necessarily care what folks in Wales think of them.' Southern – as opposed to American – exceptionalism lay behind Jim Crow segregation and the vicious, often violent campaigns against federal courts' attempts to dismantle it. Today, Dixie's enthusiasts for putting men to death often deploy the same slogan first used by the champions of slavery, and then by those who fought desegregation – 'states' rights'.

At the same time, America's federal institutions have always been aware that on some issues, the loyalty of the South to the Union still has a degree of fragility. In order to preserve the whole, they have at times been prepared to treat the states of the former Confederacy with a certain latitude. The Reconstruction era was characterised by strategic withdrawals and sleazy deals with white supremacists – such as the Georgia Assembly's passage of the Fourteenth 'equal protection' Amendment in return for the release of those being tried for assassinating G.W. Ashburn. John F. Kennedy secured the support of the Dixiecrats in his run for the US presidency by promising to promote deep-hued racists such as Columbus's Robert Elliott to the federal bench. In *McCleskey*, the Supreme Court did not assert that Baldus's analysis of the racial bias in capital punishment was inaccurate. Instead, Justice Powell's lead opinion stated that if the court were to invalidate the death penalty because its use was affected by racism, it might as well abolish the entire criminal justice system, because such disparities were equally evident elsewhere.

Arguments such as these about lynching and the death penalty are usually conducted in terms of generalities, taking the South as a whole. But Carlton Gary's trial took place in Columbus, a city where the violence and passions of the past century and a half can be documented with unusual clarity. Gary Parker told me back in 1996 that the sense of oppression that he felt in Columbus led him to believe that 'something terrible' had happened in its past. In fact many terrible things have happened there, acts of unspeakable cruelty and violence, perpetrated by white people against African-Americans and those who have tried to improve their lot. The wave of murders after the Civil War and the killing of G.W. Ashburn; the cluster of lynchings around the start of the twentieth century, culminating in the shooting of Teasy McElhaney; the Klan campaigns of the 1920s and the assassination of Dr Thomas H. Brewer: all, in their way, were acts of racial terror through which the white majority sought to enforce its dominance. The most recent incident that may fit this pattern took place as recently as 1992, when James A. Burns, the white Superintendent of the city's schools, was murdered by an unknown assailant who hid in his house while Burns was away, then stabbed him in his bed with a hunting knife. For the previous two years Burns had aroused bitter opposition by his efforts – almost four decades after *Brown vs Board of Education* – finally to desegregate Columbus's schools.

As noted in Chapter 1, the historian Victor Gatrell has observed that stories about crime and criminal justice permit 'a quest for hidden truths, when obscure people have to articulate motives, interests, and buried values and assumptions'. He illustrated his study of the changing use of the death penalty in Georgian and Regency England with what he termed a 'micro-history', an account of a murder in rural Shropshire, and the eventual execution of its perpetrator. This book has been a microhistory too, albeit with a longer span: the story not only of the stocking stranglings and Carlton Gary, but of its deep context in Columbus. It has, I hope, enabled us to look beneath the generalities described by Baldus, Zimring and Garland, and thus to see the motives and buried values still to be found in Columbus: how the past has lived in the treatment of a man whom much of the city has wanted dead for twenty-two years.

How might Columbus's history have fed into Gary's trial? There is one obvious continuity – the ongoing role of a single family, the Lands: from the lynchings of Simon Adams and Teasy McElhaney, through the States' Rights Council and the murder of Dr Brewer, to the refusal to fund Carlton Gary's defence and now, in this latest exquisite twist, to the identity of the judge who is handling his last appeals. In a place such as Columbus, whose demography, especially that of its elites, has been stable for many generations, this is not mere coincidence. Bradleys and Woodruffs have done business there for well over a century, and Lands have done (or broken) law. There is the curious process of selective recollection and forgetting through which the city has come to terms with its racist legacy, as set out in Chapter 7: an influence, to rate it at its lowest, on the formation of a common mentality, a shared attitude towards criminal justice which finds nothing much to object to in a trial conducted in the manner that Gary's was. (His state *habeas* appeal in the 1990s and the extraordinary evidence that then came to light were barely reported in the Columbus media at all.) And there are the city's ancient institutions, places where influential people from those same old families continue to gather, evolve a common political culture and indeed address their history in ways that are unlikely to be shared with outsiders. Pre-eminent still on its riverside promontory, there is the Big Eddy Club.

As I walked with my friends John and Lynn last evening, we made our way out of the residential Historic District to Broadway, the street that runs parallel to the Chattahoochee in downtown Columbus. Gene Hewell's Movin' Man, the store where Carlton Gary used to model clothes, has gone now: it closed its doors for good two years ago, bidding farewell to its customers with a live blues concert on the sidewalk. Having vowed to retire when he sold the building at a handsome profit, Gene is pursuing business interests elsewhere. The closure is by no means the only alteration since my first visit to the city in 1996. At night back then the street was almost empty, and it carried an air of menace, the only place open a scruffy, armoured liquor store. Last night it was thronged with people.

At the bottom of the street, half a block from the old theatre, stands Columbus State University's new arts complex, a magnificent edifice in glass and brick, its billboards announcing a tempting programme of forth-coming attractions. Running north for the next three blocks, every parking space was taken. There were bars and restaurants and cafés, with chairs and tables spilling onto the sidewalks, and everywhere seemed full. We wanted to hear some live music. There was almost too much to choose from: in the space of a few minutes we passed bars that had rock, jazz and blues. Finally we settled on a place where the bandstand was by the street window, so we knew what we were getting before we went in. The seven musicians were playing some bluesy electric jazz, and they were really, really good. Like the audience, some of them were white. When they took a break between sets, we talked with them for a while. Their virtuoso eighteen-year-old African-American alto player was from Atlanta, but the others had spent their lives in Columbus.

A multi-racial band re-interpreting a black musical tradition for a multi-racial audience: it seemed to be part of shifts that were not only symbolic, but real. The people on Broadway weren't out in segregated packs, and it seemed pretty clear that some of the pairs of mixed-race couples were dating. Most of them were under thirty, but things have been happening with older people too. For example, last year an African-

American, a lawyer-turned-politician, joined the Big Eddy Club, so bringing it into line with Columbus's other formerly all-white institutions, the Country and Green Island Clubs. Recently I discovered something else: that one of the first membership groups in Columbus that welcomed African-Americans was John Land's Fish House Gang. Back in the 1970s, when the city's race relations still seemed locked beneath an ice cap, the old judge and former segregationist was initiating a thaw.

Not many blocks from Broadway there are poor blacks still living in the shotgun houses and bleak housing projects of south Columbus, while affluent whites still dominate the sprawling northern suburbs. But just as the city is regenerating its geographical and cultural heart, its physical and social divisions are starting to blur. Ten years ago, the shade of Jim Crow was still palpable. Now it seems to be fading, along with the older generation of lawyers, cops and judges who tried Carlton Gary and grew up under its influence. My suspicion is that if I had asked white members of last night's audience what they thought about the Lost Cause, few would have known what I meant.

As we walked home, our ears ringing, that often-misapplied line from Faulkner formed itself in my head. To be sure, the past is never dead, and in certain senses is not even past. But neither, I reflected, is its influence static. History, and the way that history is remembered, are dynamic processes. Potent cultural symbols, as diverse as the Big Eddy Club's membership list and the Georgia state flag, shift in their substance and meaning. Men who were once abhorred – such as Dr Thomas H. Brewer – become publicly revered, with memorials erected on the spots where they died. And in the wake of such events, a young black man can walk at night, hand in hand with a young white woman, down Columbus's busiest street without being very much noticed, let alone lynched.

Historic shifts do not affect every aspect of a society evenly, and the criminal justice system, especially when it deals with the deepest trauma and the most horrific crimes, may well be the most resistant to reform. The passions and prejudices that actuated the trial of Carlton Gary have not disappeared, and in the frenzied resistance being made by the state to every aspect of his appeals, they seem very much alive. But last night, the breeze from the Chattahoochee that rustled the leaves as we turned towards my

329

friends' home felt like a wind of change. It may not be too much to hope that there will come a time when it starts to blow through Columbus's courtrooms, through the office of Georgia's Assistant Attorney General, and around the cells and echoing landings of death row.

# EPILOGUE

Having conducted further stereo microscope examinations, Dr Thomas David completed his report on the bite cast on 4 December 2006. In his view, there were 'several inconsistencies' between the cast of the bite mark found on the left breast of Janet Cofer and Carlton Gary's lower teeth, to which, David added, he had never had dental work. For example, one of the strangler's lower incisors was rotated out of alignment, while Gary's teeth were straight. In addition, the strangler had a 2–3-millimetre gap between his upper front teeth, and one of these was also rotated. Dr David said he stated this opinion 'to a reasonable degree of scientific certainty'. Gary, therefore, was 'probably excluded' as the author of the bite. The only reason David could not be absolutely sure was the quality of the bite mark 'exemplar'. He said that if he had been given the original 'positive' cast that Pullen and Smith had shown him back in 1984, he would have been able to reach a more definitive conclusion. Nevertheless, it was much more likely than not that Gary had *not* bitten Janet Cofer.

That same day, Jack Martin filed a motion with Judge Land, asking for an evidentiary hearing about the cast, in order to hear testimony from Dr David and from witnesses who had known Gary in the 1970s, who would testify that he never had a wide gap between his upper teeth, or a rotation. It also asked Land to allow fresh testimony on three other matters. The first item was the shoeprint disclosed by the former GBI agent Jim Covington, which showed (as I confirmed on my trip to see him in Americus in October 2006) that the man who stood on an air-conditioning unit in order to enter Ruth Schwob's house on the night of the terrors had size eight-and-a-half or nine feet, while Gary's are US size thirteen-and-a-half or fourteen. Secondly, Martin asked to present the reports that demonstrated a similar discrepancy between Gary's feet and the shoe size of the man who stood on Nellie Farmer's bathroom mat after killing her in Albany, New York, in 1970. Finally, Martin asked Land to hear the evidence that would show that William Smith had misled Gary's jury when he falsely stated that his namesake Detective Richard Smith had not brought copies of Gary's fingerprints back to Columbus after visiting him in jail in South Carolina in 1979. As Martin's motion pointed out, Richard Smith had told me that he not only obtained the fingerprints, he had also asked the Columbus print identification section to compare them with the strangling latents. 'The unanswered question,' Martin's motion said, 'is that if there were truly useful fingerprints matching petitioner found at the crime scenes long before Mr Gary's arrest in 1984, why were no matches made ... in 1979?'

In evaluating this request, Martin went on, the law required that the court consider the 'cumulative effect' of all the exculpatory evidence that had been hidden from Gary's trial – not just the new material, but the documents that had emerged years earlier, such as the undisclosed pre-trial statements of Gertrude Miller and the serology worksheets.

As of this writing, it seems certain that the state will oppose this motion, and that whatever its immediate outcome, the legal battle for Gary's life will continue for an unknown period. Those who wish to read updates as developments occur will find them on the HarperCollins UK news and blog website, www.fifthestate.co.uk

*David Rose*
*13 December 2006*

# NOTES ON SOURCES

Throughout the text I have quoted extensively from the numerous interviews I conducted for this book, and have usually made it clear when they
took place. I talked to most of the principal figures more than once, some
of them many times. I have not included references to the dates of
interviews in these notes, which refer only to printed and documentary
sources. This book contains no conjectured or 'made up' dialogue. It is a
work of non-fiction, not a 'non-fiction novel'. Excerpts from the trial of
Carlton Gary and his appeals hearings, as well as those of other cases, are
taken from the official transcripts.

CHAPTER ONE: THE BEST PLACE ON EARTH

4 *the gangs of Phenix City*: Margaret Anne Barnes, *The Tragedy and the Triumph of
Phenix City, Alabama*, Mercer University Press, Macon, Georgia, 1998, passim.

4 *the chemist John Stith Pemberton*: John S. Lupold, *Columbus Georgia 1828–1978*,
Columbus Sesquicentennial, Inc., Columbus, Georgia, 1978, p.52.

6 *Columbus, according to Mayor Bob Poydasheff*: http://www.columbusga.
org/mayor/m-wel.html.

6 *Ernest Woodruff and William C. Bradley*: Etta Blanchard Worsley, *Columbus on the
Chattahoochee*, Columbus Office Supply Company, Columbus, Georgia, 1951.

6 *the world's largest processor*: www.tysys.com.

8 *criticised for his record*: Ken Edelstein, '*Time* Magazine Blasts Columbus in Death-
Penalty Article', Columbus *Ledger-Enquirer*, 24 April 1991, p.A1.

11 *Bowden's pending execution*: Ken Elkins, 'Convicted Columbusite gets Celebrity
Support', Columbus *Ledger-Enquirer*, 13 June 1986, p.B1.

12 *I am Jerome Bowden*: Ken Elkins, 'Bowden is Put to Death', Columbus *Ledger-
Enquirer*, 24 June 1986, p.A1.

14 *once known as the 'millionaires' colony'*: Bruce L. Jordan, *Murder in the Peach State,* Midtown Publishing, Atlanta, 2000, pp.185–9.

14 *the heart of a social whirl*: William Winn, 'Waiting for the Strangler', *Atlanta* magazine, November 1980, pp.84–7 and 159–64.

14 *a kind of Arcadia*: ibid., p.161.

15 *By 1859 … the city is said to have contained*: Worsley, op. cit., p.265.

15 *a great railroad jubilee*: ibid., pp.183–4.

15 *the industrial production of Columbus*: Lupold, op. cit., p.30.

15 *the 1860 census*: ibid., p.27.

15 *the lawyer Raphael J. Moses*: Worsley, op. cit., pp.268–9.

15 *America's first secessionist journal*: Nancy Telfair, *A History of Columbus, Georgia 1828–1928,* Columbus Office Supply Company, 1929.

15 *all who resisted the end of slavery*: David Williams, *Rich Man's War*, University of Georgia Press, Athens, Georgia, 1998, p.45.

15 *William Scott … was run out of Columbus*: ibid., p.40.

16 *Senator Alfred Iverson*: Generally approving accounts of his career and of events in Columbus at the time of Georgia's secession can be found in the cited works by Telfair (pp.99ff) and Worsley.

16 *I think nearly all*: Lupold, p.29.

17 *The war both blasted and*: The histories by Telfair, Worsley and Williams all describe the wartime boom in Columbus's industries, although only the latter goes into detail about its disastrous effects on the less well-off. All contain detailed accounts of the battle of Easter 1865 and Wilson's putting the city to the torch, as does Lupold.

18 *Within a month of Wilson's fire*: Lupold, op. cit., pp.49ff.

19 *memory, as historians have recently*: This discussion is drawn from David Blight, *Race and Reunion: The Civil War in American Memory*, The Bellknap Press of Harvard University Press, Cambridge, Massachusetts, 2001, as well as phone conversations with and two books by W. Fitzhugh Brundage: *Lynching in the New South*, University of Illinois Press, Chicago, 1993, and *The Southern Past*, The Bellknap Press of Harvard University Press, Cambridge, Massachusetts, 2005.

19 *the Lost Cause account of the Civil War*: Blight, pp.38ff.

20 *part of the evolutionary process*: Worsley, pp.264 and 302ff.

20 *Sterling Price Gilbert*: His book was published by the University of Georgia Press in 1946. This section is on pp.13–14.

21 *Confederate Memorial Day*: Worsley, pp.304ff and Telfair, pp.151ff.

22 *a rhetoric of national reconciliation*: This is the main theme of Blight's book.

22 *an entire literary sub-genre*: Tilley's book was published in Nashville, Tennessee, by Bill Coats Ltd.

CHAPTER TWO: WE'VE GOT A MANIAC

27 *The black fiend*: Rebecca Felton, letter to the *Boston Transcript*, quoted in Philip Dray, *At the Hands of Persons Unknown: The Lynching of Black America*, Random House, New York, 2002, p.125. Felton, the wife of a Democrat US Congressman, was writing in response to criticism of a speech she made to Georgia farmers in August 1897 in which she said: 'If it takes lynching to protect woman's dearest possession from drunken, ravening beasts, then I say lynch a thousand a week if it becomes necessary.'

30 *one of the unsung heroes* and *It's always tragic*: Columbus *Ledger-Enquirer*, 18 September 1977, p.A4. Where no direct source is cited, I have summarised the details of each of the murders from testimony given at Carlton Gary's trial.

30 *serial killers*: Robert K. Ressler and Tom Schactman: *Whoever Fights Monsters*, Simon and Schuster, London, 1992, passim.

31 *The motive for the crimes*: Columbus *Ledger-Enquirer*, 26 September 1977, p.A1.

31 *By the time I was twenty-one*: 'Coroner Kilgore a Man of Convictions', Columbus *Ledger-Enquirer*, 15 October 1989, p.A1.

31 *the tension between*: Columbus *Ledger-Enquirer*, 4 October 1989, p.A1.

32 *Negroid characteristics*: Winn, 1980, op. cit., p.87.

32 *Southern rape complex*: W.J. Cash, *The Mind of the South*, Alfred A. Knopf, New York, 1941. The reference is to the 1991 Vintage edition, pp.114–17.

33 *The proud banner*: Quoted in Telfair, op. cit., p.154. Her account of the alleged lawless rampages of freed slaves is in the section that follows.

33 *Such is the explanation*: Cash, op. cit., p.117.

34 *the torture and killing of Sam Hose*: Dray, op. cit., pp.3–16.

34 *In the last speech of his life*: William S. McFeely, *Frederick Douglass*, W.W. Norton, New York, 1991, pp.378–80.

35 *Portrait in Georgia*: Jean Toomer, *Cane*, Boni and Liveright, New York, 1923. The poem can be found in the 1988 critical edition published by W.W. Norton, p.29.

36 *Jeannine Galloway*: The best and most easily accessible account of the Galloway case and the trial and appeal was written for the Columbus *Ledger-Enquirer* by Richard Hyatt, and ran for four days from 29 December 1989.

40 *a reputation for racism*: The account of the black patrolmen's firing and the events that followed is drawn from the extensive local press coverage that summer, from the legal documents filed in their civil rights case, *Sumbry vs Land*, and from interviews with those quoted.

# VIOLATION

**CHAPTER THREE: GHOST-HUNTING**

51 *And the Negro*: Carson McCullers's *The Heart is a Lonely Hunter* was first published in New York by Houghton Mifflin in 1940. This excerpt is taken from the Mariner Books edition of 2000, p.299.

53 *Reports Relating to Murders*: Records of the Assistant Commissioner for the State of Georgia, Bureau of Refugees, Freedmen and Abandoned Lands 1865–9; Reports Relating to Murders and Outrages 1866–8. National Archives and Records Service, Washington, DC, available on microfilm as NARA Roll 32 (Freedmen's Bureau), Target 2.

53 *an intense distrust*: Cash, op. cit., p.33.

53 *At the root*: Brundage, 1993, op. cit., p.6.

57 *A group of middle-aged*: Ressler, op. cit., pp.189–90.

59 *the dynasty of Woodruffs*: For background on the Woodruffs see the cited works by Worsley and Telfair, and for Kathleen's relationship with Carson McCullers, Virginia Spencer Carr, *The Lonely Hunter*, The University of Georgia Press, Athens, Georgia, 1975, pp.71–2, 317–20.

63 *Thomas Dixon's bestselling 1905 novel*: For a highly readable and scholarly account of Dixon, D.W. Griffith, *Birth of a Nation* and their impact, see Wyn Craig Wade, *The Fiery Cross: The Ku Klux Klan in America*, Oxford University Press, Oxford, 1987, especially Chapter 4, pp.119–39.

64 *Half a million negroes*: Telfair, op. cit., pp.155ff.

64 *punitive measures*: Worsley, op. cit. p.302ff.

65 *a pattern of rape, intimidation and murder*: 'Report [and Testimony] of the Joint Select Committee to Inquire into the Condition of Affairs in the Late Insurrectionary States. Made to the Two Houses of Congress February 19, 1872', vols VI and VII: Georgia. Government Printing Office, Washington D.C., 1872. The entire report is available online at http://www.hti.umich.edu/cgi/t/text/page viewer-idx?c=moa;cc=moa;sid=e6989420bda118cc39b2107121407556;rgn=full %20text;idno=ACA4911.0006.001;view=image;seq=00000003.

66 *this 'black and tan' Convention*: The quotations from the Columbus *Sun* and from Klan leaflets here and in the following section about G.W. Ashburn are taken from Worsley, op. cit., pp.308–16.

66 *the presence in the city*: See the Georgia volumes of the Select Committee report at pp.432–3 and 533–5.

66 *foul fiend in human shape*: Wade, op. cit., pp.16–17.

67 *Having travelled back to Columbus*: In addition to Worsley and Telfair, my account of the Ashburn murder is drawn from extensive testimony, especially from the Reverend John H. Caldwell, to the Joint Select Committee. Readers

who wish to learn more may type the name of Ashburn into the search box on the website cited above and will find many references; Caldwell's testimony is at pp.425–59. Another important witness was the Reverend Henry M. Turner, pp.1034–42. The committee testimony includes lengthy extracts from contemporary newspapers. The trial of Ashburn's alleged killers was covered by the *New York Times* and is now obtainable in the archives section of the paper's website, as are Ashburn's speeches to the Georgia Convention. See also Elizabeth Otto Daniell, 'The Ashburn Murder Case in Georgia Reconstruction', *Georgia Historical Review*, University of Georgia Press, Athens, Georgia, 1975, pp.296–312.

69 *flashpoints of contested memory*: W. Fitzhugh Brundage, 'Commemoration and Conflict: Forgetting and Remembering the Civil War', *Georgia Historical Review*, 1998, pp.559–74.

69 *Radical Rule*: Available at http://www.hti.umich.edu:80/cgi/t/text/page viewer-idx?c=moa;cc=moa;q1=Radical%20Rule;rgn=full%20text;view= image;seq=0001;idno=AFJ9489.0001.001;didno=AFJ9489.0001.001.

72 *The cells were dark*: The prisoners' account of their confinement was first published in *Radical Rule*, and echoed by Telfair and Worsley.

77 *black, Negroid, pubic hairs*: Winn, *Atlanta* magazine, op. cit., p.169.

77 *Chairman, Forces of Evil*: Ressler, op. cit., pp.190ff.

CHAPTER FOUR: DRAGNET

82 *Leading figures in Columbus's legal establishment*: I am indebted to research by the lawyer Jeff Ertel and his colleagues for details of the club membership, later cited in state *habeas corpus* appeal papers. These also set out details of the suspects for the murders 1978–84.

83 *It's not over yet*: Richard Hyatt, 'The Strangler Made Fear Part of Life', Columbus *Ledger-Enquirer*, 20 April 1979.

83 *A popular courthouse pastime*: Winn, *Atlanta* magazine, op. cit.

84 *Horice Adams*: Jerome Walters, 'Samples Don't Match Strangulations Evidence', Columbus *Ledger-Enquirer*, 22 June 1983, p.B1.

87 *Nine months later*: 'Police Seek Gun Stolen in Wynnton', Columbus *Ledger-Enquirer*, 24 July 1978, p.A1.

89 *held in a form*: The quotation comes from a series of articles about lynching in Columbus and the Teasy McElhaney case (see Chapter 5) by William (Billy) Winn, published by the *Ledger-Enquirer* under the rubric 'Incident at Winn's Hill' over seven days starting on p.A1 on 25 January 1987. The pieces were the product of impeccable scholarship and were beautifully written, and their

publication was itself a significant event in the history of Columbus and the evolution of local historical memory.

89 *Ma Rainey*: Sandra R. Lieb, *Mother of the Blues*, University of Massachusetts Press, Amherst, 1981, passim.

89 *details of the lynchings*: Brundage, 1993, op. cit., pp.270–80.

89 *Jesse Slayton and Will Miles*: Winn, 'Incident at Winn's Hill', part 1, and Brundage, 1993, op. cit., p.272.

90 *Simon Adams*: The account of his lynching is based on the last of Winn's articles, published on 31 January 1987.

92 *William Careker*: As well as Winn, 1987, op. cit., part 1, see Brundage, 1993, pp.111–13, and 'Talbot Citizen was Murdered', Columbus *Enquirer-Sun*, 22 June 1909, p.1.

94 *John Temple Graves:* Dray, op. cit., pp.144–5.

94 *more justice and less technicality*: Seymour D. Thompson, *Report of the Fifth Annual Meeting of the Georgia Bar Association*, 1888, pp.107–43.

95 *Are the Courts responsible for Lynchings?* John J. Strickland, *Report of the Sixteenth Annual Meeting of the Georgia Bar Association*, 1899, pp.184–90.

95 *Another speaker*: J.F. De Lacy, ibid., pp.191–8.

98 *What about the phone call:* in 'Police Work in Gary Case Good and Bad', Sunday *Ledger-Enquirer*, 31 August 1986, p.A9.

99 *all the serial killers he had ever studied*: Ressler, op. cit., pp.96–7.

CHAPTER FIVE: THE HANGING JUDGE

106 *Clock Without Hands*: This, the last of Carson McCullers's novels, is also her most political, concerning itself with the often violent political struggles of the civil rights era. It was first published by Houghton Mifflin in 1961. The quote is from the Mariner Books edition of 1998, pp.180–1.

108 *Fantasy was critical*: A.W. Burgess, C.R. Hartman, R.K. Ressler, J.E. Douglas and A. McCormack, 'Sexual Homicide: A Motivational Model', *Journal of Interpersonal Violence*, 1, 1986, pp.251–72.

108 *[Their] fantasies are:* Ressler, op. cit., pp.101–6.

111 *cold and narrow passages*: Carson McCullers, *The Heart is a Lonely Hunter*, Mariner Books edition, p.135.

112 *three such incidents*: Craig Lloyd, *Eugene Bullard: Black Expatriate in Jazz-Age Paris*, University of Georgia Press, Athens, Georgia, 2000, p.154, n.8.

113 *narrowly escaped from a lynch mob*: ibid., p.11.

113 *Norman Hadley*: 'Four Negroes were Lynched in Hamilton Monday Night', Columbus *Enquirer-Sun*, 23 January 1912, pp.1ff.

114 *Teasy McElhaney*: My account of this lynching is indebted to William Winn's 1987 newspaper series cited above. Although I read through contemporary accounts, I found only one sentence worthy of quotation that had not previously been reproduced by Winn.

117 *The trouble began*: 'Taken from Courthouse by a Mob and Lynched', Columbus *Enquirer-Sun*, 14 August 1912, pp.1ff.

127 *I don't have too much confidence*: William Winn, 'The Judge', Columbus *Ledger-Enquirer*, 30 November 1978, pp.A1ff.

127 *Chic magazine*: ibid.

128 *I'm never timid*: ibid.

128 *In another interview:* Constance Johnson, 'In Land's Case, it's Important to be a Bench Warmer', *Chattahoochee Magazine*, 10 September 1978, pp.8–9.

CHAPTER SIX: UNDER COLOUR OF LAW

129 *It was an old brick jail*: Carson McCullers, *The Member of the Wedding*, 1946. The quotation comes from the Mariner Books edition of her *Collected Stories*, 1998, p.360.

136 *a sudden signal from some unknown hand*: I am indebted here to Professor John Lupold, who has worked extensively on textile trade unionism in this period.

136 *the Klan in Columbus*: William F. Muggleston, 'Julian Harris, the Georgia Press and the Ku Klux Klan', *Georgia Historical Quarterly*, 1975, pp.284–95. This article is the source for the account of the threats to Harris and of the Klan's influence in the 1920s that follows.

138 *Thomas H. Brewer*: Once again, the starting point for my account of Brewer's life and death is the work of William Winn, who published a series of pieces over three weeks in the Sunday *Ledger-Enquirer* starting on 24 April 1988. I also rely on interviews (which are not quoted at length) that I conducted in January 2001 with some of Brewer's close associates in the NAACP, the late Columbus Mayor *pro tem.*, A.J. McClung, George Ford, Judge Albert Thompson and the city's first black police officer, Clarence White.

139 *A racist Baptist preacher*: Calvin Kytle and James A. Mackay, *Who Runs Georgia?*, University of Georgia Press, Athens, Georgia, 1998, p.249. Kytle and Mackay journeyed across the state in 1947 conducting interviews with influential people from many walks of life. The resultant book was considered too explosive to publish for fifty years. Their interview with Parson Jack, the source for most of what appears here, is at pp.245–53.

140 *black soldiers at Fort Benning*: Stephen G.N. Tuck, *Beyond Atlanta: The Struggle*

*for Racial Equality in Georgia,* University of Georgia Press, Athens, Georgia, 2001, p.81.

140 *Brown vs Board of Education:* Winn's first two articles in his 1988 series describe the local and state-wide impact of the Supreme Court decision, as does Tuck, op. cit.

141 *the Christian Civic League:* The *Georgia Tribune,* published every Thursday, carried numerous articles and advertisements publicising its activities. It is available on microfilm in the University of Georgia library in Athens.

145 *Flowers was standing:* Winn's third 1988 article, 'Shots in Rapid Succession Death to Brewer', describes the details of Brewer's murder.

147 *Land briefed the press:* Even the usually less credulous *New York Times* bought Land's line that, as its reports put it, Brewer's death had 'nothing to do with any racial matter' and that Brewer had 'threatened to get' Luico Flowers before Flowers shot him. Cf. 'Negro Leader Slain in Georgia Dispute', 18 February 1956, and 'Slain Negro Doctor Accused of Threat', published the following day. Also see Columbus *Ledger-Enquirer,* 'Flowers Under Guard at Cobb; Threat is Cited in Slaying', 20 February 1956.

147 *the Muscogee County grand jury:* Details from Winn's third article.

148 *We are looking for:* 'Luico Flowers Slain on Streets: Police Seek Unknown Assailant', Columbus *Ledger-Enquirer,* 11 February 1957, p.1; *New York Times* the same day.

150 *old South values persisted:* Tuck, op. cit., pp.143–4.

150 McNeill's *God Wills Us Free* was published by Hill and Wang, New York, 1965.


CHAPTER SEVEN: THE TRIAL

158 *the Cohiscan:* The research into the background of the judge and prosecutors cited here and below was conducted by the attorney Jeff Ertel and his colleagues and filed as part of Carlton Gary's eventual state *habeas corpus* legal brief. Ertel also obtained the Big Eddy Club's membership lists.

165 *The defence has argued:* 'Siemon Carries on Alone as Gary's Jury is Chosen', Sunday *Ledger-Enquirer,* 3 August 1986, pp.A1–2.


CHAPTER EIGHT: A BENCHMARK FOR JUSTICE

210 *Gary and his sister Miriam:* This and the rest of the description of the verdicts from Harold Connett, 'Courtroom Quiet as Foreman Reads Jury Verdict', Columbus *Ledger-Enquirer,* 27 August 1986, pp.A1ff.

214 *the necessary myths:* Blight, op. cit., especially pp.383–91. In 1913, he writes, a great reunion of the Blue and Gray armies took place at Gettysburg,

representing 'a public avowal of the deeply laid mythology of the Civil War that had captured the popular imagination … The war was remembered primarily as a tragedy that forged greater unity … not as the crisis of a nation in 1913 still deeply divided over slavery, race … and the future of the West.'

216 *Some of the jurors looked*: This and the rest of the description of the sentence verdict from Richard Hyatt, 'Gary Death Appeal is Automatic', Columbus *Ledger-Enquirer*, 4 August 1986, pp.A1ff.

### CHAPTER NINE: TO THE DEATH HOUSE

227 *he promised two interviewers*: Kytle and Mackay, op. cit., pp.242–5.

227 *a slap in the face*: Virginia E. Causey, 'The Long and Winding Road: School Desegregation in Columbus, Georgia, 1963–7', *Georgia Historical Quarterly*, 2001, pp.398–433.

228 *injunctions against planned marches*: This and other details from Jim Houston, 'Judge Elliott Reflects on Career', Columbus *Ledger-Enquirer*, 21 January, 2001, pp.A1ff.

228 *abused by agitators*: Causey, op. cit., p.401.

### CHAPTER TEN: VIOLATION

241 Herbert Packer, *The Limits of the Criminal Sanction*, Stanford University Press, Stanford, 1968, pp.231–2.

245 *Gary's life and upbringing*: My account of Gary's life is derived from interviews in prison with him, talks with members of his family, letters sent to him in prison and official prison records, legal documents filed for his appeals and 'The Puzzling Carlton Gary', an intensively researched pre-trial profile by Richard Hyatt, published by the Sunday *Ledger-Enquirer* on 13 April 1986, pp.A1ff.

248 *Porters Quarters*: the description is from Hyatt's profile, cited above.

249 *a massacre at Rosewood*: Cf Maxine D. Jones et al., 'Documented History of the Incident which Occurred at Rosewood, Florida, in January 1923', http://mailer. fsu.edu/~mjones/rosewood/rosewood.html, 1993.

### CHAPTER ELEVEN: DUE PROCESS

278 *Hyatt's profile*: Cited above.

286 *papers in the specialist journals*: For example, M. Sato and F. Ottensooser, 'Blood Group Substances in Body Fluids: Comparison of the Concentrations in Semen and Saliva', *Journal of Forensic Medicine*, 1967, pp.30–8. They conclude: 'The H substance in different semen samples from the same individual shows relatively small fluctuations in inhibition titer [concentration]. Thus, individuals with

low, high and intermediate H levels in semen can readily be differentiated. In most secretors the H content of semen is about 10–50 times as high as that of saliva.' They also comment that 'results with semen were always clear-cut'. See also R. Gaensslen, *Sourcebook in Forensic Serology, Immunology, and Biochemistry*, National Institute of Justice, Washington, DC, 1983, pp.262–327.

CHAPTER TWELVE: SOUTHERN JUSTICE AND THE STOCKING STRANGLINGS

302 *Illumination and Night Glare*, the unfinished autobiography of Carson McCullers, was published by the University of Wisconsin Press, Madison, in 1999. The excerpt, which refers to the treatment of African-Americans that she witnessed as a child in Columbus, is on p.56.

303 *It seemed to me*: 'Perfect Timing', Columbus *Ledger-Enquirer*, 26 January 2002, pp.A1ff.

313 *In the back of one*: Tim Chitwood, 'Gary Lawyer Wants Teeth as Evidence', Columbus *Ledger-Enquirer*, 19 November 2005, p.B1.

317 *Herbert Packer: The Limits of the Criminal Sanction*, op. cit.

319 *No one can doubt*: Ibid., p.237.

322 *Lynching took place in public*: I am indebted here and for parts of the following analysis to a lecture given at the University of Oxford in May 2006 by Professor David Garland of New York University: 'A Peculiar Institution: On the Forms and Functions of America's Death Penalty'.

323 *There is a special relationship*: Reverend Jesse Jackson Senior, Jesse L. Jackson Junior and Bruce Shapiro, *Legal Lynching*, The New Press, New York, 2001, p.71.

323 *Court proceedings*: Brundage, *Lynching in the New South*, op. cit., pp.256–7.

323 *The Berkeley criminologist*: Franklin E. Zimring, *The Contradictions of American Capital Punishment*, Oxford University Press, Oxford, 2003.

324 *analysed more than two thousand murders*: David Cole, *No Equal Justice*, The New Press, New York, 1999, pp.132ff.

324 *Other, later studies*: ibid., p.134.

324 *an extremely unlikely event*: Cole, op. cit., pp.135–7.

325 *some notable similarities*: Garland, 2006, op. cit.

# INDEX

tape recording of interviews 187, 188–9, 204,
258–60, 273–5
Tate, Sharon 50
Tefrey, J.S. 118
Telfair, Nancy (*also* Louise Jones DuBose) 19, 21, 32,
64, 65, 70–1, 156
Terrel County Correctional Institute 202
Theisen, Gary G. 270
Thompson, Albert 149, 161
Thompson, Seymour D. 94
Thornton, Jesse 28–9
Thurmond, Martha 49, 82, 106, 167, 176–7, 208,
210, 217, 289
Thurmond, William 49, 176
Thurmond and Lillian (CMG's uncle and aunt) 245,
246
*Time* magazine 8
Toombs, Robert 16
Toomer, Jean 35
tooth marks 267–70, 272–9, 303–10, 313–15, 318–19
Tortora, Ralph, III 296
Troup County (Georgia) 54, 55
Troy State University (Alabama) 80
*Trumpet (later Georgia Tribune)* 139
Tulane Law School (New Orleans) 158
Turner, Beleta 101–2, 243
Turner, Haywood, III 231–4
Turner, Ike and Tina 224, 276
Turner, Nat 16
Tuscaloosa (Alabama) 144
Tuskegee Institute (Alabama) 89
Tyler, Vivian 184–5
TYSYS (computing company) 6

United Daughters of the Confederacy 160
University of Florida 248
University of Georgia 59, 60
University of Iowa 324
University of North Carolina 131
University of the South (Tennessee) 159
University of Tennessee 60

Vandross, Luther 104
*Variety* (journal) 63
Victory Drive (Columbus) 5, 6
Vines, Bud 54–5
Vorys, Sater, Seymour & Pease (law firm) 271

Wade, Wyn Craig 64
Warden, Henry 306–7
Warren, Chief Justice Earl 319–20
Washington, Floyd 100–1, 153, 262
*Washington Post* 127, 135
Watt, George 323
WDAK (radio station) 142
Webb, Special Agent 256–7
Webber, Joe 29, 171–2, 176–7, 178, 184, 185

Wegel, John C. 194–5, 284–6, 289–90, 309
Wellington Hotel (Albany, New York state) 196–7,
198, 283
Wells, Beth 269
Wells, Gary 175–6, 257
Wells, Ida B. 33–4, 93
West Point (Georgia) 159
Westervelt, Robert 196–7
Wetherington, Jim 61, 80, 86, 97, 105, 261, 322
Whisnant, Mullins 37–9, 82, 162
White, Anthony 182
White, Barry 103
White, Edward D. 63
Whitley, H.T. 71, 148–9
Wiggins, Dr (hypnotist) 181
WILD (radio station) 276
Wilkins, Roy 147
Willard, Frances 35
Williams, Alma 246
Williams, Mrs Chas J. 21, 22, 33
Williams, George and Vicky 3, 4, 25–6
Williams, Hosea 42
Williams, Wayne 168, 197
*Williams vs Taylor* (US Supreme Court ruling,
2000): due diligence definition 308
Willis, R.L. 117
Willoughby, Lynn 320, 328
Wilson, James A. 271
Wilson, James Harrison 17, 18
Wilson, Joseph 20
Wilson, President Woodrow 20, 63
Winn, William 14, 83, 89, 157
witnesses, reliability of *see* identification of suspects
WOKS (radio station) 47
Women's Christian Temperance Union 35
Woodruff, George, III 60–1
Woodruff, George C., Junior 60, 76
Woodruff, George C. ('Kid'), Senior 59, 60
Woodruff, George Waldo 59
Woodruff, Harry Ernest 60
Woodruff, Kathleen K. 59–61, 97, 106, 167, 176,
177–8, 190, 192, 205, 210, 217, 263
work product privilege 235
Worsley, Etta Blanchard 15, 20, 21, 64, 70, 71, 156
Wraxall, Brian 299, 300, 301
WRBL (radio station) 22
Wright, Katharina 36
Wright, Richard 51
Wynnton (Columbus) 12, 14, 24, 27, 39, 45, 57, 58–9
Wynnton Methodist Church 184
Wynnton Road (Columbus) 49, 60

Yale University Law School 133
Young Men's Christian Association 123
Young Men's Democratic Club 249

Zimring, Franklin E. 323–4